British population history

The five studies brought together in this volume between them survey the trends and debates in English population history from 1348 to 1991, and in Scottish and Welsh population history from 1500 to 1991. For important parts of the period, British developments are set within the wider Irish and more general northwestern European context. Research over the past twenty-five years has transformed our understanding of how population has grown and declined and of why the numbers of births, deaths, marriages and migrants have risen and fallen, and has thrown much new light on the economic and social impact of these changes. The studies in this book supply introductions to these problems for readers who are not themselves demographers but who, as students, teachers, or non-specialist historians and social scientists, want to know more about what happened and what are the main topics of current debate. Full bibliographies for further study are included.

The titles included in this volume are: *Plague, population and the English economy, 1348–1530* by John Hatcher; *The population history of Britain and Ireland, 1500–1750* by R. A. Houston; *Population change in north-western Europe, 1750–1850* by Michael Anderson; and *The population of Britain in the nineteenth century* by Robert Woods. A new essay on *British population history, 1911–1991* by Michael Anderson is also included.

These titles are part of the British Economic History Society's pamphlet publications. The books by R. A. Houston and Robert Woods are available from Cambridge University Press in the series *New Studies in Economic and Social History*. Further information about this series is listed at the end of the book.

British population history

From the Black Death to the present day

Edited by

Michael Anderson
University of Edinburgh

CAMBRIDGE
UNIVERSITY PRESS

Published by the Press Syndicate of the University of Cambridge
The Pitt Building, Trumpington Street, Cambridge CB2 1RP
40 West 20th Street, New York, NY 10011-4211, USA
10 Stamford Road, Oakleigh, Melbourne 3166, Australia

First published together as *British Population History* 1996

Printed in Great Britain at the University Press, Cambridge

A catalogue record for this book is available from the British Library

Library of Congress cataloguing in publication data

HB
3583
B74

ISBN 0 521 57030 1 hardback
ISBN 0 521 57884 1 paperback

CE

Contents

1 Editor's introduction

This volume includes four previously published titles on population history, from the series Studies in Economic and Social History. To these has been added a new extended essay bringing the story from 1911 up to 1991. Between them, the five pieces of work cover English population change from 1348 to 1991; four also provide some information on Scotland and Wales, and two have an even wider geographical scope. Two of the previously published titles appeared in 1992 and one in 1988, so there is still little to add to their coverage of the literature. The fourth, John Hatcher's survey of population change in late medieval England, was published in 1977, but the basic trends which it proposes have largely been confirmed by subsequent work, and the demographic processes underlying the trends remain subject to debate.

One of the first titles in the Studies in Economic History (as it was initially titled) was Michael Flinn's *British Population Growth 1700–1850* [3]. This was published in 1970, when the broad trends in population change in the nineteenth and early twentieth centuries were quite well established, though much of the detailed analysis of the causes and regional patterning of change remained to be done. For the eighteenth century, research was well enough established for Flinn to be able to argue for quite rapid population growth in England and Scotland, representing a significant recovery from apparent population depression in the seventeenth century. However, in 1970, almost nothing was known with any certainty about population change before the 1690s.

Flinn's book, while properly cautious about the fragility of much of the evidence, portrayed a world in which population change was primarily mortality-driven. Research on the seventeenth and eighteenth centuries was highly dependent in 1970 on a relatively

limited number of summary sources which were, however, known
to have major flaws; these sources were supplemented by work on
parish registers involving many hours of tedious transcription,
compilation of monthly totals of vital events, hand-sorting, and
simple arithmetic. The resultant research showed significant
changes over time in the frequency and scale of fluctuations in the
month-by-month totals of demographic events (and particularly in
the number of burials). In the absence of any clear evidence on
underlying trends in population, it was difficult to relate numbers
of events to population trends and there was thus a temptation to
assume that the prime source of long-term population growth in
the century after 1750 was a marked reduction in the level of crisis
mortality [4; 5]. The time-consuming nature of the research
techniques (and notably of family reconstitution) severely restricted the number of case studies that were available, and this
encouraged almost all European demographers in the 1960s and
1970s to bolster inferences based on fragmentary evidence for
single countries by calling upon evidence from other parts of the
continent [see e.g. 4].

The past twenty-five years have seen major developments in
understanding and in research methods in historical demography,
and these have significantly elaborated and modified the pictures
that were being drawn even in the 1970s. One major development
has been the widespread availability of increasingly powerful
computers, which have made it possible to process huge amounts
of data in ways which were quite unthinkable even twenty years
ago. Wrigley and Schofield's highly influential *Population History of
England, 1541–1871: a Reconstruction* [25], not only rests upon
summation and direct manipulation of more than three million
months of parish register data (itself almost an unthinkable task by
manual analysis), but also exploits the power of computers to
perform complex iterative calculations in order to reconstruct
possible patterns of long-term population change. A further bonus
is the relative ease with which one can check alternative interpretations and offer revised accounts on the basis of different assumptions [e.g. 14].

Computers have also increasingly been used to facilitate and
formalise record linkage, a vital element in family reconstitution
from parish registers [see esp. 26]; analogous techniques have been

used in the analysis of medieval court rolls [16]. In addition, the developing power and sophistication of modern information technology has increased research productivity by enormously speeding calculations and the process of data exploration through rapid drawing and redrawing of graphs and computer-based maps [e.g. 2]. Computers have also provided much enhanced analytical power through the application of statistical techniques which assist in unravelling complex sets of interrelated factors, though not always in ways easily accessible to the non-specialist reader [a criticism, for example, of the otherwise very important 12]. However, in many areas, the main barrier to further progress now lies in the amount of data that can be captured for computer processing rather than in the analytical techniques themselves – and here the optical scanning of printed material is already playing a significant role (notably in work by the Cambridge Group on automating family reconstitution and at Queen's Belfast on the Irish Historical Database).

Accompanying the new techniques has been a significant shift even in the past ten years in the dominant forms of interpretation employed by historical demographers. In the study of mortality, less emphasis has been placed on famine and malnutrition as direct (or, via reduced resistance, indirect) causes of death and much more on the extent to which welfare systems and the actions of elites are able to provide security of access to food at a level which discourages mass migration and the consequent spread of disease; this applies even for the sixteenth, seventeenth and eighteenth centuries, when there can often be a clear correlation between mortality levels and harvest shortages, high prices and extreme scarcity of food [17; 23]. In parallel with these developments, improved understanding of the circumstances in which the rapid transmission of disease can occur has encouraged a greater emphasis on a range of social situations which encourage or reduce close social interaction – such as increased levels of migration and overcrowding in poor living conditions (for example, in the high mortality of London in the later eighteenth or the nineteenth centuries [7; 12]), or through the impact of declining fertility on exposure of babies to infections brought home by siblings [24, in this volume]. Increased understanding of the complexities of the long-run impact of interrelationships between different diseases has further complicated the previously largely speculative connections between nutrition and mortality [13; Lunn, and Schofield and Reher, in 20].

On the other hand, in a reaction to earlier views, the role of medicine in nineteenth-century mortality control has been more emphasised in recent research, though not, in the main, through any very positive reassessment of the consequences of direct clinical intervention by the medical profession in the treatment of disease. Rather, there has been a recognition of the possibility that growing credibility granted to the recommendations of medical practitioners and the wider propagation of advice on healthier ways of living could by themselves have played a significant role in limiting the spread of disease [7; 19; Morel in 20]. In rather similar vein, more credence is now given to the role of medical ideas in providing a persuasive rationale for social intervention and sanitary reform measures which, even if they did not always produce rapid falls in mortality, did at least help to stop mortality from rising [7; Schofield and Reher in 20; 22].

Interpretation of changing patterns of mortality has thus in recent years laid considerably greater emphasis on social, cultural and institutional factors and less on resource levels or on factors arising largely outside the system such as the arrival of new strains of disease or the consequences of climatic change. But the biggest innovation since 1980 has come from a growing recognition that another set of social changes, in the conditions under which couples could legitimately enter into child-bearing, were, for much of the present millennium, key determinants of long-run demographic trends.

This growing emphasis on Malthus's preventive rather than his positive checks was clearly signalled for the period from the sixteenth to the nineteenth centuries in Wrigley and Schofield's emphasis on marriage as the key demographic variable in their *Population History of England* [25]. A parallel hypothesis (based particularly on court roll and poll tax records), that low nuptiality was a major factor constraining population recovery after the Black Death, has subsequently become a major focus of debate in interpretations of English population change in the later medieval period [15; 16; 21], though Hatcher and Harvey [8; 10] in particular have followed Hatcher's earlier work [9, in this volume] by continuing to give primacy to mortality, basing their accounts principally on monastic mortality experience. For the period between 1500 and 1900, however, (with a few exceptions, notably [18]) there is still a fairly general consensus not only that changes in nuptiality were a crucial element in long-run English population change but also that the important role played by nuptiality change differentiates England not only from well-documented countries on the European mainland such as France and Sweden [25], but quite probably also from Scotland and Ireland, within which there were also significant regional differences in marriage behaviour [2; 11, in this volume]. These differences have been linked to different levels and structures of short- and longer-term 'security', as provided, for example, by systems of poor relief, by employment opportunities, by availability of family housing, and by kinship support [1; 2; 6]. One key implication from all this research is that it makes little sense to conceive of one single 'European demographic system' at any period in the past, and that the population history of individual regions and countries must be linked much more directly to their own separate economic, institutional and cultural histories.

Flinn began the last section of his 1970 volume with the words: 'It is clear from the foregoing that at present very little can be asserted with confidence and that much of what has been asserted in the past must now be ignored' [3: p. 50]. Progress has been rapid in the past twenty-five years, particularly with respect to the period before modern civil registration (1837 in England and Wales, and 1855 in Scotland). But, as the five publications collected in this volume clearly show, there remain many uncertainties. The authors of these works were asked to provide as far as possible non-technical guides to their periods, to help readers to identify the major issues of debate and to help them to form their own judgement and pursue more detailed studies for themselves in the extensive further readings provided. Hopefully, some of these readers will themselves be stimulated to pursue further research in population history – for there are many exciting challenges still to be met.

MICHAEL ANDERSON

Bibliography

[1] G. Alter, 'New perspectives on European marriage in the nineteenth century', *Journal of Family History*, 16 (1991): 1–5.

[2] M. Anderson and D. J. Morse, 'High fertility, high emigration, low nuptiality: Scotland's demographic experience, 1861–1911', *Population Studies* 47 (1993): 5–25 and 319–343.

[3] M. W. Flinn, *British Population Growth, 1700–1850* (1970).

[4] M. W. Flinn, *The European Demographic System, 1500–1820* (Brighton, 1981).

[5] M. W. Flinn et al., *Scottish Population History from the Seventeenth Century to the 1930s* (Cambridge, 1977).

[6] T. Guinnane, 'Re-thinking the Western European marriage pattern', *Journal of Family History*, 16 (1991): 47–64.

[7] A. Hardy, *The Epidemic Streets: infectious disease and the rise of preventive medicine 1856–1900* (1993).

[8] B. Harvey, *Living and Dying in England, 1100–1540: the monastic experience* (1993).

[9] J. Hatcher, *Plague, Population and the English Economy 1348–1530* (1977).

[10] J. Hatcher, 'Mortality in the fifteenth century: some new evidence', *Economic History Review* 39 (1986): 19–32.

[11] R. A. Houston, *The Population History of Britain and Ireland 1500–1750* (1992).

[12] J. Landers, *Death and the Metropolis: studies in the demographic history of London 1670–1830* (Cambridge, 1993).

[13] A. J. Mercer, *Disease, Mortality and Population in Transition: epidemiological-demographic change in England since the eighteenth century as part of a global phenomenon* (Leicester, 1990).

[14] J. Oeppen, 'Back projection and inverse projection: members of a wider class of constrained population models', *Population Studies*, 47 (1993): 245–267.

[15] L. R. Poos, *A Rural Society after the Black Death: Essex 1350–1525* (1991).

[16] L. R. Poos, R. M. Smith and Z. Razi, 'The population history of medieval English villages: a debate on the use of manor court records', in Z. Razi and R. M. Smith (eds.), *Medieval Village and Small Town Society: views from manorial and other seigneurial courts* (1993).

[17] J. D. Post, 'The mortality crises of the early 1770s and European demographic trends', *Journal of Interdisciplinary History*, 21 (1990): 29–62.

[18] P. Razzell, 'The growth of population in eighteenth-century England: a critical reappraisal', *Journal of Economic History* 53 (1993): 743–771.

[19] J. C. Riley, *The Eighteenth-century Campaign to Avoid Disease* (1987).
[20] R. Schofield, D. Reher and A. Bideau (eds.), *The Decline of Mortality in Europe* (1991).
[21] R. M. Smith, 'Hypothèses sur la nuptialité en Angleterre aux xiiie–xive siècles', *Annales: Economies, Sociétés, Civilisations* 38 (1983): 107–136.
[22] S. R. S. Szreter, 'The importance of social intervention in Britain's mortality decline c. 1850–1914: a re-interpretation of the role of public health', *Social History of Medicine*, 1 (1988): 1–38.
[23] J. Walter and R. S. Schofield (eds.), *Famine, Disease and the Social Order in Early Modern Society* (Cambridge, 1989).
[24] R. Woods, *The Population of Britain in the Nineteenth Century* (1992).
[25] E. A. Wrigley and R. S. Schofield, *The Population History of England 1541–1871: a reconstruction* (1981; second edition with new introduction 1989).
[26] E. A. Wrigley and R. S. Schofield, *English Population History from Family Reconstitution* (Cambridge, forthcoming).

2 Plague, population and the English economy, 1348–1530

Prepared for The Economic History Society by

John Hatcher
Reader in History at the
University of Cambridge

Contents

Figures

Tables

Acknowledgements

I am indebted to Drs T. H. Hollingsworth, E. Miller and R. S. Schofield for reading a complete draft of the text and making many valuable criticisms; and to Mr A. F. Butcher and Dr R. B. Outhwaite for advice on the passages dealing, respectively, with towns and wages and prices. The faults which remain are, of course, in no respect the responsibility of those who so kindly gave me their advice.

Note on references

References in the text within square brackets relate to the numbered items in the Select Bibliography, followed, where necessary, by the page numbers in italics, for example [131:*207*]. Other references in the text, numbered consecutively throughout the book, relate to annotations of the text or to sources not given in the Select Bibliography, and are itemised in the Notes and References section.

1
An introduction to the controversy

The two centuries which followed the Black Death of 1348–9 constitute one of the most intriguing periods in the history of population. In common with other societies in which the great mass of people was employed in agriculture, and in which technical progress was limited, the size of the population of later medieval and early Tudor England was one of the major determinants not only of both aggregate and *per capita* output, but also of the distribution of wealth and the structure of society. Just as the abundance of people prior to 1348 played a major part in reducing the standards of life of the peasantry and strengthening the power of landlords, so the progressive shortage of people in the ensuing era played a major part in undermining demesne agriculture and in bringing about a fundamental redistribution of wealth. The later fourteenth and the fifteenth centuries saw the real wage-rates of craftsmen and labourers apparently reach levels not to be exceeded until the second half of the nineteenth century. These centuries also experienced one of the most decisive shifts ever in social structure and tenurial relationships, namely the decline of serfdom and customary land tenure. But more than this there occurred within these centuries the longest period of declining and stagnant population in recorded English history. The failure of population to rise in a prolonged era of high living standards poses a severe test for many current theories concerning the causality of demographic change. In particular the experience of the late fourteenth and the fifteenth centuries would appear to conflict with the views of a powerful lobby of historians. These historians seek to interpret demographic history in neo-Malthusian terms by arguing that the size of population, and the scale and direction of its movements, were determined primarily by the standard of living and consequent so-called 'homeostatic adjustments' to the age of marriage and the size of families. In so doing they relegate disease to the status of a mere function of the standard of living. For these and other reasons the study of the demography of this era has much to commend it.

More than a generation ago John Saltmarsh and M. M. Postan sketched with bold strokes the profile of English demographic history in the century and a half after the Black Death. Postan at this stage was more concerned with evidence of economic depression than with demography, but he set his analysis firmly in the context of declining population [12]; Saltmarsh was far more explicit and stated that 'the symptoms of the fifteenth century suggest a continuous fall over a long period; not simply a population that had fallen, but one which was falling progressively' [18]. Their verdict was that after a series of drastic reductions in the third quarter of the fourteenth century population drifted downwards for a century, and few historians chose to disagree. In 1948 J. C. Russell published an extensive study of British population in the Middle Ages [39], based upon a wide range of documentary sources and demographic techniques which, although tentatively dating the commencement of the recovery in numbers from around 1430, at first appeared to lend support and unexpected precision to the thesis of substantial and prolonged decline [39]. Over the next few years Postan, in a series of pioneering studies of the indirect evidence of population movements, used changes in settlement, land values, wages, and prices, to present his case with still greater clarity and conviction [13; 14; 15]. Against such formidable weaponry, now supported by a growing body of sympathetic evidence from Europe, resistance was sparse.[1] A number of critics attempted to resurrect the 'money–price level' thesis, by claiming that a shortage of money rather than population decline was the prime mover behind the falling agricultural prices and general economic recession postulated for the century after 1380, but they did so without directly challenging the basic premise that a substantial long-term fall in the level of population had taken place [127; 129].

This premise was eventually challenged by the distinguished Russian historian, E. A. Kosminsky. In Marxian dialectics the level of population 'cannot be the chief force of development in society', and in a paper published in 1955 Kosminsky claimed that it did not 'appear to be definitely established that there was a fall in population which began in the 1320s and continued until the 1460s or 70s'; he preferred to write instead of 'the temporary fall in population' [8]. Although his resourceful arguments contained many insights and some criticisms of substance, the attempt to explain the major economic and social developments of the later Middle Ages, 'without recourse to the hypothesis of a substantial and long-drawn-out decline in England's population or to "Malthusian" speculations', found little favour with western medievalists and the Postan/Saltmarsh thesis emerged triumphant.[2]

It was perhaps inevitable, given the complexities of the subject and the deficiencies of the sources, that the ever-widening range of data revealed by subsequent studies of the medieval economy and society should have resulted in a retreat from the virtual concord of the 1940s and 50s into something which is now close to discord. Not that many historians have chosen to dispute that a significant fall in numbers occurred or that recovery was somewhat delayed; rather, there is now a distinct lack of agreement about the scale and duration of the decline, and particularly about the population trend after 1377.

One of the major sources of nonconformist beliefs is the work of J. C. Russell. Although first proffered more than a quarter of a century ago, and since subjected to much telling criticism from historians and demographers alike, Russell's speculations on the course of English medieval population continue to command widespread acceptance. Perhaps his most frequently quoted speculation is that the population of England was approximately 3.75 million in 1348, that by 1377 the Black Death and later epidemics had reduced it to 2.2 million, and that thereafter it fell very gently to about 2.1 million in 1400, at which level it remained until around 1430 when a slow recovery commenced [39: *260–81*]. It becomes evident from even a brief perusal of *British Medieval Population* that this is an extremely tentative scheme, and one which can be disputed on many grounds. It will suffice to mention only three.

Firstly, there are strong reasons for believing that Russell's estimates of English population in 1348 and 1377 are gross understatements. Since the estimate of 1348 depends upon that derived from the Poll Tax returns of 1377, adjusted to take account of intervening plagues, we shall concentrate upon the latter. (Death-rate during the Black Death and later epidemics is discussed in chapter 2.) The returns of the Poll Tax of 1377, which was levied on all persons over the age of fourteen excepting only genuine indigents, provide the medieval historian with a firm base for calculating the national population. But firm is a relative term and, in common with all medieval statistics, the adjustments and allowances that have to be made in order to transform taxpayers into population are a source of doubt and controversy. None the less, if one makes much more realistic allowances than Russell's derisory 5 per cent for evasion and fraud, for indigents who were legally exempt from taxation, and for the inevitable inefficiencies in the collection of this unique tax; and if one corrects a number of lesser imperfections in Russell's calculations, then the total number of taxpayers (1,386,196) can convincingly be transformed into a total population of 2.75–3 million.[3]

Secondly, it is a relatively simple task to demonstrate that Russell's speculations on the post-1377 population trend rest upon extremely shaky foundations. In fact they are based in part upon life-tables, derived not only from medieval but also from twentieth-century Indian sources, and in part upon the numbers of tenants listed in a sample of rural extents and surveys. Of the calculations based upon the former sources, one distinguished demographer has pointed out that 'they are not only afflicted with the uncertain-ties that beset all statistics but actually contain such curious elements of speculation and guesswork that they must regretfully be dismissed altogether' [38: *70–81*]. The dubiety of Russell's use of extents and surveys stems not only from the small size of the sample studied, but also from the artlessness of his methodology. As every agrarian historian knows, the number of tenants holding land directly from the lord of a manor need bear no direct relation to the level of population within that manor, still less to that of a wider area [13: *244*; 76: *292*]. Finally, and most ironically, Russell's view of the population trend after 1377 conflicts directly with calculations of male generation replacement rates ingeniously made by T. H. Hollingsworth from data that Russell himself collected, but was unable to utilise fully [33: *375–80*]. (Replace-ment rates are discussed below, pp. 26–9.)

Notwithstanding these flaws, the seductive charms of quantification have frequently proved too tempting for historians accustomed to courting cold favours from indirect evidence, and Russell's speculations, through widespread acceptance and repetition, have at times come perilously close to achieving the status of orthodoxy. In the last few years his estimates of national population have been described as 'the best available statistics of population' in medieval Europe [11: *19*] and they have provided the data for the medieval sections of numerous graphs of long-term population change, including those constructed by such notable historical demographers as J. D. Chambers [23: *19*] and E. A. Wrigley [43: *78*].

It is clear then that those who would see the era of severe population fall drawing to an end by the late 1370s are by no means mere uncritical supporters of the views of Russell. On the contrary a substantial body of influential opinion now rejects the possibility that numbers decreased significantly in the course of the fifteenth century. G. Duby, in his masterly survey of the rural economy of western Europe, declares that, 'Everything leads us to believe that the real fall in the rural population occurred between 1350 and 1380', and 'that the following sixty years was a period of stagnation interrupted only intermittently by catastrophes' [67: *308–10*]. A. R. Bridbury, in his controversial attempt to demonstrate economic growth in late medieval England, assumes that demographic recession was primarily confined to the period between 1348 and 1369, after which 'the shock was over ... population began to adopt itself' [2: *23*]; an opinion shared by H. A. Miskimin [123: *479*] and J. Schreiner [129: *71–2*].

J. M. W. Bean's study of the habits, incidence and impact of plague in late medieval England has been most effectual in forming and marshalling opinion against the thesis of continued population decline. Indeed his article published in 1963 has strong claims to be counted among the most influential to be written on English late medieval demography since 1950 [1]. Starting out to test Saltmarsh's conclusion that the evidence of the fifteenth century suggests 'not simply a population that had fallen, but one which was falling progressively' [18: *30*], Bean ended by claiming that 'it seems likely that the decline of the population of England had been arrested by the end of the fourteenth century and that some expansion then ensued' [1: *435*].

The growing band of historians seeking to interpret the fifteenth century as an era of prosperity and enterprise have found the hypothesis of population increase most appealing. The fearsome spectre of recurrent plague, swingeing mortality rates, and a morbid preoccupation with death, are not readily compatible with an age of vitality. F. R. H. Du Boulay, while not concerned in detail with demographic matters, writes that, 'Studies on the effects of plague have progressed from J. Saltmarsh . . . to J. M. W. Bean', and maintains that although, 'it was once thought that the death-rate from the plague was continuous enough to bring down the population without remission from 1348 until late in the fifteenth century . . . there were in fact long gaps between outbreaks which, together with their less lethal incidence, allowed momentary rises in the birth-rate' [5: *34, 182*]. Professor Lander is even more confident and concludes that, 'Everything argues against any continuous decline or even stagnation of the population', and that a slow but progressive recovery in numbers was under way by 1430 [9: *35, 46–7*].

Close examination reveals, however, that the case of those who would argue that the decline in numbers was over by 1370 or 1380, and that some measure of sustained recovery was accomplished in the ensuing century, rests not upon positive evidence of demographic vitality but upon the negative argument that fifteenth-century outbreaks of plague were neither so general, so frequent, nor so virulent as to have been able to restrain the powerful forces of recovery, still less to have effected a further significant decline. As expressed by its foremost proponent, J. M. W. Bean, this case has a number of serious flaws. In the first place it relies almost exclusively upon chronicles for evidence of plague outbreaks. Bean himself states: 'For our knowledge of the chronology of plague in England during the later Middle Ages we must rely almost completely on the evidence of contemporary chronicles, supplemented by the reference made occasionally in government records' [1: *427*]. Since he relies so heavily upon this source it is strange to find that no space is given to a discussion of possible changes in its quality. Chroniclers are not uniformly informative and those of the fourteenth and very early fifteenth centuries were far more likely to have recorded national outbreaks of plague than were those of later years. By the first quarter of the fifteenth century the tradition established by such as Walsingham,

Knighton, Higden, Adam of Usk, and the *Anonimalle Chronicle* was near extinction; the national chronicler was largely superseded by the local, who paid more attention to the affairs of the house or town to which he belonged than to those of the nation. C. Creighton, the first investigator to use chronicles systematically for evidence of plague, was well aware of the marked deterioration in quality which had taken place by the opening decades of the fifteenth century, and writes of 'the not very complete records of the time' [47: *229, 232–3*] and the views of the majority of historians are summarised by a recent commentator who writes of chronicles, 'As we move into the fifteenth century abundance is replaced by real dearth' [134: *16–17*].

Secondly, a major part of Bean's case appears to rest on the assumption that, in order to have had a significant effect on the level of population, plague had to strike through national outbreaks. Thus he maintains that the twenty-one-year gap that he finds between the 'national' plagues of 1413 and 1434 and the twenty-five-year gap between those of 1439 and 1464' must have enabled a considerable recovery of population level to occur'. But is it correct to concentrate solely on even primarily on national outbreaks at the expense of local? Can it be assumed that all the national outbreaks have been identified or that periodic epidemics of local or regional scale were of little significance in determining the level of population? There can be no doubt that a thorough search of local records will reveal a multitude of explicit references to additional outbreaks of plague and other diseases, while many more may be traced through fluctuations in the numbers of heriots, wills presented for probate, and institutions of priests to benefices.

Valuable testimony to the frequency and virulence of fifteenth-century plagues is provides by the unique obituary lists of Christ Church Priory, Canterbury, which contain details of deaths in a community of seventy-five to eighty-five monks, including special notes on most of those who succumbed to plague [22; 139]. Between 1413 and 1507 plague visited the priory at least once in every decade, saving only the 1490s (namely 1413, 1419, 1420, 1431, 1447, 1457, 1465, 1467, 1470, 1471, 1487, 1501, 1504 and 1507), and accounted for a minimum of 16 per cent of all deaths (i.e. 41 out of a total of 254 deaths).[4] It must be stressed that this is an absolute minimum figure, since in some parts of the lists the recording of deaths is extremely brief and some plague victims may have escaped record. As to the relative impact of 'national' and 'local' plagues the evidence is striking: of the fourteen years in which plague was recorded at Christ Church only four coincided with outbreaks which have hitherto been deemed national (namely 1413, 1465, 1467 and 1471); these 'national' outbreaks accounted for little more than one-fifth of all plague deaths; and more than half of all recorded plague deaths at Christ Church occurred in the two periods (1414–33 and 1440–63) declared by Bean to be free of national plagues. As we shall see later (pp. 57–8) there are grounds for believing that the number of national or extra-regional plagues has been underestimated; at least a further four outbreaks of plague at the priory (in 1420, 1431, 1457 and 1487) occurred in years for which outbreaks have been identified elsewhere in the country. Plague was not the only epidemic disease to strike the priory: three monks died in the autumn of 1435 *ex epidemia*, and an outbreak of 'sweat' in 1485 killed nine monks in the space of six days. Moreover, if we turn to the records of the city of Canterbury, we can identify at least three additional major outbreaks of epidemic disease within our period. The counting of 'national' epidemics clearly constitutes a most unsatisfactory index of mortality.

Finally, another plank in Bean's case can be shown to be insecure, namely that fifteenth-century plagues were mild because they had little immediate impact on the amounts of cloth exported from London [1: *433–4*]. The significance that Bean claims for the fact that in only one of eleven London plague years between 1407 and 1479 were cloth exports below the totals of both the preceding and the succeeding year, is rendered questionable by the fact that on the terms of this definition neither the notorious *pestis secunda* of 1361 nor the *pestis tertia* of 1368 could be counted as severe plagues.[5] Not only were cloth exports in these later fourteenth-century plague years not below the totals of both the preceding and succeeding years, they actually exceeded the average of the two preceding and two succeeding years.[6] Yet no one can doubt the virulence of these outbreaks, and we know that London was sorely afflicted by them. It is clearly dubious to attempt to measure the virulence of plague by the level of cloth exports.

The most extreme assessment to date of the incidence of plague in late medieval England was made in 1970 by J. F. D. Shrewsbury [53]. By a relentless application of hypothesis based upon a personal interpretation of the aetiology of plague, Shrewsbury denies both that England became an enzootic area in the later Middle Ages and that pneumonic plague was of more than scant significance.* He also asserts that bubonic outbreaks were unlikely to have been either frequent or severe in rural areas owing to the low density of both rat and human populations. In this way Shrewsbury is able to conclude that in all probability the national death-roll from the Black Death itself did not exceed 5 per cent, and that the vast bulk of the pestilences identified in the late fourteenth and the fifteenth centuries were not plague but other epidemic diseases, among which typhus in his favourite choice. Although he chooses not to concern himself with questions of the general course of population change, the conclusion we are invited to draw from Shrewsbury's work is similar to that to be drawn from Bean's – namely that plague could not have caused a prolonged decline in England's population. It would be out of place to conduct here a detailed refutation of Shrewsbury's analysis since this has been attempted by others, with respect both to his neglect of the major sources of historical evidence which have come to light since the 1930s, and to certain of his opinions concerning the aetiology of plague. Nevertheless it should be noted that immediate reactions to his analysis of the impact of late medieval plague have not all been condemnatory, and some historians are in danger of finding the mixture of Shrewsbury and Bean an intoxicating brew.[7]

Thus, although scarcely any positive evidence of population increase before the latter part of the fifteenth century has so far been forthcoming, the thesis of prolonged decline has been gravely weakened by increasing scepticism and the lack of recent detailed

---

*   Pneumonic plague is spread by droplet infection, in a fashion which has some similarity with the common cold or influenza; bubonic plague normally can be transmitted only through the bite of an infected flea. In addition to its greater propensity to spread rapidly, pneumonic plague has an even higher mortality rate – 99.99 per cent compared with 60–85 per cent for bubonic. An enzootic area is one in which some rats at any given moment are infected with plague; successive outbreaks do not therefore have to rely upon fresh importations of infected rats.

exposition. Indeed in the twenty-five years or so since the pioneering articles of Saltmarsh and Postan scarcely any attempt has been made to incorporate subsequent research into a thorough restatement, despite the fact that the bulk of the studies that have been written on particular aspects of late medieval economy and society have either produced evidence of low or falling population or been placed in a context which assumes such a process. Small wonder then that E. A. Wrigley should feel so bemused when surveying the demographic history of a period well outside his normal purview, that he should write on p. 77 of *Population and History* that after the Black Death, 'There then followed a very interesting period lasting perhaps a century and a quarter during which population, though now much smaller in size than in the late thirteenth century, seems not to have shown any clear tendency to rise', and then on p. 78 presents a graph entitled, 'Long-term Population Trends in England and Wales, 1000 to 1800', which shows population rising quite sharply from around 1430; or that J. Cornwall should write in 1970 of 'our virtually complete ignorance of fifteenth-century demography' [24: 42].

In fact a substantial range of direct and indirect evidence is in existence and, although it is likely that controversies over the demographic history of the later Middle Ages will rage for many years to come, this evidence enables the limits of our ignorance to be charted with some confidence.

2
Direct evidence of population change

Historical demography, a difficult pursuit in any age, is especially daunting in the English Middle Ages, a period with no parish registers, no hearth-taxes, no large-scale censuses excepting Domesday Book, and few serviceable taxation returns excepting those of 1377. Direct demographic evidence is not only sparse, it is also highly selective, and relates primarily to the mortality of the wealthy and privileged groups in society. It is most unlikely that any adequate data on birth-rates will ever be forthcoming from English sources. Nevertheless it would be displaying not only an unwarranted pessimism but also a culpable ignorance of the sophistication of modern demographic techniques to assume that no worthwhile vital statistics can be extracted from surviving records.

(i) Mortality in the Black Death and subsequent epidemics

The first and also the most devastating visitation of plague, the 'Great Pestilence' or 'Black Death' of 1348-9, has understandably exerted a fascination over successive generations of scholars, many of whom have participated in the perennially intriguing task of attempting to gauge the death-rate of that horrendous event. Precision still proves elusive, but over the years substantial advances in knowledge and technique have enabled us to proceed far beyond the overwrought imaginings and hopelessly inaccurate quantification of the chroniclers, to a position where the majority of historians are agreed upon a reasonably narrow range of probabilities.

Among the most accurate calculations that can be made, and

also among the most widely based, are those of the death-rates of the beneficed clergy. Bishops' registers contain records of the institutions of priests to benefices, and the most detailed of these registers enable vacancies caused by deaths to be distinguished from vacancies caused by resignations or exchanges. Careful calculations based upon the registers of the dioceses of Lichfield, York, and Lincoln, which are thought to be the most informative of all, yield death-rates of around 40 per cent for the year of the plague. Less informative registers, of which seven have been analysed, produce maximum death-rates of around 45 per cent. Since each diocese covered more than one county these registers provide a useful guide to the mortality of the beneficed clergy over a large part of England [33: *232–5*; 39: *220–2*]. Further, though much less significant, measures of clerical mortality are provided by average death-rates of 45 per cent in a dozen monastic houses, and of 18 per cent among bishops and 42 per cent among abbots [39: *221–6*; 132: *495–6*]. Another measure of mortality can be derived from the experience of tenants-in-chief, whose deaths and successions are recorded in a range of documents called Inquisitions *Post Mortem*. Of a sample of 505 such persons who were in possession of their inheritances in 1348, 138 or just over 27 per cent died in the year of the plague [39: *215–18*].

For an indication of the mortality of the population at large we can turn to manorial records. One method of calculating rural death-rates is from the numbers of landholdings which fell vacant during the plague year. A good series of manorial records will enable deaths to be established with a fair degree of accuracy from the payment of death-duties called heriots, and these can be compared with the number of holdings on the manor liable to render heriots on the deaths of their tenants. Sadly the disruption caused by the plague often resulted in the keeping of very imperfect records during the height of the epidemic, and in addition to good account and court rolls an accurate calculation depends upon the availability of a list of landholdings made just prior to the plague. Despite the difficulties a number of calculations have been made, of varying degrees of trustworthiness, which generally suggest very high death-rates. For example it is suggested that two-thirds of the customary tenantry of the manors of Bishop's Waltham, Hants [20: *69–70*], Downton, Wilts., and Witney [83: *196, 213*]) and

Cuxham, Oxon., died [75: *135–6*]; between 50 and 60 per cent of
those of three Cambridgeshire manors [85: *120–5*], two Essex
manors [48: *13–20*], and two east-Cornish manors [76: *102–5*];
and a third of those of the manor of Brightwell in Berkshire [83:
207–8]. Other calculations, based upon the decline in the numbers
of persons paying customary dues just before and just after the
plague, suggest average death-rates of 55 per cent on twenty-two
Glastonbury Abbey manors and 43 per cent on three Essex manors
[20: *71–1*; 39: *226–7*].

It is particularly frustrating that the most widely based data, and
probably also the most accurate, relate not to the mass of the
people but to the beneficed clergy, while the data relating to the
peasantry are extremely sparse. Accordingly it can readily be
appreciated that the task of converting these variable and scattered
statistics into a death-rate for the whole English population is
fraught with formidable difficulties. Beginning with our mortality
rates for parish priests, there are numerous problems involved in
calculating a precise death-rate from records of institutions. One
has to be especially careful to eliminate all vacancies excepting
those arising from death; in plague years the number of resignations rose sharply [132: *498–9*]. One must also take account of the
interval between the death of an incumbent and the institution of
his successor (this appears to have been at least one month); failure
to allow for this interval will have the effect of reducing the
population at risk and therefore artificially reducing the death-rate.
Pluralities and absenteeism are also complicating factors. If we are
satisfied with the accuracy of our calculations, we have to attempt
to assess the relationship the mortality of priests bore to that of the
common people. The fact that priests were on average better fed,
better housed and better educated would have tended to lower
death-rates, but the conscientious performance of pastoral duties
would have tended to raise them. The high average age of the
beneficed clergy would have led to a high 'normal' death-rate.

The 27 per cent death-rate calculated for major landholders is
clearly out of line with that suggested for the beneficed clergy and
the peasantry. There can be little doubt that this privileged group
had a greater than average chance of escaping infection; they lived
in stone houses not favoured by rats, and being more mobile than
the peasantry they could flee before the advancing plague. But

perhaps the most serious doubts on the representative nature of death-rates drawn from Inquisitions *Post Mortem* are aroused by the small size of the sample population at risk, which was a mere 505. These doubts are confirmed by the suggestion that no less than 23 per cent of heirs and heiresses died in the next plague of 1361–2, an outbreak which all other sources of evidence – literary, manorial and clerical, quantitative and qualitative – agree was far less virulent than the Black Death. The implication must be that the samples are too small to produce reliable figures for individual years.

Looking closely at the death-rates calculated from manorial sources, the likelihood is that they are at times somewhat exaggerated. In particular it is probable that on some manors two or even more heriots may have been received from the same holdings, since some of those who inherited may also have died. This would have the effect of artificially inflating the number of deaths in the original population at risk and, if it is not eliminated, of exaggerating the resulting death-rates. As for the statistics derived from customary payments, these are almost certainly over-estimates, since dead men could not continue to pay but live men could take the opportunity presented by the plague to evade payment.

The steady increase in our knowledge means that we can now begin to answer the crucial question of whether the impact of the plague was approximately uniform throughout the country, or whether some regions escaped almost unscathed. Despite the plausibility of arguments based upon scattered settlement and the consequent obstacles to the transmission of disease, it would appear that there is no reason to believe that as a rule the plague claimed fewer victims in the more remote parts of the country. Contemporaries attest that the plague spread throughout the kingdom with unabated ferocity; local studies suggest the death-rates in the Highland zone were as high as those in the more densely settled regions of lowland England; and bishops' registers suggest death-rates for the beneficed clergy of over 50 per cent in the far south-west and 48 per cent in Herefordshire [53: 56]. There would, therefore, seem to be no justification for striking a lower national average on these grounds. A further difficulty in our attempt to arrive at a national estimate stems from the fact that none of our sources provides adequate evidence of death-rates among children and adolescents, relating almost exclusively to office-holders and tenants who, in the vast majority of cases, were adults. There is some evidence from the chronicles that the first outbreak of plague, unlike many of those to follow, struck mainly at people in the prime of life, but in all honesty we must admit that this is yet another area of doubt. We must also appreciate that we have no reliable information on urban death-rates, but we know that both in the nature of bubonic plague and according to the testimony of contemporaries, the proportion dying in towns was likely to have significantly exceeded that dying in the countryside [43: *95–7*].

In some respects the range of estimates of the national death-toll espoused by historians might still be considered depressingly wide. Some historians press for a half or even more, others seek refuge in the now conventional estimate of a third and, as we have already mentioned, Shrewsbury would have the proportion of plague victims as low as one-twentieth outside East Anglia [53: *36, 123*]. Thus the elements of doubt and confusion in the evidence are reflected in the views of historians. Yet step by step the range of possibilities can be reduced. A national death-rate of below 25 per cent or above 55 per cent would appear most unlikely. In addition to the data rehearsed above there are literally hundreds of mid-fourteenth-century records of manors, towns and other communities throughout the country which bear testimony, with a lack of precision but a compelling force, to a death-rate of at least 30 to 35 per cent; yet when we look at England in the 1350s a death-rate of more than a half would not appear to be compatible with the progress of the economy and the behaviour of prices and wages (see pp. 53–60 below). Until more evidence of rural death-rates is forthcoming great weight must be attached to a revised average death-rate of around 35 to 40 per cent for beneficed clergy. In fact it is fitting that it should provide the mid-point of the most judicious estimate of the national death-rate in 1348–9 in the present state of knowledge: 30 to 45 per cent.[8]

Information on the toll of ensuing epidemics is far less satisfactory. For 1361–2 we have the 23 per cent for heirs and heiresses mentioned earlier, and 14 per cent for beneficed clergy in the diocese of York. For 1369 the rate for heirs and heiresses falls to 13 per cent, and the same figure is recorded for the beneficed clergy of York Diocese [39: *27–18*; *222*]. For the fourth major national outbreak of 1375, and for outbreaks thereafter, we have as yet no reliable statistical evidence whatsoever.

In assessing the incidence of plague we must not neglect a most valuable index compiled by Russell from Inquisitions *Post Mortem*, namely the time of year at which tenants-in-chief died [39: *195–9*]. Russell's findings demonstrate a remarkable transformation in the seasonal pattern of mortality in the century after 1348, and provide a strong indication that this transformation was caused by the virulence of bubonic plague and other summer diseases. The pre-Black Death pattern with, as one would expect, the heaviest mortality in the winter months was succeeded by one in which the heaviest mortality was concentrated in the period from late July to late September. Furthermore Russell found that as the pattern in the years after 1348 which did not experience large-scale epidemics was also markedly different from that in the pre-plague period it was likely that plague had become endemic. The samples upon which these findings are based are of necessity modest, but once again there is ample scope to enlarge them by using evidence contained in wills and bishops' registers.

(ii) Replacement rates

Even for a period which was afflicted repeatedly by virulent epidemics on a national and local scale, estimates of the incidence of disease can provide only an imperfect guide to fluctuations in the size of the nation's population. Knowledge of mortality needs to be supplemented by knowledge of fertility. In this respect one of the most promising avenues of investigation to be opened up in recent years is the calculation of generation replacement rates: that is the number of children, usually male, surviving the death of one or other of the parents, usually the father. Replacement rates are, of course, not a perfect substitute for birth-rates, and may at times tell us more about infant and childhood mortality than about birth, but since they are the closest the medievalist is ever likely to get to birth-rates they are too valuable to spurn. By far the best series of replacement rates is that calculated by T. H. Hollingsworth from

Table I *Male generation replacement rates calculated from inquisitions* post mortem

Period	Deaths	Sons calculated	Replacement rate
Up to 1265	347	568	1.64
1266–90	568	718	1.26
1291–1315	1043	1335	1.28
1316–40	1093	1535	1.40
1341–65	1348	1332	0.99
1366–90	761	619	0.81
1391–1415	696	558	0.80
1416–40	769	628	0.82
1441–65	631	695	1.10
1466–90	887	1076	1.21
1491–1505	673	1359	2.02

Sources: Russell [39: *240–2*]; Hollingsworth [33: *375–80*].
Note: When assessing the value of these data the following factors should be borne in mind: (1) uncertainty as to the precise point in time to which each replacement rate refers; (2) the rates do not fully reflect the effects of crisis mortality years when a series of deaths might occur in the same family in a very short space of time; (3) children conceived but not born at the time of death of the father are not recorded; (4) some of the recorded sons would not survive into adulthood; (5) daughters who had entered nunneries were not recorded.

the data extracted by Russell from Inquisitions *Post Mortem* [33: *375–80*]. On the death of a tenant-in-chief an inquest was held to determine, *inter alia*, the heir to the landholdings. The report of the inquest could take three forms: first, a statement concerning the sole or eldest son, or his heir or heirs; second, if there were no sons, a list of all surviving daughters; third, a statement that there were no direct heirs. Thus if there were at least one son the inquest did not have to report how many sons there actually were, but fortunately if there were no sons the report had to list all the daughters. Using an ingenious method, Hollingsworth has managed to calculate male generation replacement rates by allocating sons on the basis of the data concerning daughters. It must be readily admitted that the results of these calculations are speculative, but Inquisitions *Post Mortem* are among the most trustworthy of extant sources for information concerning heirs. Furthermore, even if there are doubts concerning the precise orders of magnitude, the relative changes are significant, and the samples upon which they are based are large enough and the results consistent enough to warrant serious consideration.

It will be noted that not a single positive replacement occurs in any twenty-five-year period between 1341 and 1440, while even if five-year periods are used only one positive replacement occurs, namely 1386–90 (1.14). If these replacement rates were applied to the nation as a whole, the population of England would have fallen with virtually no remission for a century, at a rate which Hollingsworth estimates would have totalled 50 per cent; and almost 20 per cent of the decline would have occurred after 1377. But clearly they are not readily applicable. Tenants-in-chief were a small and highly favoured section of society, and their living standards were far in excess of those of the mass of people; on the other hand they were perhaps more likely than the population at large to suffer violent deaths in the frequent hostilities of the times. Weighing all the factors, Hollingsworth has estimated on the basis of the replacement rate evidence that England's population as a whole may well have declined by around two-thirds in the century after the Black Death [33: *380–8*].

The imaginative attempt by Professor Thrupp to coax accurate replacement rates from manorial court rolls must be deemed to have failed; sadly so because direct evidence of the demographic history of the peasantry is almost wholly lacking [40]. Even long series of detailed manorial court records are capable of yielding a far less comprehensive and accurate picture of the life of medieval rural communities than many present researchers would wish. On the death of a customary tenant who held by impartible tenure there was necessity to record only the direct heir, while even the entail of a partible inheritance resulted only in the listing of sons already of age. To believe that all or even most of the extra sons ineligible to inherit will be able to be traced in other proceedings of the court is surely to be unrealistically optimistic. Even if difficulties over the inconsistent use of surnames are discounted, it must be admitted that the deficiencies of the rolls themselves did not remain constant. In the fifteenth century even the most efficiently administered manors witnessed some deterioration in the standard of management, and villagers for their part were less likely than their predecessors of the thirteenth century to welcome the opportunity of inheriting a customary holding, and some no doubt took positive steps to avoid having to inherit. Furthermore, it was inevitable that the information available to the court was often imperfect, and the incentive for court officials to be diligent was frequently lacking. These and other inevitable sources of 'leakage' mean that the number of sons that can be identified must almost invariably be an understatement.[9]

S. Thrupp's pioneering method of using sons named as beneficiaries in wills as a means of calculating male replacement rates probably produces more useful results, and in so far as the factors making for the under-enumeration of sons in wills may well be more constant than in court rolls the trend may well have some significance [40: *114–18*]. In fact the replacement rates calculated from both court rolls and wills follow a trend similar to that followed by replacement rates calculated from Inquisitions *Post Mortem*. The rates from court rolls fall sharply between the later thirteenth century and the mid-fifteenth, while those from fifteenth-century wills remain well below unity until the closing decades of the century. But it comes as no surprise that the rates themselves are unrealistically low. Indeed it has been computed that the rates calculated by Thrupp would have produced a fall of about 60 per cent per generation in the century or so after the Black Death, with the result that, on the basis of 2.2 million in 1377, the population of England by about 1470 would have stood at an incredible 142,000! [33: *222–3*].

Notwithstanding, S. Thrupp has taught us that manorial court rolls should not be discarded for together with wills they can almost certainly be made to yield valuable demographic data. An examination of succession to partible patrimonies based upon excellent series of court rolls has potentially rewarding possibilities, and the use of wills in great numbers, using beneficiaries to calculate replacement rates, is a promising avenue of investigation.

Finally, in passing, attention should be drawn to the direct demographic evidence which can be derived from the obituary book and ordination lists of Christ Church Priory, Canterbury [22; 139]. The full and continuous recording of both ordinations and deaths at the priory between 1394 and 1504 permit the calculation not only of crude death-rates, but also of the size and age-structure of the monastic population, and hence of life-tables. Inevitably there are shortcomings, not least the small size of the population at

risk (generally between seventy-five and eighty-five monks), and
the fact that it was not representative of the population at large.
Many difficult methodological problems need to be solved before
the Christ Church data can be presented in the most accurate and
informative manner, but preliminary analysis reveals high and
fluctuating levels of mortality in the priory.[10]

Turning first to the simplest of calculations, crude death-rates,
we find that they range from as low as the mid-twenties per
thousand in the healthiest decades to as high as the mid-forties per
thousand in the unhealthiest. Over the 110-year period covered
they averaged more than thirty per thousand. Not only are such
levels high, the wide fluctuations they exhibit are characteristic of a
community experiencing waves of epidemic disease, an observation borne out by the information contained in the obituary book
of time and cause of death. These rates were not unduly influenced
by changes in the age-structure of the monastic population, since
the average age of the community varied between the relatively
narrow limits of the mid-30s to early 40s, and tended to drop in
times of high mortality as new monks were ordained to take the
places of those who died. During the course of the fifteenth
century Christ Church monks were ordained at an average of 17 to
19 years, and died at an average age of somewhat less than 50
years.

Comparative data are hard to come by, but it is significant that a
preliminary attempt to construct a life-table for the cohort of just
under 80 monks who were ordained between 1395 and 1423
produces expectations of life that are, age for age, as low as, or
even lower than, those calculated for men and women at an
average age of 25 years during the 'worst period' at Colyton,
between 1625 and 1699 when there was a surplus of burials over
baptisms and 'population was apparently falling' [45]; farmers in
Crulai at an average age of 27 in the 'crisis' period of 1675 to 1742
[26: *176 ff.*]; and male members of the British peerage aged 20
years at any time from the beginning of calculations in 1550 [32:
56]. Moreover, the incidence of death did not follow an orderly
progression according to advancing years; in fact the mortality
level of the 25–34 years age-group was frequently in excess of that
of the 35–44 years age-group, and sometimes even in excess of that
of the 45–54 years age-group. If such a characteristic obtained in

England at large it would have severely restricted the growth potential of the population. Indeed even if no allowance is made for the abundant food of excellent quality and the impressive standards of hygiene and medical care enjoyed by the monks, the Christ Church data provide still further evidence that the population of England declined throughout much of the fifteenth century.

3
Economic evidence of population change

The study of the demographic history of the Middle Ages provides confirmation of the aphorism that 'necessity is the mother of invention'. Faced with scarce and imperfect sources of direct evidence of population medieval historians have ingeniously sought to utilise a wide range of indirect evidence, including prices and wages, the occupation and value of land, and the prosperity of the urban and industrial sectors. Yet indirect evidence, by its very nature, is imprecise and difficult to interpret and consequently extreme care must be exercised in its use. A striking instance of the need for caution is provided by the experience of the later fourteenth century.

(i) The later fourteenth-century economy

There are many aspects of the economic and social history of the later fourteenth century which remain extremely puzzling, and the formulation of satisfactory explanations will occupy historians for many generations to come. In the first place the Black Death and the immediately ensuing waves of devastating epidemics which, as far as it is possible to judge at present, must have led to a reduction in population of at least a third and more probably almost a half, had few of the debilitating effects that one has been led to associate with the population decline of the later Middle Ages. Indeed the often quoted epithet 'depression' fits the facts of the fifteenth century far better than those of the later fourteenth, while 'economic growth' can justifiably be applied to the later fourteenth century but not to the fifteenth. A remarkable buoyancy in agriculture was emulated by the fortunes of many towns and many branches of industry and commerce. The immense loss of life in plagues inevitably caused disruption and setbacks in production, but in greater part these appear to have been short-lived.

One of the most striking features of the thirty and more years following 1348 was the resilience that the agrarian economy displayed in the face of recurrent plague. Although blows had been struck at the prosperity of 'high farming' at least as early as the second decade of the fourteenth century, blows which were redoubled in 1348–9, 1360–2 and 1368–9, the era refused to be brought to a summary demise, and by the end of the third quarter of the century large numbers of landlords, perhaps even the majority, were enjoying revenues not decisively below those received in pre-plague years. Naturally the precise timing of the post-Black Death recovery and its extent and composition varied from estate to estate and from region to region, but with a few exceptions a peak of seigneurial prosperity was reached before many years of the fifteenth century had elapsed.

The most frequently quoted illustration of this phenomenon is the fortunes of certain estates of the higher nobility situated in East Anglia, Denbigh, Monmouthshire, Somerset and Dorset, whose yields in the 1370s were found by G. A. Holmes to have been less than 10 per cent below those of the 1340s [79: *ch. 4*]. Yet many other equally striking examples can be given, and many more doubtless remain to be discovered. The vast and widely scattered estates of the Duchy of Lancaster, still to be studied in their entirety, provide much complementary evidence; from the Honour of Tutbury's estates in Staffordshire and Derbyshire, for example, we learn of the re-leasing of many previously vacant tenements in the 1360s and 70s, and of rent receipts from a group of manors which in the same period were no more than 10 per cent lower than in 1313 [57: *74–81*]. Ecclesiastical estates, as we might expect, enjoyed fortunes no less propitious than these, and we learn that the manorial revenues of the bishopric of Winchester in the later fourteenth century 'remained remarkably (though also precariously) high' [16: *588–9*]; that the estates of Ramsey Abbey enjoyed an 'economic recovery [in] the 1370s and 1380s' [88: *259–65*]; that the first signs of difficulty in securing tenants for vacant holdings on Crowland Abbey estates were encountered as late as 1391 [85: *152–3*]; and that the income of Christ Church Priory, Canterbury, reached 'its highest recorded level' in 1411 [93: *194*]. Even more impressive evidence of buoyant demand for land is forthcoming from both ecclesiastical and lay estates in south-western counties [70: *253–7*; 76: *ch. 6*].

Late medieval England was a predominantly peasant economy, and with perhaps three-quarters of the population consisting of peasant farmers and farm labourers, and a relatively static technology, changes in the level of population ought to have been reflected in the competition for land, and particularly in the amount of land under cultivation and the value placed upon it. The tell-tale signs of a low or falling population are consequently vacant holdings, arable reverting to rough pasture, low or falling rents and entry fines, the accumulation of rent arrears and so on. The historian's dilemma regarding the later fourteenth century is that none of these things appear to have happened on a scale commensurate with a population decline of around 35 to 50 per cent. At present the most plausible resolution of this dilemma appears to lie in overpopulation before 1348 and a marked increase in *per capita* output and income afterwards, which combined to offset the characteristically depressive effects of the decline in absolute numbers. In the case of agriculture increased costs in the form of wages and equipment may have been balanced by the fact that prices of farm produce in the thirty years after the Black Death were maintained at very high levels, and output per acre may well have risen. (For wage and price data, see below pp. 53–60.)

There are many good reasons why the reduction in population should have led to a rise in *per capita* output. It is now generally agreed that England, along with many parts of Europe, was suffering from some degree of overpopulation in the early fourteenth century, and that diminishing returns had long since begun to operate in many sectors of the economy. There is widespread evidence of the cultivation of poor soils at this time, of holdings far below the optimum size, and of an abundance of labour which inevitably produced chronic under- and unemployment. The subsequent reduction in population must have led to increased productivity by restoring a more efficient balance between labour, land and capital. The reduction in population must also have led to a sharp increase in *per capita* wealth and consumption. In simple terms, the survivors inherited the property of those who had perished and, when presented with a sudden increase in wealth at a time of recurrent plague and considerable uncertainty, it is not surprising that they chose to spend on a greater scale than their predecessors. Demand was further stimulated by the increasing earnings of labourers and peasants; and there is also the possibility that these groups had a greater propensity to consume than landlords and others who suffered a relative reduction in income. The 'outrageous and excessive' expenditure of the lower and middle classes was one of the favourite themes of the moralists of the age, and we can take as representative the sentiments of Henry Knighton, a canon of Leicester, who wrote in 1388 of 'the elation of the inferior people in dress and accoutrements in these days, so that one person cannot be discerned from another in splendour of dress or belongings, neither poor from rich nor servant from master' [5: 67]. With the trappings of the cherished hierarchy of status under such determined assault Parliament attempted, with a series of notably unsuccessful sumptuary statutes beginning in 1363, to restrain conspicuous expenditure and regulate personal possessions according to occupation and income [123: 486–90; 130].

The urban sector was inevitably a prime beneficiary of this increase in *per capita* consumption. For large numbers of towns the early fourteenth century brought the onset of difficult trading conditions, and for a time the Black Death seemed likely to precipitate a major long-term crisis. Yet within a decade or so of the first plague many towns, particularly the larger centres, were showing signs of strong recovery. Some well-known examples of revived fortunes or new growth in the late fourteenth century include York, Newcastle, Norwich, Boston, Lynn, Coventry, Southampton and Bristol, and doubtless many more will be found to add to this list.[11] Evidence of the output and trade of individual commodities is limited but none the less highly suggestive. The development of the English woollen textile industry is a remarkable instance of rapid growth in the face of rapid population decline. The average annual exports of English woollens rose from less than 2000 cloths in the early 1350s to over 40,000 cloths between 1390 and 1395, while the number of cloths supplied to the home market may well have doubled. Although this industrial development inevitably reduced the exports of raw wool, in terms of both weight of wool and value, combined exports of raw wool and cloth reached a peak in the last decade of the fourteenth century comparable with previous peaks in the first and sixth decades.[12] The production of tin, also a leading export commodity, used primarily in the manufacture of pewter, followed an upward path similar to that of cloth. The effect of the Black Death on tin output was little short of catastrophic, but after many setbacks production had risen by the late 1380s to levels barely below the highest hitherto recorded [106: *155–9*]. Further quantitative evidence of economic resilience comes from wine imports, albeit greatly influenced by the current state of hostilities in the Hundred Years War, which suggest that the turn of the century saw a return to prosperity in the wine trade with demand, as also in the case of tin, seemingly not greatly affected by steep increases in price [109: *30–4*].

(ii) The fifteenth-century economy

These propitious times were not to persist, however, and at some point in the late fourteenth century or early fifteenth, depending upon the particular region or sector of the economy concerned, decline set in. By the mid-fifteenth century a severe contraction had occurred in almost every sector of the economy. Why the later fourteenth-century boom came to an end, and why the reversal was of such dramatic proportions, are difficult questions to which only speculative answers can be given. We can be certain that England's economy, and in particular her overseas trade, was gravely injured by wars with France, Spain and the Hanseatic League, and it is possible that a progressive shortage of money may have assisted in the promotion of recession. A further possibility is that the continuing fall in the population, and the consequent increasingly acute shortage of labour may eventually have undermined the buoyancy of the economy, and may have encouraged a shift towards a relatively prosperous self-sufficiency. But if doubts exist about the causes they do not exist about the consequences. On the vast majority of the rural estates that have been studied aggregate rents, rents per acre, and the amount of land under cultivation declined, to reach a nadir around the mid-century or somewhat later. One by one, with very few exceptions, the older and larger urban centres eventually succumbed to economic and demographic retrenchment as the fifteenth century wore on. Exports of wool and cloth, expressed in terms of value, followed a fluctuating but nevertheless distinctly downward course, with a reduction of almost a third comparing 1381–1400 with 1451–80. The production, and probably also the export, of tin followed a similar but less erratic and even steeper downward course. Poundage receipts from duties levied upon the import and export of miscellaneous goods (which, unsatisfactory though they are, probably give a further clue to commercial and industrial prosperity) reached a nadir in the 1450s and 60s, fully 50 per cent below the opening two decades of the century. Wine imports too were more than 50 per cent lower on average between 1450 and 1470 than they had been between 1400 and 1420 [15: *193*]. Thus, even if full account is taken of the compensation to be found in the development of new industrial centres and of the likelihood of grave inefficiency in the collection of customs and other dues during the civil war period, one is forced to conclude that the first sixty or seventy years of the fifteenth century, in aggregate terms at least, bore far more resemblance to Postan's tale of 'recession, arrested economic development and declining national income' [12: *161*] than to Bridbury's proclamation of an 'astonishing record of resurgent vitality and enterprise' [2: *24*].

When considering the significance of such data for the reconstruction of the history of population, it must be stressed that fluctuations in industrial output and commercial activity can normally provide only the vaguest of hints, while even the assistance given by prices, wages and agrarian evidence is sometimes oblique and very difficult to interpret. Yet these downward shifts in economic activity were so general in scope and so dramatic in scale as to be incompatible with a modestly rising or even a stable population. In the absence of population decline the contraction in economic activity must have been accompanied by comparably dramatic reductions in output per head, and by reductions in income to match. In the light of the considerable evidence we have of the well-being of the mass of fifteenth-century Englishmen such a proposition is wholly untenable.

(a) Agriculture and the land

Since the great bulk of Englishmen gained their livelihood by working the land it is essential that we pay careful attention to the testimony, drawn from most parts of the country, of a severely depressed land market, including retreating cultivation, low and falling rents, and wide gaps between the profits that landlords claimed and the incomes that they actually received. For most estates and regions the descent from the post-Black Death peaks of demand for land was under way before 1400, precipitated by, or coinciding with a sharp fall in the price of agricultural commodities and a further rise in wage-rates. Once begun the downward trend usually continued with only occasional respite until the bottom of the trough was reached in the middle of the fifteenth century or a little later. There were notable exceptions but this general pattern appears to have been followed in the great majority of the regions of the country that have so far been studied, while even the exceptional regions experienced a sympathetic mid-century recession.

Before we embark on our brief tour of rural England it should be noted that the authors of the estate and regional studies which are our guides had differing interests and therefore concentrated upon different aspects of agrarian history; some, for example, have dwelt upon landlords' incomes to the neglect of the amount of land under cultivation or the level of rents per acre, while the prime interests of others have lain in social rather than economic matters. Nevertheless we can make some use of most studies.

Northern England is no longer a closed book. The fortunes of the Percy family are well enough known: despite the sparseness of manorial documentation it appears that its income between 1416 and 1470 from lands in Cumberland fell by between a quarter and a third, and from lands in Northumberland by up to a half, while that from lands in Yorkshire fell by between a fifth and a quarter after 1443 [55: *12–42*]. Still in the far north, we learn that Durham Priory found it extremely difficult, and on occasion impossible, to lease manors in the late 1430s and the 1440s, even at substantially reduced rents [64: *ch. 8*], while the landed revenues of the bishops of Durham appear to have suffered to an even greater extent [64: *283n.*; 95: *69–70*]. Conditions in the north-west were scarcely more prosperous, for the agrarian economy of the West Riding, as exemplified by the estates of Bolton Priory, experienced a severe mid-fifteenth-century depression with a marked contraction of arable farming [81: *180–3*]. Cheshire and north Shropshire, if we may judge from the estates of the Earls of Shrewsbury and Princes of Wales, after some buoyant decades in the later fourteenth century, displayed abundant evidence of progressive agrarian contraction in the course of the first half of the fifteenth [87]. It has been estimated that the terms on which farms on the Duchy of Lancaster estates were let, already declining by 1400, fell a further 20 per cent in the first seventy-five years of the fifteenth century [13: *237*]. That portion of the vast inheritance situated in Staffordshire and Derbyshire appears to bear out this figure, and although some initial resistance to decline was offered in upland pastoral regions, these eventually followed the path trodden by lowland manors since Henry IV's reign and likewise experienced falling rents and abandoned holdings [57: *94 ff.*; 58: *84*; see also 94: *216–17, 248–50, 265–6*].

The fifteenth century was a period of acute agricultural recession in the Midlands. Inadequate documentation is a problem for Leicestershire, but we can be certain that a fall of only 15 per cent in the customary rents due to Leicester Abbey between the rental of 1408 and that of 1477 masks a far more serious state of affairs in which revenues from wool sales, sales of tithe corn, and demesne leases may well have fallen by a half or more [77: *85–8*]. The decline in demand for land on the Worcestershire, Gloucestershire and Warwickshire estates of the bishopric of Worcester was so severe that by the 1430s tenants were able to withhold the payment of rent on a grand scale, with the result that arrears mounted relentlessly [68]. Complementary evidence from south Warwickshire and Herefordshire suggests that the bishops' problems were shared by other landlords [6: *161–73*; 90: *173–5*], while an apparent decline of nearly 50 per cent in the agricultural profits of the Earls of Stafford from their Gloucestershire estates suggests that bad management also played a part [16: *597*]. We also learn that on Westminster Abbey manors in Gloucestershire and Worcestershire 'such demesne rents as were not stationary in the first half of the fifteenth century were falling' [74: *23*]. Moving eastwards, we find a severe agricultural depression in south Lincolnshire, occasioned by an inability to find tenants for many holdings

[72], while Ramsey Abbey, with estates situated mainly in Huntingdonshire and west Cambridgeshire, was experiencing 'the deepest and most prolonged depression in manorial revenues ... revealed for any period in the abbey history', and by the 1450s and 1460s the accumulation of debt 'was often phenomenal' [88: *265–6, 292–3*]. Crowland Abbey, whose estates were largely in Lincolnshire, Huntingdonshire, and Northamptonshire, was in a state of 'economic confusion' in the fifteenth century and was suffering in particular from a continual loss of tenants [85: *145–55*].

Although it may well prove to be the case that southern counties did not experience as deep an agricultural recession as the rest of England, there are many indications that here too demand for land generally declined significantly in the course of the first half of the fifteenth century. The Berkshire manors studied by R. J. Faith displayed symptoms of falling demand for land occasioned by falling population [69], while in Sussex evidence of decline may be drawn from the estates of Battle Abbey [91: *368–9*], the Percies [55: *17–21*], and elsewhere [94: *217*; 59: *69–72*; 60]. The agricultural profits of the bishopric of Winchester, derived predominantly from manors in Hampshire, undoubtedly suffered to some extent, and the 'comparative resilience' that they displayed may well have owed much to the avaricious energies of Cardinal Beaufort [16: *597*]; most other landlords in Hampshire seem to have fared less well [98: *421–3*]. The recession in Wiltshire and Somerset, as elsewhere, appears to have affected arable farming to a somewhat greater extent than pastoral. Nevertheless the rent roll of the Wiltshire manors of the Duchy of Lancaster generally decreased between *c.* 1400 and *c.* 1470, with receipts from some manors falling by 25–30 per cent, and we learn that leases on the Somerset and Wiltshire manors of Glastonbury Abbey fell by about a third over the same period, with an even greater decline registered in the level of entry fines exacted from customary tenants [86: *ch. 9*; 99: *40–2*; 13: *237*].

The evidence briefly recited above clearly suggests that England experienced a deep and widespread agricultural recession in the fifteenth century, a recession which took the form of falling demand for land and falling aggregate production. Yet it would be unrealistic to expect that fifteenth-century England did not have its exceptional regions and exceptional landlords, or that the agricultural recession plunged landlords from affluence to penury. It was inevitable, given the diversity and complexity of the English economy, that demand for land should have been sustained or even enhanced in some regions, and that some landlords, by a combination of diligence, cupidity and good fortune, should have managed to stabilise or even increase their revenues. But, whereas it is essential that full weight must be given to each example of 'prosperity' that comes to light, it would be quite erroneous to attempt to create a new orthodoxy from the unorthodox, or to imagine that untypical upward movements in rents or landlords' revenues were invariably the result of upward movements in the level of population. In a recent attempt to argue that the fifteenth century was not a landlord's purgatory, it has been tentatively suggested that declining incomes were more a sign of incompetent management than of adverse economic circumstances, and that efficiently administered estates, such as those belonging to Christ Church, Canterbury, the Archbishop of Canterbury, Tavistock Abbey, and the Greys of Ruthin, were capable of producing stable or even increasing profits [9: *ch. 2*]. But a close examination of these and other 'prosperous' estates reveals a number of instances in which the degree of 'prosperity' has been exaggerated or based upon inadequate evidence, but no indication of general demographic vitality.

Kent is frequently cited, along with other Home Counties, as a region which escaped the general agrarian depression of the fifteenth century. Kentish agriculture undoubtedly benefited from close proximity to London, for London continued to grow rapidly in the later Middle Ages. Whereas the capital accounted for 2 per cent of the assessed wealth of the country in 1334, by 1515 it accounted for nearly 9 per cent [19]. Yet the most that can be said for Kentish agriculture is that the decline in its fortunes was not as severe as that experienced by most other counties, and that its recovery was stronger and began earlier – in other words its experience differed by degree rather than by kind.

We should not be misled into believing that the rebuilding at immense cost of the nave and the great tower of Canterbury Cathedral was the product of a rising income enjoyed by Christ Church Priory. Indeed, contrary to what has been claimed, far from being immune to the common afflictions of fifteenth-century landlords, the priory suffered the common fate of declining income. The record gross revenues of £4100 in 1411 should be seen in the context of only £2382 received in 1437, £2116 in 1454 and £2060 in 1456 – this much can be learnt from Smith's study which touched only lightly on the fifteenth century [93: *13*]. Conclusive evidence of decline is provided in a recent study of the late medieval fortunes of the priory in which we are told that the gross manorial charge, taking no account of arrears, fell by 22 per cent between 1410 and 1469, and that, although many examples of temporary recoveries in rent levels occurred during this period, the over-all trend was unmistakably downwards. Furthermore, we learn not only that rents were depressed in the middle decades of the century, but also that the priory's income suffered acutely at this time from the accumulation of arrears [62: *95–125*].

Such evidence, firmly based upon the direct testimony of manorial accounts, suggests that the picture that has emerged from F. R. H. Du Boulay's study of the comparatively poorly documented estates of the archbishopric, situated predominantly in the same region, may well be too optimistic. In the absence of an adequate range of reeves' and receivers' accounts Du Boulay was forced to rely primarily upon valors for evidence of long-term fluctuations in the archbishopric's income [65]. In fact only four valors survive for a period of two and a half centuries, namely for 1291, 1422, 1446 and 1535. Thus evidence of the extent of the decline, if any, in income in the decades preceding 1422 and succeeding 1446, is completely lacking, a grave weakness since the trough of the decline in the value of Christ Church Priory's lands was not reached until the late 1460s. It has often been noted that valors can be a notoriously treacherous source: in particular they are statements of potential income and not of the revenues which were collected or even ultimately collectable.[13] It is significant therefore to find that according to the best of the surviving series of receivers' accounts the average annual amount actually received by the archbishops' officials from the bailiwick of Otford, which according to the valors should have been worth £346 in 1422 and £413 in 1446, was no more than £303 in the 1450s, £262 in the 1460s, and £308 in the 1470s.[14] Clearly we should pay close attention to Du Boulay's judgement that the estate passed through 'a phase of mid-century doldrums … when it became rather harder to make satisfactory leases' [66: *220, 225*].

Similar doubts can be expressed about some of the claims

concerning the basis of the prosperity of the Greys of Ruthin, whose lands lay for the most part in the east Midlands [80]. While it is evident that this noble family benefited greatly from the longevity of heads of the house, a rare absence of minorities, prudent management, and skilful avoidance of the major pitfalls of war and politics, there is insufficient evidence for us to be certain that income from the individual manors which comprised its landed estates did not decline in the course of the fifteenth century. Inevitably the small cluster of extant sources, comprising in the main a single valor dated 1467–8 and two receivers' accounts from the mid-1440s, reveals little about agrarian trends in the first half of the century, but it should be noted that the amounts entered under 'decays of rent' in 1467–8 indicate that a decline of 15 per cent had taken place in this source of income since the last rental had been composed. Furthermore, although comparison with an extent made in 1392, of certain of the manors while they were in the hands of the Hastings family, suggests that their yield had not fallen by 1468, we are warned that the 'Hastings estate was in some disrepair by 1392', and that the value of these manors 'may therefore have been lower than usual' [80: *28–9*]. Thus the fortunes of the fifteenth-century Greys cannot be held to have depended upon a rising demand for their lands, still less upon the recovery of population. Similarly, the Hungerfords' rapid social and economic advance appears to have owed far more to good political judgement and high salaries from the holding of office in royal bureaucracies, than to profits forthcoming from their extensive Wiltshire rent-rolls and sheep farms. For the Hungerfords, as well as the Percies, the key to wealth lay in the accumulation of more lands rather than the extraction of greater profits from existing lands [82; 86].

The land market of the south-west displayed exceptional resilience in the later Middle Ages, yet even here there were some severely depressed areas. The prosperity of east and central Cornwall and east Devon, where rents rose to new heights in the fifteenth century and scarcely any vacant holdings were to be found, must be balanced against the more conventional fortunes of west Cornwall and south Devon, where rents fell and vacant holdings abounded. Moreover the economy of the whole region experienced a significant downturn in the middle decades of the

fifteenth century. Although it would be unwise to discount completely the possibility of a less than average decrease in the
population of the south-west, the buoyancy of the local economy
would seem to have played the major part in the maintenance of
land values. The increasing rent rolls enjoyed by landlords fortunate to have estates in the prosperous parts of the south-west were
less the result of land-hunger than of a selective demand for
favourably sited fertile soils; the rents of poor and ill-sited soils
stagnated or declined. The contrasts between the fortunes of
different parts of the region were heightened by high levels of
mobility among the population. For these reasons it would be
unwise to argue for general demographic vitality from the fortunes
of the south-west [70; 71; 76; 78].

After our examination of the English economy in the second half
of the fourteenth century it is scarcely necessary to warn against
any simple correlation between the level of population and the
level of economic activity, even in the agrarian sector. In addition
our knowledge of the agrarian sector is perforce composed of the
experience of a series of individual estates, and there were many
factors, other than the numbers of people, which could affect the
receipts, rent levels and occupation of holdings on a single estate.
For example, the landlord who adopted flexible and imaginative
policies to cope with changed economic circumstances might
compete successfully for tenants with his more conservative peers.
It must also be stressed that the land market was constrained by
custom, and that for a time some landlords successfully used their
seigneurial authority to force tenants to remain on their holdings
and pay, in both money and labour, rents in excess of the true
market value of the land. On the other hand it is essential that we
should not regard peasants as mere flotsam drifting on the tide of
economic fortune and seigneurial authority. On the contrary the
peasantry frequently took steps to exploit the power that declining
demand for land had given them, including refusal to pay rents or
other dues, and the abandonment of holdings on a grand scale if
the terms of the tenancies were not acceptable [7]. Some account
must also be taken of the adverse effects of border raids and
military campaigns on the economies of estates situated in the far
north and west, although they do not appear to have been decisive
[64: 274–5; 87: 560].

In spite of the difficulties of interpretation, however, the great weight of the agrarian evidence, the scale and uniformity of the changes in the occupation and value of land between the late fourteenth century and the late fifteenth are such as to be virtually incapable of explanation without recourse to population decline. The thesis of fifteenth-century population decline, supported as it is by the direct demographic evidence discussed earlier, is further strengthened by the contention of those who have studied the phenomenon of the deserted village, that the most rapid depopulation of all occurred between 1450 and 1485 [56: *11–17*], and by the well-attested conclusion that retreating cultivation took place alongside a dramatic increase in the average size of holdings and a dramatic decrease in the numbers of labouring poor [17: *139 ff.*]. Furthermore, firmer and more precise evidence of the course of population is beginning to emerge from the painstakingly detailed study of manorial court rolls, a new and promising venue of research into medieval society. A by-product of the intimate knowledge which follows from the massing of minute data on individual and families is that researchers are able to make informed projections of the probable course of population on the manors they have studied. In the two such studies which have so far been published the authors are in no doubt that the population of their manors declined substantially. E. A. DeWindt tells us that, 'It is definite . . . that Holywell [Hunts.] was experiencing a decline in resident population from as early as the second decade of the fourteenth century and on into the 1450s.' The scale of this decline was prodigious: 64 per cent between 1300 and 1450 [63: *166–71*]. J. A. Raftis has found a somewhat different chronology at Warboys (Hunts.), but a similar trend. A partial recovery in population took place on this manor after the Black Death, but from 1370, 'a steady and prolonged decline set in. This was most drastic after 1400, so that by the mid-fifteenth century the population would seem to have been less than one half of that one hundred and fifty years earlier' [89: *68*].

There would, therefore, appear to be no doubt that there were substantially fewer people in the countryside in the mid-fifteenth century than there had been fifty or sixty years before. If one is not inclined to accept that the population of England declined during this period, the only possible alternative explanation must lie in a truly prodigious expansion of the non-agrarian sectors of the economy which gave employment to those who were clearly no longer on the land. It is not a difficult task to demonstrate that such an explanation has no substance whatsoever.

(b) Towns, trade and industry

In order for the urban, industrial and commercial sectors of the economy to have offered any compensation for decline in the rural population the numbers absorbed by them would have had to grow not only relatively but absolutely. In order for these sectors to have offered complete compensation they would have had to grow at a rate approximately nine times greater than the rate at which numbers in the agricultural sector were falling. Thus, for the sake of argument, in order to compensate for a fall of only 10 per cent in the agricultural population the numbers living in towns and employed in industry and trade would have had to almost double. While it is possible that the non-agricultural sectors continued in the fifteenth century to grow relative to the agricultural, and just possible, although most unlikely, that they grew a little in absolute terms, growth on any greater scale simply cannot be contemplated. We have already noted the sharp decline recorded in the first half of the fifteenth century in those branches of industry and overseas trade for which data exist, and even the most optimistic commentator on the fortunes of the late medieval urban sector readily admits that, 'most provincial towns had many fewer inhabitants after the Black Death than before it' [2: 62]. Those who take a more pessimistic view would see the period from *c.* 1420 to *c.* 1550 as one of relentless urban economic decline and demographic attrition [111].

With towns as with agriculture, however, the more closely one looks at the evidence the more one appreciates that generalisations are hazardous. Not only does account have to be taken of the varying fortunes of the older towns, large and small, but also of the many industrial villages which grew into sizeable settlements in this period. Looking first at the older centres, there can be little doubt that there was a substantial overall decline in both their populations and their prosperity. Of the dozen or more leading towns of late fourteenth-century England, all with populations of 4000 or more, fewer than half, most notably London, Colchester, Salisbury and Newcastle, appear to have successfully resisted substantial decline as the fifteenth century wore on. Of the forty or so towns with populations in 1377 of between 1000 and 4000 those which resisted decline or advanced to new peaks of population and prosperity – for example Exeter, Plymouth, Worcester, Reading and Ipswich – were far outnumbered by those which succumbed. This is not to say that a great many of these older towns did not continue to enjoy a fair measure of trade, rather that in terms of both total population and aggregate economic activity there were few which did not contract between the later fourteenth century and the close of the fifteenth.[15]

There are clear signs that changes in the distribution of wealth and in consumption patterns profoundly affected the structure of the late medieval economy; in particular they led to shifts in the location of industries, and to changes in the nature of the industries themselves and the articles which they produced. We must not be over-impressed, therefore, with evidence of contraction in the older urban centres, for this contraction was undoubtedly compensated to an appreciable extent by growth in newer centres and in rural industries. Just as the expanding cloth industry, based primarily upon the production of cloth suitable for the mass market, provided the foundation of the prosperity of most of the older towns which resisted the general decline, so it also encouraged the spectacular development of many villages into thriving towns. Notable examples of such development in the south-west include Totnes and Tiverton; in Suffolk and north Essex, Hadleigh, Maldon, Lavenham, Nayland, Long Melford, Sudbury and Coggeshall; in the West Riding, Leeds, Bradford, Halifax and Wakefield; and in the Cotswolds, Castle Combe, Stroudwater (& district) [2: *112–13*; 102; 108; 110]. Some of the metal trades also enjoyed substantial growth. The manufacture of pewter, to satisfy the fashionable desires of the gentry, bourgeoisie and richer peasant alike, was one of the few exclusively urban industries to expand rapidly [107: *ch. 2*], while the primarily rural iron-working industries of north Worcestershire and south Staffordshire stimulated the development of Birmingham and its environs [6: *86–7*].

In light of the evidence of variations in agrarian and industrial prosperity recited above it should come as no surprise to learn that profound changes took place in the regional distribution of population and wealth in later medieval England. A comparison of the distribution of taxable wealth between counties in 1334 and 1515 reveals that the position of counties south of a line from the Severn estuary to the Wash improved markedly *vis-à-vis* that of counties to the north [19]. The most impressive performances were recorded by Cornwall, Devon, Somerset, a group of counties surrounding London, namely Middlesex, Surrey, Kent and Hertfordshire, and the clothworking counties of Essex and Suffolk. We know that peasant families were surprisingly mobile [7: *32–5;* 84], and a comparative study of the 1377 Poll Tax returns and Tudor subsidy and muster returns will doubtless reveal that a major redistribution of population accompanied this redistribution of wealth. More detailed investigation will also reveal that major redistributions of population and wealth took place within as well as between counties.

Thus in the England of the fifteenth century, as in the Britain of the 1920s and 30s, the depression was punctuated by instances of striking growth and development. These instances helped to balance the decline taking place in other centres of industry and trade, but even the cloth industry did not grow at a rate sufficient to have offered significant compensation for the overall decline in the rural population. We have learnt that the major concentrations of clothworkers provided a strong stimulus to the economies of their hinterlands, but in national terms the impact was much more limited. It has been estimated, on the basis of stable home demand, that the cloth industry employed 23–26,000 more people at the end of the fourteenth century than at the beginning [101: *261 n.*]; but even allowing for further increases thereafter it is probable that at the very most an additional 2 per cent of the population found some employment in clothworking. Much of this employment was, moreover, of a part-time character, consisting of the labour of peasant families who continued to devote most of their time to farming.

Since our primary concern is the reconstruction of the course of the national population we have dwelt upon absolute size and absolute levels of production and employment, and have freely used such words as 'depression', 'recession', 'decline' and 'contraction'. But we should not forget that the most valid measure of economic prosperity results from dividing the total numbers of people into such aggregates. The 'depression' of the fifteenth century was no ordinary depression since it did not involve falling *per capita* output, falling living standards or rising unemployment. A careful distinction needs to be made, therefore, between changes in the total area of land in cultivation, the total size of the urban sector, the total output of industry, the total amount of goods imported and exported, and these changes measured in terms of the size of the prevailing population of England. That the fall in population generally exceeded the fall in production is suggested by the behaviour of real wages.

(iii) Wages, prices and the supply of money

Much expert attention has been devoted to the interpretation of medieval and early modern wage and price data, and many attempts have been made since Professor Postan's pioneering article in 1950 to utilise them for demographic purposes. Fortunately the accumulation of a wide range of direct and indirect demographic evidence means that it is no longer necessary to attach prime importance to these data, and yet if they are employed with discretion they can still play a useful supporting role. Discretion must be employed, however, since wages and prices are blunt instruments in the hands of the historical demographer, and although they are fully capable of reflecting large-scale shifts in the level of population, they are much less informative in less spectacular periods. The level of population was undoubtedly a major determinant of the level of wages and prices, but other factors may have played a part, including the amount of money in the nation and the speed with which it circulated. The prices of foodstuffs were also influenced by such diverse, and to us frequently obscure, factors as changes in the size of the non-agrarian sectors of the economy, in the balance between pastoral and arable farming, in the levels of exports and imports, and in the weather and the state of technology; while wages were influenced by custom and legislation as well as by the supply of labour and the demand for it. Nor should we neglect, given the experience of our own times, the fact

Table II *Wage-rates, 1301–1540*

| | Piece-rates for threshing and winnowing 3 rased quarters of grains (wheat, barley, oats) | | | Daily wage-rates of craftsmen and labourers | | | | | | | |
| | | | | Average of rates on 8 Winchester Manors | | | | Rates paid for building work in Westminster | | | |
	(a) Westminster manors d.	(b) Winchester manors d.	(c) Thorold Rogers d.	(d) Carpenter d.	(e) Thatcher and helper d.	(f) Labourer d.	(g) Tiler and helper d.	(h) Carpenter d.	(i) Labourer d.	(j) Mason d.	(k) Tiler and helper d.
1301–10	6.51	3.85	—	2.82	3.19	1.49	6.19				
1311–20	8.01	4.05	—	3.41	3.55	1.87	6.44				
1321–30	6.68	4.62	—	3.39	3.78	1.84	5.91				
1331–40	7.35	4.92	—	3.18	3.82	1.78	5.73				
1341–50	7.41	5.03	—	2.96	3.73	1.86	4.70	3.89	2.12		
1351–60	13.02	5.18	—	3.92	5.00	2.85	6.25	6.06	3.08	6.13	9.00
1361–70	12.76	6.10	7.20	4.29	5.95	3.25	7.01	7.94	4.27	6.52	11.92
1371–80	12.23	7.00	8.70	4.32	5.98	3.19	6.89	6.00	3.39	7.35	10.50
1381–90	10.82	7.22	9.03	4.40	6.01	3.35	7.54	6.42	3.33	7.21	10.00
1391–1400	10.44	7.23	7.66	4.13	5.85	3.30	7.36	5.68	3.46	6.48	11.51
1401–10	11.00	7.31	8.37	4.64	6.31	3.53	8.17	—	3.33	6.67	12.50
1411–20	12.40	7.35	8.50	4.51	6.40	3.69	8.50	6.22	4.00	6.67	11.88
1421–30	10.00	7.34	8.13	4.52	6.19	3.83	8.56	6.77	3.84	6.67	12.99
1431–40	13.00	7.30	9.75	4.75	6.89	3.87	8.81	7.00	4.87	6.67	13.20
1441–50	13.00	7.33	9.13	5.18	8.19	4.11	9.24	8.17	4.91	6.67	13.17
1451–60	—	7.25	8.75	5.23	8.24	4.03	9.60	7.57	4.64	6.67	12.74
1461–70	—	—	8.50	—	—	—	—	8.00	4.42	6.67	13.00
1471–80	—	—	8.00	—	—	—	—	7.45	4.06	6.67	13.00
1481–90	—	—	7.00	—	—	—	—	6.63	4.03	6.67	12.31
1491–1500	—	—	9.25	—	—	—	—	6.27	4.00	6.67	11.50
1501–10	—	—	11.63	—	—	—	—	6.66	4.07	6.67	12.75
1511–20	—	—	10.00	—	—	—	—	6.64	4.02	6.67	12.24
1521–30	—	—	11.25	—	—	—	—	7.61	4.04	6.67	—
1531–40	—	—	12.25	—	—	—	—	8.00	4.00	6.67	—

Sources: Beveridge [118: 28; 117: 38], Thorold Rogers [128: *I, 320; IV, 525*].

that prices can exert a powerful influence on wages just as wages can exert a powerful influence on prices.

Yet even having regard to all these reservations it cannot be denied that the behaviour of wages between 1350 and 1500 offers strong supporting evidence of substantial long-term population decline. Data from many parts of the country, a small selection of which is printed in Table II, suggest a striking uniformity of change in the course of the last 150 years of the Middle Ages. With occasional reverses both day- and piece-rates for both agricultural and building work climbed upwards to reach a peak somewhere between 1430 and 1460. Sadly the series of agricultural wages are the least satisfactory, but an increase of around 50 to 75 per cent between 1340–9 and 1440–9 in wages paid for threshing and winnowing is indicated, and the true rate may well have been higher.[16] The many good series of building workers' wages record increases over the same century of between 75 and 100 per cent for craftsmen, and 100 and 125 per cent for labourers.[17] Of especial significance is the fact that substantial increases were often recorded in the fifteenth century. This evidence suggests a severe shortage of labour in late medieval England, a suggestion for which there is abundant confirmation in a multitude of non-quantifiable sources, ranging from the frequent reiterations of the Statutes of Labourers to the complaints of individual employers as far apart as the Cornish tin mines and the fertile lowlands of southern Sussex [106: *63–5*; 61: *93, 98*].

Taking the period as a whole, the course of prices generally ran counter to that of wages. But although the century and a half after the Black Death has frequently been termed an era of falling agricultural prices a detailed appraisal of the evidence, some of which is contained in Table III, shows that this is only partly true. In fact grain prices in the second quarter of the fourteenth century were the *lowest* they were ever to be, while in the third quarter of the same century they were maintained at levels comparable with the *highest* ever hitherto seen. From the mid-1370s, however, grain prices began to fall sharply and by the 1380s and 90s a decline of 25 to 30 per cent had taken place. The opening decades of the fifteenth century saw a partial recovery before prices turned downwards again in mid-century; by the closing decades a hesitant recovery was under way. During the same period the prices of

Table III   *Wheat prices, 1301–1540*

| | Decennial means in shillings per quarter | | | | | |
| | Exeter | | Westminster | | 'Eng. average' | |
	s.	Index (1341–50) =100	s.	Index (1341–9) =100	s.	Index (1341–50) =100
1301–10					5.7	119
1311–20	8.4	168			7.9	164
1321–30	6.4	128			6.8	142
1331–40	5.4	108			5.2	108
1341–50	5.0	100	4.3	100	4.8	100
1351–60	7.1	122	7.2	167	7.0	146
1361–70	8.3	166	9.0	209	8.0	167
1371–80	6.8	136	6.8	158	6.7	140
1381–90	5.5	110	5.0	116	5.2	108
1391–1400	5.1	102	5.4	126	5.5	115
1401–10	6.5	130	7.7	179	6.4	133
1411–20	6.3	126	6.9	161	5.8	121
1421–30	5.7	114	6.1	142	5.5	115
1431–40	7.3	146	8.8	205	7.3	152
1441–50	5.4	108	6.1	142	4.9	102
1451–60	6.4	128	6.9	160		
1461–70	6.3	126	6.3	147		
1471–80	6.2	124	7.8	181		
1481–90	6.9	138	7.6	177		
1491–1500	6.0	120	6.1	142		
1501–10	7.3	146	7.3	170		
1511–20	6.8	136	7.6	177		
1521–30	8.6	172	8.4	195		
1531–40	8.4	168	7.8	181		

Sources: Beveridge [116; 117: *38*; 118: *28*]. The dating used by Beveridge has been altered to conform with the usual practice of dating an account by its closing Michaelmas.

livestock and dairy produce, although falling, displayed greater resilience than those of grains, probably due in part to changes in tastes brought about by the improved living standards of the masses [128; *i, 452, iv, 381*; 115: *163*; 15: *209*]. For an over-all view we cannot at present do better than study the behaviour of the price of the Phelps Brown/Hopkins 'composite unit of consumables', composed 80 per cent of foodstuffs and drink and 20 per cent of textiles and fuel, which fell sharply in the later 1370s, recovered somewhat in the first quarter of the fifteenth century, and then plunged to new post-Black Death lows between 1440 and 1479 [125].

The effects of these divergent price and wage movements upon the real wage-rates of common people were dramatic. Staying with the researches of Professor Phelps Brown and Sheila Hopkins we learn that the real wage-rates of Oxford building craftsmen, taking the 1340s as a base, had risen by almost 50 per cent by the last quarter of the fourteenth century and almost 100 per cent by the later fifteenth century, at which time they were higher than they were ever to be again before the later nineteenth century (see Figure 2, p. 77). Naturally these precise figures cannot be applied to the whole community. Indeed since England was primarily a peasant economy wages comprised only a fraction of the real income of the population as a whole; nevertheless they do provide further indications of a general rise in living standards. To use the language of the economist, the real wage was a measure of the marginal productivity of labour, and this in turn must have been closely related to the welfare of the population at large.

Argument about the precise weighting to be given to the various factors which may have played a part in causing these movements in wages and prices is certain to continue, but it is most unlikely that falling population, which reduced the supply of labour relative to that of capital and land, was not of prime importance in the fifteenth century as well as the later fourteenth. Half of the rise in real wage-rates recorded by the Phelps Brown/Hopkins index occurred after 1400, and as we have seen from our glance at the fortunes of towns, industry and commerce, they could not have been forced up to these levels by a rising demand for labour in these sectors. On the contrary, the rising wages of the first seventy-five years of the fifteenth century must be interpreted in the context of substantially declining economic activity and the presence of strong deflationary pressures in the economy. In like fashion the behaviour of agricultural prices fits well into a context of falling population. In particular we should note that food became cheaper in a period when the acreage under cultivation shrank and *per capita* consumption probably increased substantially. By the mid-fifteenth century annual fluctuations in price caused by variations in the quality of the harvest were among the narrowest in recorded history. That this abundance was not assisted by grain imports is clear from both statutes and customs accounts. Between 1394 and 1467 successive Acts of Parliament shifted national policy decisively from the complete prohibition of grain exports to free exports and a prohibition on imports, save only in times of exceptional scarcity. That this shift in policy was occasioned by economic rather than political considerations is exemplified by the many petitions to Parliament which complain, as in 1437, that 'farmers could not sell their corn at a profitable rate', and as in 1445, that 'the counties on the sea could not sell the bulk of their corn other than by oversea traffic'. The growing export trade in grain is a further indication of abundance [105: 131–56].

On a priori grounds alone, however, it would be unwise to place the explanation for price movements solely on population and other 'real' factors; prices may be influenced by the quantity of money in circulation as well as by shifts in supply and demand. Indeed a number of historians have argued that a shortage of money was the prime factor behind the falling prices of the later Middle Ages, and some have gone so far as to suggest that the shortage of money exerted so powerful a depressive influence over the whole economy that it was instrumental in causing the falling production and trade of the fifteenth century [123; 127; 129]. In support of their arguments we find that the annual average output of coin from English mints plunged dramatically after the mid-fourteenth century and fell by a further 50 per cent comparing 1350–1417 with 1418–60, and that frequent complaints were made about the shortage of specie by groups of merchants and tradesmen [121: 410–14; 123: 474–7]. Moreover one notes that the periods of lowest mintings, 1375–1407 and 1438–60, were also periods of low prices.[18]

It is possible therefore that the supply of money may have exercised same influence over price levels, and that its contraction may have contributed in some measure to the economic recession of the fifteenth century. But it is scarcely credible that money supply was a more important influence than population decline on the level of prices and economic activity in late medieval England, and inconceivable that it could be decisive, as some argue, in the face of a recovery of population [123: *479*; 129: *71–2*]. It is far from proven that the contraction in the total stock of money was by itself sufficiently great to have forced prices down. The output of the mints is a very poor guide to the total stock of money, even in the long term. If, as is frequently maintained, England had a balance-of-payments surplus in the later Middle Ages, foreign coin would have been drawn into the country and augmented the native money supply. It is also probable that credit was used more extensively as time went by, and that this helped to compensate for a fall in the total stock of coins [119; 126], and it is possible that a fall in the total stock of money may have been offset to some extent by an increase in the velocity of circulation of remaining coins. Another major criticism of those who would seek to negate the importance of real factors is that as far as prices are concerned it is not the total stock of money in the country which is the crucial measure, rather it is the stock of money per unit of output and to a lesser extent the stock of money per head [122: *91–2*]. From what we know of the output of most goods in the fifteenth century, and of the probable course of population, we can be certain that the decline in the stock of money per unit of output and per head was far less than the decline in the total stock. This may well explain why signs of really acute monetary shortage, for example the widespread adoption of barter, do not appear to be present in fifteenth-century England.

In this century the English currency displayed a remarkable degree of stability, in marked contrast with Continental currencies [119: *419–21*]. It is improbable that it could have done so in the face of dire monetary scarcity, since immense pressures would have built up in favour of debasement. Moreover, despite claims to the contrary, there does not appear to have been an acute shortage of bullion in fifteenth-century England. On the contrary visitors to these shores frequently commented upon the huge quantities of silver and gold plate held in both private and institutional hands, and confirmation of these comments can be found in wills and inventories [137: *28–9, 42–3, 77–8*; 107: *50–1, 60–1*]. If it was felt necessary the Crown could have induced the owners of plate to sell to the mint on favourable terms, thereby greatly increasing the amount of coin in circulation. But the most telling argument of all against relying solely upon monetary explanations is the behaviour of wages, which continued to push upwards during the middle decades of the fifteenth century, commonly believed to be the period of greatest monetary dearth. We can conclude, therefore, that if a shortage of money was exercising a deflationary pressure on the fifteenth-century economy, the behaviour of wages is truly remarkable since it testifies to a growing shortage of labour in conditions normally liable to have produced unemployment. The only satisfactory explanation would seem to lie in a continuing decrease in the size of the population.

4
Why was the population decline so protracted?

Economic conditions in the fifteenth century were without doubt conducive to an expansion of population: land and food were cheap and abundant, while labour was scarce and well-rewarded. Conditions such as these, according to a multitude of demographers and historians from Malthus at the close of the eighteenth century to the flourishing French school of our own times, should have led to a rising birth-rate and a falling death-rate. The age of marriage should have fallen in response to the availability of land and work, marriages should have become more fertile in response both to improved standards of nutrition and to a lessening of the burdens of parenthood, and the infrequency of subsistence crises should have led to a lowering of the mortality schedules of infants, adolescents and adults alike.[19] In the words of Malthus in the 1790s: 'Plenty of rich land to be had for little or nothing is so powerful a cause of population as generally to overcome all obstacles' [36: *I, 304*], and of Goubert in the 1950s: 'The price of wheat almost always constitutes a true demographic barometer' [28: *468*]. If population had expanded apace in the fifteenth century historians would certainly have had few difficulties in explaining why! Yet, as we have seen, it is manifest that such expansion did not take place. In the light of the evidence at present available to us there would appear to be an overwhelming case for assuming that the level of mortality was the prime determinant of the size of the population, and also for assuming in turn that the level of mortality was not primarily determined by economic factors.

The size of a population is, however, a function of its fertility schedule as well as its mortality schedule, and the severe epidemics

of the period sent violent tremors through the social and economic
fabric which may well have led to profound changes in attitudes to
many aspects of life including marriage and procreation. Accordingly, some historians would seek to explain the failure of numbers
to recover by the widespread practising of prudential checks.
Professors Helleiner and Duby have tentatively suggested that the
improved living conditions of the masses 'so far from promoting
early marriages and high marital fertility, may have produced the
opposite effects' – namely that, eager to defend their new-found
prosperity, peasants and artisans delayed marriage and deliberately
limited the size of their families, and that young men increasingly
married older women [30: *69–71*; 67: *309–10*]. It will be noted that
these arguments have some similarity to those put forward by E. A.
Wrigley with reference to later seventeenth-century Colyton [44].
Infanticide practised upon female babies is also mentioned as a
possibility. Sylvia Thrupp has tentatively suggested that some
people may have sought to evade family responsibilities by entering
the Church or leading itinerant lives [40: *118*]. But the lack of
sufficient evidence to prove or disprove such hypotheses is high-
lighted by the fact that Duby espouses precisely the opposite view
and argues not only for a 'reduction in the relative numbers of
landless labourers', but also that 'peasants settled on their land
were probably more careful to limit their families' than were those
who led itinerant lives [67: *309–10*].

    A fundamental criticism of hypotheses which stress delayed
marriages and family limitation is that they would appear to turn
logic on its head, by requiring prudential checks to be applied in an
era when wives and children could be supported, and indeed
owing to the acute shortage of labour could often be self-supporting, and abandoned and not re-applied in the subsequent era
of drastically declining living standards from *c.* 1520 onwards.
Moreover, such evidence as there is seems also directly against
them. One of the immediate effects of plague in the fourteenth
century – as Hume, Sussmilch and Malthus noted with the
epidemics of the eighteenth century – appears to have been an
upsurge in the number of marriages.[20] J. Hajnal's analysis of the
Poll Tax returns of 1377 suggests that the prevailing marriage rate
was high, and that it conformed to the normal 'non-European'
pattern [27: *116–20*]. As for the view that young men may

increasingly have married older women, we can only reflect that Titow has argued, with more conviction and a stronger foundation of evidence, that land *scarcity* in the thirteenth century frequently drove young men to marry widows [96]. Indeed it seems more logical to believe that the population fell despite an increase in the marriage rate and fertility than to believe that it fell, or failed to recover, because of a decrease in the marriage rate and fertility. But it must be admitted that there are scarcely any reliable data on these basic aspects of medieval life, and that there is a pressing need for more research.

Postan would see the level of population both influencing and being influenced by 'upward and downward trends in medieval agriculture'. He entertains the possibility that population, which in his view began to fall before the Black Death and may have continued to fall after the power of plague had waned, was influenced by a long-term agrarian crisis and decline in the productivity of the soil. In Postan's own words, 'the continual inability of men to repair the damage done to the land in previous centuries may have been one of the causes of delayed recovery' [17: *38–9*; see also 14: *233–6*; 16: *569–70*]. So it may, but before one could allow soil exhaustion a leading role the case would have to be made in greater detail, and low productivity of the soil would have to be reconciled with low prices for agricultural produce and a striking freedom from subsistence crises.

Having placed the emphasis upon high mortality caused by disease we must now explore the mechanisms through which it could have operated upon late medieval society. At the outset it must be stressed that it is mistaken to assume that demographic decline could only be effected by national epidemics of spectacular proportions. On the contrary there is every reason to believe that the cumulative impact of lesser and local epidemics could be decisive, the more so if the young were afflicted in disproportionately high numbers. From the last quarter of the fourteenth century plague increasingly occurred in the form of innumerable widely scattered local outbreaks. Notwithstanding, in little more than a century after 1377 England experienced at least fifteen outbreaks of plagues and/or other epidemic diseases of national or extra-regional proportions; namely, 1379–83, 1389–93, 1400, 1405–7, 1413, 1420, 1427, 1433–4, 1438–9, 1457–8, 1463–4,

1467, 1471, 1479–80 and 1485. As most of these outbreaks have received detailed attention in other works it is necessary to comment only upon those that have not. Although not noted by chroniclers as a national outbreak, there is considerable evidence that 1420 saw severe epidemics in many parts of the realm, including Norfolk, Kent, London, Scotland and the north of England [33: *316*; 47: *221–2*; 53: *143, 150*]. In 1427 the cause of the high mortality was not plague but 'a certain rheumy infirmity called *mure* [which] invaded the whole people, and so infected the aged along with the younger that it conducted a great number into the grave' [47: *398*]. In the closing years of the 1450s, we learn, a 'great and grievous plague' afflicted Kent and many other parts of England [139: *67*].

Much more attention must be paid than hitherto to diseases other than plague, for there can be no doubt that they played a major part in raising the death-rate in the fifteenth century, as they did in all centuries of pre-industrial England. The outbreak of 1427 was only one of many fatal pulmonary epidemics in the 1420s; and we know that between 1389 and 1393 famine-sickness and dysentery were rife; that many deaths were precipitated in 1438–9 by the one major famine of the century; and that in 1485 the cause of the high mortality was the 'sweat'. As yet we know little of the precise incidence of diseases such as typhus, diphtheria, measles, dysentery and the various pox and fevers, and scarcely anything about such mysterious afflictions as 'styche' and 'ipydyme'; nor should tuberculosis, appropriately called the 'Great White Plague', a mass killer in all eras, be ignored. Small wonder that William Langland portrayed the late fourteenth century as an age of

> fevres and fluxes,
> Coughes, and cardiacles, crampes and tothaches
> Rewmes and radegoundes and roynouse scalles,
> Byles, and bocches and brennyng agues;
> Frenesyes, and foule yveles . . .
> . . . pokkes and pestilences'
> (*Piers Plowman*, B Text, Passus xx, 80–4, 97)

Also worthy of special attention is the vexed question of whether bubonic plague exhibits a preference for the younger age-groups.

Contemporaries were in no doubt whatsoever that in many of the major epidemics victims were not only selected mainly from the young but also from the male sex. Commentator after commentator from many parts of Europe remarked on the disproportionately large numbers of children and adolescent males who died in the 1360–2 outbreak: the anonymous chronicler of York reports that it was known as '*la mortalite des enfauntz*'; Knighton wrote that the 'great and less died, but especially young men and children', the northern Chronicle of Melsa termed it '*secunda pestilentia . . . que dicta est puerorum*'; and a London chronicler recorded that 'especially it raged among Young Men and Children, being less fatal to Women'. Moreover, *The Brut*, the *Polychronicon* and John of Reading all remarked that men died in far greater numbers than women. De Chauliac, who was among the most reliable of contemporary reporters on medical matters, relates that in France 'a multitude of boys, and a few women were attacked', a view confirmed from as far afield as Poland [47: *203, 206*; 53: *127–9, 136–8*; 50: *180*; 30: *11*].

The markedly different characteristics ascribed by chroniclers to some later outbreaks clearly demonstrate that it is wrong to dismiss their testimony concerning the age-selective impact of epidemics, as has recently been done, on the grounds that they were misled because 'children were so much in evidence as a result of the birth- and death-rate changes brought about by the first plague' [46: *591* n.]. The epidemic of 1369 was termed by more than one observer as a pestilence 'of men and the larger animals' [141: *i, 309*], and while certain outbreaks of the later 1370s and the early 1380s were seen to rage 'chiefly among children' [138: *ix, 14, 21*], others were seen as killing 'both men and women without number', 'an infinity of both sexes', and 'sparing no age or sex' [141: *i, 319*; 47: *219*].[21] The 1390–1 pestilence, which was so prolonged and so severe as to warrant comparison with the Black Death itself, naturally attracted much detailed comment from contemporaries. Walsingham called it 'a great plague, especially of youths and young children who died everywhere in towns and villages in incredible and excessive numbers' [141: *ii, 186*], while the anonymous continuator of Ranulph Higden confirmed that it killed more young than old [138: *ix, 237–8*]. Adam of Usk reporting on the epidemic of 1400 described it as a plague which 'prevailed through all England and specially among the young, swift in its attack and carrying off many souls' [131: *207*].

Modern medical opinion, however, is by no means as certain as late medieval chroniclers that plague frequently strikes hardest at the young and the male sex; in fact many specialists maintain that no group is inherently more vulnerable [51: *209*; 53: *138*]. None the less, R. Pollitzer does admit that differences in death-rate might follow from differences in risks of exposure [52: *503–4*]; children were perhaps more likely to come into contact with rats and fleas because they played on floors and in streets among dirt and rubbish. It must be admitted, however, that plague is not only an extremely complex disease, but our medical knowledge of its nature and behaviour is also unsatisfactory because it has been gathered largely from the study of a handful of small outbreaks in this century. The whole subject is further complicated by the strong possibility that there were many strains of *Pasteurella pestis*. Additional explanations of the susceptibility of the young may lie in the fact that those who recover from an attack of plague usually acquire immunity to infection thereafter [49: *440*], and in the possibility that those who live through an outbreak without becoming infected may, through natural resistance, be less likely to become infected in subsequent outbreaks. Death-rates would therefore tend to be higher among those who had not previously been exposed to infection.

Whereas it is possible, albeit probably misguided, to dismiss the chroniclers as ill-informed and the tale of the Pied Piper of Hamelin as unsubstantiated legend, hard statistics culled from London burial registers present a much more formidable obstacle to the sceptical. Such statistics, from the parish of St Botolph's Without Bishopsgate during the 1603 plague outbreak, have recently been published by M. F. and T. H. Hollingsworth [31]. Using registers which record age at death as well as allowing sex to be deduced from Christian names, the Hollingsworths found not only that mortality was highest among those aged under twenty-five, but also that 'the men were much more affected by plague than the women'. They found also that the general shape of the mortality curve from the plague of 1603 was decidedly downwards from a high level, from probably over 50 percent for the youngest children to no more than 10 per cent at ages over sixty. Although the age-structure of the population at risk has of necessity to be calculated on the basis of a series of assumptions, the resultant differences in death-rate are of such an order of magnitude that they must reflect the actual effects of plague. As in the Middle Ages, however, seventeenth-century plagues did not invariably exhibit identical characteristics and a more superficial analysis of London plagues after 1603 suggests a considerable measure of diversity. Whereas the 1625 plague in St Botolph's parish 'seems to be probably of the same type' as that of 1603, evidence of the 1605 outbreak in St Margaret's, Westminster, suggests a more uniform spread of victims.

In addition, a large proportion of the other diseases likely to have been prevalent in late medieval England display a preference for young victims, including smallpox, measles, scarlet fever and diphtheria. Moreover, there is evidence that at this time tuberculosis was particularly fatal to adolescents and young adults [22]. Attention has already been drawn to the distorted pattern of age-specific mortality found in Christ Church Priory in the fifteenth century, and extensive calculations from Inquisitions *Post Mortem* have revealed that the death-rates of the under-thirty age-group were disproportionately high in the century and a half after the Black Death [38: 70–5]. We should note also that the prevalence of diseases which sought out the young relates convincingly to the persistence of negative replacement rates (discussed above pp. 30–3). Finally we can draw further support for our contention from the pulpit. Moralists are always ready to interpret the phenomena of an age, and a later variant on the common theme that plague was a visitation from God to punish man for his sinfulness was that the excessive mortality among children was due to their misbehaviour:

it may be that [for] vengeaunce of this synne of unworschepynge and despysynge of fadres and modres, God sleeth children by pestylence, as ye seeth al day. ffor in the olde lawe children that were rebelle and unbuxom to here fadres and modres were ypunysched by deth, as the fyfthe boke of holy wryt wytnesseth.
(Quoted in G. R. Owst, *Literature and Pulpit in Medieval England* [Cambridge, 1933] p. 464.)

It would clearly take some very sophisticated demographic analysis to calculate the precise effects of age- and sex-selective mortality, and the firm data from which such an analysis could be made are unlikely ever to be forthcoming in adequate quantities from medieval sources. But it is clear that if such conditions did exist they would have compounded the impact of the prevailing high level of mortality. Frequent visitations of epidemics which not only killed substantial numbers but also left in their wake distorted age- and/or sex-structures would severely inhibit the ability of the population to reproduce itself. Thus instead of merely a temporary raising of the mortality schedule, the fertility schedule might be lowered for a decade or more as depleted cohorts reached marriageable and child-bearing age.[22] Such an effect would also help to explain the lack of close correlation which sometimes occurred between major outbreaks of plague and economic fluctuations, and which is puzzling to historians.

It is for further research to determine the significance that should be assigned to age- and sex-specific mortality, and the concept remains at present little more than a plausible solution to some of the many perplexing problems posed by the apparent behaviour of population in the later Middle Ages. Nevertheless, the attention of historians should be drawn to the extraordinarily jagged population pyramid of Lichfield in 1695, as presented by Gregory King [27: *182*], and to the recently published study of the demographic history of the Pacific Islands, in which it is argued that age-selective mortality, rather than massive outbreaks of disease, was responsible for the substantial long-term decline in the population of several islands [37].

5
Population in early Tudor England

The half century between 1475 and 1525 remains very much a no-man's-land between the main interests of medievalists and early modernists, and it has consequently failed to receive the attention that it merits. Nevertheless both schools of historians have tended to agree that the origins of the demographic explosion of the sixteenth and early seventeenth centuries lay in the last quarter of the century, more especially in the decade 1475 to 1485 [16: *570*; 4: *193*; 24: *44*]. This view would appear to have some truth in it, for at this time, or somewhat earlier, there are the first signs that the long decline in numbers was at last slowing and perhaps even being reversed.

In so far as it is possible to generalise from a wide diversity of regional experience and short-term local ebbs and flows, most economic indicators appear to have reached the bottom of their downward spirals around the middle decades of the fifteenth century. Moreover the direct demographic evidence strongly supports a similar chronology. Replacement rates calculated from Inquisitions *Post Mortem* at last moved above unity after 1445, albeit only marginally and tentatively at first, while those based upon wills show an increase in the numbers of sons surviving their fathers from the 1460s (see above pp. 30–3). But it would be wrong to assume that the population increased rapidly and continuously thereafter, for there are many signs that this early vitality was temporarily undermined some time before the end of the century.

The tendency for the demand for land to quicken in the last quarter of the fifteenth century has been noted in a large number of estate and regional studies, and this quickening has frequently been explained by reference to an expanding population. Such statements as 'the population trend was at last showing marked signs of recovery' [81: *183*] and 'by the 1490s an increasing population deprived the tenants of their ultimate sanction, easy migration' [68: *32*] are frequently encountered. The most spectacular increases in rents, both arable and pastoral, are to be found in the counties around London, but evidence of an arresting or reversal of the familiar downward trend is widely based in both England [55: *41–2*; 62: *119*; 64: *273*; 65] and Europe [30: *20–5*]. The later fifteenth-century upswing in England's industrial and commercial activity was of even more substantial proportions. The average increase in recorded imports and exports, already rising before the accession of Henry VII, was fully 100 per cent by the accession of Henry VIII twenty-four years later [113]. This remarkable feat was equalled, perhaps even exceeded, by the performance of some major industries [106: *158–9*]. The fact that prices did not move decisively before the second decade of the sixteenth century need not preclude a modest increase in population, for the gross under-utilisation of land in the late fifteenth century meant that food production could be increased without difficulty or substantially enhanced costs; while the failure of wage-rates to move upwards in a period of rapidly expanding industrial employment seems to imply an increasing supply of labour, perhaps provided in part by the countryside.

For further indications of the movement of population we can turn to the incidence of disease. Sadly there are no English sources to compare with the German chronicler who was so impressed by the evidence of growth that he wrote in 1483 that 'within these twenty years there has not been any real pestilence; and seldom is there a couple but they have eight, nine, or ten children' [30: *24*]. Instead we have only curt references to outbreaks of disease, and the translation of an imperfect epidemiological record into a demographic trend is a most speculative undertaking. Until more research is carried out on the incidence of disease and the level of replacement rates it would be foolish to be dogmatic; none the less there are grounds for believing that the mortality rate may have eased appreciably from time to time in the later fifteenth century. It is possible that the lengthening gaps between major plague outbreaks may have been reflected in some abating of the frequency and virulence of local outbreaks. If one is forced to be specific, the later 1440s and the 1450s and the late 1480s and the 1490s may well have been relatively healthy by the standards of the times.

Yet we must be careful to distinguish any early tentative upward movements in numbers from the well-documented progressive population pressure experienced under the later Tudors and early Stuarts. Evidence is mounting which suggests that in many areas the recovery in the land market was not strong, that it often petered out before 1500, and sometimes went into reverse. It may well prove true that, with the exclusion of those regions benefiting from proximity to London or other expanding food markets, many arable rents did not move sharply upwards before the 1520s [21; 73].[23] Looking to the major towns we find the persistence and, in many cases, the intensification of economic and demographic retrenchment. Judging by the well-documented experience of Coventry, where in the early 1520s a quarter of all the property was vacant and the total population was well on the way to being less than a half of what it had been in 1434 [111: 6–8], we would be ill-advised to dismiss the laments of contemporaries about the decay of England's towns and cities as wild exaggerations.[24] There is more than a grain of truth in such claims as '300 and more dwellings [had] decayed within a few years' before 1487 and 1488 in Gloucester, that 800 ruined houses existed in Bristol in 1518 and over 900 in 1530, and that in 1512 'many and the most partie of all the Cities, Boroughs and Townes corporate wythin this realme of Englande be fallen in ruyn and decaye'.[25]

Nor should the likelihood of an intermittent slackening in the incidence of disease be allowed to create the impression that the closing decades of the fifteenth century and the opening decades of the sixteenth were positively salubrious. The mid-1460s, the early and late 1470s, and the years at the turn of the century saw severe outbreaks of plague in many parts of the country, and in the autumn of 1485 there occurred the first, and by far the most lethal, outbreak of the strange disease known as the English Sweat, which according to chroniclers spread over much of England killing 'young and old and of all manner of ages' in great numbers [47: 240–3, 237–43, 282–8]. It seems probable that these waves of disease temporarily brought to an end or even reversed the tentative recovery.

Yet by the second quarter of the sixteenth century the indications of a marked quickening in population growth become evident. By the 1520s sharp increases had taken place in the prices of foodstuffs, real wages had fallen by a third, and the struggle for land which was to characterise the next hundred years and more was growing in ferocity. By the 1530s contemporaries tell us that the times were less disease-ridden than they had been hitherto, and the earliest series of parish registers, commencing in the 1540s and 1550s, suggest that birth-rates were extremely high.

This is not to say that society was forced against the final limits of subsistence within a short space of time. On the contrary the long decline in population stretching back perhaps almost two hundred years, and the economic contraction of the first three-quarters of the fifteenth century, had created a great deal of slack. Although the testimony of Italian visitors to England on these matters is somewhat suspect owing to the very high density of population in their native lands, it is interesting to learn that a Venetian wrote in the later 1490s that

Agriculture is not practised in this island beyond what is required for the consumption of the people; because were they to plough and sow all the land that was capable of cultivation, they might sell a quantity of grain to the surrounding countries ... The population of this island does not appear to me to bear any proportion to her fertility and riches. I rode ... from Dover to London and from London to Oxford ... and it seemed to me to be very thinly inhabited; but, lest the way I went ... should have differed from the other parts of the country, I enquired of those who rode to the north of the kingdom, i.e. to the borders of Scotland, and was told that it was the same case there; nor was there any variety in the report of those who went to Bristol and into Cornwall   [137: *10, 31*]

It is also instructive to learn that well-informed English statesmen likewise felt that the country was seriously underpopulated in the 1530s [140: *iii, 5*]. Indeed the *Dialogue* between Cardinal Pole and Thomas Lupset, as composed by Thomas Starkey, refers at considerable length to the 'grete lake of pepul and skaresenes of men' and to the view that 'in tyme past many mo have byn nurychyd therin, and the cuntrey hath byn more populos, then hyt ys now' [135: *72–6*]. It was claimed that 'batyl and pestylens, hungur and darth' were not the principal causes of this lack of people, rather it was an avoidance of marriage and procreation.

Consequently the answer was 'to intyse man to thys lauful maryage and couplyng togydur', and the suggested means of enticement were to repeal the law of chastity in the Church, limit the numbers of serving men that might be kept, since serving men do not marry, give those who marry a house and a portion of the waste lands at a nominal rent, grant tax reliefs and privileges to those who had five children, and impose a swingeing tax on bachelors [135: *145–52*].

After reading these deliberations one is tempted to speculate that, in order to resist the fall in real wages which followed upon the tendency of the population to increase when the power of disease abated, people were delaying marriage and limiting their families. Such measures, however, could have provided only a palliative, and before 1600 real wages had plunged to the lowest level ever and commentators were increasingly arguing that England was overpopulated [120: *293*].

6
Conclusion

Having come this far it is difficult to resist the temptation to engage in the popular sort of guessing at the population of England over the broad sweep of almost half a millennium of history from Domesday to the subsidies of the third decade of the sixteenth century. Domesday Book presents the historical demographer with a set of problems similar to those presented by the 1377 Poll Tax returns. A raw total of about 275,000 persons mentioned in Domesday has to be converted into the national population. Each person is usually taken to be the head of a household, and a multiplier of just under five would appear appropriate to convert them into families. In addition allowance has to be made for four northern counties and at least two major cities omitted from the survey, and for the likelihood of unrecorded sub-tenants and landless men. By these means the 275,000 becomes an estimated 1.75–2.25 million [4: *45*; 17: *28–9*]. Our next landmark is the Poll Tax, which for reasons outlined above indicates that there were approximately 2.5 to 3 million people in England in 1377 (see p. 18). Our next calculation is extremely speculative, since it involves estimating the loss of population between 1348 and 1377. If we simply add up the death-rates of the four major epidemics between these dates, and assume a static population in the intervening years, then population would have fallen by 65–75 per cent. But to do so would be unrealistic, and substantial allowance must be made for demographic recovery between outbreaks; a net decline of 40–50 per cent might therefore be in order (see above pp. 25–9). If so, England's population in 1348 might well have lain within the range of 4.5 to 6 million, with the balance of possibilities pointing to the higher reaches of this range. Moreover it is unlikely that the population in 1348 was not somewhat lower than it had been at its peak, which was probably around the turn of the thirteenth century.

We move to firmer ground with recent attempts to coax national population figures from the tax returns and muster certificates of the 1520s. As with all pre-census material the use of these records requires considerable judgement; in particular estimates have to be made of the number of people omitted from the tax returns because they were too poor or too young, or from the muster certificates because they were too young or too old. J. Cornwall's resourceful methodology has led him to conclude that the population of England around 1522–5 was of the order of 2.3 million [24]. This figure might well be a little too low since Cornwall, by using Gregory King's age-structure data from the late seventeenth century, a period of relatively low fertility, may well have over-estimated the proportion of the population liable to military service. We would thus appear to be justified in suggesting a range of 2.25 to 2.75 million for this date. As we have seen there is good reason to believe that population in the 1520s was somewhat above its lowest point, which was probably reached in the mid-fifteenth century when England may have contained only 2 to 2.5 million people. If this is so then population in the mid-fifteenth century was scarcely, if at all, higher than it had been in 1086, and it had fallen by at least 60 per cent since the Black Death. Furthermore, it is unlikely that the population level of 1377 was exceeded until the second quarter of the sixteenth century.[26] It does not need to be stressed that all these figures are highly speculative, and that the chart of population flows illustrated on p. 77 has even scantier claims to accuracy.

In this account a number of variables have been discussed at some length, including the level of population, the standard of living, the level of economic activity, and the incidence of disease. A plausible attempt can be made to represent graphically the relationship between two of these variables, the level of population and the standard of living, over five centuries of pre-industrial England. Admittedly the population levels portrayed are little more than judicious guesswork and the standard of living is really the real wage-rates of building craftsmen in southern England, but the patterns which they trace in Fig. 2 are in such stark contrast to each other that doubts as to precise accuracy need not be of central importance. It can be seen at a glance that high population coincided with low living standards, and low population with high living standards, and that as population rose so living standards fell, and that as population fell so living standards rose. It can also be seen that in the seven hundred years portrayed by Figs 1 and 2 there were two protracted periods of sharply rising population and two protracted periods of falling, stagnant, or only slowly rising population.

In some respects the relationship that is portrayed between population and real wage-rates could be held to be Malthusian in the long run. Malthusian crises could be postulated for the early fourteenth and mid-seventeenth centuries, and explained in terms of the sharply declining living standards of the preceding eras. Subsequent recoveries in population might be held to have been stimulated by high living standards. Yet it could also be argued that the duration of such cycles, with periods of both rising and falling or stagnant population often exceeding 100 years, was so long as to bring into question whether the relationship between living standards and numbers of people was truly Malthusian. Certainly these time-spans are far removed from the immediacy of the response suggested by Malthus himself and recently by historians, who would portray the demographic experience of pre-industrial Europe in the following terms: 'Whenever in relation to population, land was abundant, birth-rates rose in excess of death-rates and people became more numerous', and 'An amelioration of the conditions of existence, hence a survival, and an increase in economic opportunity had [i.e. before the Industrial Revolution] always been followed by a rise in population'.[27] Likewise the Malthusian checks to a society which appeared gravely to exceed the tolerable limits of existence could be long delayed. The well-known experience of the thirteenth century was repeated in the later sixteenth and early seventeenth centuries, when population continued to rise in the face of a mounting scarcity of food and an appalling slump in living standards.

The lack of a close correlation between living standards and death-rates can be discovered time and gain in pre-industrial societies. The Black Death itself struck England after a significant improvement in living standards had taken place, and in the

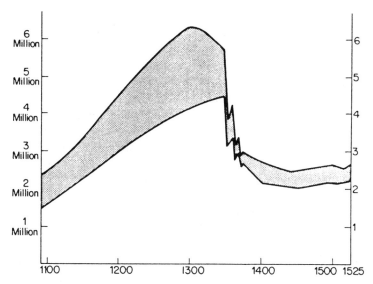

Figure 1 *Long-term flows in English population, 1086–1525 showing the ranges between plausible estimates*

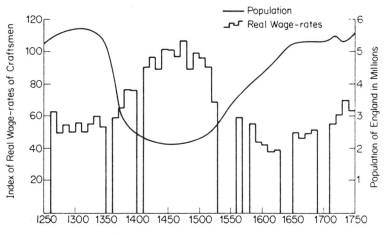

Figure 2 *English population and the real wage-rates of craftsmen, 1250–1750*

The line graph of population is based upon the author's estimates. The bar graph of real wage-rates is based upon Phelps Brown and Hopkins [125].

sixteenth century it seems probable that the highest national mortality occurred in the late fifties when living standards still had a long way to fall. It is also noteworthy that the decades of notoriously low living standards at the turn of the sixteenth century were relatively healthy, and that in the later seventeenth and early eighteenth centuries the virulence of successive waves of epidemics in England and in Europe bore little relationship to the state of the harvest [23: 87–96; 34; 42].

Thus evidence drawn from many periods and many parts of pre-industrial Europe confirms the conclusion to be drawn from late medieval England, namely that mortality was not simply a function of the state of the harvest or the level of real wages. This is not to say that there were not innumerable local subsistence crises during which the death-rate rose sharply, for we know that many maladies associated with malnutrition did increase in incidence in times of scarcity; rather that the national population trend was not in the long run invariably determined by such crises. In the long run the major killers were frequently the epidemic and infectious diseases, and these usually varied in incidence according to a wide range of non-economic factors, including the habits of bacteria, fleas, lice, and rats.*

We would conclude therefore that the prime determinant of the course of population in pre-industrial England was mortality rather than fertility, and that changes in real wages were often merely a secondary influence. Yet we would not go so far as to claim that swings in mortality were invariably exogenous. Our understanding of the demographic experience of pre-industrial England may be advanced if we cease to regard mortality as either a Malthusian agent or an exogenous force, and instead acknowledge that these two broad categories of mortality coexisted. The ineluctable logic of the Malthusian cycle, in which mortality is a function of

---

* It should be noted that this view is by no means generally accepted. The overwhelming conclusion of the contributors to the Third International Conference of Economic History was that the demographic experience of pre- and early industrial societies was very largely a function of the pace and character of economic change. D. E. C. Eversley (ed.), *Third International Conference of Economic History, Munich, 1965*, Paris (1972). A recent econometric analysis by R. Lee does, however, lend support to the views we have expressed ('Population in Preindustrial England: An Econometric Analysis', *Quarterly Journal of Economics*, LXXXVII, 1973).

economic change, cannot be overthrown; other things being equal, high living standards did encourage population growth and low living standards did inhibit population growth or bring about decline. But this model is far too simple to cope with the complexities of historical experience: 'other things' frequently did not remain equal. Epidemic and infectious diseases, only distantly if at all related to economic conditions, were a complicating factor, an additional dimension which has to be superimposed upon the basic Malthusian model. In pre-industrial England the progress of the Malthusian cycle was frequently gravely distorted by epidemic disease. Thus, although population may well have begun to fall, for Malthusian reasons, before 1348, we should not be misled into seeing plague as the inevitable result of dreadful living conditions. Overcrowding and poor sanitation doubtless assisted in the spread of the disease, but there is no reason to suspect that susceptibility to plague is enhanced by malnutrition, and we must entertain the possibility that the second pandemic would have swept through even a prosperous Europe. Certainly it is inconceivable that mortality induced by low living standards could have reduced England's population by more than half and then delayed recovery, despite rising living standards, for almost two centuries. In spite of the protestations of generations of historians there remains much truth in the view that the arrival of plague was a turning-point in history.

Finally we must do something to correct an impression given in this account, and in much of the writing on this period, that living standards can be assessed solely in terms of the amount of goods that a man's wage would purchase. In these terms the fifteenth century was truly the golden age of the English labourer. Yet, as we have seen, these high living standards were not due to any decisive advances in techniques or in the structure of the economy, but to the simple fact that there were fewer people to share the resources of the nation. Moreover, this situation did not result from a once-and-for-all fall in the population, the effects of which have been likened to 'a sort of Marshall Aid on a stupendous scale' for the survivors [2: *91*]. Rather, living standards were maintained and improved further by the persistence of very high death-rates which stopped the population from recovering. Clearly an age which relies for its prosperity upon large numbers of its members dying at an early age, and suffering the frequent losses of spouses, children, relatives, friends and colleagues, is somewhat less than golden. Can we wonder that a preoccupation with death and putrefaction is encountered so frequently in the artistic, literary and religious movements of the age [133; 136]? The problems involved in calculating the material well-being of fifteenth-century Englishmen are formidable enough, but those involved in attempting to balance the result against their physical and mental health and their expectation of life are such as to try the skills of even the most imaginative and resourceful of cliometricians. But the impossibility of quantification is no excuse for neglect.

Notes and references

Unless otherwise indicated, London is the place of publication. The abbreviation *E.H.R.* represents *Economic History Review*.

1 Generally sympathetic statements are to be found in W. Abel, *Die Wüstungen des ausgehenden Mittelalters* (Jena, 1943); 'Wüstungen und Preisfall in spätmittelalterlichen Europa', *Jahrbüch für Nationalökonomie und Statistik*, CLXV (1953); J. Schreiner, *Pest og prisfall i senmiddelalderen* (Oslo, 1948); K. F. Helleiner, 'Population Movement and Agrarian Depression in the Later Middle Ages', *Canadian Journal of Economics and Political Science*, LV, (1949); and in various contributions to the 'Histoire économique: moyen âge' section of the *Rapports du IXᵉ Congrès international des sciences historiques* (Paris, 1950).

2 For a further statement by Kosminsky, somewhat less sceptical of long-term population decline, see 'Peut-on considérer le xiv et le xv siècles comme l'époque de la décadence de l'économie européenne?' *Studi in onore di Armando Sapori*, 2 vols (Milan, 1957) I, pp. 550–69. The most forceful statement by Kosminsky on this subject, also the earliest, was published in *Voprosi Istorii* in 1948.

3 For general criticisms of Russell's methodology and final estimate, see *Cambridge Economic History of Europe*, vol. I, pp. 561–2; Titow [20: *67–8, 84–5*]; J. Krause, 'The Medieval Household: Large or Small?', *E.H.R.*, 2nd ser., IX (1957). Where local sources exist which permit detailed testing of completeness, the 1377 tax returns are frequently shown to be deficient. For example, S. Thrupp has found that the London returns often omitted apprentices, adolescent children and single women [114: *49–50*]; and M. J. Bennett concludes that a study of a range of complementary sources relating to the clergy in north-west England in the later fourteenth century 'casts doubt upon the high degree of accuracy always claimed for the 1377 returns': 'The Lancashire and Cheshire Clergy, 1379', *Transactions of the Historical Society of Lancashire and Cheshire*, CXXIV (1973) p. 3. Lesser under-

enumerations arise from Russell's underestimating the population of Cheshire; see Cornwall [24]; and from his failing to note that the tinners of the south-west were exempt from tax: see J. F. Willard, *Parliamentary Taxes and Personal Property, 1290–1334* (Cambridge, Mass., 1934) pp. 118–20. On the other hand, Russell ascribes the full number of children to the clergy, which is surely taking too literally contemporary complaints of clerical non-celibacy! It is widely appreciated that the first census of 1801 was also seriously defective: Glass and Eversley [27: *223 n. 10*].

4 The data contained in this paragraph differ from those presented by Bean [1: *430, 432–3*] largely because Stone's chronicle [139] has been used to amplify and extend the obituary book.

5 1361 and 1368 were the peak plague years in London (Creighton [47: *203, 205–16*]; Shrewsbury [53: *126–9, 133–4*]). Some chroniclers reserved the title *pestis tertia* for the outbreak of 1375.

6 Total exports of cloth were as follows: 1359–1479 cloths; 1360–1550; 1361–1496; 1362–1144; 1363–1544; 1366–1931; 1367–3219; 1368–2756; 1369–2497; 1370–3181 (Carus-Wilson and Coleman [103: *76–8*]).

7 For generally critical reviews see Morris [51]; P. A. Slack, *English Historical Review*, LXXXVII (1972) 112–15; and R. M. S. McConaghey, *Medical History*, XV (1971) 309–11. The review by P. Laslett in *The Times* (21 February 1971) is much more favourable, and Bridbury [46: *591–2*] finds the arguments of Bean and Shrewsbury concerning the habits and incidence of plague plausible.

8 Far more data, of an admittedly imprecise nature, could be compiled by comparing the numbers of heriots, reliefs, wills, etc., in normal years with those in plague years. This would give widely based indications of the scale of the increase in death-rate, although not of the rate itself.

9 It is significant that the male replacement rates computed by S. Thrupp from later thirteenth-century court rolls are appreciably lower than those recorded from censuses of the same date by H. E. Hallam, 'Some Thirteenth-Century Censuses', *E.H.R.*, 2nd ser., X (1958). Illegitimacy and entry into the Church, further sources of under-enumeration, are discussed by Thrupp.

10 The data presented below have been prepared with the assistance of Mr P. Atkinson. The author hopes to publish an article on the demography of the priory.

11 A general study of late medieval towns is sorely needed, but see *inter alia*: Bartlett [100]; E. M. Carus-Wilson, 'The Medieval Trade of the Ports of the Wash', *Medieval Archaeology*, VI–VII (1962–3); *Historic Towns*, ed. M. D. Lobel and E. M. Carus-Wilson (1975) vol. II.

12 Calculated using the formula and figures given in Bridbury [2: *32–3*],

with adjustments to take account of the changes in the price of wool specified in T. H. Lloyd, *The Movement of Wool Prices in Medieval England*, supplement no. 6 to *E.H.R.* (1973).

13 For critical assessments of valors see: C. D. Ross and T. B. Pugh, 'Materials for the Study of Baronial Incomes in Fifteenth-century England', *E.H.R.*, 2nd ser., VI (1953) 185–94; R. R. Davies, 'Baronial Accounts, Incomes, and Arrears in the Later Middle Ages', *E.H.R.*, 2nd ser., XXI (1968) pp. 213–18. It should also be noted that the structure and purpose of valors differed from estate to estate.

14 Calculated from Table 2, Du Boulay [65: *434*]. The calculations were based upon three surviving accounts for the 1450s, seven for the 1460s and five for the 1470s.

15 For example, Bartlett [100]; J. W. F. Hill, *Medieval Lincoln* (Cambridge, 1965) chapter 13; *Bridgewater Borough Archives, 1468–85*, ed. R. W. Dunning and T. D. Tremlett, Somerset Record Society, LXX (1971) pp. xii–xiii; *Historic Towns*, ed. M. D. Lobel (1969) vol. I; *Historic Towns*, ed. M. D. Lobel and E. M. Carus-Wilson (1975) vol. II; and A. F. Butcher's and C. Phythian-Adams's papers on Canterbury and Coventry respectively, presented to the 1971 Urban History Conference at York University, England.

16 It should be noted that the frequently quoted Winchester series of piece-rates for threshing and winnowing understates the rate of increase after 1400. The series has to be based on fewer and fewer manors, for as the fifteenth century progressed demesnes ceased to be cultivated; almost without exception it is the high-wage manors which ceased to be represented. A rate of around 7·4d. to 7·5d. between 1430 and 1460 would appear to be more accurate representation.

17 The daily wage-rates of building craftsmen and labourers in southern England rose, respectively, from 5d. to 6d. and from 3d. to 4d. in the opening decades of the fifteenth century: Phelps Brown and Hopkins [125]. Rates paid for similar work in Cornwall rose, respectively, from 4d. to 6d. and from 3d. to 4d. in the 1430s: Hatcher [76: *291*].

18 It should be noted, however, that the 20 per cent debasement of 1464 and the subsequent marked upturn in total coinage produced no more than a brief flurry in prices.

19 For a discussion of current thinking concerning fluctuations in pre-industrial populations see Wrigley [43: *62–106*]. It is also instructive to note the similarity between factors used to explain the 'demographic explosion' of the eighteenth and early nineteenth centuries and those ruling in fifteenth-century England. See, for example, Wrigley [43: *146–80*]; H. J. Habakkuk, 'English Population in the Eighteenth Century', *E.H.R.*, 2nd ser., VI (1953); M. Drake (ed.), *Population in Industrialization* (1969).

20 The evidence is slight, but some continental chronicles refer to the

frequency of marriages after the Black Death and the Curé of Givry married forty-two couples between 14 January and 24 February 1349, whereas in the previous year he had not conducted a single marriage service: *Cambridge Economic History of Europe*, vol. I, p. 675.

21 On these points see also Creighton [47: *207, 219*] and Shrewsbury [53: *136–8*].

22 The precise effects of distorted sex-structure, and to a lesser extent age-structure, would depend on the proportion of the population which was unmarried. A sizeable reservoir of single persons who subsequently married would help to lessen the impact on fertility. If we accept Hajnal's thesis (above p. 62) then the proportion of single persons of marriageable age was unlikely to have been high; furthermore with a succession of epidemics any reservoir would soon be drained.

23 It must be admitted, however, that rent movements are a poor indication of possible population increase at this time since the lassitude of the preceding era had encouraged many landlords to grant long leases, and lulled numbers of landlords and tenants into believing that security of tenure at fixed rents and entry fines was the prerogative of all. Time was needed to adjust to changing conditions.

24 In addition to the records and histories of individual towns much of value can be gleaned from John Leland (*The Itinerary of John Leland, 1535–43*, ed. L. Toulmin-Smith, 5 vols., 1907–10), and from Tudor statutes, which list more than fifty cities and towns which had fallen into decay (see in particular the statutes of 4 Henry VII, c. 16; 6 Henry, VIII, c. 5; 7 Henry VIII, c. 1; 25 Henry VIII, c. 13; 27 Henry VIII, c. 1; 32 Henry VIII, c. 18, 19).

25 W. H. Stevenson, *Calendar of the Records of the Corporation of Gloucester* (1893) no. 59; *Select Cases before the King's Council in the Star Chamber*, ed. I. S. Leadam, Selden Society, xxv (1910) p. 146; G. R. Elton, *Reform and Renewal: Thomas Cromwell and the Common Weal* (Cambridge, 1973) pp. 107–8; *Statutes of the Realm*, 3 Henry VIII, c. 8.

26 Many estimates would have 2·8 to 3 million people in the England of 1500. What is more, since these estimates are based upon the assumption that there were only 2·25 million people in 1377, they imply an *increase* between these two dates of around a third. The thesis that we have outlined runs directly counter to this by arguing for a *decrease* between these dates of around a quarter. Current estimates of the level of population in the early sixteenth century are reviewed in Tucker [41: *209–11*], and Clarkson [3: *25–7*].

26 The quotes are drawn from Y. S. Brenner, *A Short History of Economic Progress* (1969) p. 5, and D. S. Landes, 'Technological Change and Development in Western Europe, 1750–1914', *Cambridge Economic History of Europe*, vol. VI, Pt I (Cambridge, 1965; repr. 1966) p. 274.

Select bibliography

A comprehensive bibliography of all the topics touched upon in this book would be inordinately long. We have, therefore, provided full details of the sources which have been cited in the text, and for ease of reference these have been arranged in sections, each section being prefaced by brief critical comments. Unless otherwise indicated, London is the place of publication. The abbreviation *E.H.R.* represents *Economic History Review*.

General studies

All students of the later medieval economy should begin with the works of Postan. Some of his most important studies have been collected together in *Essays on Medieval Agriculture and General Problems of the Medieval Economy* and *Medieval Trade and Finance* (Cambridge, 1973). Saltmarsh's article is also invaluable. Major assaults on the theses of Postan and Saltmarsh have been made by Kosminsky and Bridbury, who dispute that the later Middle Ages experienced a severe depression, and by Bean, who argues that the population decline was probably over by the close of the fourteenth century. Hilton's work places a welcome emphasis on the peasantry, and Du Boulay's on social history.

[1] J. M. W. Bean (1963) 'Plague, Population and Economic Decline in England in the Later Middle Ages', *E.H.R.*, 2nd ser., xv.
[2] A. R. Bridbury (1962) *Economic Growth: England in the Later Middle Ages*.
[3] L. A. Clarkson (1971) *The Pre-Industrial Economy in England, 1500–1750*.
[4] H. C. Darby (ed.) (1973) *New Historical Geography of England* (Cambridge).
[5] F. R. H. Du Boulay (1970) *An Age of Ambition*.
[6] R. H. Hilton (1975) *The English Peasantry in the Later Middle Ages* (Oxford).

[7]   R. H. Hilton (1969) *The Decline of Serfdom in Medieval England*.
[8]   E. A. Kosminsky (1955) 'The Evolution of Feudal Rent in England from the XIth to the XVth Centuries', *Past and Present*.
[9]   J. R. Lander (1970) *Conflict and Stability in Fifteenth-Century England*.
[10] E. Miller (1964) 'The English Economy in the Thirteenth Century', *Past and Present*, 28.
[11] H. A. Miskimin (1969) *The Economy of Early Renaissance Europe, 1300–1460* (Princeton, New Jersey).
[12] M. M. Postan (1939) 'The Fifteenth Century', *E.H.R.*, IX.
[13] M. M. Postan (1950) 'Some Economic Evidence of Declining Population in the Later Middle Ages', *E.H.R.*, 2nd ser., II.
[14] M. M. Postan 1950) 'Histoire économique: moyen âge', *Rapports du IXe congrès international des sciences historiques* (Paris).
[15] M. M. Postan (1952) 'The Age of Contraction', in *Cambridge Economic History of Europe*, vol. II (Cambridge).
[16] M. M. Postan (1966) 'Medieval Agrarian Society in its Prime: England', in *Cambridge Economic History of Europe*, vol. I, 2nd ed. (Cambridge).
[17] M. M. Postan (1972) *The Medieval Economy and Society: An Economic History of Britain, 1100–1500*.
[18] J. Saltmarsh (1941) 'Plague and Economic Decline in England in the Later Middle Ages', *Cambridge Historical Journal*, VII.
[19] R. S. Schofield (1965) 'The Geographical Distribution of Wealth in England, 1334–1649', *E.H.R.*, 2nd ser., XVIII.
[20] J. Z. Titow (1969) *English Rural Society, 1200–1350*.

Demography

Russell's remarkably resourceful statistical study contains much of great value and remains a standard text, but sadly it has not been revised to take account of the research and debate which have taken place since its publication in 1948. Helleiner has provided a stimulating survey of European developments. Thrupp has introduced ingenious methods for charting population change; Cornwall has attempted to estimate England's population in the 1520s; and Blanchard has gathered evidence from parts of the north and Midlands which indicates the persistence of low levels of population into the sixteenth century. Ohlin has made some perceptive criticisms of work done on medieval demography. Although they deal only in part with the later Middle Ages, the works of Chambers, Hollingsworth (1969) and Wrigley (1969) are highly recommended.

[21] I. Blanchard (1970) 'Population Change, Enclosure and the Early Tudor Economy', *E.H.R.*, 2nd ser., XXIII.

[22] Canterbury Cathedral MS. D 12, Obituary Book of Christ Church Priory.
[23] J. D. Chambers (1972) *Population, Economy, and Society in Pre-Industrial England* (Oxford).
[24] J. Cornwall (1970) 'English Population in the Early Sixteenth Century', *E.H.R.*, 2nd ser., XXIII.
[25] F. J. Fisher (1965) 'Influenza and Inflation in Tudor England', *E.H.R.*, 2nd ser., XVIII.
[26] E. Gautier and L. Henry (1958) *La population de Crulai, paroisse normande* (Paris).
[27] D. V. Glass and D. E. C. Eversley (eds) (1963) *Population in History: Essays in Historical Demography.*
[28] P. Goubert (1952) 'En Beauvaisis: Problèmes démographiques du XVIIIᵉ siècle', *Annales*, VII.
[29] B. F. Harvey (1965) 'The Population Trend in England between 1300 and 1348', *Trans. of the Royal Historical Society*, 5th ser., XVI.
[30] K. Helleiner (1967) 'The Population of Europe from the Black Death to the Eve of the Vital Revolution', in *Cambridge Economic History of Europe*, vol. IV.
[31] M. F. and T. H. Hollingsworth (1971) 'Plague Mortality Rates by Age and Sex in the Parish of St. Botolph's Without Bishopsgate, London, 1603', *Population Studies*, XXV.
[32] T. H. Hollingsworth (1964) 'The Demography of the British Peerage', supplement to *Population Studies*, XVIII.
[33] T. H. Hollingsworth (1969) *Historical Demography.*
[34] E. Jutikkala and M. Kauppinen (1971) 'The Structure of Mortality during Catastrophic Years in a Pre-Industrial Society', *Population Studies*, XXV.
[35] R. Lee (1973) 'Population in Preindustrial England: An Econometric Analysis', *Quarterly Journal of Economics*, LXXXVII.
[36] T. R. Malthus (1958 edn) *An Essay on Population*, 2 vols. (ed. M. P. Fogarty).
[37] N. McArthur (1968) *Island Populations of the Pacific* (Canberra).
[38] G. Ohlin (1966) 'No Safety in Numbers: Some Pitfalls of Historical Statistics', in *Industrialization in Two Systems: Essays in Honor of Alexander Gerschenkron*, ed. H. Rosovsky (New York).
[39] J. C. Russell (1948) *British Medieval Population* (Albuquerque).
[40] S. Thrupp (1965) 'The Problem of Replacement Rates in Late Medieval English Population', *E.H.R.*, 2nd ser., XVIII.
[41] G. S. L. Tucker (1963) 'English Pre-Industrial Population Trends', *E.H.R.*, 2nd ser., XVI.
[42] G. Utterström (1954) 'Some Population Problems in Pre-Industrial Sweden', *Scandinavian Economic History Review*, II.
[43] E. A. Wrigley (1969) *Population and History.*

88   *John Hatcher*

[44] E. A. Wrigley (1966) 'Family Limitation in Pre-Industrial England', *E.H.R.*, 2nd ser., XIX.
[45] E. A. Wrigley (1968) 'Mortality in Pre-Industrial England: The Example of Colyton, Devon, over Three Centuries', *Daedalus*, 97.

Disease

The standard works on the medical aspects of plague are by Hurst and Pollitzer. Creighton's book, despite errors on medical matters, is still a useful guide. Shrewsbury's book also contains much of value, although many of its conclusions are extremely controversial; Morris's review essay should be read as a corrective. Ziegler has provided a good readable introduction to the first outbreak of plague.

[46] A. R. Bridbury (1973) 'The Black Death', *E.H.R.*, 2nd ser., XXVI.
[47] C. Creighton (1965 edn) *A History of Epidemics in England* I.
[48] J. L. Fisher (1943) 'The Black Death in Essex', *Essex Review*, LII.
[49] L. F. Hirst (1953) *The Conquest of Plague: A Study of the Evolution of Epidemiology* (Oxford).
[50] W. MacArthur (1948–9) 'The Identification of Some Pestilences Recorded in the Irish Annals', *Irish Historical Studies*, VI.
[51] C. Morris (1971) 'The Plague in Britain', *Historical Journal*, XIV.
[52] R. Pollitzer (1954) *Plague* (Geneva).
[53] J. F. D. Shrewsbury (1970) *The History of Bubonic Plague in England* (Cambridge).
[54] P. Ziegler (1969) *The Black Death*.

The economy

The vast bulk of our knowledge of late medieval economic developments is contained in the studies of particular manors, estates, towns, industries, trades, and regions, some of which are listed below. For an overview see, in addition to the works listed in the first section, the works of Duby, Carus-Wilson (1967), Carus-Wilson and Coleman, and Power and Postan (eds).

Agriculture and agrarian society

[55] J. M. W. Bean (1958) *The Estates of the Percy Family, 1416–1557* (Oxford).
[56] M. W. Beresford and J. G. Hurst (eds) (1971) *Deserted Medieval Villages*.
[57] J. R. Birrell (1962) 'The Honour of Tutbury in the Fourteenth and Fifteenth Centuries', Birmingham University M.A. thesis.

[58] I. S. W. Blanchard (1967) 'Economic Change in Derbyshire in the Later Middle Ages, 1272–1540', London University Ph.D. thesis.

[59] P. F. Brandon (1962) 'Arable Farming in a Sussex Scarp-foot Parish during the Late Middle Ages', *Sussex Archaeological Collections*, c.

[60] P. F. Brandon (1963) 'The Common Lands and Wastes of Sussex', London University Ph.D. thesis.

[61] J. A. Brent (1968) 'Alciston Manor in the Later Middle Ages', *Sussex Archaeological Collections*, cvi.

[62] M. N. Carlin (1970) 'Christ Church, Canterbury, and its Lands, from the Beginning of the Priorate of Thomas Chillenden to the Dissolution, 1391–1450', Oxford University B.Litt. thesis.

[63] E. B. DeWindt (1972) *Lands and People in Holywell-cum-Needingworth: Structures of Tenure and Patterns of Social Organization in an East Midlands Village, 1251–1457* (Toronto).

[64] R. B. Dobson (1973) *Durham Priory, 1400–1450* (Cambridge).

[65] F. R. H. Du Boulay (1964) 'A Rentier Economy in the Later Middle Ages: the Archbishopric of Canterbury', *E.H.R.*, 2nd ser., xvi.

[66] F. R. H. Du Boulay (1966) *The Lordship of Canterbury: An Essay on Medieval Society*

[67] G. Duby (1968 edn) *Rural Economy and Country Life in the Medieval West.*

[68] C. Dyer (1968) 'A Redistribution of Incomes in Fifteenth-Century England?', *Past and Present*, 39.

[69] R. J. Faith (1962) 'The Peasant Land Market in Berkshire', Leicester University Ph.D. thesis.

[70] H. P. R. Finberg (1951) *Tavistock Abbey: A Study in the Social and Economic History of Devon* (Cambridge).

[71] H. S. A. Fox (1975) 'The Chronology of Enclosure and Economic Development in Medieval Devon', *E.H.R.*, 2nd ser., xxviii.

[72] H. E. Hallam (1967) 'The Agrarian Economy of South Lincolnshire in the Mid-Fifteenth Century', *Nottingham Medieval Studies*, xi.

[73] B. J. Harris (1969) 'Landlords and Tenants in the Later Middle Ages: The Buckingham Estates', *Past and Present*, 43.

[74] B. F. Harvey (1969) 'The Leasing of the Abbot of Westminster's Demesnes in the Later Middle Ages', *E.H.R.*, 2nd ser., xxii.

[75] P. D. A. Harvey (1965) *A Medieval Oxfordshire Village: Cuxham, 1240–1400* (Oxford).

[76] J. Hatcher (1970) *Rural Economy and Society in the Duchy of Cornwall, 1300–1500* (Cambridge).

[77] R. H. Hilton (1947) *The Economic Development of Some Leicestershire Estates in the Fourteenth and Fifteenth Centuries*, (Oxford).

[78] D. J. B. Hindley (1958) 'The Economy and Administration of the Estates of the Dean and Chapter of Exeter Cathedral in the Fifteenth Century', Exeter University M.A. thesis.

[79] G. A. Holmes (1957) *The Estates of the Higher Nobility in Fourteenth-century England* (Cambridge).

[80] R. I. Jack (ed.) (1965) *The Grey of Ruthin Valor: The Valor of the English Lands of Edmund Gray, Earl of Kent, drawn up from Ministers' Accounts of 1467–68* (Sydney).

[81] I. Kershaw (1973) *Bolton Priory: The Economy of a Northern Monastery, 1286–1325* (Oxford).

[82] J. L. Kirby (1939) 'The Hungerford Family in the Later Middle Ages', London M.A. thesis.

[83] A. E. Levett and A. Ballard (1916) 'The Black Death on the Estates of the See of Winchester', in *Oxford Studies in Social and Legal History*, vol. v.

[84] R. P. McKinley (1969) *Norfolk Surnames in the Sixteenth Century*, Leicester University Department of English Local History, Occasional Papers, 2nd ser., II (Leicester).

[85] F. M. Page (1934) *The Estates of Crowland Abbey* (Cambridge).

[86] R. C. Payne (1939) 'The Agricultural Estates in Wiltshire of the Duchy of Lancaster in the 13th, 14th, and 15th Centuries', London University Ph.D. thesis.

[87] A. J. Pollard (1972) 'Estate Management in the Later Middle Ages: The Talbots and Whitchurch, 1383–1525', *E.H.R.*, 2nd ser., XXV.

[88] J. A. Raftis (1957) *The Estates of Ramsey Abbey: A Study in Economic Growth and Organization* (Toronto).

[89] J. A. Raftis (1974) *Warboys: Two Hundred Years in the Life of an English Medieval Village* (Toronto).

[90] A. F. Roderick (1938) 'Agrarian Conditions in Herefordshire and the Adjacent Border during the Later Middle Ages', London University Ph.D. thesis.

[91] E. Searle (1974) *Lordship and Community: Battle Abbey and its Banlieu, 1066–1538* (Toronto).

[92] B. H. Slicher Van Bath (1963) *The Agrarian History of Western Europe, A.D. 500–1850*.

[93] R. A. L. Smith (1943) *Canterbury Cathedral Priory: A Study in Monastic Administration* (Cambridge).

[94] R. Somerville (1953) *The Duchy of Lancaster, 1265–1603*.

[95] R. L. Storey (1961) *Thomas Langley and the Bishopric of Durham*.

[96] J. Z. Titow (1962) 'Some Differences between Manors and their Effects of the Condition of the Peasants in the Thirteenth Century', *Agricultural History Review*, x.

[97] G. H. Tupling (1927) *The Economic History of Rossendale*, Chetham Society, new ser., LXXXVI (Manchester).

[98] *Victoria County History: Hampshire*, vol. v (1912).

[99] *Victoria County History: Wiltshire*, vol. IV (1959).

Industry, towns and trade

[100] J. N. Bartlett (1959) 'The Expansion and Decline of York in the Later Middle Ages', *E.H.R.*, 2nd ser., XII.

[101] E. M. Carus-Wilson (1967 edn) *Medieval Merchant Venturers.*

[102] E. M. Carus-Wilson (1959) 'Evidences of Industrial Growth on some Fifteenth-Century Manors', *E.H.R.*, 2nd ser., XII.

[103] E. M. Carus-Wilson and O. Coleman (1963) *England's Export Trade, 1275–1547* (Oxford).

[104] O. Coleman (1963) 'Trade and Prosperity in the Fifteenth Century: Some Aspects of the Trade of Southampton', *E.H.R.*, 2nd ser., XVI.

[105] N. S. B. Gras (1967 edn) *The Evolution of the English Corn Market from the Twelfth to the Eighteenth Century* (New York).

[106] J. Hatcher (1973) *English Tin Production and Trade before 1550* (Oxford).

[107] J. Hatcher and T. C. Barker (1974) *A History of British Pewter.*

[108] H. Heaton (1920) *The Yorkshire Woollen and Worsted Industries* (Oxford).

[109] M. K. James (1971) *Studies in the Medieval Wine Trade* (Oxford).

[110] B. McClennaghan (1924) *The Springs of Lavenham* (Ipswich).

[111] C. Phythian-Adams 'Coventry and the Problem of Urban Decay in the Later Middle Ages' (unpublished paper submitted to the 1971 Urban History Conference).

[112] E. Power and M. M. Postan (eds) (1933) *Studies in English Trade in the Fifteenth Century.*

[113] P. Ramsey (1953) 'Overseas Trade in the Reign of Henry VII: The Evidence of the Customs Accounts', *E.H.R.*, 2nd ser., VI.

[114] S. Thrupp (1962) *The Merchant Class of Medieval London* (Ann Arbor, Michigan).

Wages, prices and money supply

The articles by Phelps Brown and Hopkins provide the best introduction. Thorold Rogers remains, after more than a century, the fount of most data, with Beveridge's articles providing a valuable supplement. Miskimin, Robinson, and Shreiner emphasise the importance of money supply in creating the economic conditions of the later Middle Ages, while Postan and Cipolla minimise it.

[115] W. H. Beveridge (1927) 'The Yield and Price of Corn in the Middle Ages', *Economic History*, II.

[116] W. H. Beveridge (1929) 'A Statistical Crime of the Seventeenth Century', *Journal of Economic and Business History*, I.

[117] W. H. Beveridge (1936) 'Wages in the Winchester Manors', *E.H.R.*, VII.

[118] W. H. Beveridge (1955) 'Westminster Wages in the Manorial Era', *E.H.R.*, 2nd ser., VIII.

[119] C. Cipolla (1963) 'Currency Depreciation in Medieval Europe', *E.H.R.*, 2nd ser., XV.

[120] D. C. Coleman (1956) 'Labour in the English Economy of the Seventeenth Century', *E.H.R.*, 2nd ser., VIII.

[121] Sir John Craig (1953) *The Mint: A History of the London Mint from A.D. 287 to 1948* (Cambridge).

[122] M. Friedman (1965) 'The Supply of Money and Changes in Prices and Output', in *The Controversy over the Quantity Theory of Money*, ed. E. Dean (Boston, Mass.).

[123] H. A. Miskimin (1964) 'Monetary Movements and Market Structure, Forces for Contraction in Fourteenth and Fifteenth Century England', *Journal of Economic History*, XXIV.

[124] E. H. Phelps Brown and S. V. Hopkins (1955) 'Seven Centuries of Building Wages', *Economica*.

[125] E. H. Phelps Brown and S. V. Hopkins (1956) 'Seven Centuries of the Prices of Consumables, Compared with Builders' Wage-Rates', *Economica*. Both [124] and [125] are reprinted in E. M. Carus-Wilson (ed.), *Essays in Economic History*, vol. II (1962).

[126] M. M. Postan (1959) 'Note', *E.H.R.*, 2nd ser., XII.

[127] W. C. Robinson (1959) 'Money, Population and Economic Change in Late Medieval Europe', *E.H.R.*, 2nd ser., XII.

[128] J. Thorold Rogers (1866–1902) *A History of Agriculture and Prices in England*, 7 vols (Oxford).

[129] J. Schreiner (1954) 'Wages and Prices in England in the Later Middle Ages', *Scandinavian Economic History Review*, II.

Contemporary comment and social developments

Medieval chronicles are an important source of information on outbreaks of disease, but they rarely refer in detail to economic and social matters. By the later fifteenth and the early sixteenth centuries, however, contemporaries were commenting much more extensively on such matters, and the *Italian Relation* [137] and Thomas Starkey [135] are good examples of this welcome development. Huizinga and Crawfurd stress the impact of recurrent waves of disease on artistic and social attitudes.

[130] F. E. Baldwin (1926) *Sumptuary Legislation and Personal Regulation in England* (Baltimore).

[131] *Chronicon Adae de Usk, A.D. 1377–1421*, ed. E.M. Thomson (Oxford, 1904).

[132] C. G. Coulton (1945) *Medieval Panorama* (Cambridge).

[133] R. Crawfurd (1914) *Plague and Pestilence in Literature and Art* (Oxford).

[134] G. R. Elton (1969) *England 1200–1640*.

[135] *England in the Reign of King Henry the Eighth*, (1878) ed. S. J. Herrtage, Early English Text Society, extra ser., xxxii.

[136] J. Huizinga (1955 edn) *The Waning of the Middle Ages*.

[137] *Italian Relation of England: A Relation or rather a True Account of the Island of England* ed. C. A. Sneyd, Camden Society, xxxvii (1847).

[138] *Polychronicon Ranulphi Higden, Monachi Cestrensis* ed. C. Babington and J. R. Lumby, 9 vols, Rolls Ser. (1865–96).

[139] W. G. Searle (ed.) (1902) *The Chronicle of John Stone, Monk of Christ Church, 1415–71*, Cambridge Antiquarian Society, xxxiv.

[140] *Tudor Economic Documents* (1924) ed. R. H. Tawney and E. Power, 3 vols.

[141] Thomas Walsingham (1836–4) *Historia Anglicana*, ed. H. T. Riley, 2 vols, Rolls Ser.

3 The population history of Britain and Ireland 1500–1750

Prepared for the Economic History Society by

R. A. Houston
University of St Andrews

For D.C.C., T.C.S. and E.A.W.

Contents

Tables

Note on references

References in the text in brackets are detailed in the Bibliography. The author's name and date of publication are followed, where necessary, by the page numbers in italics.

Author's preface

Population history is a large, complex and expanding area of research. For the non-specialist, unfamiliar terms, copious statistics and convoluted arguments also render it one of the most potentially confusing. Awareness of these potential difficulties explains the aims and layout of this pamphlet. Readers will not find a flat exposition of different points of view. Debates and uncertainties have been made explicit but the problem of synthesising substantial quantities of complicated material make it essential to differentiate possibly significant areas of disagreement from pointless bickering. Tables have been kept to a minimum. Population totals are discussed only briefly because structures and trends, and the reasons behind them, are more relevant to social and economic historians. The implications of demographic structures and trends are dealt with in passing. References in square brackets may indicate that an outline of the argument under discussion can be found in the work cited, not that its author necessarily espouses the viewpoint. Certain technical terms may require fuller explanation than can be offered in the text. Readers should consult Roland Pressat's *Dictionary of Demography*, a new edition of which has been prepared by Christopher Wilson (1988).

R. A. HOUSTON
Department of Modern History
University of St Andrews

Introduction

Most histories of Britain are histories of England. The quality of information about Scotland, Wales and Ireland is generally far inferior to that about England before the nineteenth century. Abundant sources and a well-established tradition of genealogy and of local social and economic history have made English historical demography more advanced than Scottish or Irish. The existence of specialist research bodies, notably the Cambridge Group for the History of Population and Social Structure, founded in the 1960s, has given population history a firm grounding. With the publication in 1981 of *The Population of History of England, 1541–1871* by two members of the Cambridge Group, England's demographic history moved onto a different plane. For that reason, England is treated as a benchmark in this book, a relatively well-documented and fairly well-studied country with which its near neighbours can be compared. Scotland, Wales and Ireland are not less interesting or important: far from it. They are simply less well researched.

Before *The Population History of England* a number of local studies of population, economy and society existed and some attempts at a general interpretation had been made. Working in the 1950s and 1960s, J. D. Chambers, M. Drake, D. Eversley and H. J. Habakkuk made the greatest contribution to English historical demography at this time, K. H. Connell to Irish. More sophisticated methods such as family reconstitution (see Chapter 2) were being developed in France by L. Henry during the 1950s and P. Goubert's magisterial 1960 study of *Beauvais et le Beauvaisis* is acknowledged as a landmark. With much 'fact' disputed and various theories of population dynamics in competition, *The*

Population History of England set out to provide a comprehensive interpretation from scratch. A similar attempt had been made in 1977 by M. W. Flinn and his collaborators (mostly T. C. Smout and R. Mitchison for the seventeenth and eighteenth century sections) in *Scottish Population History from the Seventeenth Century to the 1930s*. Serious source problems and some unfortunate methodological assumptions made this overview less satisfactory. Irish historians have followed up Connell, checking and reworking his findings. Efforts at synthesis have been confined largely to articles which struggle with difficult sources, outline population trends and speculate cautiously on dynamics (Goldstrom and Clarkson, 1981; Daultrey, Dickson and Ó Gráda, 1981).

The early modern period witnessed no 'demographic revolution' of the kind which transformed European fertility in the later nineteenth century (partly through the dissemination of effective contraception), or the large improvement in adult life expectancy during the last 50 years (partly through better medical care). In many ways, the sixteenth, seventeenth and eighteenth centuries were very different from modern times. Most noticeably, in the early modern period expectation of life at birth was half what it is in late twentieth century Britain. In others, such as the relatively late age of first marriage and the prevalence of small, simple families it is easier to identify with them. However, the centuries between the end of the middle ages and the dawn of the industrial revolution clearly command attention. They saw wars and invasions in Britain and Ireland as elsewhere in Europe but they also witnessed the demise of plague as a serious killer and, in some areas, of short-term mortality crises related to famine and disease.

There were important similarities between certain aspects of family and demography in Britain and Ireland, aspects they shared with much of north-western Europe (Hajnal, 1983). However, there were equally significant regional and perhaps 'national' differences in the way elements of the demographic system fitted together. The ancient parts of the early modern British Isles and Ireland had very different social structures. Despite a trend towards political and legal assimilation, and towards cultural integration, significant differences remained even in 1750 and we should not be surprised to find these reflected in demographic behaviour (Houston and Whyte, 1989). Both trends and the reasons behind them varied considerably between regions of the British Isles. Historical demographers now doubt if there was such a thing as a 'European demographic system', and except at a simple level there was no common demographic regime across England, Wales, Scotland and Ireland between 1500 and 1750.

The aim of the next section of this pamphlet is to discuss sources for early modern demographic history and the ways of exploiting them. Population structures and trends are then outlined before the dynamic components of fertility, nuptiality, mortality and migration are discussed. A substantial chapter on the relationship between demographic behaviour and its economic and social context concludes the pamphlet. Approximately equal space is given to Scotland and Ireland, where possible. On some topics, such as nuptiality, relatively more attention is given to these areas because of the need to outline sources, methods and explanations which have received little attention in existing literature. Yet, with the best will in the world there is no making up for the absence of sources and research for Scotland and Ireland. It is possible to present the facts for England and to discuss competing interpretations, though readers should not infer from this that English sources are absolutely reliable. For Scotland and Ireland it is more a question of trying to establish the facts and then conjecture about explanations. Wales is mentioned only occasionally.

1
Sources and methods

Sources

Two principal types of source are used by historical demographers. The first is records of ecclesiastical events – baptisms, marriages and burials. The second is listings of all or part of a local population drawn up for religious, military or fiscal reasons. Unfortunately, the sources used by historians of population were almost never compiled for strictly demographic purposes. Furthermore, interpretation of these sources is complicated by the ecclesiastical, administrative and legal differences between England and other parts of the British Isles. Hampered by suspicion and evasion, secular institutions had less access to reliable information than the church but the latter's interests were even further removed from the concerns of modern demographers than those of the flimsy early modern state. Human frailty compounds problems of omission: early modern numeracy was questionable, age-rounding to, say, multiples of 10 years was common, and reported ages may have been under- or over-stated according to circumstances. Source problems are much more serious than for nineteenth and twentieth century demography (Wrigley, 1966; Willigan and Lynch, 1982). We should be wary of early modern sources and adopt a degree of agnosticism about the results derived from them. We need to know whether the data are *reliable* – consistently measured – and *valid* – meaningful indicators of the concepts we wish to explore.

Except briefly during the 1650s, England had no civil registration until 1837, Scotland until 1855 and Ireland until 1864. The first national census was not conducted until 1801 (to all intents and purposes not until 1821 for Ireland). In the absence of these basic centralised sources for modern demography, early modern historians rely primarily on parish registers. In 1538 Thomas Cromwell, Henry VIII's famous minister, ordered that all parishes in England should keep records of baptisms, marriages and burials. Some parishes obeyed immediately but others took decades before commencing registration. Some registers were kept only intermittently and incompletely, others have not survived the ravages of damp, rodents, fire or carelessness. The Cambridge Group has more than 500 parish register counts for England. Parish registers can be supplemented by other sources. From 1629, for example, the London bills of mortality give yearly deaths from various causes in 130 city and adjoining parishes.

In Scotland, types of source are broadly similar. Edinburgh's Greyfriars' burial ground had an official keeper of the register from 1658, paid by the town council, and both Edinburgh and Glasgow have well-kept bills of mortality for the first half of the eighteenth century. These documents are especially welcome in view of the poor quality and survival of many Scottish parish registers. In common with much of Europe, Scotland's baptism and marriage records began earlier than those for burial, and those burial registers which were kept tend to under-record the deaths of infants and children; those they do record are sometimes denied even a name. Some parish registers began to be kept during the 1550s and 1560s but are few before the seventeenth century and those which survive are rarely complete (Flinn, 1977, *46–8*). For the upland areas of northern and western Scotland, the Highlands and Islands, statistics are almost wholly absent until the eighteenth century, a serious shortcoming in view of tantalising suggestions that this region, like seventeenth century Ireland, possessed rather different nuptiality patterns from the Lowlands (Houston, 1988, *19*; Ó Gráda, 1979). In some respects, the quality of Scottish registers is superior to that of English. Women kept their maiden name after marriage and are identified by it in baptismal and, sometimes, burial registers. This makes record linkage of baptisms less ambiguous than where the father only is mentioned since a statement of relationships to the living makes it easier to link deaths to earlier events. Burials of those unable to pay mortcloth dues (for hire of the pre-burial winding sheet) and clerk's fees are noted 'poor' in the better-kept registers, allowing analysis of socially-specific mortality in famine years such as 1698.

Similarly with Ireland, our understanding of pre-census demography depends on a handful of comparatively well-kept parish registers and listings of inhabitants conducted for taxation, military or ecclesiastical reasons. For Ulster, the registers of the established (anglican) church of Ireland are the best kept before the nineteenth century (Macafee, 1987). Approximately 100 Irish catholic registers survive for the eighteenth century but most state only names at baptisms and marriages, and most relate to towns in the east of Ireland. The seventeenth century is a wasteland as far as catholic registers are concerned – only those of Wexford town survive and are currently being analysed. Many protestant (church of Ireland) registers were destroyed by fire in 1922. In Wales too, survival and quality of registers is poor – though no worse than in Scotland or Ireland – and there are none in the Cambridge Group's sample. Projects are afoot in Ireland and Scotland to study elite genealogies, though these are typically much more informative about males than females. Lack of consistently and accurately recorded vital events seriously limits the statistical techniques which can be applied to sixteenth and seventeenth century Scottish data.

Even when parish registers survive, it is not always certain what proportion of vital events they record. Some 'marriage' registers are in fact lists of the couples whose banns were proclaimed but who may have married later or not at all. Changes in fashion could have a marked effect on registration. Clandestine marriages (not celebrated in accordance with the requirements of the established church) may have accounted for a sixth of all marriages among those born in 1666, but a generation before or after, levels of 4–5 per cent were more common (Schofield, 1985b, *14*). A similar trend is clear in early eighteenth century Scotland when, in the Edinburgh area at least, clandestine or 'irregular' marriage was fashionable. The main problem is that parish registers record ecclesiastical rather than vital events (Smout, 1981). If, for example, baptism was delayed there is a chance that infants who died very young would not be recorded. Fortunately, in Scotland the interval from birth to baptism was short during the second half of the seventeenth century and the first half of the eighteenth century. For example, 93 per cent of children in Haddington

1653–8 were baptised within a week, 94 per cent of Kilmarnock infants 1740–51. For England the interval is slightly longer – though not damagingly so until the late eighteenth century – and there was considerable variation between baptismal customs in different parishes.

Urbanisation had less of a detrimental effect on registration than is commonly assumed, at least before the later seventeenth century. London registers between 1580 and 1650 'are of a high standard of accuracy' (Finlay, 1978, *112*). This can be established by various methods. One, developed by the French demographer Bourgeois-Pichat, allows the extent of under-registration of infant deaths to be measured by comparing the numbers of children recorded as dying ('from birth trauma, congenital defect and functional inadequacy' – endogenous causes) during the first weeks of life with what is biologically likely (Schofield and Wrigley, 1979, *73*). All other deaths are caused by environmental or 'exogenous' causes. If this 'biometric' analysis shows levels of endogenous mortality to be too low then the register from which the figures were derived is probably defective. It also helps to know the number of stillbirths and, since there was no statutory require- ment to register stillbirths before 1927, any register which contains plausible numbers is likely to be generally well-kept.

Religious divisions were similarly less serious before the second half of the eighteenth century than is sometimes claimed. In England, under-registration caused by withdrawal from the an- glican church varied geographically but is estimated to have increased generally over the eighteenth century. Dissent flourished more noticeably in England than in Scotland and from the 1640s in London religious fragmentation and the growth of sects affected registration (Finlay, 1978). The spread of English dissent in the period after the restoration of the monarchy of 1660 was particu- larly rapid. The effect of religious differences on Scottish registra- tion was not significant until after 1689–90. For example, the small numbers of Independents in the 1650s and Quakers in the 1660s seem to have been prepared to present their children for baptism in the established church in the city of Aberdeen. Political and military problems, for example in the collection of the hearth tax, were more serious in the 1690s in areas sympathetic to the ousted Stuart dynasty. In early eighteenth century Edinburgh those attending Episcopalian meeting houses, as opposed to the Presbyterian kirks, were still supposed to register deaths with the keeper of the city's mortality register. The number of communicants attending the established church in one densely peopled central Edinburgh parish remained constant from the 1730s to the 1770s, implying an acceptance of its offices.

For one religious group, distinctive practices have proved beneficial to the historical demographer. Quakers did not baptise their children, therefore all entries in the records of their monthly meetings are of births. In addition to registers of vital events, Friends kept family genealogies. What is more, Quakers only pass out of observation because of death, because they left England or because they had ceased to be Quakers rather than because of moving from a parish (Eversley, 1981, *58–60*; Landers, 1990, *35–6*). This makes family reconstitution easier and makes it possible at all for Ireland where early parish registers are rare and in England at times when anti-clericalism, non-conformity and clerical laxity seriously limit the value of anglican registers.

The second main source of demographic information is the listing of inhabitants. Listings which provide the ages of household members are a particular boon to historians because techniques are available to estimate mean age at first marriage, age gap between spouses and the age of servants – all important demographic indicators. The first reliable and complete English age listing is for the then rural parish of Ealing (Middlesex) in 1599. The only reliable listings for Scotland before the mid eighteenth century relate to urban communities and even these lack the detail and comprehensiveness of their English counterparts. A 1755 'census' of Scotland carried out by Alexander Webster in connection with his work on clerical pensions has been extensively used as a benchmark for population totals and, more recently, to provide other demographic statistics (Mitchison, 1989). Webster's diligence in collecting, analysing and presenting these figures does not bear too close an examination. For Wales there are several partial listings of indeterminate quality, notably those for St Asaph's diocese in northern and central Wales during the 1680s. These, along with hearth tax schedules, have received little attention.

Where more than one listing of inhabitants survives during a period of a few years, it may be possible to estimate the extent of population turnover between the dates. The movement of vagrants and apprentices has been extensively studied from the records of the former's punishment and the latter's indentures (Clark and Souden, 1987). More detailed figures about geographical mobility by age, status and gender can be gleaned from the biographical details furnished by those who gave evidence before the church courts of England, from settlement certificates (introduced in England from 1662) and from Scottish 'testificates' issued by the church to movers (Clark, 1979; Houston, 1985). Voluntary and involuntary movement of British people to the New World can be studied from convict transportation records, contracts of indentured service, port records and passenger lists (Galenson, 1981; Ekirch, 1987).

Methods

Ways of exploiting these sources have become increasingly sophisticated in the last three decades. Traditional approaches used contemporary estimates of population, such as those of Gregory King or William Petty; or documents showing the number of communicants or taxpaying households which were then inflated by a suitable multiplier to give total population; or multiplying baptism or burial totals by a constant birth or death rate to give a total for a parish. The first national exercise of this kind was carried out by John Rickman, director of the 1801 British census. Rickman used aggregates of baptisms, burials and marriages from sample years to estimate population totals in 1570, 1600, 1630, 1670, 1700 and 1750. This method provides approximate figures for English population but it is imprecise, open to criticism and tells us little more than total numbers. Birth totals cannot be subjected to a single multiplier because changes in the age structure of fertile women mean they are not constant; death rates too vary according to age structure and type of environment. The problem with communicant lists such as those of 1563 or the famous Compton 'census' of the 1670s is estimating the age at which communion took place, the proportion of the population not included, and the extent of religious non-conformity. Population listings generally cover only one age group, geographical area, occupation or religion. Alldridge's valuable study of Chester, using parish rate (local tax) books and listings highlights the problems. One projection of the population in 1692 is 34 per cent lower than that for the same year using a different source (Alldridge, 1986, *122–7*).

Contemporaries could be highly perceptive and well-informed but they could also be selective in their use of evidence and inaccurate in their conclusions. The famous novelist and journalist Daniel Defoe overestimated London's early eighteenth century population by a factor of two. The way in which contemporaries collected quantitative material is sometimes frustratingly unclear. Arthur Dobbs wrote of northern Ireland in 1725: 'From several returns made to me of the number of persons in each family, in a great many contiguous parishes in the county of Antrim, I find the medium to be 4.36 to a family' (Clarkson, 1981, *22*).

For Ireland and Scotland, serious source deficiencies mean that traditional methods continue to be used, albeit in a more sophisticated way, though Macafee and Morgan have shown that partial family reconstitution can be done with eighteenth century Ulster registers (Morgan, 1976; Macafee, 1987). Daultrey *et al.* (1981) have tested Irish hearth tax schedules and have been able both to distinguish between data of widely differing reliability and to identify the main regional trends in the better series. Attempts to identify and explain structures and trends rely heavily on comparisons with better documented historical populations and on the creation of more or less plausible scenarios. Scottish and Irish demographic history before the nineteenth century, like Dutch, 'emphasizes the investigation of macrodemographic questions in a regional context' and depends on 'resourceful use of flawed and imperfect data' (De Vries, 1985, *661*). As De Vries points out for the Netherlands, fertility, nuptiality and mortality rates are 'based largely on fragmentary and indirect evidence. Any general statements should be thought of as hypotheses awaiting confirmation rather than as the conclusions of systematic research' (1985, *663*). Some use has also been made of population theory as a way of defining aims and content. These theories are best seen as a set of hypotheses to be tested rather than moulds into which historical data are to be crammed. What follows should be treated as a set of 'controlled conjectures' based on sporadic and imperfect evidence,

especially as far as Scotland and Ireland are concern
absolute proof is difficult to establish, historical demog
have to eliminate the impossible or create likely paran
possible.

There is still merit in traditional approaches, especially when
documentation is suspect or too fragile to bear the weight of
demanding methods. However, these approaches have increasingly
been complemented, and indeed superseded, by new methods
which allow more accurate quantification of a wider range of
demographic variables. Population totals at different dates are
useful but without an idea of what produced them we cannot go
much further. Family reconstitution and aggregative analysis help
us to understand why population changed and how it was made
up.

Family reconstitution involves amassing all the information
about vital events in individuals' lives. Numbers of family genealogies are created which can then be analysed to calculate demographic measures such as the age at first marriage, the number of
children from every 1,000 born who died before the age of one
year (infant mortality rates), and the number of children a woman
bore between marriage and the end of her fertile period. The
technique is appropriate only to parishes with well-kept registers
and even then is better suited to some than others. Family
reconstitution is possible for London though the high level of
geographical mobility and small parishes means that age at marriage, age-specific marital fertility and adult mortality cannot
generally be calculated because age at marriage, at the birth of
children and at death are unknown. By contrast, record linkage is
easier and more productive in a large rural parish like Cartmel in
north-west England since mobility can occur without people
moving out of observation. Parishes whose inhabitants share a
small number of surnames cannot be reconstituted because it is
frequently impossible to link vital events accurately – a common
problem in Wales.

Because of the strict rules governing the linking of names in
family reconstitution, only a minority of the population of a parish
can be used for some demographic measures (Wrigley, 1966). In
English studies completed to date, age-specific marital fertility
rates use just 16 per cent of legitimate live births because mothers

have to be born locally for their ages to be known. High levels of geographical mobility mean that adult mortality is also based on small percentages of the total population. Between a third and a half of those born in an English parish also married and died there, in contrast with France where nearly four-fifths did so. Infant mortality rates, on the other hand, are based on roughly 80 per cent of legitimate live births (Wrigley and Schofield, 1983, *158*). Family reconstitution is much more representative than is sometimes asserted. For example, the fecundability of women excluded from age-specific marital fertility calculations is the same as those on whom the statistics are based. And studies which have followed movers over parish boundaries – and therefore out of observation in conventional reconstitutions – have found close similarities with stayers. However, mobility creates a bias – specifically, a 'censoring effect' – of which we must be aware. While movers and stayers may have the same age-specific vital rates, those who marry latest and those who survive longest have most chance of escaping inclusion in age at marriage and adult mortality estimates because they are more likely to have moved.

Family reconstitution sets rules of observation which defines the population at risk and therefore offers census-like information on delineated subsets of the population without full census data. It details the dynamics behind population trends. However, it is time consuming, localised and provides small numbers of events from which to generalise. Recent publications use data from just 13 English parishes (Wrigley and Schofield, 1983). For Scotland, full family reconstitutions have proved difficult though some partial ones are available for a handful of parishes and recent work on Fife promises to produce more usable statistics from this method. In order to obtain a broad picture of demographic development, another technique has been used.

Aggregating monthly or annual totals of baptisms, marriage and burials has a long pedigree stretching back to Rickman in the early nineteenth century and before (Wrigley, 1966). These aggregative analyses formed the model for Wrigley and Schofield in their magisterial *Population History of England* (1981, *15–154*, *195–9*). First, a new sample of 404 parish registers was drawn from the nearly 10,000 English parishes. The quality and coverage of these was checked and adjustments made to ensure that the sample, though not random, was as representative of size, geographical location, social structure and ecological type as possible. Baptisms, marriages and burials were inflated into national series, including an adjustment for London, and then these ecclesiastical events were converted into vital rates by applying demographic models to make allowances for under-registration of births, marriages and deaths at different periods. Armed with a known age structure in 1871 and a set of life table estimates of the age structure of mortality, it is possible to step backwards, five years at a time, by making each age-group five years younger and adding those estimated to have died or emigrated in between. This technique, 'back projection', gives population totals, age structures and net migration estimates every five years back to 1541. These can be used to calculate growth rates as well as measures of fertility, mortality and nuptiality (Schofield, 1985a, *583–4*; Trussell, 1983, *307–10*; Flinn, 1982, *450–1*; Gutmann, 1984).

Both methods and results have provoked criticism, scepticism and sometimes even hostility. Review articles by Flinn, Gutmann, Henry and Blanchet, and Trussell are particularly helpful on technical aspects. While an important part of the *explanation* of changing population depends on flawed estimates of wages and prices (outlined in Chapter 6 below), discussion here is confined to possible problems in Wrigley and Schofield's *description* of population size, structures and trends. One concern is over the number and distribution of parishes. Aggregative analyses from 530 parishes were whittled down to the 404 which form the core of the study in the years 1662–1812. But, the further back in time, the fewer parishes are included: just 45 at the starting date of 1541 (Flinn, 1982, *448–9*). What is more, an eighth of all parishes in the sample are from Bedfordshire, none at all from Cornwall. That the four northernmost counties provide just 13 parishes (3 per cent of the sample) is a serious defect in view of the possible similarities and differences between Scottish and English demography.

Criticisms have also been made of aspects of the methodology. Estimates for 1541–1630 are particularly tentative because plausible numbers of births and deaths for the 95 years before 1541 have to be 'invented' in order to create a 1541 population (Henry and Blanchet, 1983, *807–10*). The weakest links in the chain are the migration estimates which are residuals and depend on questionable assumptions about continuities in the age structure of emigration (Guttmann, 1984, *15–16*). This issue is dealt with by Oeppen (1991), who shows that the fluctuations in net migration estimates are an artifact of the statistical method originally used in Wrigley and Schofield (1981). However, Oeppen also finds that the total volume of migration is the same 1541–1866 and that the effect on population totals is negligible. Henry and Blanchet (1983, *815–18*) draw attention to the large margin of error in estimates of proportions never married over time but allow that the trends identified by Wrigley and Schofield are probably correct. Summing up the main strain of criticism, Flinn opined: 'readers will note with some apprehension the enormous distance between the raw data and the final levels and rates' in *The Population History of England* (1982, *457*).

Yet, we should not allow these clouds of criticism to obscure the merits of back projection, population modelling and other statistical and theoretical tools. The methodologies have the great advantage of being rigorous and open to scrutiny and replication. Those who read through the 700-odd pages of *The Population of History of England* will be impressed by the intellectual effort involved, by the clarity of the exposition, and by the willingness to acknowledge potential shortcomings in data and findings. Those who have tried alternative assumptions and projections – for example, vital rates before 1541, age structures of mortality, under-registration at different periods – have been impressed by the sturdiness of the results (Henry and Blanchet, 1983). By identifying and allowing for deficiencies in the sources Wrigley and Schofield offer a much higher standard of transparency and accuracy than earlier work. The results have an internal consistency which is encouraging in a subject where context is everything. The pooled data on fertility and mortality available from the 13 reconstituted parishes are, for example, close to those achieved by back projection. Indeed, many of the criticisms levelled at the authors are answered by Wrigley and Schofield in the new preface to the 1989 edition of *The Population History of England*. Their publications since 1981 have used constructively some of the alternative suggestions raised by their critics. It seems fair to concede the authors' claim that 'the main outlines of the population history of England seem to be remarkably robust in the face of quite large errors or uncertainty in the data' (1989, *xvi*). The latest demographic tool to become available is computer microsimulation. Programs such as CAMSIM randomly assign characteristics in accordance with assumed distributions based on demographic probabilities. This creates model populations which can be used to estimate the chances that, for example, a father is survived by one or more sons (Laslett, 1988). This is useful in discussing the role of inheritance in family formation. Another possibility is to estimate the numbers of eligible husbands available for the remarriage of widows, indicating whether remarriage chances were determined by demographic or cultural and economic factors. Microsimulation is particularly useful for modelling kin universes which are almost impossible to recreate by conventional methods. Family, career and business strategies could also be influenced by changing demography. For instance, young women in England around 1800 had twice as many living cousins as in 1700 (Laslett, 1988, *15*). With microsimulation, studies of historical demography may be entering a new phase of development which promises to address a host of hitherto inaccessible problems.

2

Structures and trends

When population estimates were merely an obligatory backdrop to more 'important' topics such as politics, religion and warfare, historians concerned themselves almost exclusively with overall numbers. Estimating population size from scratch is, in fact, a more difficult exercise than when the demographic parameters are known. The size and composition of a population are, after all, a direct function of fertility and mortality, and are indirectly influenced by nuptiality and migration. Nevertheless, an idea of population structures and trends can set the stage for an analysis of the motors of change.

For England, robust figures exist for five-year intervals beginning in 1541. Those used here are from Oeppen (1991) and are very slightly higher than those presented by Wrigley and Schofield (1981, *528–9*) because a more reliable statistical technique was used on the data. The main reason for the adjustment is a different set of net migration estimates (see Chapter 5). England had some 3.02 million people in 1541, a figure which rose almost without interruption to reach 5.47 million in 1656. Thereafter a period of stagnation or slight decline set in. Population did not exceed the 1656 level until the 1730s but then grew at a modest rate to reach 5.90 million in 1751 and more rapidly to 8.70 million by 1801. Population growth rates peaked at just under 1 per cent a year in the third quarter of the sixteenth century and at their lowest a century later were − 0.25 per cent. Between 1541 and 1751 yearly growth rates averaged under 0.5 per cent.

These trends can be explained almost wholly by changes in fertility, measured by the gross reproduction rate (GRR), and mortality, of which expectation of life at birth (e_0) is a good overall indicator (see Pressat, 1985, for these and other definitions). Proportional changes in these two measures will be equally important in changing the intrinsic growth rate (*r*) (Wrigley and Schofield, 1981, *228–48*). There is no reason to believe that one is inherently more powerful than the other. For the period 1571–1611 fertility and mortality were stable, combining to give an intrinsic growth rate of 0.85. During the following 60 years fertility fell and mortality rose in equal proportions to produce a fall in *r*. The main factor in population growth 1671–91 was fertility while between 1691 and 1751 mortality exerted the most significant impact. How and why fertility and mortality changed, and the contribution of migration to population trends, are discussed in Chapters 3–5.

Estimates of total population in Ireland and Scotland rely mainly on taxation records. Multiplying the number of households, hearths or taxpayers by a suitable figure gives population totals. The trick is in identifying the relationship between a house's physical characteristics such as the number of hearths and the number of inhabitants. Surviving schedules of the 1691 tax on hearths levied in Scotland show 2 hearths per household in Edinburgh, just under 1.5 in the rest of the Lowlands and 1.2 in the Highlands. Allowance must be made for legitimate exemption and evasion. The second variable is the proportion of the total households which paid tax: the range is 60–67 per cent here. We also need to know the average size of a house. Using figures from the 1790s and assuming no change in household size over the eighteenth century, mean household size was roughly 4.5, ranging from less than 4 in Clackmannan to nearly 6 in Sutherland. Finally, if we assume that the areas without surviving hearth tax returns had the same ratio of population to those with extant schedules as they do in Webster's 1755 census, we can estimate the population of Scotland at 1.23 million in 1691. This is 3 per cent lower than in 1755 and implies a miniscule growth between the dates. A period of serious mortality in the 1690s when population fell by perhaps 10–15 per cent was followed by half a century of modest growth of perhaps 0.3 per cent a year, comparable with that of contemporary England (Tyson, 1992).

Earlier estimates for Scotland are largely conjectural, though it may be possible to identify periods of change. Population growth seems to have been fastest in the late sixteenth and early seven-teenth century, if we can judge from indirect, unsystematic and possibly subjective literary sources. There is no evidence of serious pressure of population until after *c.* 1570 and the balance of probability is that famines, wars and disease kept growth rates low between the early fourteenth century and the mid sixteenth. Poverty, for example, was not as apparent as in English and European towns for much of the century. However, legislation in 1574, 1579 and 1592, coupled with contemporary comments, create the impression of prevalent vagrancy and begging. The real wages of Edinburgh labourers fell sharply from the 1560s, con-firming the pressure of population on resources.

Scotland experienced similar growth rates to Ireland's average of 0.2–0.4 per cent a year 1687–1755 though with marked short-term fluctuations. Numbers in Ireland stagnated from 1687, when the first reasonably reliable hearth tax returns become available, until 1706. Strong growth, touching 2 per cent a year, followed in most counties until the famines of 1727–9, 1740–1 and 1744–6 dam-pened it down (Dickson *et al.*, 1982, *156–75*; Daultrey *et al.*, 1981, *622–7*). The difference became even more marked thereafter, with Ireland's population growing at three times the Scottish rate 1755–1801. Moving backwards in time, Cullen and others have pre-sented some ingenious political arithmetic for the seventeenth century (Cullen, 1981, *90–4*). Cullen believes that numbers may have doubled between 1600 and 1712, with fluctuations in growth rates mainly caused by changes in immigration: fastest growth came 1600–40 and 1652–9. Irish growth rates in the seventeenth century were much faster than either England or Scotland (Clarkson, 1981, *25–7*). Ireland in 1500 was probably lightly populated and experienced less growth than other areas of Europe in the sixteenth century. The best recent estimates of Irish popula-tion are approximately 800,000 people in 1500, one million in 1600 and 2 million by 1687. There were slightly less in 1700 but perhaps 2.4 million in 1750 and 5 million by 1800. These figures should be treated with extreme caution. Eighteenth century sources for Ireland are treacherous enough but those for the seventeenth are like quicksilver and earlier estimates almost purely conjectural.

Irish population was more directly affected by war than Scottish or English. The towns of Armagh and Galway were devastated in the early sixteenth century and the ruthless Elizabethan conquest and plantation of Munster may have caused a regional fall in population, against the European trend. There were further dislocations during the 1640s and 1650s, including the storming of Drogheda and Wexford, and in Ulster 1689–91. In parts of Ulster these upsets and the end of rapid immigration reduced nuptiality and fertility dramatically in the first half of the eighteenth century compared with *c.* 1660–89 (Morgan, 1976, *13–14*; Cullen, 1975). Dickson claims that these wars 'cancelled out the natural increase of many years' (1988, *97*). However, wars were not the only factor: regional population trends were closely related to wider economic and political circumstances (Macafee and Morgan, 1981).

Within these national pictures there were marked local and regional variations. Certain types of community grew more quickly than others. 'Open' parishes with ample pasture and opportunities for industrial work tended to experience the fastest increases. Areas of the Cambridgeshire fens and of north-west England saw rates of growth in the Elizabethan period double those of Norfolk and Suffolk (Smith, 1978, *228*). In the north of England during the eighteenth century mining and industrial communities mushroomed. However, there is no guarantee that particular types of community will experience growth. Husbands warns against ecological determinism while arguing that 'proto-industrial' and urban communities were the real engines of growth in south-east England between the 1520s and 1670s (Husbands, 1987). Kussmaul shows that this was even more so in the following century (Kussmaul, 1990, *142–4*). Numbers could fall as well as rise within a region. The most buoyant Scottish region 1691–1755 was the western Lowlands with 12 per cent growth, the least so the northeast Lowlands where population fell by 6 per cent.

Throughout Britain and Ireland, towns of 10,000 or more grew faster than the population as a whole from the mid sixteenth century (Table 1). A threshold as high as 10,000 is needed because of the difficulty of distinguishing smaller urban centres in the sources though there are also positive reasons for choosing it (Wrigley, 1985). The rate of change varied over time and may be linked to changes in real incomes. The largest Scottish towns in 1500 – traditional provincial centres – also headed the hierarchy in

Table 1 *Proportions living in towns of 10,000 or more and total population of those towns in thousands*

	Scotland		England		Ireland	
	000s	%	000s	%	000s	%
1500	13	1.6	80	3.1	0	0
1550	13	1.4	112	3.5	0	0
1600	30	3.0	255	5.8	0	0
1650	35	3.5	495	8.8	17	1.1
1700	53	5.3	718	13.3	96	5.3
1750	119	9.2	1021	16.7	161	7.0
1800	276	17.3	1870	20.3	369	7.4

Source: Whyte, 1989a, 22.

1700: Edinburgh, Glasgow, Aberdeen, Perth, Dundee. Comparisons between tax assessments in 1639 and 1691 show that, except for Edinburgh and Glasgow, many of the larger towns experienced declining population though other smaller centres did grow. The fastest rates of increase probably occurred in the small towns which proliferated in this period (Whyte, 1989a, 26). Even in 1700 Scotland's largest city, Edinburgh, had no more than 40,000 inhabitants and probably closer to 30,000 though the figure depends on what parts of the metropolis are included. Dublin grew quickly from around 20,000 in 1650 to 130,000 in the 1750s, becoming the second largest town in the British Isles but with only a fifth of London's population. Cork was the second largest Irish city with 12,000 people around 1650 and 70,000 inhabitants in the mid eighteenth century.

English urbanisation before the eighteenth century was dominated by London. The metropolis was 13 times larger than the second biggest city (Norwich) in 1600, 19 times larger in 1700 (Wrigley, 1985, 686). London's multiple advantages as court, port and capital city help to explain its dramatic growth and a share of national population – 5 per cent in 1600, 11.5 per cent in 1700 – without parallel in contemporary Europe. London's share of England's population more than doubled in the sixteenth century and nearly doubled again 1600–1700. London had to draw in 900,000 immigrants between 1600 and 1700 to grow from 190,000 to 550,000, and by doing so consumed 80 per cent of the natural increase in England's population. Other English towns fared less well in the sixteenth century leading some scholars to speak of an urban crisis. However, old established provincial centres, ports, and new leisure and industrial towns flourished after *c.* 1660. Bristol had about 21,000 inhabitants in 1700, 50,000 in 1750 and Liverpool more than trebled in this period to 22,000 in 1750. The growth of towns like this accounts for nearly all the doubling of proportions urban 1670–1800 (Wrigley, 1985). English urbanisation was a reflection of, and a stimulus to, agricultural improvement and the expansion and diversification of industry and commerce.

Vital events in large towns followed different seasonal patterns from rural areas. In the countryside, marriages peaked in April and May in pastoral parishes, in September and October in arable ones, following the rhythms of the agricultural year. Conceptions also tended to be clustered in the slack agricultural seasons. Mortality followed a similar seasonal pattern to baptisms, clustering in January, February and March. Towns (and rural industrial parishes) had a flatter curve through the year for all vital events (Wrigley and Schofield, 1981, *288, 293, 299*; Kussmaul, 1990). Population turnover peaked at the main hiring fairs of Whitsunday and Martinmas. These patterns prevailed in Scotland and Ireland too.

Other superficial similarities are apparent between regions of the British Isles. Taxation schedules and communion rolls indicate that mean household size in Lowland Scotland was comparatively small at between four and five people; composition was simple (Flinn, 1977, *196*; Tyson, 1985, *125–6*). Household formation depended on the north-west European norm of economic independence, at least in the Lowlands. In other respects, such as the preponderance of females in the population, and the higher proportion of female-headed households in towns as opposed to rural areas, Scottish households are unexceptional in a north-west European context (Houston, 1979; Tyson, 1988). Eighteenth century English observers were inclined to believe that Irish households were larger than English but Clarkson suggests they may have been of similar size (1981, *20–4*).

Finally, we can consider age structures. Demographers and economists conventionally present age distributions in terms of dependent versus productive members of the population. Those aged 14 years or less and those aged 60 and above are viewed as net consumers of resources, those 15–59 either self-supporting or net producers. Fortunately, these conventions correspond with the most significant indicators of population composition. A country with relatively high fertility will have a younger age distribution than one with low fertility. Between 1541 and 1751 the proportion of English population aged 60 and over changed little: the lowest figure (just over 7 per cent) was in 1566, the highest (just over 10 per cent) 1716. The proportion aged 14 or under peaked in 1556 at nearly 37 per cent; the lowest proportion of children came in 1671 – just under 29 per cent (Wrigley and Schofield, 1981, *443–50, 528–9*). The point to note is that while the age structure is 'young' compared with modern western countries, it is nothing like as imbalanced as some developing countries where children may account for more than half the population. A relatively light 'dependency burden' has important implications for the balance between population and resources, and thus for the standard of living of all age groups.

The only semi-reliable estimate of age structure in contemporary Scotland is given in Webster's 1755 census. Even he was forced to make assumptions, from the clergy's returns which he used, about the age structure of those too young to be examined on the catechism (Mitchison, 1989, *71*). Webster's figures are likely to be far less precise than ones derived from back projection for England but they indicate perhaps a quarter of the population aged 10 years or less and just over two-fifths aged 20 or less. If we can lay any weight on these estimates, the population age structure was not very different from contemporary England. Reporting of advanced ages in historical populations is often seriously inaccurate and proportions elderly are not offered here. The age structure of the Irish population was probably younger than that of England or Scotland because (as we shall see in Chapter 3) of its high, fertility-dominated growth rates *c.* 1600–1750.

Describing population structures and trends is valuable in itself. To explain them we must analyse different combinations of mortality, nuptiality, fertility and migration.

3
Nuptiality and fertility

The medieval and early modern church made it extremely easy to marry. Boys could marry at fourteen, girls at twelve throughout Britain, except between 1653 and 1660 when England's civil marriage ordinance raised the minimum age of consent to sixteen and fourteen years for males and females respectively. Until 1753 in England (and much later in Scotland and Ireland) there were four different paths: an exchange of oaths before witnesses, an exchange of statements of intent to marry followed by sexual intercourse, a licence from the church authorities dispensing with banns, and church marriage preceded by the publication of banns. With rare exceptions, the bulk of England's population, and probably also those of Scotland and Ireland, waited some ten years after puberty before marrying. Only one English bride in eight was a teenager when she first married 1600–1749. The reasons for this are discussed in Chapter 6. The present section is concerned with the effects of decisions to marry or remain celibate, to reproduce within or outside wedlock. It is almost wholly concerned with women since their reproductive behaviour is much more significant to population dynamics than that of men.

Nuptiality

Until the 1960s many historians believed that women married relatively early in the past. Partly, they based their ideas on literary evidence and partly on elite social groups. Unless backed up by other evidence, contemporary writing may provide a distorted view of social behaviour. It has also been clear that until the end of the seventeenth century the aristocracy behaved completely differently from ordinary people in their marriage patterns. Women of the British peerage usually married as teenagers and only two out of every five remained unmarried at age 20. Their husbands were aged 22–24 years: five or more years older (Hollingsworth, 1964).

The technique of family reconstitution has provided new figures on the nuptiality of ordinary men and women. Between 1600 and 1799 family reconstitutions for 13 English parishes generate estimates of mean age at first marriage for women. Figures for 1550–99 cannot be given because the late start of many parish registers truncates the population in observation and thus biases age at marriage downward. The 13 parishes cover a wide range of ecological types from an isolated pastoral community (Hartland, Devon) through a commercial agricultural village (Terling, Essex) and a textile centre (Shepshed, Leicestershire) to a large market town (Banbury, Oxfordshire) (Wrigley and Schofield, 1983, *158–9*). Results are presented in Table 2.

Changes in age at marriage are important for the following reason. In populations with natural fertility (see below), fertility is largely a function of age and is highest in the twenties when women produce approximately 0.4 live births a year on average. Given prevailing adult mortality, a union will produce about four live births. Therefore, if age at first marriage rises or falls by one year, the total fertility of a marriage will change by approximately 7 per cent. When age at marriage falls, women begin bearing children younger which, in addition to increasing total fertility, shortens the mean length of generation and thereby accelerates population growth.

In the age of the industrial revolution, changes in the age at marriage dominated changes in fertility attributable to nuptiality. However, the numbers of women who remain celibate throughout their reproductive careers also has a powerful impact on total fertility. For all its merits, family reconstitution has little to offer on the proportions who never marry. Aggregative back projection fills the gap. For women born before the middle of the eighteenth century this other influence on nuptiality, celibacy, was far more important. Some 5 per cent of those born around 1566 never married by the end of their childbearing span (i.e. before the 1610s) but among the cohort born in 1616 22 per cent remained celibate. Some explanations of changes in nuptiality are offered in

Table 2   *Mean age at first marriage for men and women in 13 English parishes (by marriage date)*

	Men	Women
1600–49	28.1	25.6
1650–99	28.1	26.2
1700–49	27.2	25.4
1750–99	25.7	24.0

Source: Wrigley and Schofield, 1983, *162*.

Chapter 6. For the present, it is worth noting that changes in the proportions of women never married did not occur at the same time as changes in age at first marriage for women, and that until the early eighteenth century changes in celibacy dominated the movement of fertility (Goldstone, 1986, *10–11*; Weir, 1984; Schofield, 1985b).

Some tentative estimates of age at marriage and proportions never married in Scotland are available. Mean age at marriage derived from statements about age and marital status among a thousand court deponents shows a mean age at first marriage of 26–27 years for Lowland adult women giving evidence 1660–1770 and celibacy to the end of the fertile period of at least 11 per cent (Houston, 1990, *63–6*). The age at marriage figure finds support from partial family reconstitutions of two parishes. One is the Highland community of Laggan where age at first marriage for women born before 1800 was approximately 27–30 years (Flinn, 1977, *279*). The other is the large parish of Kilmarnock in the mid eighteenth century where just 57 women have been traced at birth and marriage. Those living in Kilmarnock town married at a mean age of 23–24 years, rural women at 26–27. Preliminary results from a study of eighteenth century Fife indicate an age at first marriage for women in the mid-20s. Permanent spinsterhood in a sample of west central Lowland and western Border parishes was comparatively high at perhaps 20–25 per cent (ignoring extreme figures) (Flinn, 1977, *276, 280*). Taking 11 per cent as a minimum and 25 per cent as a maximum, these figures are broadly comparable with late seventeenth and early eighteenth century England. They imply a substantial constraint on overall fertility. However, they seem to have been less variable in the long term than in

England. Mean age at first marriage for Scottish women stayed at 26–27 during the later eighteenth and first half of the nineteenth century while in England the range was 23–27. Celibacy too remained high in Scotland (Houston, 1988, *19*). There is some unsubstantiated literary evidence of early marriage in the western Highlands and Islands (Flinn, 1977, *279*). For Ireland, the most reliable nuptiality and fertility figures relate to Quakers. Eversley compares these systematically with English Quakers, and contends that Irish Friends' demographic behaviour was different from their Irish catholic or protestant counterparts in degree rather than in kind. Irish Quaker women married earlier and had shorter intervals between births than English Quakers (Eversley, 1981, *64–5*). Mean age at first marriage for Quaker women 1650–99 was 22.7 years and 23.2 for 1700–49. Their husbands were four and a half years older in both periods. This distinguishes Irish Quakers from their rural counterparts in southern England. Women first married there at 24.9 years 1650–99 and 26.3 years 1700–49; their husbands were 28.6 and 28.1 years old respectively. Irish Quaker women started reproducing at a younger age and in their most fecund years.

Other estimates reinforce this picture. Among 121 marriages in the church of Ireland registers for the linen weaving parish of Killyman in Ulster 1771–1810, mean age at first marriage for women was 22 years, for males 26 years; half the women were married by their 21st birthday (Macafee, 1987, *152, 155-6*). An even lower figure of 18 or 19 years for women is offered for Blaris, Lisburn in the late seventeenth and early eighteenth century though there are serious source problems here and a censoring effect in the family reconstitution which would lower mean age at first marriage (Macafee and Morgan, 1981, *56*).

Literary evidence lends weight to the picture of relatively early marriage in Ireland. Sir William Petty and other observers believed that 'Irish women marry upon their first capacity' and noted a stress on the fertility of unions apparently not found in England (Ó Gráda, 1979, *285*). Petty had local knowledge of Dublin and Kerry, and was better informed than most contemporaries who followed a derivative and cavalier tradition of writing which based images of Ireland less on personal observation and empirical enquiry than on literary conventions and ethnocentric cultural prejudices about *all* non-English societies – specifically, that the women would enter the loose bonds of marriage while still young, would be naturally fecund, and would bear large numbers of children with ease.

Recent work by David Dickson lends credence to the idea that seventeenth-century Irish women did marry for the first time at a comparatively early age but firmly within the bounds of the north-west European marriage pattern (Dickson, 1990). Listings from county Dublin and Munster in the 1650s contain a substantial proportion of unmarried female servants with a median age of 25–26 years, showing early and universal marriage cannot have existed. An estimate of age at first marriage can be made by subtracting the reported age of the first child listed from that of the mother then subtracting a further year to allow for marriage to first birth interval. A median age at first marriage for women of 22–23 years can be suggested which is consistent with the Quakers and the other estimates given above. At the same time, the age gap between spouses was wider than in England at slightly more than five years, implying that Irish men married for the first time in their late twenties. Ó Gráda concludes that 'in Ireland early marriage was the norm and age at marriage roughly constant long before' the eighteenth century (1979, *285*; Dickson *et al.*, 1982, *173–4*). It may also be that female celibacy was relatively low but marriage patterns were not those of eastern or southern Europe. What is more, the similarity between Quaker, church of Ireland and Irish catholic nuptiality indicates that the causes lie in economic circumstances rather than in the cultural behaviour of Ireland's indigenous population. This reinforces Eversley's picture of clear differences between English and Irish Quaker nuptiality (1981, *86*). Irish Quakers behaved in this way because they were Irish rather than because they were Quakers.

The age at which women first marry has a powerful impact on total fertility. Early first marriage probably explains much of the rapid and sustained population growth in Ireland during the seventeenth century and again in the eighteenth century. However, it has been estimated that in late sixteenth century England 25–30 per cent of all marriages were remarriages. This figure fell over time to reach 10 per cent in the mid nineteenth century. Divorce was difficult and expensive to obtain; most unions were ended by death or, occasionally, desertion. Contrary to expectation, only a small part of the reduction in remarriages was related to a fall in adult mortality. The likelihood of being bereaved depended on mortality, that of remarrying on social or economic circumstances. Problems of source and method make analysis of remarriage from family reconstitutions difficult. Just 423 widowers and 295 widows can be studied from the available reconstitutions; the market town of Gainsborough provides half the widows and two-thirds of the widowers while 70 per cent of cases come from the eighteenth century (Schofield and Wrigley, 1981). Of those whose age at remarriage is known, nearly a half of widowers and just over a third of widows remarried within a year though the mean interval nearly doubled or both sexes between the late seventeenth and late eighteenth centuries. Age at bereavement was not a significant influence on remarriage chances but the more dependent children a man or woman had the longer he or she would wait to remarry.

To a limited extent, changes in the composition of the population could affect nuptiality. By moving into towns as servants and apprentices, young adults had their marriages delayed by formal or informal means. One girl in ten aged 15–24 would have been working in one of the four main Scottish towns at the end of the seventeenth century (Whyte and Whyte, 1988, 97). Imbalances between young men and women may have had a similar effect. London-born girls could expect to marry younger than their immigrant peers in the Elizabethan and early Stuart period but a century later growing sex imbalances among the nubile population made it harder for young women there and in other large towns to find a husband.

Legitimate fertility

The most striking features of English marital fertility are its comparatively low level, its stability over time and its homogeneity across space. The total marital fertility ratio varied just 1 per cent above and below its 1600–1799 average in different half centuries (Wrigley and Schofield, 1983, 169). Unpublished work by Christopher Wilson shows a marriage to first birth interval of approximately 19 months in 16 parishes 1550–1749. The interval for all subsequent births was 31 months; both figures were stable over the two centuries. Fecundability (the probability of a woman conceiving in one menstrual cycle) and fecundity (the physiological capability of a couple to produce a live birth) can vary – in response to changes in nutrition or health, for example – but it is almost impossible to investigate these changes in historical populations. The prolonged, debilitating malnutrition needed to change fecundity in closely studied modern populations was unlikely to have been present in early modern Britain. Those women exposed to the risk of starvation would probably have been among those too poor to have married anyway. The most potent influence on marital fertility was infant-feeding practice. Mothers who breastfed their children tended to wait longer before conceiving another child – and gave their infants a much better chance of surviving to reach their first birthday. Marriage order affected fertility 'almost entirely in a substantially reduced fertility of widower/widow remarriages' (Schofield and Wrigley, 1981, *225*).

For Ireland, we must again use the Quakers and patchy local studies to represent the population as a whole. Quaker morality forbids pre-nuptial fornication and all recorded births were legitimate. Age-specific marital fertility was consistently and appreciably higher for Irish Quakers than for southern rural English Friends for all age cohorts, 1650–1749. Birth intervals were clearly shorter for Irish Quakers than English, except after five or more children had been born. In particular, marriage to first birth interval 1650–1749 was 6–7 months less than English Quakers at about 15 months and 4 months less than Wilson's estimate (Eversley, 1981, *65, 72–3*). Subsequent birth intervals were shorter for English than Irish Quakers (25 months compared with 27–28 months) but both are less than Wilson's 31 months. Completed family size was larger too for Irish Quakers: just under 7 compared with just over 4 for southern English Quakers and just over 5 from English family reconstitutions (Wrigley and Schofield, 1983, *176*; Eversley, 1981, *76*). For late eighteenth century Killyman, Ulster, Macafee reports marriage to first birth intervals of about one year and subsequent intervals of 24–30 months (1987, *157*). Sterility increases with age but the figure of 10 per cent of married couples who are involuntarily sterile found by Eversley for Irish Quakers appears to be average for early modern populations (1981, *79*). If, as seems likely, Quakers are representative of the bulk of the population, Ireland's comparatively low age at first marriage and high marital fertility in the seventeenth and early eighteenth century were powerful forces behind population growth compared with England's.

The short marriage to first birth interval among Irish Quakers finds similarities with that among a small sample from the town of Kilmarnock in Scotland. The marriage to first birth interval was 13.3 months 1730–53 compared with 15.9 months for Irish Quakers, 19.9 for southern English Friends 1700–49, and about 19 months for 16 English parishes 1550–1749 (Flinn, 1977, *287*). Taking all higher birth orders together, intergenesic intervals at Kilmarnock were almost identical to English Quakers and slightly above Irish. If Kilmarnock is at all representative of Scottish marital fertility, the similarities with Ireland are intriguing. Total marital fertility would also have been higher in Scotland than in England, balancing out some of the effect of higher Scottish mortality (see below). One reason for the shorter birth intervals in Ireland compared with England may be the higher fecundity of women there – as contemporaries claimed. Another explanation might be that breastfeeding was less extensively practised by Irish Quakers though this cannot account for the shorter marriage to first birth intervals. We might also expect that infant and child mortality would be higher among children weaned earlier but there is no clear evidence of this except among Irish Quaker children aged 1–9 years and then only 1700–49 but not 1650–99 (Eversley, 1981, *80*). Kilmarnock aside, we can say nothing useful about Scottish marital fertility before the late eighteenth century. However, pronounced regional variations in both legitimate and illegitimate fertility during the nineteenth century are again fascinating. If carried back into earlier centuries they would contrast strongly with England's relative homogeneity.

There is virtually no material on overall Scottish fertility before the eighteenth century. Tyson's reasonably reliable estimate of the crude birth rate for Aberdeenshire 1691–5 is 29 per 1,000 (1985, *126*). Mitchison offers a higher rate of 35 per 1,000 for Scotland as a whole based on Webster's 1755 census age structure and model life tables (1989, *71*). Both estimates are significantly lower than Hollingsworth's very approximate 41 per 1,000 in the 1750s – a figure which is hard to square with other nuptiality and fertility parameters (Mitchison, 1989, 66). They are, however, close to the English levels of 32 per 1,000 in the 1690s and 33 in the 1750s. Potentially, a woman might have up to 30 children during her childbearing span between the ages of roughly 15 and 45: assuming no breastfeeding or severe mortality among the newly born. There are prominent historical examples of large families and high fertility but these are unusual. One seventeenth century English clergyman's wife, Elizabeth Walker, bore 11 children during her life while Charles I's queen Henrietta Maria produced seven children between autumn 1628 and spring 1639. Putting children out to wetnurses, a practice among elements of the upper classes, explains the latter example. But even in 'reference' communities with no deliberate birth control the average maximum number of live births by the end of a woman's reproductive career is under nine, the average birth interval is approximately 30 months, and the actual maximum birth rate around 50 per 1,000. Because of relatively late marriage, breastfeeding, and biological factors women in such communities are only pregnant for a sixth of their reproductive years (Bongaarts, 1975). The most potent factor in controlling total fertility was nuptiality.

Whatever their desires, couples do not seem to have limited the number of children born to them. In particular, 'parity-specific' birth control was not an option. In other words, parents could not decide to have a set family size and then achieve just that number. It was possible to space births by practising primitive contraceptive methods such as abstinence or withdrawal, or by increasing the length of time a child was breastfed and thereby inhibiting (if not absolutely preventing) conception. The age pattern of marital fertility in a natural fertility population is determined largely by physiology. If family limitation is practised, fertility will fall more rapidly with age and rising parity. Demographers use a measure (m) of the difference between a 'natural' fertility regime and one in which contraception is practised to indicate birth control. A m value of less than 0.2, characteristic of seventeenth and eighteenth century English marital fertility, means that no parity-specific birth control was being used. Other telltale signs are absent from England. If a notion of parity exists there will be a replacement effect as women whose children have died will continue child-bearing longer in order to replace them. No such effect has been found for 1600–1799 and indeed Wilson concludes that 'while the existence of family limitation in pre-industrial England cannot be ruled out, it is highly unlikely that it was of any significance in determining the overall patterns of marital fertility' (Wrigley and Schofield, 1983, *169–70*; Wilson, 1984, *240*).

Nor is there any clear evidence that parents sought to maximise the number of children they had, either as a way of increasing the family labour supply or securing for their old age. For one thing, children in both Scotland and England tended to leave home just as they were becoming most productive (in their mid-teens) and to use their earnings from working as servants and apprentices once they had left home to establish economic independence and set up their own household rather than remitting money to their parents (Kussmaul, 1981). Labour needs were met by hiring strangers rather than kin. For another, help for the aged and infirm was mainly provided by the community rather than by family members in England with no guarantee that parents could rely on their offspring for support, though this may have been expected. In Scotland the role of family and neighbourhood support and of informal charity was probably greater than in England but there is no evidence of a stress on fertility or of a desire to have a large family for practical reasons. In any case, high levels of geographical mobility militated against kin-based support, at least in the Lowlands. There is, however, evidence of Highland seasonal workers and domestic servants, working in the Lowlands, remitting to the home family in the later eighteenth century.

Illegitimate fertility

Most births took place within marriage. However, a 'procreative career' may begin before marriage and persist after the death of the last spouse; it may even exist within marriage but not with the spouse, difficult though it is for demographers to identify this in the past. Births outside marriage have attracted considerable attention from historians because of their implications for social life and personal relations (Laslett *et al.*, 1980). Yet, while pre-nuptial conception was quite common, at least in England, bastardy was not.

The ratio of illegitimate births to all births in 98 sample parishes rose in the last quarter of the sixteenth century to peak at 3.4 per cent in the early 1600s. Bastardy ratios fell thereafter to reach a nadir of 0.9 per cent 1655–9 before beginning a steady rise to reach 3.1 per cent 1750–4 and 5.3 per cent in the early 1800s (Laslett *et al.*, 1980, *14*; Wrigley, 1981, *157*). Trends in pre-nuptial pregnancy followed a similar path. In 16 parishes with well-kept registers, 31 per cent of legitimate first births were conceived within eight months of marriage 1550–99, 23 per cent 1600–49, 16 per cent 1650–99 and 22 per cent 1700–49 (Laslett *et al.*, 1980, *23*).

Bastardy is often treated as a pathological phenomenon or as an indicator of changing moral standards. Its recording is a function of the perceptions of church and community, its definition clouded by different interpretations of what constituted a marriage. For those born around 1666 roughly 14 per cent of marriages were 'clandestine' (not celebrated in accordance with the requirements of the established church) though 4–5 per cent is more usual for seventeenth and early eighteenth century England (Schofield, 1985b, *14*). However, historians now believe that most English bastard-bearers were ordinary women who decided to begin having sex in anticipation of marriage, conceived but then became the victims of social and economic dislocations or personal misfortunes which prevented them marrying. This would explain the late sixteenth century rise in illegitimacy which came at a time of serious dearths and of pressure of population on a relatively inelastic economy. An explanation predicated on an economic downturn is less obviously successful in accounting for the long rise in illegitimacy from the mid seventeenth to the early nineteenth century, during which period conditions were generally buoyant. The trough of the 1640s and 1650s was more the result of underreporting by neighbours and officials in response to draconian penalties introduced during the English revolution rather than a sign that puritan morality had been accepted by the populace (Laslett *et al.*, 1980, *158–91*).

Legitimate and illegitimate fertility can be seen as elements of the same social practice: both marital and extra-marital births were the result of a market in procreative unions. Courtship intensity varied over an individual's life and this may explain why illegitimacy levels in England tended to change with general fertility levels, why having a bastard did not prevent subsequent marriage, why trends in illegitimacy and pre-nuptial pregnancy moved together, why there was apparently an inverse relationship between age at first marriage for women and bastardy ratios, and why the age when women bore bastards was close to age at first birth within marriage (Laslett et al., 1980, 467–9).

Bastardy ratios were higher in Scotland and also less changeable. Illegitimate births were roughly 4 per cent of all births 1660–1750. A similar proportion of legitimate first births were conceived before marriage – much lower than in England (Mitchison and Leneman, 1989, 164, 168). There were marked regional variations even in the late seventeenth century. In aggregate, the relatively low levels mean that the effect on overall fertility was slight. Nationally, there was a slight downward trend 1660–1750 in both illegitimacy and pre-nuptial pregnancy but levels were more stable than in England. This finding lends further weight to the idea that nuptiality and fertility varied much less in Scotland than in England c. 1660–1750. The social background of illegitimacy was also different from that of England. Scotland may have possessed two distinct groups of extra-marital procreators: one intending marriage who began to have sex before marriage and another who did so without any strong prospect of marriage. The reasons for this, and their significance, are not yet clear (Mitchison and Leneman, 1989, 176). The low level of extra-marital sexual activity has sometimes been attributed to the action of a strong brand of protestantism working through parish 'courts' called kirk sessions. The differences between Scotland and England may also be related to sources, those for Scotland causing historians to underestimate pre-nuptial pregnancy though it is hard to believe that the marked divergence between the societies can be wholly explained in this way.

Illegitimacy was low in Ireland during the eighteenth century. Among the few figures available, Macafee cites 2 per cent bastardy among anglican births at Loughgall, county Armagh, 1707–29. In the second half of the eighteenth century three catholic parish registers reveal illegitimacy of less than 3 per cent and pre-nuptial pregnancy of about 10 per cent (Connolly, 1979, *8, 18–19*). Much more work is needed but it may be that early and more general marriage thanks to easier economic conditions removed some of the reasons for illegitimacy. The Counter-Reformation may have brought about changes in sexual practices and other aspects of behaviour during the seventeenth century but it would be too simplistic to relate low illegitimacy solely to the influence of the catholic church.

4
Mortality

For most age groups, levels of mortality in early modern Britain were much higher than in the nineteenth and twentieth centuries. Mortality could vary explosively in the short term in local areas. As many as a quarter of the population might be carried away by spectacular bouts of disease and famine during a two to three year period. Individual parishes had their own rhythms of mortality with huge local variations in the pattern and timing of fluctuations (Dobson, 1989a, *280*). Charting those patterns provides important insights into the reasons for mortality trends and fascinating detail about their social and economic significance. But the main task facing the historical demographer is to establish the overall level of mortality which tended to vary much less at regional and national levels.

Mortality crisis

The main text on Scottish population history sees mortality as the principal motor of demographic change before the nineteenth century (Flinn, 1977). This interpretation follows a historiographical tradition which stresses the significance of violent, short-term fluctuations in death rates for overall mortality. Flinn and his collaborators relied principally on inference from these short-term trends. Population grew 'naturally' because of a surplus of births over deaths but growth was periodically curbed by bouts of severe mortality caused by famine and disease. 'Mortality in the seventeenth century tended to fluctuate violently in the short run, and there is little doubt that it was primarily the changing pattern of mortality fluctuations that determined whether population would grow, stagnate or decline' (Flinn, 1977, *4*).

Irish historians have been more cautious about linking mortality crises to underlying death rates. But, as Clarkson remarks, 'the Malthusian spectre hangs heavily over popular perceptions' thanks to memories and folklore of the severe famine of the 1840s (1988, *220*). Certain periods witnessed serious crises, most notably that of 1740–1 which may have killed a quarter of a million people and there were other periods of famine in the 1620s, 1640s, 1650s and 1720s (Clarkson, 1988; Gillespie, 1988, *77–89*). The 1740–1 famine, occasioned by abnormal weather, simultaneous failure of all foods and lack of imports due to shortages abroad, led to destocking of farm animals, abandonment of farms and widespread vagrancy (Dickson, 1988, *97, 103–4*; Post, 1985).

Short-term mortality indices can certainly be used to identify periodic crises which were a distinctive feature of early modern Britain and Europe. Scotland and Ireland seem to have experienced mortality crises at different times from England and until later in their histories. Mortality crises had important social repercussions and could exert a powerful short-term influence on demographic and economic trends. Perhaps a fifth of the population of Aberdeenshire may have died during the crises of the 1690s (Tyson, 1986, *50*). However, there are a number of problems with an argument which relates short-term mortality crises to overall levels of mortality over long periods. Some shortcomings can be demonstrated by reference to English and European experience, others on more methodological and theoretical grounds. Part of the explanation for variations in mortality may be statistical. Most English parishes were small and there would have been large random variations in vital events from year to year. Half the parishes in Kent, Essex and Sussex in the seventeenth century had less than 200 inhabitants (Dobson, 1989b, *399*). Scottish parishes tended to be larger but random variations cannot be ruled out. Scottish figures should also be treated with caution since recording of deaths was rarely consistent or complete and periods of high mortality may have encouraged more diligent registration. In some cases 'surrounding years' may be only one or two each side of the crises. Even in a run of high mortality, experience was very varied, some areas being unaffected, others suffered once, certain locations frequently. The worst hit areas of Scotland in the famine of 1697 was the north-east, in 1699 the south-east. In England, France and Spain during the sixteenth and seventeenth centuries chronologies of growth and stagnation are not necessarily linked to mortality crises (Souden, 1985, *239–40*). Crude death rates may move down when the incidence of crises increases, as in late sixteenth century England.

Overall, it seems unwise to equate evidence of mortality fluctuations or crises with overall levels of mortality, population trends or mechanisms of change. Peaks in mortality in some years do not mean that mortality over time was high except in the very short term. England's population fell by more than 5 per cent between 1556 and 1561 as the crude death rate soared to over 50 per 1,000 in 1557. Expectation of life during the 5-year period centred on 1556 was roughly 15 years or a third less than that for the quinquennia 1551 or 1561 (Wrigley and Schofield, 1981, *230, 234*; Oeppen, 1991). However, the crises of the late 1550s were only a 'blip' in the steadily rising e_0 and hardly dented strong population growth. The significance of the underlying mortality and fertility regime is shown in the effects of the 1690s' dearths in Scotland. The slow growth of 1700–55 was almost certainly a continuation of a relatively high mortality and low fertility regime which existed in the seventeenth century. Famine and disease reduced total numbers in the 1690s but had no lasting effect on growth rates in the long term. As Souden reminds us, 'there is not a necessary relationship between moving totals of deaths and medium-to-long-term measures of mortality, between variance and level' (1985, *234*). These and other methodological problems were recognised by Flinn and his collaborators but were largely ignored in formulating their interpretation. It may be that mortality is the main dynamic variable in Scottish population history and the principal reason why population did not rise very quickly over the long term. But there is little reason to believe this on the evidence presented.

Levels of mortality

The principal difference between mortality patterns in the twentieth century and those in the seventeenth is that a much higher

Table 3 *Infant and child mortality in 13 English parishes (rates per 1,000) and expectation of life at birth in years (e_0) among the whole population (both sexes)*

	$_1q_0$	$_4q_1$	$_5q_5$	$_5q_{10}$	e_0
1600–49	161.3–162.3	89.3	41.2	25.2	36.4
1650–99	166.7–169.7	101.5	40.0	24.2	33.9
1700–49	169.2–195.3	106.5	40.6	22.8	34.5
1750–99	133.4–165.5	103.5	33.2	20.7	36.5

Source: Wrigley and Schofield, 1981, *252–3*; 1983, *177*.

percentage of all deaths occurred amongst the young in the past. Table 3 gives the most recent (and robust) estimates for England from 1600 onwards. Infant and child mortality come from family reconstitution studies, expectation of life at birth (e_0) from back projection estimates. The figure $_1q_0$ is the number of deaths among infants below one year of age per 1,000 live births. The other quotients relate to child age groups. A range is given for infant mortality because under-registration has to be taken into account. Life expectancy at birth of England's population was higher than in contemporary Europe (and Scotland) partly because infant and child mortality was relatively low. An earlier study showed that infant mortality in eight English parishes fell 1550–99 to 1600–49 but that of children aged 1–4 rose sharply and of 5–9-year-olds even more so (Schofield and Wrigley, 1979, *67, 95*). The fall in expectation of life at birth between the first and second half of the seventeenth century was caused by a rise in early child mortality, the eighteenth century rise by improving infant mortality.

Variation in infant and child mortality between different types of community was enormous. Infant mortality in the market town of Gainsborough (Lincolnshire) was three times the level of that in the coastal parish of Hartland and child mortality between five and nine years old was double. The role of infant and child mortality in determining total life expectancy is striking. Expectation of life at birth in a relatively 'healthy' parish like Hartland may have been as high as 50 years 1600–1749 compared with just 30 years in Gainsborough (Wrigley and Schofield, 1983, *179*). In wealthy central London parishes 1580–1650 expectation of life at birth was roughly 35 years but in the poorer suburban and riverside parishes with large numbers of incomers the figure was nearly a third lower (Finlay, 1981a, *107–8*). The worst non-urban infant mortality was found in marshy coastal and estuarine parts of south-east England where water-borne infections and malaria created levels of 250–300 per 1,000 (Dobson, 1989a, *265*).

Quoted life expectation at birth of, say, 35 years does not mean that everyone died at that age. Once a person had survived infancy and childhood they could expect to live through several decades of adult life. Men who became London freemen in the mid sixteenth century, at an average age of about 26 years, could expect to live a further 28 years (Rappaport, 1989, *69*). Between 1550 and 1749 male expectation of further life at age 30 among reconstitution populations was 28.4 years at its worst (1650–99) and at its best 30.4 years in the first half of the eighteenth century (Wrigley and Schofield, 1981, *250*). Women's life expectancy was almost identical. Adult life expectancy varied much less than infant or child over time and most changes in expectation of life at birth (and most geographical variations) are attributable to changing mortality of those aged 10 or less.

Historical demographers must again extrapolate from Irish Quaker mortality to that of the population of Ireland as a whole. Age-specific adult mortality of English and Irish Quakers was similar 1700–49. There was little to choose between infant mortality 1650–1749 or that of children 1650–99 but Irish Quaker child mortality at ages 1–9 was much higher than English 1700–49. Infant and child mortality among southern rural English Quakers was slightly better than that among English family reconstitution populations, possibly because unhealthy market towns are included in pooled data for the 13 parishes. For infants and children as well as adults there was little improvement in Irish Quaker mortality until the nineteenth century, though more recent work has suggested a fall in mortality in parts of Ulster from the mid eighteenth century (Eversley, 1981, *80*; Macafee, 1987, *146*).

Expectation of life at birth was apparently lower in Scotland than England. Using the age structure given in Webster's 1755 census and model life tables, Mitchison has calculated a life expectancy at birth of 31 or 32 years compared with 36 or 37 for England (Mitchison, 1989, *71*). Much of this difference was accounted for by different levels of infant and child mortality – infant mortality of over 220 per 1,000 compared with 170–190 in England 1700–49 – though adult mortality was also higher in Scotland (Wrigley and Schofield, 1983, *177*). The crude death rate for Scotland was 31 per 1,000 compared with 26 for England in the 1750s. There is evidence of increasing adult life expectancy among elite Edinburgh-based lawyers ('advocates'). The period 1650–1749 saw an important fall in adult mortality similar to that occurring among certain European elites. Expectation of life at age 30 among advocates entering their professional association 1650–99 was 27.4 years compared with 33.9 years 1700–49 (Houston, 1991). These figures relate to adults from a privileged elite. Mitchison (1989, *71*) has estimated expectation of life at age 30 of 25.8 years for both sexes from Webster's 1755 census age structure and model life tables. This means that adult life expectancy for advocates was at least a third better than for the population at large. In Scotland there may have been wide divergences in the mortality of social groups of a kind well documented on the Continent – notably in seventeenth century Geneva – but not apparently found in England at so early a date. Expectation of life at birth among British peers was lower than for the population at large during the seventeenth century, only slightly better 1700–49 but clearly superior in the second half of the eighteenth century (Hollingsworth, 1964, *56*).

Differences between the mortality of social groups are strongly related to living conditions. Plague, for example, was no respecter of status once caught but those who lived in well-built brick houses had much less chance of being infected by rat fleas than poorer people who inhabited crowded and inferior dwellings. Whether differential mortality also highlights social attitudes is much less clear. It has been claimed that infant and child mortality rates obtaining in early modern Britain show that children were not valued. This view can be challenged on a number of fronts. First, there is now overwhelming evidence from diaries and autobiographies to show that parental affection was not new to the eighteenth century. Second, urban poor relief provisions and regulations governing servants and apprentices clearly demonstrate the value placed on the health of children and youths, albeit partly for economic reasons (Houlbrooke, 1984, *127–56*; Wrightson, 1982, *104–18*).

More sinister is the possibility that female infants and children suffered greater neglect than male (Wall, 1981; Finlay, 1981b). Wall thinks that higher female infant mortality after a number of births to a family is at least suggestive of differential neglect in some parishes. Yet, the evidence is far from conclusive. In fact, a study of eight English parishes 1550–1749 found that there was a slight, 'normal' surplus of male infant and child deaths compared with female. Far more important than sex to life chances was parental wealth with poorer children more likely to die young than those from better-off backgrounds. Most important of all was environment: infants and children living in congested and insanitary communities had high mortality (Finlay, 1981b, 70–1, 76; Wall, 1981, 136–7). Mortality differences were a direct result of living conditions and infant-feeding practices, and an indirect effect of levels of wealth. Finally, there is intriguing evidence for England that infant mortality was high for first births, much lower for second, third and fourth births, but rose sharply for higher birth orders (Wrigley and Schofield, 1983, 180–1).

If the demographic experience of urban dwellers differed from their rural counterparts growing urbanisation might have a significant effect on demographic trends by changing the composition of the population. Towns were, for example, significantly less healthy environments than rural areas. There were just 0.87 births for every death in London 1580–1650 (Finlay, 1981a, 59). Infant and child mortality, already severe in early seventeenth century London, worsened in late century and continued to rise into the eighteenth century (Landers, 1990, 41–2). Given urban/rural mortality differences, an increase in London's share of English population from 5 per cent to 10 per cent (as happened 1600–1700) would reduce national e_0 by one year (Wrigley and Schofield, 1981, 415, 472–6). London and other towns certainly helped to restrict population growth in the later seventeenth century but the net effect of urban growth should not be exaggerated. The lower the starting level, the smaller the effect on national population of urban growth. The compositional effect of urbanisation on mortality, or nuptiality and fertility, would have been significantly less in England than in the Netherlands, where more than 30 per cent of the population lived in towns of 10,000 or more in 1600, the effect even more limited in Scotland and Ireland (De Vries, 1985, 666–7).

Causes of death

Describing changing levels of mortality is difficult enough with intractable early modern sources. Explaining the observed structures and trends is considerably more of a problem. Parish registers only rarely give cause of death and their descriptions can confuse as much as they enlighten. Urban bills of mortality may be more forthcoming. In London, experienced but non-specialist 'searchers' cursorily examined a corpse and reported the reason for death to the clerk of the bills. Descriptions such as 'the pox' (smallpox) or 'a bloody flux' (dysentery) are readily identifiable, and the symptoms of bubonic plague hard to miss. But, among the 150 other descriptions used, 'fever' or 'dropsy' could be almost anything; 'blasted and planetstruck' is intriguing if nothing else (Galloway, 1985, *491*).

Yet, even where causes of death are not given it is possible to piece together a plausible explanation from indirect indicators because each disease has its own etiology and epidemiology. A time-consuming, if potentially fascinating, piece of detective work is to follow systematic differences in mortality patterns at a local level. For example, Dobson finds an extensive coverage of moderate mortality peaks in south-east England in the 1670s and 1680s covering all ecological and environmental types. Looking at the duration and seasonality of mortality, she identifies gastric diseases such as typhoid, dysentery and salmonella (Dobson, 1989b, *418–19*).

Another killer has been tracked down in south-west England. The very high death rates at Colyton between November 1645 and November 1646 suggest that a highly morbid disease was present. The mortality, perhaps a fifth of the population during that year, was confined to that parish and was probably not caused by an airborne infection which would have spread more widely. Its slow passage through the parish further indicated an insect-borne infection. Certain diseases tend to kill victims in particular age groups or at specific times of the year. Typhus kills mainly adults in the winter and is carried by human lice; dysentery spread by flies is a summer disease. Both can be ruled out for Colyton. Seasonality and the clustering of deaths in certain households show that plague was present (Schofield, 1977).

Plague is a high-profile disease which commentators were likely to record because of its symptoms and urban focus, and because of the fear it induced. But it was clearly not equally serious everywhere and its overall effect on mortality may have been less than is assumed. The last serious outbreak of plague occurred in Scotland 1645–9 when it may have killed as much as a fifth of Scotland's urban population (Flinn, 1977, *147*). However, less than 12 per cent of the population of seventeenth century Scotland lived in towns of 2,000 or more inhabitants and since plague was primarily an urban disease the effect on population totals may have been less severe than urban mortality figures and contemporary alarm suggests (Whyte, 1989a, *28, 33*). The same point can be made for England. In 1604 the Durham mining parish of Whickham lost perhaps a fifth or a quarter of its population, a proportion comparable with the London epidemic of 1563. However, between 1580 and 1650 plague accounted for just 15 per cent of all deaths in London and the proportion of national deaths would have been lower still (Finlay, 1981a, *111–32*; Slack, 1985). The worst mortality crisis in early modern England was actually caused by the influenza epidemic of 1557–9. Plague's disappearance, from Scotland after the 1640s, and from England after the 1660s, may have been compensated for by other killers such as dysentery, measles, influenza or pulmonary complaints, while smallpox probably became endemic in parts of England and all over the Scottish Lowlands from the 1670s and 1680s (Flinn, 1977, *115, 158, 163–4*). If smallpox was truly a universal childhood disease in the eighteenth century this would distinguish Scotland (and Sweden) from England where it was mainly endemic in London.

Starvation is apparently well documented for certain periods such as 1596–8 or 1623–4. Yet, it is by no means certain that the main killer in famine years was hunger since the social dislocations upon which contemporaries remarked so forcibly may have increased the likelihood of catching morbid diseases (Walter and Schofield, 1989, *53–4, 67–8*; Flinn, 1977, *179*). Sir Robert Sibbald wrote of the 1690s famines in Scotland: 'Everyone may see death in the faces of the poor that abound everywhere; the thinness of their visage, their ghostly looks, their feebleness, their agues and their fluxes threaten them with sudden death' (Flinn, 1977, *170–1*). In the spring of 1700 when the worst of the dearth was over, the

Scottish church ordered a token fast because of 'the great and unusual sickness and mortality throughout the land'. Famine mortality tends to affect extensive areas simultaneously, whereas disease mortality spreads slowly in a wave-like motion from one community to another. Starvation deaths usually occur close to the periods of highest prices, as in Munster 1740–1. Later mortality peaks are likely to be the result of disease epidemics. Typhoid and dysentery were killing people in Edinburgh in the autumn of 1741 when food supplies were returning to normal after the serious shortages of the previous harvest year (Post, 1985, *241–2*). Galloway believes that an increase in London deaths 1640–1750 among middle and older age groups in times of grain price surges was because they migrated into the city and died from diseases to which they had no immunity (1985, *500*). Other connections between nutrition and mortality are discussed in Chapter 6.

An allegedly common female experience was death in childbed. A woman who went through an average six or seven full-term pregnancies would run a 6–7 per cent chance of dying in childbirth. Maternal mortality accounted for a maximum of 20 per cent of all female deaths between the ages of 25 and 34, 11–14 per cent aged 20–24 and 35–44. To appreciate how little effect death in childbed may have had on women's attitudes, a large English village of 1,000 inhabitants, where a quarter were women aged 15–49, would experience only one maternal death on average every third year. Women must have been aware of the risks but may have seen them as distant. Maternal mortality in eighteenth century London was, however, 30–50 per cent higher than elsewhere in England. While the risks of dying in childbed were much greater for women than in the twentieth century, so too were those of dying from many other causes (Schofield, 1986, *259–60*). Finally, higher female mortality in the childbearing years should be set alongside higher male mortality in those years thanks to occupational risks – coal-mining accidents in north east England or plague deaths among south-east dock workers, for example.

Quantifying the relative importance of different causes of death is notoriously difficult. Landers shows that nearly a half of deaths among London Quaker children aged 5–9 were from smallpox and that this disease is important in accounting for the rise in child mortality in the early eighteenth century (1990, *54–5*). Ten times as many deaths were attributed to smallpox as to typhus in the London bills of mortality 1630–1730 (Appleby, 1975, *15*). The number of deaths from typhus remained fairly constant over this period but its relative significance as a killer decreased as the population of the city more than doubled. Some 20 per cent of reported deaths at Dublin 1661–1745 were attributed to smallpox (Ó Gráda, 1979, *288*).

Different age groups were susceptible to different diseases. Jones argues that the decline in infant mortality in rural north Shropshire from the late seventeenth century was thanks to a reduction in winter respiratory infections in the first three months of life. The doubling in mortality of those aged 6–11 months 1711–60 was mainly the result of smallpox, measles and other diseases (1980, *244–9*). For contemporary London, Landers posits that gastric and respiratory diseases particularly affected the under-twos while smallpox and other infections were the main killers above that age (1990, *58–9*). Substantial improvements in infant and child mortality did not begin until the second half of the eighteenth century (Riley, 1987; Landers, 1990). It is probably safe to say that most deaths in the early modern period were from infectious diseases rather than from accidents, non-infectious ailments and old age as in the twentieth century.

5

Migration

Historians once believed that population was essentially immobile before the economic changes and transport developments of the nineteenth century. Research in the last three decades has radically modified this perspective. Four out of every five witnesses before the church courts of Elizabethan Buckinghamshire said they had moved at least once in their lives. Over seventeenth century England as a whole, between a half and two-thirds of a parish's population would be renewed every 12 years. Between 1681 and 1686 approximately 40 per cent of household heads in parishes of central and north Wales had moved. Evidence from the Weald shows that better-off people moved shorter distances than the poor. An extreme example of this pattern was the mobility of vagrants: usually young, single males moving long distances in search of subsistence. Vagrancy was a crime punishable by whipping and return to parish of origin. Those caught in the southeastern counties in the late sixteenth and early seventeenth centuries were drawn from all over England (Clark and Souden, 1987, 29–34).

Important changes were taking place over time, with the mid seventeenth century representing a watershed. Improved economic conditions substantially reduced concerns about vagrancy in the second half of the seventeenth century and probably also long-distance subsistence migration itself. This was part of a wider trend towards less frequent, shorter distance and more formalised movement. In the diocese of Bath and Wells, lifetime immobility increased from a third of church court deponents in the early seventeenth century to a half in the later century. This change was, however, much less pronounced in East Anglia. Apprentice migration fields contracted dramatically and the system itself fell into decay. Between 1486 and 1750 the average distance travelled by provincial recruits to London companies was halved from 212 km to 111 km. The proportion of young men of known origin coming from the northern counties fell from 51 per cent 1486–1500 to 4 per cent in the 1740s while the share from London and the Home Counties grew from 28 per cent to 72 per cent (Wareing, 1980, *243–4*). Norwich and Southampton saw a 90 per cent reduction in the number of formal enrolments 1600–1700. Formal apprenticeship survived longer in the north of England and in Scotland but even here by the early eighteenth century it became increasingly confined to the wealthier trades and professions. Apprentices were becoming more local in their origins, as were agricultural servants whose movement was more institutionalised by the Settlement Acts after 1662. The later seventeenth century also saw greater seasonal mobility to meet the changing labour needs of a more specialised agriculture: for example, Welsh girls who came to work in the market gardens around London. In short, the sixteenth and early seventeenth centuries in England were characterised by 'a relatively ill-defined and undifferentiated system of migration. More basic, localised movement shaded into longer-distance travelling. Crude subsistence or push factors were a vital part of the migration matrix. Pull factors were not matched to the precise needs of the economy' (Clark and Souden, 1987, *32*).

Recently, the emphasis in research has switched from mobility towards stability (Boulton, 1987). Even in communities experiencing rapid growth by immigration, such as London in the late sixteenth and early seventeenth century or the contemporary mining parish of Whickham, there was a core of long-established inhabitants (Rappaport, 1989; Wrightson and Levine, 1989). This is not to deny the problems of assimilation for movers and host communities alike, or to question the existence of a high level of population turnover. It is to suggest that among certain (predominantly middling) sections of local communities there was considerable stability and continuity and that this has implications for the distribution of wealth and power within society.

Scotland shares many of the structures found in England. Geographical mobility within Scotland was extensive from an early date. The existence of servants in husbandry and a large land-poor class of 'cottars', both of whom moved frequently over short distances, coupled with the growth of towns and the evidence of extensive vagrancy from the later sixteenth century clearly indicate this. Population turnover occurred mostly among young, single people three-quarters of whom stayed less than three years in a parish; it was linked to the rhythms of agricultural life (Houston, 1985). Like England, most parishes would also possess a stable core. Some 45 per cent of completed tenancies in Angus (1650–1714) were less than five years long though 65 per cent of renewals were by sitting tenants (Whyte, 1989b). Taking into account adult mortality levels this implies a degree of permanence.

Most movement was local and over distances which people could walk in a day. Longer-distance migration involved apprentices and seasonal workers. Edinburgh was the only town with a truly national catchment area for apprentices in the period 1583–1700. Other towns had more localised recruitment areas and it was only in the early eighteenth century that Glasgow, on the way to becoming the largest Scottish city, began to make inroads into Edinburgh's appeal (Houston and Withers, 1990). Distances moved, and possibly population turnover as well, increased in eighteenth century Scotland. Vagrancy remained a problem well into the eighteenth century. Seasonal migration of Highlanders – who made up a third of Scotland's population in 1755 – to the Lowlands during the summer is documented from the later seventeenth century and may have existed before. Transhumance was practised on the Scottish Border in the sixteenth century but died out in the seventeenth (Kussmaul, 1990, *44*). Given the importance of geographical mobility, the presence of clear regional variations in illegitimacy, and the possibility of significant differences between Highland and Lowland demography, generalisations about 'Scottish' population (like Dutch) 'may obscure a series of distinctive regional demographic processes that were linked together by migration' (De Vries, 1985, *682*).

A similar suggestion has been made for England. The south-east and south-west differed substantially from each other in the extent of male and female migration, the sex ratio among movers and the proportion of local moves. A half of Devon's church court deponents in the seventeenth century were still living in the parish of their birth. This compares with a third of men and a quarter of

women from Somerset and Wiltshire. Further east the proportions
who never moved fell to a fifth of males and a sixth of females
(Souden, 1987, *315–17*). There must also have been a net movement of males to the south-eastern counties (except London) and
of females to the south-west because differences in the sex ratio at
birth and burial in these regions are too large to fit observed
demographic parameters. The spread of pastoral husbandry in the
west of England during the late seventeenth century reduced the
need for agricultural workers in general and for men in particular.
Depopulation would follow unless industry was introduced to mop
up the surplus labour (Kussmaul, 1990). Contrasting rates of
regional population growth may be explained by differential migration. North Wales experienced faster growth *c*. 1550–*c*. 1670 than
the south, possibly because of English immigration. Regional
variations in Irish growth rates, notably the buoyancy of Ulster and
Munster in the seventeenth century, may also be related to
immigration from Scotland and England (Macafee and Morgan,
1981; Dickson *et al.*, 1982, *156–69*). The eighteenth century saw
the beginnings of a substantial redistribution of population from
the north to the central Lowlands of Scotland.

Most population turnover and seasonal migration had little
impact on levels and distribution of people. Permanent movement,
to towns or from one region to another, certainly did. Towns were
unhealthy environments which needed large numbers of immigrants to maintain their populations, let alone sustain the growth
apparent *c*. 1550–1800. The effect of migration on the population
of Chester can be gauged for various periods between 1585 and
1702. The population was the same at both dates but movement
into the town diminished the effect of higher mortality 1597–1606;
it converted a natural loss into a net gain 1637–9. Out-migration
turned a birth surplus into a net loss 1616–18 (Alldridge, 1986,
130). The age and sex structure of migration also influenced
marriage chances: if nubile women were over-represented their
marriage would be delayed at their new abode –as in seventeenth
century London (Clark and Souden, 1987, *23*). However, across
England as a whole, Kussmaul finds the net effect of selective
migration on nuptiality was weak (1990, *158–63*).

Mobility could therefore contribute to regional demographic
differences and thus to national structures and trends. However,

there was no effect on total numbers until movers left the country altogether. Permanent migration overseas certainly existed in the sixteenth century and before but the volume of emigration increased significantly in the seventeenth century. Scots were engaged in overseas trade, notably with the Netherlands, the Baltic and the north-west Atlantic coast from the medieval period and can be found as soldiers, farmers, petty merchants and 'professionals' in eastern Europe in the sixteenth and seventeenth centuries. For the middle classes, contacts with European universities were extensive, notably Leiden for law in the seventeenth century. Movement of Scots to the New World was comparatively unimportant before the second half of the eighteenth century. Something like 6,000 left for that destination before 1700, some voluntarily as religious refugees during the 1640s and 1690s, others transported by Oliver Cromwell in the 1650s or by Charles II in the 1670s and 1680s. Convict transportations were increasing from the late seventeenth century but only a few hundred left 1718–75 (Ekirch, 1987, *23–7*). As early as 1740 groups of families began to leave the western isles for the Americas, often led by lesser gentry (Houston and Withers, 1990).

Such numbers are dwarfed by the volume of movement to (and from) Ireland in the seventeenth century. The initial settlement of Ulster involved some 14,000 Scots before 1625 (Flinn, 1977, *8*). In the 1650s, 24,000 Scots went there, and a total of perhaps 100,000 Scots during the seventeenth century. Some 130,000 people left Scotland for north America and Ireland during the seventeenth century. Movement of Scots to England is harder to quantify except for specific groups: the 1,600 men who loaded coal onto the ships bound for London from Newcastle ('keelmen') were almost all Scots-born in the seventeenth century; in the late seventeenth century Scots were prominent in itinerant trading and in London hairdressing and tailoring.

In contrast with the nineteenth century, early modern Ireland was almost certainly a net receiver of people from Scotland and, to a lesser extent, England. One estimate has over a quarter of Ireland's people 'of Scottish and English blood' in 1733. Almost all the Irish Quakers of the seventeenth century were of English extraction. Ulster people moved back to Scotland in periods of political and religious upset during the seventeenth century and at times of severe famine such as the 1620s. There is also evidence of emigration to north America of small farmers and craftsmen from Ulster in the 1720s, 1740s and 1750s (Clarkson, 1988, *231*). Ireland was attractive to Scots because they had more capital and better agricultural techniques than natives, and because political restrictions kept catholics from the land. Taking into account differing perceptions of acceptable living standards, these reasons may explain why Scots moved to Ireland and Irish to Europe and America (Macafee and Morgan, 1981). Military defeats in 1603, 1652 and 1691 prompted an exodus not only of individual Irish officers and soldiers to Europe but also of whole companies or regiments. Irish were a major component of white emigration to the West Indies from the mid seventeenth century and Ulster Scots of movement to north America before 1760. The volume of migration into Ireland was much lower in the early eighteenth century than in the seventeenth. The same is true of emigration from Ireland where one rough estimate is 1–2 per 1,000 in the seventeenth century, 1 per 1,000 in the eighteenth.

Needless to say, English net migration estimates are both more precise and more robust. The figures in Wrigley and Schofield showed migration moving in cycles and peaking in the 1650s. Recent work by Oeppen (1991) has flattened out these 'waves' and presented a more reliable set of estimates. Net emigration was at its highest in the mid sixteenth century and declined almost without interruption until the beginning of the nineteenth century. At 1.7 per 1,000, the net migration rate was higher in the 1560s than at any time between 1541 and 1866. Net migration exerted a powerful influence on population growth during the century *c.* 1650–*c.* 1750 when intrinsic growth rates were low. England's population fell by 385,000 1656–86 and migration accounted for a substantial proportion of this, also slowing early eighteenth century growth significantly (Wrigley and Schofield, 1981, *228*; Oeppen, 1991). At other periods the net loss was lower and the effect on growth rates attenuated. Movement abroad did not merely effect total population. Most English emigrants to the New World were young adults who would have married and reproduced in the colonies. Their movement therefore reduced total fertility among the remaining population. In addition, since most English emigrants were single men their departure may have slightly reduced marriage chances for resident women and thus further limited population growth. Military emigration from seventeenth century Scotland may also be related to the relatively late age at first marriage for women.

Recent work has sought to revise upwards numbers of emigrants. However, in discussing migration estimates, we must be careful to distinguish figures of net from gross emigration or immigration, and those which cover specific groups or destinations from total estimates. Net migration is the total movement out of a country less the numbers who enter it. Between 1630 and 1699, for example, a net total of some 544,000 people left England, 70 per cent of them destined for the New World. Back projection calculations give this figure, including estimates of deaths at sea and by soldiers and traders abroad, but do not show the absolute numbers entering or leaving. Other sources can help here. Indentured servants were young women and men (in a ratio of 1:4 1650–1780) who, like apprentices, agreed to work for a master during a fixed period in return for a paid passage, their keep while serving and certain rights on completion of the indenture (Galenson, 1981). Between 300,000 and 400,000 of these young adults (nearly three-quarters were aged 15–24) left for British colonies 1650–1780, making up perhaps a half to three-quarters of all white settlers of the American colonies. A further quarter of Britons moving to the New World 1718–75 were forcibly transported convicts – made up of approximately 36,000 English, 13,000 Irish and 700 Scots – with an age and sex composition similar to that of free servants (Ekirch, 1987, *23–7, 116*). Most went to the Chesapeake.

There may have been a substantial outflow to the New World colonies compensated for by movement from other parts of Britain or by protestant refugees from Europe. England probably received more Scots people, and possibly also Welsh, than it gave to these regions whereas Ireland was a net recipient of migrants: the commentator Reynel estimated in 1674 that 200,000 people had been 'wasted in repeopling Ireland' (Wrigley and Schofield, 1981, *224*). Knowing the numbers who arrived in the colonies does not show how many stayed there because individuals and families sometimes returned to England, especially in the seventeenth century (Cressy, 1987).

Most migration was voluntary and drawn from a broad spectrum of society: labourers to lairds. However, recent work has shown how complex were the motivations of emigrants. Even the supposedly 'religious' movers to New England in the first half of the seventeenth century had important family and economic reasons for leaving their homeland and Cressy concludes that 'the movement to New England appears untidy, fractured and complex rather than rational, purposeful and coherent' (1987, 74). To a degree, emigrants may have been responding to specific changes in the economic climate at home but there is no evidence that they were driven out by an acute pressure of population on resources. Desire for betterment rather than mere subsistence characterises most movement. For example, the settler population of early seventeenth century Munster mostly comprised skilled artisans and farmers (Canny, 1985, 13). English emigrants to the north American colonies were more literate than their counterparts left behind, suggesting above-average status. Criminals were dispatched to the Americas and there was some settlement by soldiers, in parts of Ulster for example, but emigrants were definitely not the dregs of society. As Sir George Peckham remarked in 1583, people emigrated 'in hope thereby to amend their estates' (Galenson, 1981, 112–13).

Inferring motivation is difficult. However, both the timing of emigration and the composition of migrant groups suggest that narrowing opportunities to improve, or at least maintain, individual or family fortunes at home rather than absolute want were the principal incentives. Furthermore, the overall volume of emigration from Scotland and England grew in the first half of the nineteenth century at a time of economic expansion rather than contraction and stagnation. Those who emigrated seem to have responded positively to better opportunities perceived in new lands. It is true that movement of Scots to Ireland in the 1690s was caused mainly by adverse economic conditions in Scotland and that in the 1770s Scots were more likely to leave Britain for negative reasons – such as landlord exploitation – than were English emigrants. However, emigration should be seen as a positive response more than as a sign of desperation. The *effect* of emigration may have been to improve the balance between population and resources for those remaining but this was probably not the *cause* except in the short term. Migration was a way of preventing any imbalance becoming too serious rather than a simple reaction to over-population. Other means of achieving an equilibrium are discussed in the following chapter.

6

Population, economy and society

Up to this point, we have dealt mainly with the purely demographic components of population structures and trends. Human beings did not, of course, marry, procreate and die in a vacuum. The decisions which they made as individuals or as a society could both reflect and effect their environment. Migration is an example. During the early modern period, their understanding of, and control over, that environment was much weaker than for many modern populations. However, they were by no means wholly victims of circumstances.

In any population, human or animal, there must at some point exist a balance between the demand for food and the ability of an environment to provide it. Several early modern commentators, of course, recognised this, but none developed the idea as clearly as Thomas Malthus. In his *Essay on the Principle of Population*, first printed in 1798 and in subsequent editions, Malthus posited that while food production could only increase arithmetically, population could show compound or geometrical growth. Over time, population growth rates would therefore exceed the rate of increase in agricultural output and living standards would be likely to fall. One way in which population and resources could be brought back into balance was by progressive immiseration, starvation and disease: what Malthus called a 'positive' check. Much more likely was that people, realising their living standards were threatened, would adopt some means of checking population growth before the ravages of high mortality were felt. Malthus called this a 'preventive' check and saw a reduction in nuptiality as the mechanism which would eventually bring population back into line with food supply (Schofield, 1983).

Where do England, Scotland and Ireland fit into this scheme? A demographic regime is an internally coherent population system defined in social and economic terms as well as simply demographic ones. In order fully to understand its functioning and to explain changes in the relative significance of its components we must look beyond purely demographic factors. Economic, social, cultural, legal and ideological considerations may come into play. Throughout, the difference between short- and long-term effects, between simultaneous and lagged ones, and between the relative strengths of relationships is important (Schofield, 1985a, *578–9*).

Mortality

Historians traditionally fell into two camps when it came to explaining population growth rates. In the 1970s the orthodox view was that population and resources would be kept in a sort of balance by periodic outbreaks of famine, war and disease. Some of these would be the direct result of over-population, others accidental. Nuptiality and fertility were felt to be much too slow to respond in the short term to changes in scarcity and plenty, and could not vary enough to make the necessary adjustments (Flinn, 1977). This turned out to be a dangerous assumption to make on both theoretical and empirical grounds. Opposing this view were authorities such as Connell, Habakkuk and Krause who focused on the preventive check which was seen to work through nuptiality and fertility. Changes in nuptiality can indeed have a rapid and pronounced effect on fertility which, for England at least, varied more than mortality over long periods. Wrigley (1981) has shown that three-quarters of the increase in population growth in England in the second half of the eighteenth century can be attributed to rising fertility consequent on a substantial fall in the age at first marriage for women. Studies of the eighteenth century have dominated discussion of the role of nuptiality and fertility in demographic change. However, mortality was of great importance, accounting equally with fertility for changing rates of population growth in England between 1551 and 1751. There are two main issues. First, could people, as individuals or as a society, influence their own life chances at all, and, if so, by what means? Second, was mortality an integral component of the demographic and economic system, linked positively or negatively to other variables such as food supplies and nuptiality?

At first sight, mortality may seem largely exogenous, or linked only weakly, to economic change. This is particularly true of England. Just 16 per cent of short-run mortality variation from the sixteenth to the early nineteenth century was associated with price changes and the long-term relationship was 'disorderly and frequently contrary to expectation' (Schofield, 1983, 276–7, 282). In England, mortality did respond to short-term monthly and annual changes in food prices up to 1640. During the following century the relationship weakened then disappeared altogether (Wrigley and Schofield, 1981, 285–355, 368–77, 412–17). Galloway has shown for England 1675–1755 that just a quarter of fluctuations in deaths of those over age five were associated with fluctuations in grain prices (compared with nearly a half in France) and that the magnitude of the mortality increase in the year of harvest failure and in the following year was only half that of France (1985). Long-run trends in scarcity and plenty shown by wage rates were not related to mortality in early modern England.

England conquered the problem of famine at an early stage in her development. What is more, recent work suggests that the importance of famine in the late sixteenth and early seventeenth century has been overestimated and defences against it underrated. Even in years of serious shortage such as 1597–8 when mortality was 26 per cent over its long-term trend, only 28 per cent of parishes in the Cambridge Group sample suffered from subsistence crises (Walter, 1989, 79). Walter identifies vulnerability to famine increased by 'the weakness of local ecologies, fragile surpluses, poor and unfavourable market integration' and economic specialisation (81) while 'the more mixed the economy the greater were the defences against harvest failure' (92). The last serious famines in the 1620s seem mainly to have affected certain northern pastoral areas. Indeed, Walter cautions against exaggerating vulnerability to famine in England because of extensive formal and informal support mechanisms (1989, 92–116). English agriculture expanded sufficiently between the late fifteenth and early nineteenth century to cope with a fourfold increase in population. By the end of the seventeenth century wheat prices moved in unison, demonstrating that a national market existed for that grain (though not others) (Walter and Schofield, 1989, *9–10*). English poor relief, codified in laws of 1597 and 1601, was based on compulsory rating of better-off parishioners and was very effective nationally by the 1630s.

This does not necessarily mean that nobody starved. 'Hidden hunger' may still have haunted sections of the population. In communities with extreme wealth polarisation, such as the cloth areas of Essex during the 1629 trade slump, poor-law rating alone could not cope. Nor does it mean that agricultural productivity was always sufficiently elastic to meet the needs of a growing population. In periods when population grew at more than 0.5 per cent a year the greater proportional fall in real wages suggests otherwise. If population grew at more than 1 per cent a year then food prices would rise at 1.5 per cent per annum – as in the late sixteenth century (Wrigley and Schofield, 1981, *404*). The most fertile period for the dissemination of agricultural improvements in England came between 1660 and 1740. They were stimulated by falling profitability and changing demand structures rather than by the pressure of population – which was in fact much weaker than a century before (Kussmaul, 1991). Agricultural change came about more in response to changing population composition – more urban and rural non-agricultural workers – than to growth itself.

In Scotland and Ireland, low agricultural productivity, restricted marketing and inadequate poor relief undoubtedly contributed to continued vulnerability to famine, notably in Scotland in the 1690s and in Ireland in the 1720s and 1740s (Dickson, 1988; Post, 1985). In some Scottish towns recorded burials during the dearth years 1623–4 were up to eight times as high as surrounding years (Flinn, 1977, *6–7*). However, it is difficult to argue that a Malthusian 'positive check' was truly an integral part of Scotland's demographic and economic system. Crises like the 1690s may have helped alleviate any population pressure but the unexpected nature of the famine of 1695–9 is shown by the passing of an act by the Scottish parliament in early 1695 to subsidise grain exports at a time of low prices (Flinn, 1977, *165*). Ireland too was a net exporter of grain in the 1700s and 1710s though there were heavy imports in the second quarter of the eighteenth century (Clarkson, 1988, *223*; Dickson, 1988, *101*). By the early eighteenth century there was no close connection between grain prices and mortality in Scotland (Flinn, 1977, *211*).

In both Scotland and Ireland, poor relief was permissive rather than obligatory, based on voluntary donations and landowners' charity. For most of the period before 1750, Scottish landowners steadfastly refused to be rated. Some East Lothian parishes did have effective poor relief in the 1690s and this protected them from the worst effects of famine mortality but it was not until well into the eighteenth century that provisions worked efficiently over large areas of Scotland. The shortages of 1740–1 were dealt with much more effectively than those of the 1690s by supplying grain to markets, providing substantial voluntary relief and creating employment.

Irish poor relief in the early eighteenth century was essentially private and local, based on the charity of landlords, clergy and neighbourly 'generosity of the have-littles towards the have-nots' (Dickson, 1988, *105–6*). The parish as a unit of government and administration never really took root in Ireland because of the late development of the established (but minority) church of Ireland as an effective ecclesiastical organisation. New means of relief were being tried in Ulster in the late 1720s though their effect was limited. In parts of Ireland, absence of a resident landlord may have prevented employment projects and sales of subsidised grain being implemented (Flinn, 1977, *7*, *13*; Post, 1985, *146–7*, *176–7*). Problems were exacerbated because in Ireland doctrinal divisions followed those of wealth and poverty: catholics were usually poorer than protestants. This illustrates the point that hunger is not solely related to harvest shortages but is tied to a range of other entitlements which may worsen or ease its burden. The fact that Ireland escaped lightly from the European famines of the 1690s and relatively lightly in 1708–10 may also show that an element of meterological luck was involved.

Most subsistence crises were not a structural part of the demographic and economic regime but were accidental. Admittedly, in Scotland the problems of sort-term grain shortage were exacerbated by chronically low net grain yields, limited transport and marketing mechanisms, and a relatively ineffective poor-relief system before the eighteenth century. The example of Shetland suggests that people could cope with one dearth year, even if it involved bad harvests, shortage of fish and cattle disease (1663), but that runs of bad years like 1633–5 or 1693–6 in these islands elicited statements about widespread deaths from starvation (Flinn, 1977, *114*, *130*). Admittedly too, Scotland was not 'a region of a larger international economy' as was the Netherlands. This had important implications for the overall standard of living and for the existence for some brief periods of a negative relationship between food prices and population size since the demographic/economic system was more likely to be closed (De Vries, 1985, *679–81*). Again, the problems of securing grain from external sources improved in the eighteenth century. Yet, there is little point in piling up examples of local subsistence crises since this does not allow systematic measurement of the strength or consistency of the relationship between prices and mortality. Recent work by Gibson and Smout (1992) has given an outline of wages and prices in some areas of Scotland, but without firm evidence on changing levels of underlying mortality there is no way of proving a long-term connection between the variables.

Harvest failures had wide-ranging effects in societies where a half or more of household expenditure went on food stuffs (Walter, 1989, *81–6*). Having access to grain markets might be of little help if people had no money to buy. Communities specialising in pastoral agricultural products or in industrial production may have been unable to sell their products to those spending their all on grain. Cumbria in the 1620s was particularly vulnerable. There were social as well as economic implications, one noted by the Scotsman David Calderwood during the autumn of 1621: 'Every man was careful to ease himself of such persons as he might spare, and to live as retiredly as possibly he might. Pitiful was the lamentation not only of vaging [wandering] beggars, but also of honest persons' (Flinn, 1977, *122*). The closer a farmer was to subsistence under a regime of low net yields, the less likely he would be to have a surplus which could be used to feed employees or to sell. If he had to go into the market during a dearth to buy food for workers whose contracts included diet, the effect could be disastrous. Furthermore, in societies where a half of family expenditure went on grain-based foods, changes in grain prices would have a disproportionate effect on income for non-food purchases and demand for non-agricultural goods and services (Wrigley, 1989).

The comment about wandering beggars also reminds us that higher mortality in years of shortage may have been partly due to disease. Social as well as biological links may have existed between dearth and death (Walter and Schofield, 1989, *18–20, 53–4*). From one angle, economic diversification and good welfare provisions might not protect a population against a surge in mortality associated with social upheaval: England in 1742 is a clear example (Post, 1985, *93, 279*). Better urban than rural poor relief in Scotland and Ireland encouraged an influx of beggars: between 1740 and 1741 a mortality index for rural Munster rose 53 per cent, for urban Munster 90 per cent (Post, 1985, *152, 245*). In that sense, good poor relief could have an adverse effect on a community's overall mortality. Public policy which reduced unemployment, migration, vagrancy and begging had the best chance of minimising the risk of epidemic disease.

Poor-relief provisions would help to alleviate starvation but could do little to prevent disease mortality unless they encouraged the poor to remain in their parishes. Medical intervention was largely ineffective in dealing with morbid diseases at this time, with the possible exception of inoculation which was being tried out in the 1740s and 1750s (Porter, 1987). Once a person was infected there was little chance effectively to change the disease's course. Other biological links have recently been questioned, notably the commonly posited relationship between malnutrition and disease morbidity. A link between malnutrition and higher case fatality for tuberculosis, diarrhoea, measles and some respiratory infections exists. The biological effect of poor nutrition on the chances of contracting, or dying from, other diseases is highly questionable (Post, 1985, *273*). Plague, smallpox, malaria and typhoid were so virulent that chances of survival had little to do with nutrition. The short-term link between prices and fertility in England was less through amenorrhoea resulting from malnutrition than through foetal loss during pregnancy (Wrigley and Schofield, 1981, *363–6, 368–73*). Finally, similarities between the mortality of a privileged group such as peers and ordinary English people before 1750 support the notion that nutrition and medical care can have played little part in explaining life expectancy.

Looked at in another way, the relationship may seem paradoxical. Economic 'progress' rather than backwardness may have increased mortality since the development of overseas trade, urban growth and the integration of domestic markets may have accelerated the distribution of disease pathogens by increasing the volume of contacts between carriers and potential victims. If part of England was vulnerable to subsistence crises, the more densely settled south-east was prone to disease epidemics, a pattern which seems to have persisted until the 1720s (Schofield, 1983, *287*; Dobson, 1989b). Rising real income may increase mortality by drawing more people into towns to fulfil demand for goods and services (Wrigley and Schofield, 1981, *415*). In Scotland, the proliferation of market centres in the second half of the seventeenth century, coupled with comparatively rapid urbanisation 1650–1750, may help to account for the shift from epidemic to endemic smallpox and other diseases. We might speculate that seasonal migration from Highlands to Lowlands from the later seventeenth century may have exposed more Highlanders to the endemic smallpox of the Lowlands, thus integrating disease pools and raising mortality in Highland areas contributing to the flows.

A further paradox hinted at above is that economic specialisation may have increased vulnerability to famine. Growing dependence on a particular food could have this effect. For example, potatoes were an important but not yet staple food in parts of late seventeenth century Ireland. Described, by the commentator Madden in the 1730s, as a substitute food for a quarter of the year, potatoes took hold in Munster and were the main winter diet of the cottier and lesser tenant classes in many parts of Ireland by the 1690s and perhaps earlier – except in Ulster where porridge and root vegetables were preferred. Failure of both cereal crops and potatoes during 1740–1 certainly contributed to the severity of famine in south-west Ireland (Post, 1985, *97*). The potato was of less importance in Scotland before the mid eighteenth century.

Growing dependence on a particular type of production could have a similar effect. Areas of Scotland which specialised in pastoral husbandry might be particularly unfortunate. Most Hebridean islands grew grain for subsistence but those such as Mull which concentrated on cattle-raising suffered badly from the 1690s' dearths. After 1700 Highlanders were exposed to the adverse effects of uncertain markets which allowed them to sell cattle and buy grain (Walter and Schofield, 1989, *33*). If demand for livestock fell, those in specialist cattle-raising regions would have less money to buy grain. People could make choices about work and lifestyle but it was not always possible to control the demographic outcomes of these decisions.

The potential for human action can be illustrated by efforts to prevent plague. The reasons behind the disappearance of plague from Britain during the seventeenth century are the subject of considerable debate (Slack, 1985). Some argue that human beings had little control over plague and that changes in the disease itself or in the rat population which carried it must explain its demise. Mortality from disease is a function of three things: exposure to infection, levels of resistance and the frequency and virulence of different strains of pathogen (Landers, 1990, *30*). However, in the case of plague we have to understand the four main stages in its spread in order to judge the role of different agencies in banishing its scourge. The transmission of the most common form of plague, bubonic, depends on the existence of a pool of resistant rats and fleas who can carry the disease without dying of it. Plague epidemics of the sixteenth and seventeenth centuries seem to have been the result of periodic reintroductions from abroad – possibly from the Netherlands which had worldwide trade connections. At this point, humans could prevent the transmission of plague by quarantine measures. Once introduced into Britain, plague spread from town to town at a pace which suggests that humans rather than rats transmitted the disease, or perhaps rats on baggage and bulk food carts. At this second stage too, people could throw up sanitary cordons to prevent the entry of infected persons into their communities (Slack, 1985).

The coherent suite of policies – at household, local and national level – which had developed to counter plague by the middle of the seventeenth century focused on the actions of people. The importance of rats was not understood until the end of the nineteenth century. This meant that if steps were taken early on, plague deaths could be prevented, but that efforts to curb an epidemic in its two latter stages would be much less successful. Once introduced into a community, plague took root in suburbs and back alleys away from main centres of intercourse, pointing to rats as the bearers of disease. At the level of the household, the lack of correlation between mortality and household size, and the way plague left some houses unaffected, suggests that the frequency of human contact was much less significant than the numbers and movements of rodents carrying infection. For this reason, attempts to quarantine infected households were likely to prove unsuccessful once plague had a grip. There was, admittedly, an element of chance in all this: restrictions on movement prevented serious mortality at Exeter in 1665–6 but not at Norwich, at Linlithgow but not at Leith in the 1640s (Slack, 1985; Flinn, 1977, *137*).

As noted above, levels of mortality from disease depend in part on the extent of human exposure and resistance to infections. Diseases which killed readily in one period may be much less deadly in another or many disappear altogether from a country over time. Riley has recently claimed that the eighteenth century mortality decline was the result of fewer and less severe epidemics because 'a medicine of avoidance and prevention' developed to reduce human contact with disease (1987). Biological hypotheses about disease morbidity and mortality changes are extremely difficult to test: Riley's fails to document changing deaths by cause and by transmission vector or to assess the value of medical advice and intervention. Reductions in mortality may be attributable to changes in human action but they may also be the result of factors over which men and women had no control. Changes in diseases and immunological adjustments by humans may have taken place, though while the adjustment may have been 'mutual', changes in microbe genetics occur much more rapidly than among human. Before *c.* 1750 the modest rate and scale of changing mortality is consistent with this explanation (among others), but probably not after that date.

The role of resistance is clearly illustrated in the age structure of mortality in late seventeenth and early eighteenth century London. Adult life expectancy above age 30 differed little between London Quakers and anglicans living in rural parishes and small market towns. However, infant, child and young adult mortality was much higher in the metropolis. Among south London Quakers all those aged 10 years or older who died from smallpox were immigrants to the city. Native-born adults had high levels of immunity but incomers did not. Much excess urban mortality was occasioned by 'the action of density dependent immunising infections' (Landers, 1990, *52, 54, 59*).

Not all diseases confer immunity. Some gastric and respiratory fevers could be 'debilitating, recurrent and progressive' (Dobson, 1989b, *418–19*). Commenting on the increase in background mortality across south-east England *c.* 1640–1720, Dobson writes of 'an epidemiological crisis fuelled by pathogens and peoples moving across the countryside and oceans' (1989b, *421*). For example, malaria may have been brought into south-east England by Dutch settlers in the sixteenth century. Diseases nurtured in south-east England went with emigrants to the New World. New diseases being introduced between the mid sixteenth and the mid seventeenth centuries would affect children above the age of weaning and this would explain the marked worsening of mortality among those aged 1–9 years compared with that of infants (Schofield and Wrigley, 1979, *67–9*). Children fed at the breast are much less likely to become infected by water- and food-borne gastric diseases than those fed artificially. In addition, human breast milk contains antibodies which confer a degree of immunity on the suckling infant. English infants whose mother died soon after birth, and who were deprived of breast milk, were three times as likely to die by age one than the general infant mortality rate (Wrigley and Schofield, 1983, *183*).

Finally, wholly exogenous factors such as weather also played a role. A fall of 1° C in summer temperature reduced annual mortality by 4 per cent (Wrigley and Schofield, 1981, *384–98*). Endemic respiratory infections or typhus increased as a result of lower winter temperatures while higher summer ones facilitated the diffusion of bacteria causing dysentery and typhoid. The late seventeenth century 'ice age' created these conditions.

In conclusion, mortality was only partly endogenous to the economic and demographic regime. For England it is clear that mortality was not 'regularly and substantially affected by changes in living standards' (Wrigley and Schofield, 1981, *354*). It does not seem to have acted as an equilibriating mechanism. In some areas, such as agricultural improvements and poor relief, people acted with varying degrees of success to prevent excessive strain on resources being corrected by mortality. For Scotland and perhaps Ireland, abrupt short-term adjustments through mortality may have occurred in times of famine – as occasionally happened in England. It is unclear whether a long-term equilibrium between population and resources was maintained by mortality in Scotland and it almost certainly was not in Ireland. Overall, it seems that mortality was only weakly integrated into the economic system and for most purposes it should be seen as an independent variable.

Nuptiality

North-west European societies of the sixteenth, seventeenth and eighteenth centuries differed fundamentally both from contemporary eastern and southern Europe and from peasant or tribal societies in the modern world. The most important difference lay in the nature of the early modern household and in the preconditions of family formation (Hajnal, 1983; Smith, 1981; 1984). Social and cultural norms dictated that couples wishing to marry and procreate should possess sufficient resources to establish independent households. Those households would normally be economically and physically separate from those of kin. This explains the contrast between the large, sometimes complex households characteristic of eastern and southern Europe – numbering 10–15 souls and often including more than one married couple – and the small, simple nuclear family households found in north-western Europe. It also explains why women waited until they were roughly 23–26 years old before marrying for the first time and why, over the early modern period as a whole, one woman in eight never married. In eastern Europe almost all women were married by age 20. Couples joined existing, large households made up of their kin.

The time between puberty and marriage in Britain and Ireland was filled for the majority by a period working in another household as a servant or apprentice. Servants were typically young, single men and women aged 15–25 who worked in agriculture or, for females, as domestics in return for board and lodging. In the late seventeenth and early eighteenth centuries 18 per cent of England's population were servants: most of the relevant age group (Kussmaul, 1981). Apprentices signed a contract binding them to work for a master for a set period in return for training and keep. Average age at indenture for London apprentices in the late sixteenth and early seventeenth centuries was 18 or 19 years, in seventeenth century Newcastle and Edinburgh approximately 15 or 16 years. Young men served terms of 5–7 years on average, meaning they would be in their early to mid twenties when they started working as journeymen and making their own living. Apprentices were prevented from marrying and the institution checked early marriage. There was no formal restraint on servants marrying. Service was an opportunity for not marrying and for saving to reach the accepted threshold of economic independence necessary to marry.

In early modern Britain, marriage formation was linked to economic opportunity but the precise relationship varied regionally. We noted in Chapter 2 that between 1551 and 1751 fertility and mortality contributed almost equally to changes in England's intrinsic growth rate. However, movements in fertility were twice as large as those in mortality during these two centuries. In Chapter 3 we saw that nuptiality was the main force behind changing fertility. Why should age at first marriage and proportions never married alter? The simple answer is that people married on the expectation of economic independence and continued well-being. Their changing perceptions of economic opportunity provide the key. However, recent research has painted a more complicated picture of nuptiality's context.

Armed with estimates of changing population over time, and of the relative significance of fertility and mortality in those trends, and equipped with an indicator of changing economic opportunity it has already been possible to demonstrate for England the lack of a long-term connection between scarcity and plenty, and mortality. When the same economic indicator is set alongside changes in nuptiality and fertility the association is clear and striking. Over the long term, the curves representing real wages and the gross reproduction rate move in waves separated by 30–40 years. When population rose at more than approximately 0.5 per cent a year, real wages fell. After a period during which English society became aware of the worsening balance between population and resources, levels of nuptiality would fall either by raising age at first marriage for women or by increasing the proportion of women never married, or both. This reduced fertility and brought growth rates down. In times of plenty when growth rates were less than 0.5 per cent, nuptiality would also adjust to improved economic opportunities and the cycle would begin again (Wrigley and Schofield, 1981, *402–14, 466–80*). Flinn contends that demographic–economic interactions must be arranged in a linear hierarchy, but within a demographic system relationships can operate in both directions (1982, *455*). This seems to be the case in early modern England for both positive and negative feedbacks existed within the system.

As Malthus suggested, there were long, slow fluctuations in the rate of population growth in England which were associated with the standard of living. While the long-term relationship between nuptiality and price fluctuations is clear, that between the variables in the short term is no less marked. A doubling of grain prices in any one year produced a lasting reduction in the 'normal' number of marriages over a five-year period of more than a fifth (Schofield, 1983, *282*). Rises in mortality associated with disease epidemics had the predictable effect of raising nuptiality in the short-term though this was more through remarriages rather than by creating more openings in the economy for first marriages. The net effect on fertility was slight because a widow remarrying would not necessarily have had any more children than if her husband had remained alive.

Wrigley and Schofield's interpretation of population-resource links is surprisingly traditional and lacking in statistical sophistication compared with their analysis of purely demographic relationships – perhaps because theories which link population to resources are still rudimentary. For example, is the long time-lag believable; what components of nuptiality were affected by changing real wages; and did changes in the social and occupational composition of the population influence the relationship? Weir ((1984) and modified by Schofield (1985b)) has addressed these questions, arguing that a change in the economic climate affected only a part of the population and, until the eighteenth century, had most influence on the chances of ever marrying rather than on age at marriage. The main effect of a growth in real wages was a reduction in celibacy. Marriage depended on economic independence gained either by the transmission of property from older to younger generation or through the pooling of labour resources of husband and wife. When times were hard, fewer people could surmount this threshold and may have been denied the chance to marry. Differential effects may have existed. For example, adverse economic circumstances may reduce marriage chances but if conditions affect female employment opportunities particularly badly they may be encouraged to marry because of the difficulties of subsisting as single women. Economic differences between regions may have exaggerated or reduced such changes. In pastoral areas with more regular employment for women the effects of an economic downturn may have been attenuated.

Studies of socially specific trends in nuptiality are rare for the early modern period. One, of Colyton in Devon, demonstrates two important points. First, male and female marriage ages did not move in tandem. Second, trends in age at first marriage for women from labouring backgrounds were very different from those of gentry or the poor 1550–1750. For the period 1538–1799 an almost identical proportion of gentry, crafts and labouring women never married by age 45 (just over 5 per cent) but nearly 13 per cent of women who were poor or who came from impoverished families never began reproductive careers (Sharpe, 1991).

Goldstone (1986) reinforces and refines the contention that until the middle of the eighteenth century changes in nuptiality were mainly caused by rises or falls in the proportions of women ever married rather than by changes in age at first marriage. For the period up to c. 1750 he identifies two types of marriers. First, 'traditional' marriers covering a wide range of ages whose behaviour changed relatively little over time because they were always above the threshold of economic independence – probably because they relied on transfers of wealth before parental death or on the inheritance of property. Second, 'non-marriers' whose proportion of the population changed significantly over time. Among the cohort born 1604–28 22 per cent never married by age 45 compared with 12 per cent for 1704–28 (Goldstone, 1986, 17). Marriage chances for this group were determined by the opportunity for personal saving, itself primarily related to changes in real income. Those close to the conventional threshold of economic independence were most vulnerable to changing economic circumstances. Goldstone argues that 'for the cohorts born before 1700 swings in the proportion ever married clearly were large, independent of changes in the age at first marriage, and dominated the movement of fertility' (1986, 10). For example, a 50 per cent increase in real wages between the early seventeenth and early eighteenth centuries had almost no effect on age at first marriage for both sexes. Whether the shift to age at marriage as the main determinant of changing fertility in the middle of the eighteenth century constitutes a 'revolution' is more debateable since the responsiveness of nuptiality *as a whole* to real wage trends remained similar over long periods.

Goldstone has made a further contribution by using a more geographically extensive and complete series of agricultural and industrial prices as a proxy for real wages. Measuring the economic environment in a pre-statistical age is notoriously difficult and historians have to use a range of more or less reliable indicators. Best known of these is the Phelps Brown and Hopkins index of wages and prices. This suffers from long periods of missing data, especially in the first half of the seventeenth century. Goldstone's alternative series fills this gap and shows that real wages did not begin to rise until the 1650s while the gross reproduction rate rose from the 1670s. A lag of 15–20 years between changes in real wages and population is more believable than Wrigley and Schofield's 30–40 years because it would take ordinary people a decade or two to accumulate savings as servants or apprentices and then during a period of working independently as labourers or journeymen (Goldstone, 1986, *7–8, 15*).

It is fortunate that Goldstone and others have reworked the Phelps Brown and Hopkins index, for it has been heavily criticised. Wrigley and Schofield acknowledge that 'the statistical base of the real-wages index is partial, limited and fragile' (1981, *354, 407–8, 411–12*). Others have reworked and updated the wage and prices indices, leaving the trends intact but adjusting the level and fine-tuning the timing of changes in direction. By substituting retail for wholesale prices as the basis of his index, Rappaport has shown that during the sixteenth century in London real wages declined only half as much as Phelps Brown and Hopkins believed. Short-comings in the real wage series are most apparent in the long run since they do not fully reflect changes in consumption pattern or the amount of work available, especially for women and children whose contribution to the total family budget was often consider-able but whose work opportunities were much more volatile in the long-term than those of adult males (Snell, 1985; Rappaport,

1989). However, if changing demand for female and child labour worked in the same direction as that for adult males the resulting fluctuations in family income would have been more extreme. It should be stressed that, in spite of revisions to the wage and price series, and in spite of debates over the time-lag between changing real wages and population growth rates, the long-term relationship between the variables in England is very striking and of great importance.

The population–resource equation is complicated for England by the presence of institutional factors which could influence demographic behaviour. An unusual feature of England in the seventeenth and eighteenth centuries was the blending of economic individualism with social and political collectivism. Economic and residential independence at marriage existed alongside a compulsory community welfare system which supported families at points when there were too many dependent mouths to feed (Smith, 1981). By contrast, the poor-relief system in Scotland may have discouraged early marriage because poorer couples perceived that surplus resources in the society were scanty and that they would have to shoulder the potential burden of poverty by themselves, or with informal help from equally impoverished neighbours or kin. In Ireland, abundance of resources compensated for lack of an effective poor-relief scheme under most economic conditions.

Finding the resources to create a new household depends, in an agrarian society, on access to land. The most obvious mechanism linking population and resources would be deaths in the older generation releasing property for sons to marry. Improving life expectancy in eighteenth century France was associated with reduced nuptiality because there were fewer 'dead men's shoes' to fill (Schofield, 1989, 299). For this reason, the laws and customs relating to inheritance of property have been seen as important determinants of household structure and demographic behaviour. 'Impartible' inheritance, where land passes intact to one person (usually the eldest son), may restrict the number of new households, while delaying marriages and encouraging migration among other children. Partible inheritance divides land and may have had the reverse effect. The role of partible and impartible inheritance has been hotly debated but it was less important in Britain than elsewhere in Europe and nowhere should it be viewed deterministically (Smith, 1984). In Scotland most land was owned by a relatively small number of landowners and worked by tenant farmers, with their live-in single servants, and cottagers who received use rights in exchange for family labour on the main farm. Continuity of tenure was possible and owner-occupation was increasing during the sixteenth and late seventeenth century but the main factors determining availability of land were landlord policy and the market in leasehold farms. Cottars who, with their families, made up the majority of the Lowland population, were wholly dependent on tenant farmers (Houston and Whyte, 1989, *3–20*).

In Ireland, the issue was an abundance of land and ample opportunities for the cheap acquisition of farms. Buoyant real wages in Dublin during the seventeenth century reflected the shortage of skilled labour and the generally healthy state of the economy. Under certain circumstances, rapid population growth is not incompatible with a rising standard of living. Conceivably, Irish labour productivity grew sufficiently in the seventeenth and early eighteenth centuries to cope with population increase (Dickson *et al.*, 1982, *175*). Most agricultural labourers were married and had their own plots of land. There were large numbers of single female servants with a median age in the mid-20s in listings from county Dublin and Munster in the 1650s (Dickson, 1990). However, with age at first marriage for women in the low 20s, it seems that the constraint placed on nuptiality by a decade of service between puberty and marriage was less important in Ireland than in England or Lowland Scotland.

Landholding systems were more complex in England and there were many more small owner-occupiers, at least before the later seventeenth century. Recent research has shown that even where impartible inheritance was practised, parents made every effort to provide as generously for other children (both while still alive and in their wills) as for the one inheriting land (Wrightson, 1982). Given the ease of contracting marriage, and the weak parental or communal control over household formation for most people, inheritance cannot have been an important factor in adjusting population to resources. England's economy contained a large wage-labour component from the sixteenth century, if not before, and most land changed hands by purchase or sale rather than by inheritance from kin. Perhaps a third of England's population in the seventeenth century depended on wage-labour and could therefore have little expectation of inheriting property. At the same time, roughly two-fifths of fathers would have had no surviving sons at their death and a further fifth would have had no children at all to succeed them; some, of course, would have had more than one son (Schofield, 1976, 153). This means that niches would be created within the economic system but that they would be filled by marriage or purchase rather than by inheritance. For some groups such as copyholders (a form of manorial land tenure), marriage may have been linked to property inheritance. But for much of English society, demographic, and possibly economic, events in the household from which marriers came may have had little direct effect on the formation of a new family (Smith, 1981, 602).

The prevalence of wage-labour and growing non-agricultural employment opportunities highlights the importance of the wider economy. England and Scotland slowly became more urbanised 1500–1750 and in addition more rural dwellers worked in some form of industry such as mining or textiles. By 1750 a sixth of England's population lived in large towns and a further quarter were rural industrial workers. In other words, more niches were available for those wishing to marry and establish new households outside a purely agrarian context. Some historians have argued that the expansion of these industrial employments could short-circuit the usual wait for inheritance or the time spent between puberty and marriage working as a servant in husbandry or as a domestic servant in one of the growing towns (Levine, 1977). Expanding domestic and overseas demand fostered an increase in textile output not from factories but by increasing the number of traditional family production units. Because start-up costs were low and specialist skills were not needed, couples could marry at an early age. Some have sought the reasons for accelerating population growth in Ireland after the middle of the eighteenth century in the effect of rural industry on nuptiality (Dickson et al., 1982, 173–4).

In reality, the picture is much more complicated. Rural domestic industry, sometimes called 'proto-industry', certainly expanded in parts of Britain and Ireland: in the west country, midlands and north of England, especially between 1660 and 1740. Total nuptiality was greater in rural industrial parishes (and in market towns) than in agricultural communities. However, it has proved impossible conclusively to link the economic makeup of a parish with age at first marriage for women (Houston and Snell, 1984; Kussmaul, 1990, *141–4*). Nor was rural industry always connected with faster population growth. The 66 parishes in north-east Scotland which had stocking-knitters in 1761 and the 33 where the spinning of linen yarn was widely practised had significantly lower population growth rates over the eighteenth century than the region's small towns. English parishes which had dual industrial and agricultural employments rather than solely industrial ones could maintain a high age at marriage (Kussmaul, 1990, *141–2, 154, 157–8*). Other explanations of any apparent connection between domestic industry and population growth are possible. Entrepreneurs who controlled some forms of rural domestic industry may have chosen to establish ties with parishes which were already growing rapidly because abundant labour supply would keep down costs (Kussmaul, 1990, *139*).

The key to understanding the uneven impact of proto-industrialisation on population trends lies in the context in which proletarianisation took place. If increases in the numbers of wage-dependent workers occurred against a background of rising unemployment, nuptiality would be reduced because more people would not reach the socially acceptable economic threshold for marriage. This was clearly the situation in 1550–1650 when population growth outran employment opportunities. Eighteenth century economic expansion created a much more favourable climate for marriers. However, in England, trends in age at first marriage appear to have followed regional or national economic fortunes rather than strictly local ones. The same may be true of regions of eighteenth century Ireland (Macafee, 1987).

Turning from the specific role of inheritance and rural domestic industry to the general, long-term relationship between population and resources, Scotland's population may not have responded to changing economic circumstances in the same way as England's. No estimates of nuptiality exist for the sixteenth and early seventeenth century. However, the population pressure of the second half of the sixteenth century may have provoked a major change in diet from one with a large meat component to a mainly cereal-based one. What grains were consumed – oats in the form of meal – are generally seen as inferior foods: the English ate wheat bread. With stable agricultural output, a given amount of land could support more mouths under crops than under pasture (Gibson and Smout, 1992). Opportunities to farm new land were strictly limited. Wage and price series for the sixteenth century are scanty but the real wages (expressed as oatmeal purchasing power) of Edinburgh labourers and masons fell sharply c. 1560–c. 1590. Assuming that a dietary change of this nature represents a reduced standard of living, Scottish society may have opted for more people at the expense of quality of life. The shift from a meat-dominated diet to a largely grain-based one during the later sixteenth century may reflect a decision to tolerate a high fertility (or at least a *stable* nuptiality and fertility?) regime and not to make the sort of adjustments elsewhere in the demographic system which happened in early modern England. Purely economic responses to population growth were probably also inadequate since until the eighteenth century agricultural productivity remained low, overseas trade small in scale, industrial diversification slight. The situation in England and Scotland, where between roughly 1560 and 1620 the economy failed to expand sufficiently to mop up surplus population, was partly corrected in the 1620s and 1630s in Scotland but imbalances may have persisted much longer north of the border. As a pure speculation, it may be that the imbalance in Scotland after c. 1560 was caused by autonomous improvements in mortality.

A simultaneous rise in marriage age in the late sixteenth century cannot be ruled out but there is no way of telling. Stability in age at first marriage over long periods does not necessarily prove the absence of a connection between real wage trends and nuptiality. Rural real wages in Scotland were stable 1680–1770 and did not follow the cycles apparent in England. Real wages were increasing in early eighteenth century Glasgow and those of Edinburgh labourers were rising strongly 1740–80, though those of their employers such as masons were easing (Houston, 1988; Gibson and Smout, 1992). The near trebling of proportions urban may indicate growing real incomes 1650–1750: towns provided goods and services on which people could spend their surplus income. But the demand which urban growth reflects may have come from a restricted section of Scottish society: from the rural middling and upper ranks, and from the urban population itself. The absolute standard of living remained lower in Scotland than England and wealth was more obviously polarised between mercantile, professional and landed classes and the bulk of Scotland's people. Furthermore, the dietary changes of the later sixteenth century were partially reversed in the second half of the eighteenth in prosperous parts of the central Lowlands, lending credence to the idea that adjustments of population and resources were not achieved through nuptiality in Scotland. A high and stable age at first marriage for women over long periods adds weight to this hypothesis. Extensive and possibly unvarying female celibacy over long periods suggests that adjustment was not obtained through this mechanism. In 1782, J. M'Farlan's *Inquiries Concerning the Poor* set out projects to encourage Scotland's poor to marry as a way of fostering population growth and economic change. Late marriage and high celibacy persisted until the second half of the nineteenth century as embedded customs which had outlived the economic circumstances which brought them into being.

The relative inflexibility of marriage ages in Scotland and, probably, Ireland may reflect economic circumstances more than different cultural norms. If Quakers can be taken to represent Ireland's population as a whole, age at first marriage for women rose steadily from the early 20s *c.* 1600 to the late 20s *c.* 1800. This may show 'frontier' conditions giving way to more 'normal' constraints on nuptiality. Scotland may have had less leeway in the economic and demographic system than England or Ireland. Low gross grain yields, of the kind known to characterise Scottish agriculture, involve a high mean annual variation in net yields left for human consumption (Wrigley, 1989, *258–9, 263*; Whyte, 1979). Gibson and Smout show substantial annual and decadal variations in real wages. Sharp variations from year to year in the standard of living will render the population more susceptible to famine and associated diseases. In such an environment, and without extensive non-agricultural employments, the great uncertainties in obtaining the economic independence on which marriage depended might encourage an extremely cautious nuptiality response: women marrying late and a high percentage never at all. Without the cushion of adequate poor relief, couples would be doubly reluctant to marry. This combination, as much as the role of extreme protestantism, may also explain the low levels of pre-nuptial pregnancy obtaining in Scotland before the second half of the eighteenth century. To speculate, Scotland's high celibacy and late age at first marriage for women may be linked to mortality in the same way as France's – as mortality falls, age at marriage and proportions never married will rise – implying a *relatively* high expectation of life at birth given available economic resources.

What all this means is that although England, Scotland and Ireland clearly fit into the north-west European marriage pattern, they did so in distinctive ways. Whatever the imperfections in wage and price series, the link between nuptiality and fertility on the one hand, and economic opportunity on the other, seems firmly established for England. It was not paralleled in Scotland. The method of adjusting population to resources was quite different: changes in diet, migration and (possibly) mortality. For early modern Ireland the balance between population and resources was less of an issue. If there was a response within the system it lay in migration possibly coupled with a gently rising first marriage age for women.

All the above are variations on the 'preventive' check but the role of Malthus' main mechanism, nuptiality, varied. Even in England, the preventive check was only effective over a long time-span: Lee estimates that only a quarter of population growth in one genera-tion would be self-corrected by a real wage response (Wrigley and Schofield, 1989, *xxvii*). Nor was the mechanism always efficient: it tended to 'over-shoot'. Differences in power relations between employers and employees meant that between *c.* 1650 and 1750 when population stagnated and real wages rose, farmers' demand for live-in servants rather than expensive wage labourers held back nuptiality and exerted a 'dysfunctional' check (Schofield, 1989, *303–4*).

The implications for what was perceived to be an acceptable standard of living, and on demand for non-agricultural products, are profound. In Scotland, a low-pressure nuptiality and fertility regime created a lower equilibrium level of population than obtained in Ireland. In that sense, an adjustment had been made but the balance achieved was precarious and the relative standard of living for the bulk of Scotland's people was low, both in terms of diet and possession of material goods (Weatherill, 1988). In England equilibrium was achieved at an even lower level relative to available resources which allowed a high and growing standard of living (Wrigley and Schofield, 1981, *459–61*). In Ireland the resources for marriage were easily available but social and political factors kept wealth polarised and the average standard of living low. While emphasising the broad sweep, we must be aware that there may be important regional variations and that further research on Scotland and Ireland is badly needed.

Conclusion

Pre-industrial societies are often lumped together as undifferentiated entities. The demographic histories of regions of the British Isles illustrate above all the great complexity and diversity of those societies. Much weight is often placed on England's distinctiveness. In certain respects this may be correct. The way population and resources were actively kept in balance by changes in nuptiality and fertility may well be unique in Europe, as may England's relatively benign mortality regime. However, other parts of the British Isles have a claim to distinctiveness. Ireland's population in the seventeenth and early eighteenth centuries was characterised by higher fertility than England's or Scotland's mainly because of an earlier age at first marriage for women but also different practices thereafter which produced higher marital fertility than in England. Child mortality may also have been higher in Ireland than in England, infant mortality higher in Scotland than in other parts of Britain and Ireland. Given that fertility was already high in Ireland, improvements in mortality may well account for the rapid population growth from the mid eighteenth century. Before that date, the difference in mortality regimes is probably more marked between Scotland and England. Relatively late marriage between the mid seventeenth and mid eighteenth century, and the possibility that marriage age and proportions ever married changed much less than in England, strengthen the impression that Scotland's place within the spectrum of north-west Europe's demographic behaviour was significantly different from England's or Ireland's. Mortality may well have been the main dynamic force.

We have dealt only in passing with the long-term economic consequences of population structures and trends. Much has been written about the role of England's low-pressure demographic regime in creating savings and other preconditions for the industrial revolution. Yet, Scotland industrialised at the same time as England from a different demographic background and a much lower standard of living. This should warn against treating demography as a determinant of economic change without considering other factors such as distribution of wealth or cultural decisions about the relative values of 'goods' such as standard of living compared with marriage and a family. Other fields are open for research. Since the publication of *The Population History of England* in 1981, most work on that country has sought to refine the basic picture presented by Wrigley and Schofield or to relate their findings to the broader context of English society. Future work is likely to follow the same path. The possibility of regional variations in demographic patterns, the reasons behind changes in mortality and the precise relationship of nuptiality to economic opportunity are all likely to attract attention. Deeper investigation of customs surrounding infant feeding and child care may eventually explain important aspects of fertility and mortality variations. The publication of Wrigley and Schofield's volume presenting the results of family reconstitutions may well close one important chapter in English historical demography and open another.

In the rest of Britain and Ireland historians have barely begun to scratch the surface. If English historical demographers have written with one eye on the industrial revolution they must surely bend the other to the varied economic, social and demographic experiences of adjacent regions. Readers may find the tentative generalisations about population, economy and society, not to mention the lack of definite demographic statistics, on Ireland, Scotland and Wales, frustrating. Yet, these are now the true frontier lands of British historical demography. If the population history of England drew in the pioneers of the 1960s and 1970s that of the rest of Britain must attract those of the future.

Bibliography

Alldridge, N. (1986) 'The population profile of an early modern town: Chester, 1547–1728', *Annales de Démographie Historique*.

Anderson, M. (1988) *Population change in north-western Europe, 1750–1850* (London).

Appleby, A. B. (1975) 'Nutrition and disease: the case of London, 1550–1750', *Journal of Interdisciplinary History* 6.

Appleby, A. B. (1978) *Famine in Tudor and Stuart England* (Liverpool).

Bongaarts, J. (1975) 'Why high birth rates are so low', *Population and Development Review* 1.

Boulton, J. P. (1987) *Neighbourhood and society. A London suburb in the seventeenth century* (Cambridge).

Canny, N. (1985) 'Migration and opportunity: Britain, Ireland and the New World', *Irish Economic and Social History* 12.

Clark, P. (1979) 'Migration in England during the late seventeenth and early eighteenth centuries', *Past & Present* 83 or in Clark and Souden (1987).

Clark, P. and Souden, D. C. (eds) (1987) *Migration and society in early modern England* (London).

Clarkson, L. A. (1981) 'Irish population revisited, 1687–1821', in Goldstrom and Clarkson.

Clarkson, L. A. (1988) 'Conclusion: famine and Irish history', in Crawford.

Connolly, S. J. (1979) 'Illegitimacy and pre-nuptial pregnancy in Ireland before 1864: the evidence of some Catholic parish registers', *Irish Economic and Social History* 6.

Crawford E. M. (ed.) (1988) *Famine: the Irish experience, 900–1900* (Edinburgh).

Cressy, D. (1987) *Coming over. Migration and communication between England and New England in the seventeenth century* (Cambridge).

Cullen, L. M. (1975) 'Population trends in seventeenth-century Ireland', *Economic and Social Review* 6.

Cullen, L. M. (1981) 'Population growth and diet, 1600–1850', in Gold-
    strom and Clarkson.
Daultrey, S., Dickson, D. and Ó Gráda, C. (1981) 'Eighteenth-century
    Irish population: new perspectives from old sources', *Journal of
    Economic History* 41.
De Vries, J. (1985) 'The population and economy of the preindustrial
    Netherlands', *Journal of Interdisciplinary History* 15.
Dickson, D. (1988) 'The gap in famines: a useful myth?', in Crawford.
Dickson, D. (1990) 'No Scythians here: women and marriage in seven-
    teenth-century Ireland', in MacCurtain, M., and O'Dowd, M.
    (eds), *Women and society in early modern Ireland* (Edinburgh).
Dickson, D., Ó Gráda, C. and Daultrey, S. (1982) 'Hearth tax, household
    size, and Irish population growth, 1680–1800', *Proceedings of the
    Royal Irish Academy* 82.
Dobson, M. J. (1989a) 'Mortality gradients and disease exchanges:
    comparisons between old England and colonial America', *Social
    History of Medicine* 2.
Dobson, M. J. (1989b) 'The last hiccup of the old demographic regime',
    Continuity and Change 4.
Ekirch, A. R. (1987) *Bound for America. The transportation of British convicts
    to the colonies, 1718–1775.*
Eversley, D. E. C. (1981) 'The demography of the Irish Quakers, 1650–
    1850', in Goldstrom and Clarkson.
Finlay, R. A. P. (1978) 'The accuracy of the London parish registers,
    1580–1653', *Population Studies* 32.
Finlay, R. A. P. (1981a) *Population and metropolis: the demography of
    London, 1580–1650* (Cambridge).
Finlay, R. A. P. (1981b) 'Differential child mortality in pre-industrial
    England', *Annales de Démographie Historique.*
Flinn, M. W. (ed.) (1977) *Scottish population history from the 17th century to
    the 1930s* (Cambridge).
Flinn, M. W. (1982) 'The population history of England, 1541–1871',
    Economic History Review 35.
Galenson, D. (1981) *White servitude in colonial America* (Cambridge).
Galloway, P. R. (1985) 'Annual variations in death by age, deaths by cause,
    prices, and weather in London, 1640 to 1830', *Population Studies* 39.
Gibson, A. and Smout, T. C. (1992) *Prices, food and wages in Scotland,
    c1550–1780* (Cambridge).
Gillespie, R. (1988) 'Meal and money: the harvest crisis of 1621–4 and the
    Irish economy', in Crawford.
Goldstone, J. A. (1986) 'The demographic revolution in England: a re-
    examination', *Population Studies* 49.
Goldstrom, J. A. and Clarkson, L. A. (eds) (1981) *Irish population,
    economy, and society* (Oxford).

Gutmann, M. P. (1984) 'Gold from dross?' Population reconstruction for the pre-census era', *Historical Methods* 17.

Hajnal, J. (1983) 'Two kinds of pre-industrial household formation system', in Wall, R. (ed.), *Family forms in historic Europe* (Cambridge).

Henry, L. and Blanchet, D. (1983) 'La population de l'Angleterre de 1541 à 1871', *Population* 38.

Hollingsworth, T. H. (1964) 'The demography of the British peerage', *Population Studies* supplement to volume 18, no. 2.

Houlbrooke, R. A. (1984) *The English family, 1450–1750* (London).

Houston, R. A. (1979) 'Parish listings and social structure: Penninghame and Whithorn (Wigtownshire) in perspective', *Local Population Studies* 23.

Houston, R. A. (1985) 'Geographical mobility in Scotland, 1652–1811: the evidence of testimonials', *Journal of Historical Geography* 11.

Houston, R. A. (1988) 'The demographic regime, 1760–1830', in Devine, T. M. and Mitchison, R. (eds), *A Social History of Modern Scotland*, volume 1.

Houston, R. A. (1990) 'Age at marriage of Scottish women, c.1660–1770', *Local Population Studies* 43.

Houston, R. A. (1991) 'Mortality in early modern Scotland: the life expectancy of advocates', *Continuity and Change* 5.

Houston, R. A. and Snell, K. D. M. (1984) 'Proto-industrialization? Cottage industry, social change and industrial revolution', *Historical Journal* 27.

Houston, R. A. and Whyte, I. D. (eds) (1989) *Scottish society, 1500–1800* (Cambridge).

Houston, R. A. and Withers, C. W. J. (1990) 'Migration and the turnover of population in Scotland, 1600–1900', *Annales de Démographie Historique*.

Husbands, C. (1987) 'Regional change in a pre-industrial society: wealth and population in England in the sixteenth and seventeenth centuries', *Journal of Historical Geography* 13.

Jones, R. E. (1980) 'Further evidence on the decline in infant mortality in pre-industrial England: north Shropshire, 1561–1810', *Population Studies* 34.

Kussmaul, A. (1981) *Servants in husbandry in early modern England* (Cambridge).

Kussmaul, A. (1990) *A general view of the rural economy of England, 1538–1840* (Cambridge).

Landers, J. (1990) 'Age patterns of mortality in London during the "long eighteenth century": a test of the "high potential" model of metropolitan mortality', *Social History of Medicine* 3.

Laslett, P. (1988) 'La parenté en chiffres', *Annales ESC* 43.

Laslett, P., Oosterveen, K. and Smith, R. (eds) (1980) *Bastardy and its comparative history* (London).

Levine, D. (1977) *Family formation in an age of nascent capitalism* (London).

MaCafee, W. (1987) 'Pre-famine population in Ulster: evidence from the parish register of Killyman', in O'Flanagan, P. Ferguson, P. and Whelan, K. (eds), *Rural Ireland, 1600–1900: modernisation and change* (Cork).

Macafee, W. and Morgan, V. (1981) 'Population in Ulster, 1660–1760', in Roebuck, P. (ed.), *Plantation to partition* (Belfast).

Mitchison, R. (1989) 'Webster revisited: a re-examination of the 1755 "census" of Scotland', in Devine, T. M. (ed.), *Improvement and enlightenment* (Edinburgh).

Mitchison, R. and Leneman, L. (1989) *Sexuality and social control. Scotland, 1660–1780* (Oxford).

Mokyr, J. and Ó Gráda, C. (1984) 'New developments in Irish population history, 1700–1850', *Economic History Review* 37.

Morgan, V. (1976) 'A case study of population change over two centuries: Blaris, Lisburn 1661–1848', *Irish Economic and Social History* 3.

Ó Gráda, C. (1979) 'The population of Ireland, 1700–1900: a survey', *Annales de Démographie Historique*.

Oeppen, J. (1991) 'Back-projection and inverse-projection: members of a wider class of constrained projection models', *Population Studies* 45.

Outhwaite, R. B. (ed.) (1981) *Marriage and society* (Cambridge).

Porter, R. (1987) *Disease, medicine and society in England, 1550–1860* (London).

Post, J. D. (1985) *Food shortage, climatic variability, and epidemic disease in pre-industrial Europe. The mortality peak in the early 1740s* (Ithaca).

Pressat, R. (1985) *The dictionary of demography* (English edition edited by C. Wilson, Oxford).

Rappaport, S. (1989) *Worlds within worlds: structures of life in sixteenth-century London*.

Riley, J. C. (1987) *The eighteenth-century campaign to avoid disease* (London).

Schofield, R. S. (1976) 'The relationship between demographic structure and environment in pre-industrial western Europe', in Conze, W. (ed.), *Sozialgeschichte der Familie in der Neuzeit Europas* (Stuttgart).

Schofield, R. S. (1977) 'An anatomy of an epidemic: Colyton, November 1645 to November 1646', in *The plague reconsidered. A new look at its origins and effects in 16th and 17th century England*. Local Population Studies supplement.

Schofield, R. S. (1983) 'The impact of scarcity and plenty on population change in England, 1541–1871', *Journal of Interdisciplinary History*

14 or in Rotberg, R. and Rabb, T. K. (eds) (1985) *Hunger and history: the impact of changing food production and consumption patterns on society* (Cambridge).

Schofield, R. S. (1985a) 'Through a glass darkly: *The Population History of England* as an experiment in history', *Journal of Interdisciplinary History* 15.

Schofield, R. S. (1985b) 'English marriage patterns revisited', *Journal of Family History* 10.

Schofield, R. S. (1986) 'Did the mothers really die? Three centuries of maternal mortality in "The World We Have Lost" ', in Bonfield, L., Smith, R. M. and Wrightson, K. (eds), *The world we have gained: histories of population and social structure* (Cambridge).

Schofield, R. S. (1989) 'Family structure, demographic behaviour, and economic growth', in Walter and Schofield.

Schofield, R. S. and Wrigley, E. A. (1979) 'Infant and child mortality in England in the late Tudor and early Stuart period', in Webster, C. (ed.), *Health, medicine and mortality in sixteenth-century England* (Cambridge).

Schofield, R. S. and Wrigley, E. A. (1981) 'Remarriage intervals and the effect of marriage order on fertility', in Dupâquier, J. *et al.* (eds), *Marriage and remarriage in populations of the past* (London).

Sharpe, P. (1991) 'Literally spinsters: a new interpretation of local economy and demography in Colyton in the seventeenth and eighteenth centuries', *Economic History Review* 44.

Slack, P. (1985) *The impact of plague in Tudor and Stuart England* (London).

Smith, R. M. (1978) 'Population and its geography in England, 1500–1730', in Dodghson, R. A. and Butlin, R. A. (eds), *An historical geography of England and Wales* (London).

Smith, R. M. (1981) 'Fertility, economy and household formation in England over three centuries', *Population and Development Review* 7.

Smith, R. M. (1984) 'Some issues concerning families and their property in rural England, 1520–1800', in Smith, R. M. (ed.), *Land, kinship and life cycle* (Cambridge).

Smout, T. C. (1981) 'Scottish marriage, regular and irregular, 1500–1940', in Outhwaite.

Snell, K. D. M. (1985) *Annals of the labouring poor. Social change and agrarian England, 1600–1900* (Cambridge).

Souden, D. (1985) 'Demographic crisis and Europe in the 1590s', in Clark, P. (ed.), *The European crisis of the 1590s* (London).

Souden, D. (1987) ' "East, west – home's best?" Regional patterns in migration in early modern England', in Clark and Souden.

Trussell, J. (1983) 'Population under low pressure: reviews of *The population history of England*', *Journal of Economic History* 43.

Tyson, R. E. (1985) 'The population of Aberdeenshire, 1695–1755: a new approach', *Northern Scotland* 6.

Tyson, R. E. (1986) 'Famine in Aberdeenshire, 1695–99: anatomy of a crisis', in Stevenson, D. (ed.), *From lairds to louns* (Aberdeen).

Tyson, R. E. (1988) 'Household size and structure in a Scottish burgh: Old Aberdeen', *Local Population Studies* 40.

Tyson, R. E. (1992) 'Contrasting regimes: population growth in Ireland and Scotland during the eighteenth century', in Houston, R. A., *et al.* (eds), *Conflict and identity in the social and economic history of Ireland and Scotland* (Edinburgh).

Wall, R. (1981) 'Inferring differential neglect of females from mortality data', *Annales de Démographie Historique*.

Walter, J. (1989) 'The social economy of dearth in early modern England', in Walter and Schofield.

Walter, J. and Schofield, R. (eds) (1989) *Famine, disease and the social order in early modern society* (Cambridge).

Wareing, J. (1980) 'Changes in the geographical distribution of the recruitment of apprentices to the London companies, 1486–1750', *Journal of Historical Geography* 6.

Weatherill, L. (1988) *Consumer behaviour and material culture in Britain, 1660–1760* (London).

Weir, D. (1984) 'Rather never than late: celibacy and age at marriage in English cohort fertility, 1541–1871', *Journal of Family History* 9.

Whyte, I. D. (1979) *Agriculture and society in seventeenth century Scotland* (Edinburgh).

Whyte, I. D. (1989a) 'Urbanization in early-modern Scotland: a preliminary analysis', *Scottish Economic and Social History* 9.

Whyte, I. D. (1989b) 'Population mobility in early modern Scotland', in Houston and Whyte.

Whyte, I. D. and Whyte, K. A. (1988) 'The geographical mobility of women in early modern Scotland' in Leneman, L. (ed.), *Perspectives in Scottish social history* (Aberdeen).

Willigan, J. D. and Lynch, K. A. (1982) *Sources and methods of historical demography* (London).

Wilson, C. (1984) 'Natural fertility in pre-industrial England, 1600–1799', *Population Studies* 38.

Wrightson, K. (1982) *English society, 1580–1680* (London).

Wrightson, K. and Levine, D. (1989) 'Death in Whickham', in Walter and Schofield

Wrigley, E. A. (ed.) (1966) *An introduction to English historical demography* (London).

Wrigley, E. A. (1981) 'Marriage, fertility and population growth in eighteenth-century England', in Outhwaite.

Wrigley, E. A. (1985) 'Urban growth and agriculture change: England and the continent in the early modern period', *Journal of Interdisciplinary History* 15.

Wrigley, E. A. (1989) 'Some reflections on corn yields and prices in preindustrial economies', in Walter and Schofield.

Wrigley, E. A. and Schofield, R. S. (1981) *The population history of England, 1541–1871: a reconstruction* (London). Revised paperback edition 1989.

Wrigley, E. A. and Schofield, R. S. (1983) 'English population history from family reconstitution: summary results, 1600–1799', *Population Studies* 37.

4 Population change in north-western Europe, 1750–1850

Prepared for The Economic History Society by

Michael Anderson
Professor of Economic History
University of Edinburgh

Contents

List of figures

Acknowledgements

I could never have written this book without the help of many friends, students and colleagues, far too numerous to mention by name. I owe, however, special debts to Tony Wrigley and Roger Schofield, who have so patiently answered my many questions about their work over the years, to Ann-Sofie Kälvemark who at a critical point in my career made me aware of the rich opportunities that were present in the Swedish writings on historical demography, and to Rosalind Mitchison with whom I have so greatly enjoyed teaching a course on Western European demography and from whom I have learnt so much. Leslie Clarkson, Rab Houston and Elspeth Moodie made many helpful comments on earlier drafts of this book; for this I am very grateful even though I have at times been too stubborn to follow their wise advice. One invaluable source of counsel, Michael Flinn, in whose footsteps I have followed in so many ways, had sadly and prematurely died before the writing got under way. Through the generosity and kindness of his family, who gave most of his books and offprints to his old department in Edinburgh, I have nevertheless been able to benefit from the mass of material he collected and even, at times, from his trenchant marginalia. I should like to place on record here my appreciation of the generous gift of this material; it has made my task infinitely easier and more pleasurable.

Note on references

Numbered references in the text within square brackets relate to the entries in the Select Bibliography.

1
The problem

Between 1750 and 1850 the population of north-western Europe almost doubled. Rises on this scale had happened in the twelfth and thirteenth centuries, and also in the later fifteenth and sixteenth, but these periods had been punctuated by major crises, and had ended with setbacks in the hunger and plagues of the fourteenth and seventeenth centuries. As late as the 1690s Scotland and the Nordic countries experienced famines which reduced the population of parts of Scotland by at least 15 per cent and of some areas of Finland by over a quarter. The first half of the eighteenth century saw continuing problems. The Great Northern War of 1699–1721 brought dislocation and starvation to much of Scandinavia; perhaps a fifth of adult male Finns died. Smallpox killed a third of the population of Iceland in 1707. Many areas of France experienced famine in 1708–10. Plague rampaged through Denmark, Sweden, Finland and parts of Germany in 1708–12. England's population fell briefly in the 1720s and most of Europe experienced crisis in the early 1740s [2b; 3; 7; 16; 18].

By contrast, after 1750, there was a change, and after 1815 a very marked one (though the old world had not totally disappeared: Ireland experienced a disaster when the potato crop failed in the 1840s, and Finland a devastating crisis as late as 1867–8). In general, however, the period 1750–1850 was free from major demographic catastrophes, and even the lesser setbacks had little long-term effect. More strikingly, perhaps, this century of expansion was followed by more than a century of further growth. In many ways, between 1750 and 1850 Europe broke free from the demographic constraints of an earlier age [cf. 3; but see 43; 59].

How and why did this growth of population come about? What

was its real significance? Our understanding of these problems has been transformed by work of the last twenty years. In this short book some of the issues and controversies that have emerged are outlined. Inevitably, in covering half a continent, some of the subtlety of local variation has been lost, and this is regrettable since an important lesson of recent research has been the demonstration of regional and international variations. Nevertheless, there are many similarities between the countries of our area; in particular, their late marriage patterns differed markedly from the Mediterranean and Eastern regions of the European continent [2a]. The significance of this special pattern of marriage behaviour provides a coherence and ultimately a conclusion for our theme.

2

Sources and methods

Historical demography must, as a minimum, start from two kinds of information: numbers of people alive at different times, and the numbers of demographic events (births, deaths and migrations) experienced over time. Ideally, of course, more is required. To *understand* population development we need more data on the *mechanics* of changes than we can get from simple counts (and, in particular, information on the age of patterns of deaths and migrations, the distributions of ages at which women bore children, changes in marriage ages and proportions ever marrying, and causes of death and how they were distributed across the population). To *explain* the changes we need to relate demographic information to its climatic, biological, economic and social contexts.

Unfortunately, for much of our period, really detailed basic information is often lacking; sometimes there is hardly any information at all. (The best general survey is [27]; see also [3; 6; 11; 15; 23].) In particular, over most of our area, regular, reliable, centrally organised population counts began only in the early nineteenth century. The main exceptions are the Nordic countries, though even here the accuracy of the earliest censuses has been questioned (Sweden's first census probably missed at least 60,000 people).

Elsewhere, regular censuses date from the early nineteenth century (for example every ten years from 1801 in England and Wales and in Scotland, but in Ireland effectively only from 1821). The French government made useful population counts in the 1690s, but then there is nothing of much use until the unstandardised collections of 1801 and 1806, followed, with more refined methods, by regular quinquennial counts from 1816. The conquests of the Napoleonic period led to the first nationally organised counts in Belgium and the Netherlands, in the Helvetic Republic (comprising most of modern Switzerland) and in some of the Germanic States. Thereafter, regular censuses began in Belgium in 1829, in the Netherlands in 1839, and in Switzerland in 1850. The first pan-Germanic census was in 1852.

Many of these early censuses are unsatisfactory since they failed to use two key aids to reliable counting: the collection of complete lists of the population including names and addresses; and the conducting of the whole census on one day. As a result, sometimes only very impressionistic estimates were made and, since the central authorities often did not even know how many communities existed, they had no check on the completeness of the data provided. Equally serious, the failure to complete the count of a country on a single day led to omission and double counting (the 1771 Dachsberg census of Bavaria was spread over ten years; the first British census of 1801 was spread over seven weeks). In addition, evasion was encouraged by widespread suspicion, sometimes justified, that censuses were to be used for taxation or military conscription purposes, though encouragement of overcounting was sometimes induced by beliefs (supposedly widespread in Ireland in 1831) that enumerators were to be paid according to the number of people they recorded [14b]. Even in the mid-nineteenth century many infants were under-reported and ages inaccurately stated.

Nevertheless, these early national censuses represent magnificent feats of organisation, equalled by few of the privately organised surveys which preceded them (the only clear exception is the count of the population of Scotland conducted in 1755 by Alexander Webster [11]). Most other pre-census population estimates come from counts of houses made for local taxation purposes, counts of adult males eligible for military conscription, or counts by church authorities of numbers of communicants. All these have unknown levels of omission, evasion and exemption; they also require us to guess appropriate 'multipliers' to inflate counts of houses or of adult males or of communicants to total population figures. As we shall see below, this inevitably leads to debate.

Regular efficient population counts had long been preceded by attempts to record quasi-demographic events. The church in many areas began the systematic recording of all baptisms in the late medieval period, and this gradually spread to marriages and burials as well (see e.g. [27; 6; 11; 23; 30]). Initially, however, these registers usually recorded not the demographic events of births and deaths but ecclesiastical events such as baptism, or burial in consecrated ground, or payments to church authorities; this led to major omissions – for example, of children who died before they could be baptised. Even 'marriage' registers are sometimes registers of *intention to* marry; they thus include reference to marriages which did not take place and record intent in the parish both of the bride and of the groom, thus leading to double counting.

By 1750, however, over most of Western Europe some parish records were kept; in some cases (e.g. France from 1579, the Nordic countries except Iceland from the 1730s) counts from the registers were regularly returned to central or local authorities. However, comprehensive central collection of information for demographic purposes (on births and deaths rather than burials and baptisms) generally came much later. Vital registration was secularised in France in 1792 but was for a long time very disorganised. Except during the Commonwealth, England and Wales had no State system until 1837 and even then births were under-registered. Scotland had to wait until 1855, Ireland until 1864. Even the excellent Swedish system needed modification in 1858.

The detail in which information was recorded varied widely [7; 11; 29; 30]. In mid-eighteenth-century England, for example, burial registers for adults frequently contain only a name and date, though the names of husbands of married women, and of at least one parent of children, are usually given. For baptisms and marriages more detail is often provided, but English information is minimal compared with that available in France or Sweden. In France, for example, a marriage register typically contained information on the names, ages, occupations and parents of the couple and also names of witnesses. French baptism registers nearly always gave enough detail to make the identification of parents unambiguous. Swedish registers by the 1820s were comprehensive and were supplemented by a continuously updated household register and by registers of in- and out-migration.

However, many registers are lost or incomplete. In Sweden,

most places have surviving records of good quality and coverage. The other Nordic countries also have reasonable records, though in both Denmark and Finland up to 10 per cent of births were sometimes missed, and death recording was sometimes erratic, particularly for infants [31; 32]. In France, too, record quality, coverage and survival was high; infant and child deaths, however, were under-recorded especially in the mid-eighteenth century, and there were similar problems after the Revolution.

Elsewhere the position was less satisfactory. In Scotland, even where they had once been kept, most old parish registers have been lost or destroyed and the survivors are often of poor quality [11]. Welsh records raise many problems, but in England, Germany, Belgium and Switzerland there are many surviving registers which seem conscientiously kept, though the communities covered are unevenly spread across the country, and urban areas are poorly represented.

English registers, though, have other problems, relating especially to births and deaths (for a useful summary see [7, chaps 1–5]). Firstly (and between 1780 and 1820 in particular) baptisms by nonconformist ministers increased rapidly, and there was a steady expansion in the use of nonconformist burial grounds; relatively few of these nonconformist records survive, and indirect methods of estimation must be used. One recent estimate suggests that about 9 per cent of all children in the 1780s and about 16 per cent in the 1830s were baptised by nonconformist ministers; for burials the shortfalls are about 5 per cent and about 14 per cent respectively [7].

Secondly, over the eighteenth century in England the gap in time between birth and baptism steadily increased; by the 1790s the median gap was probably at least a month. This delay is important because high infant mortality meant that many children died before they could be baptised; since the burial of unbaptised children often went unrecorded, burial registration is also deficient. In the years 1750–1800 this factor alone may have reduced baptisms by 7 per cent below their 'proper' level and burials by 5 per cent; for 1800–37 the deficits were even higher.

Finally, rapid urban growth, and absenteeism among clergy led to widespread omissions from the English registers, especially of baptisms. Wrigley and Schofield estimate that about 5 per cent of births in the 1750s were not recorded by any church and by the early nineteenth century around one fifth [7]. In all, Wrigley and Schofield suggest that nonconformity, delayed baptism, and non-registration for other reasons, led to the Anglican registers by the early nineteenth century recording less than three-quarters of all births and deaths – though these estimates have been subjected to some criticisms [see e.g. 55]; comparable figures for the 1750s are about 87 per cent of births and 93 per cent of deaths.

In spite of these problems, dramatic progress has been made in the exploitation of parochial records. We can distinguish two broad strategies, one based on 'family reconstitution', the other on forms of 'aggregative analysis' (a useful introduction is in [29]).

'Family reconstitution' begins by abstracting all baptisms, burials and marriages from a lengthy parish register run. The entries are sorted by name. Then, taking each marriage record in turn, an attempt is made to add to it information on the births and deaths of the couple, and on the births, deaths and marriages of their children. Where a complete record can be assembled it is possible to calculate a wide range of information including the ages of the couple at marriage, their ages at the birth of each of their children, and the birth intervals between children, and between marriage and the first child. Once these data are assembled for all possible couples in the community under study, a wide range of statistics relating to fertility, mortality (and especially infant and child mortality), age at marriage, and to some extent migration, can be derived.

Family reconstitution demands high-quality records. Omissions in birth recording distort estimates of fertility. Migration means that information on age at death or year of birth (and thus age at marriage) cannot be obtained (though Swedish records allow migrants to be traced to the registers of other parishes) [30]; also, if only records on non-migrants are used, there are questions about the representativeness of the group analysed. In addition, where only a small number of names was used in a community, it is impossible to relate each entry in a register to a single person or family, and as a result many 'ambiguous' entries arise. This is not a major problem in the detailed French and Scandinavian registers, but it causes difficulties in England and the Netherlands, and is a major barrier to work on Wales.

These problems mean that, even in France, the proportion of families on which information can be collected is often quite low, though the size of the 'reconstitutable minority' varies according to the topic under study. In thirteen English reconstitutions about 80 per cent of legitimate live births could be used for the calculation of infant mortality, but age-specific fertility rates could be calculated for only 16 per cent of all married women [9]. This accentuates another difficulty of community-based studies: because demographic events are inherently variable between families and over short periods of time, small numbers of observations mean that computed differences between places and periods may result from random fluctuations rather than reflecting 'real' differences in behaviour [28].

It is not, however, easy to expand the number or scale of family reconstitutions since the work is time-consuming and computerisation has proved, until recently, difficult. In Germany, Sweden and Belgium the work of earlier generations of genealogists has been utilised to speed the task [33; 34; 81]. In Germany, for example, over 100 '*Ortssippenbücher*' exist; these 'Collections of family histories of the residents of a particular place' provide genealogies on all residents in a village in as far as these can be compiled from village records [82; 83].

Nevertheless, several hundred communities in Western Europe have now been reconstituted for our period (see [3] for examples to 1979), though the scatter of parishes covered is uneven, with communities often selected because of good records or personal interest rather than as part of an overall plan; the main exceptions here are a major French project for the systematic analysis of a representative sample of forty communities spread across the entire country, and Swedish work on a large, statistically stratified sample of parishes from the south of the country [22; 43]. In England, by mid-1986, nearly thirty parishes had been reconstituted by the Cambridge Group alone, although some of these reconstitutions have not been wholly successful and most do not go past 1837 (when parish registration falls off markedly in completeness) while some stop at 1811.

Family reconstitution is invaluable but it has limitations. In particular, unless population mobility is low it cannot produce statistics which require knowledge of 'numbers at risk'. It thus provides good information on infant mortality but not on the death rates of adults, allows estimation of average ages at marriage but not of proportions ultimately marrying, and is little help in determining the population of a community, let alone national populations. As a result, alongside family reconstitution, work has continued on 'aggregative analysis'. The basis of aggregative analysis is simple: take a high-quality register of reasonable continuity; count, for each year, the numbers of baptisms, burials and marriages. The resulting figures (and particularly the differences between numbers of baptisms and burials) provide important clues about long-run population change; study of short-run fluctuations in burials shows patterns of mortality crises; examination of the seasonality of the burials, and study of correlations of changes in baptisms and marriages with changes in burials, provide clues about the causes of the crises.

Beginning from the late medieval period with the compilation of urban 'Bills of Mortality', contemporary interest in population developments led by 1800 to quite widespread official counts of burials, baptisms and marriages. The collected data on the Nordic countries is generally of high quality but the French system largely broke down after the Revolution and remained suspect to the end of our period. Information was assembled by Rickman at the 1801 British census and extended, for England and Wales, at subsequent censuses up to 1841, but the English information is of little real use to the historical demographer [10], and the Scottish material was recognised as almost worthless at the time [11].

Historical demographers have therefore recently returned to the parish registers and instigated new series of counts. For Scotland, the fragmentary registers of over one hundred parishes have been used to construct a rough index of mortality fluctuations [11]. For France, there is an excellent scheme to analyse a representative sample from the parish registers of 413 places in mainland France for the period 1740–1829 [22]. For England the Cambridge Group has estimated national totals of births, deaths and marriages from a sample of 404 high-quality Anglican parish registers [7].

The Cambridge study is a path-breaking one but questions have been raised about sample quality and about the assumptions and techniques used in the analysis [e.g. 55; 54]. The sample is unevenly spread over the country, is skewed towards larger parishes, and excludes London; as a result, major (though superficially reasonable) adjustments have had to be made to the data. Beyond this, as we have seen above, allowance is required for those births, burials and marriages which left no record in the Anglican registers. The cumulative impact of the adjustments for non-representativeness and for non-recording is very large indeed. For example, the number of baptisms *recorded* in the 404 parishes rose by 40 per cent between 1750 and 1800. However, after adjustment for gaps in registration, parish size bias, and the omission of London, the estimated *national total* of Anglican baptisms rose by only 33 per cent; after correction for nonconformity, birth-baptism interval change, and residual non-registration, the *estimated rise in births* is 58 per cent. Some other adjustments, notably for marriages between 1800 and 1837, produce even larger differences. However reasonable the adjustments may be, the end results are only as good as the assumptions made, and a considerable margin of error must be assumed [see especially 55].

Wrigley and Schofield, however, go beyond the raw totals of events. For some years demographers have been experimenting with procedures for deriving population numbers (and also rates of mortality, fertility and nuptiality) from totals of births, deaths and marriages. Wrigley and Schofield's procedure, 'back projection' [7], a development of the 'inverse projection' technique invented by Lee (*Population Studies*, 1974), is based on a simple idea: if one starts from a known census population, then, subtracting the number of births from the previous year and adding the number of deaths gives an estimate of the population at the start of that year. In a world with no emigration, cumulating this process would produce estimated populations backwards, on an annual basis, as far as the beginning of the records of births and deaths.

Unfortunately, because we cannot ignore emigration, a more complex computer-based solution must be employed. It exploits a general demographic observation: regardless of the *level* of mortality, fertility, nuptiality and migration in any year, the *shares* of events between different age groups tend to vary in highly predictable ways. Making suitable assumptions about these shares allows us to proceed as follows: Take the number of persons alive and aged, say, 10–14 at the 1871 census. Then, from the total of deaths between 1866 and 1871, and the assumed age distribution of those deaths, we can estimate the number of deaths of children who had been aged 5–9 in 1866. Adding these dead children to the numbers alive aged 10–14 in 1871 gives a figure for the number of children aged 5–9 in 1866. Repeat this procedure for 1861–6 for children aged 0–4 in 1861; this gives an estimate of the number of 0–4 year olds alive in 1861. A similar procedure can be used across all other age groups. The same procedure for earlier years builds population estimates back in time.

There are, however, two complications. Firstly, the method gives no estimate of the numbers alive in the oldest age group in 1866, the oldest two age groups in 1861, and so on; this is because all members of this age group are assumed to have died by 1871. For each year, therefore, we must estimate the number of very old persons alive so that they can be fed into the 'top' of the model and gradually work their way back to their births. The solution adopted by Wrigley and Schofield is based on the numbers originally born into any age cohort and the mortality experience of the whole society over the lifetime of that cohort; this clearly makes a number of assumptions, but these are not especially problematic for scholars of the 1750–1850 period since the population age structure can be checked back in censuses as far as 1821.

The second complication deals with migration. When any cohort is followed back to age 0–4, the next preceding five-year period will be that during which its members were born. If one adds to the numbers computed as alive at 0–4 at any date the estimated deaths of their age peers during the five years before that date, one gets the numbers who 'should' have been born during the preceding five years. The difference between this figure and the numbers actually 'known' to have been born indicates the extent of emigration by members of the cohort over their lives. Using a standard distribution of the ages at emigration, the migrants can be added to the numbers estimated as alive at the different periods of the cohort's life; the computer program then makes adjustments and produces new estimates of numbers alive and dying in each age group in each year.

The results give both population totals and age estimates. These are a dramatic advance on anything previously achieved, though only as good as the assumptions made in calculating the original numbers of demographic events, and those made by the model. Wrigley and Schofield describe their work as a 'reconstruction' of the population of England and stress the inevitably approximate status of the results. Some scholars have been highly critical of what one has called 'a sand of mere assumption and historical speculation' [Razzell, *New Society*, 1981] but this is unfair; all historical knowledge is reconstruction based on judgements about the extent and direction of bias in surviving records, and on historians' interpretations of their meaning and significance. Certainly, as we have seen, some of the judgements used are open to question, but this is true of all assessments of historical data.

More significantly, Lee (*Population Studies*, 1985) has challenged certain aspects of the logical status of the model (though for our period, his alternative calculations using 'inverse projection' produce very similar results). This, however, illustrates a vital point. In back projection all the evidence and all the assumptions are open to inspection; alternative estimates can be made on other premises. So far such work does not markedly challenge Wrigley and Schofield's conclusions for our period. Nevertheless, their results, like all those we shall be discussing in this book, must not be treated as 'facts'; they are merely the best estimates currently available.

3
Population change 1750–1850

In 1750 the population of north-west Europe was between 60 and 64 million; by 1850 it was around 116 million. As Table I and Figure 1 show, this dramatic expansion, unprecedented since the sixteenth century, was not evenly spread across the continent. At one extreme, Finland's population almost quadrupled in this period and, before its collapse in the famine of the late 1840s, Ireland's probably grew over three and a half times. At the other extreme was France (and probably Switzerland and the Netherlands); France in 1750 had two-fifths of the population of our area, but her population seems to have grown by less than 50 per cent to 1850, reducing her share to three-tenths of the total. Between the extremes, the population of England and Wales expanded 2.9 times, from about 6.1 million in 1750 to 17.9 million in 1851.

Some of the figures used here involve substantial revisions of earlier estimates. The English population data from Wrigley and Schofield's back projection exercise [7] have modified considerably figures based on Rickman's parish register summaries [see 10]; they show in particular slower growth in the 1760s, but faster growth to the end of the century. Allowances has also been made for under-recording at the early censuses and this raises the early-nineteenth-century figures somewhat.

For Ireland, the problems are greater. Kenneth Connell, the pioneer of Irish demographic history, accepted the censuses of 1821, 1831 and 1841 as the best estimates available for the period [12]; recently, some scholars have suggested substantial under-enumeration at the 1821, 1841 and (by inference) 1851 censuses, though they have been happier with 1831. Other writers have suggested over-enumeration in 1831 and have used the remaining

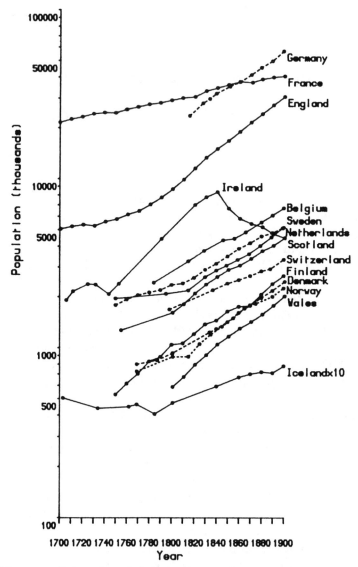

Figure 1   *Estimated populations of selected countries, 1700–1900*

NOTE
The population figures on the vertical axis are plotted on a logarithmic scale. The effect of this is to ensure that population changes of the same *relative* magnitude produce similar vertical variation on the graph regardless of the initial absolute values. Population growth at a constant rate will produce a straight line

Table I   *Estimated populations of north and west European countries,*
c. 1750–c. 1850 (millions)

	c. 1750	*c.* 1800	*c.* 1850
Norway	[0.7]	0.9	1.4
Sweden	1.8	2.3	3.5
Finland	0.5	1.0	1.6
Denmark	[0.7]	0.9	1.4
Iceland	0.0	0.0	0.1
Germany	[18.4]	(24.5)	(35.0)
Netherlands	[1.9]	(2.1)	3.1
Belgium	[2.2]	[2.8]	(4.4)
Switzerland	(1.4)	(1.7)	2.4
France	24.5	29.0	35.9
Scotland	1.3	1.6	2.9
Wales	[0.3]	0.6	1.2
England	5.8	8.7	16.7
Ireland	2.4	[5.2]	6.7
Total	61.9	81.3	116.3

Notes: The figures for Germany are for the 1914 boundaries less Alsace and Lorraine.

The figures for other countries are for the borders of 1850.

Figures in square brackets are very approximate, usually based to some degree on long-term extrapolation or analogy.

Figures in round brackets are based on interpolation between two reasonably sound figures.

For details of the sources and bases of the estimates for France, Ireland, Scotland and England see text. The remaining figures are from B. R. Mitchell, *European Historical Statistics* (1980), modified where appropriate in the light of data or discussions in [4; 16; 17; 19; 21; 25; 26].

figures relatively unchanged. There is at present no obvious resolution to this debate [a useful summary is in 13]. The figures used here accept the 1831 data and assume that the other censuses were as deficient as the English enumerations of the same dates (probably a conservative assumption); this puts the figures into the midband of the range of recent estimates.

There is even greater debate over Ireland's population before 1821. The main sources are estimates of the numbers of houses derived from the collection of hearth tax. Contemporaries believed that the pre-1790 figures were too low through laziness, ignorance and corruption of the collectors; recent research tends to ignore the figures between 1753 and 1791 altogether. Connell assumed that the earlier figures were as at least as bad as those of the 1780s; he suggested inflation factors of 50 per cent for 1725 and 1753, and 20 per cent for 1791 [12]. Recent work has been less pessimistic, with under-recording estimated at between 14 per cent and 34 per cent for the earlier years and between 10 per cent and 20 per cent for 1791 ([14a]; Daultry *et al.*, *Journal of Economic History*, 1981).

There is also debate for Ireland for this period over the appropriate multiplier to convert houses to people. Connell assumed average household sizes rising from 5.25 to 5.65 between 1725 and 1791 [12]. Detailed research by Daultry and his colleagues suggests a figure of around 5 for 1725 and 1753 but 4.7 for 1744 and 5.8 for 1791 [and see 14a]. The figures used here are from the middle of Daultry's range of estimates and produce a markedly lower 1753 population than Connell's (2.385 million compared with Connell's 3.191). In consequence, growth between 1753 and 1791 is much faster than Connell estimated and growth between 1791 and 1821 is slower, which fits with much contemporary comment suggesting a decline in growth even before the Famine (see also [47; 13]).

Finally, major modifications have recently been made to earlier estimates for France as a result of analysis of the relationship between inter-censal growth on the one hand and the difference between recorded births and recorded deaths on the other [22; 23]. As a result, French population is now believed to have been significantly higher in the mid-eighteenth century than earlier scholars assumed (around 25 million in 1750 as opposed to 21 million); the pace of growth after 1750 is thus even slower than was once thought.

In spite of the tentative nature of the figures, some general statements about the course of population movements can be made. The forty years after 1750 saw most populations growing slowly, typically on a long-run growth rate of around 0.5 per cent per annum but with some setbacks (Swedish population fell, for example, by around 75,000 in the famine of 1772–3). If recent estimates are correct, however, the populations of Ireland and Finland were on a faster growth trajectory. Ireland growing between 1753 and 1791 at 1.7 per cent per annum, Finland on a fluctuating path of around 1.5 per cent per annum until the setback of 1788–90. England's population, though growing at around 0.5 per cent per year in the 1750s and 1760s, thereafter accelerated to exceed 1 per cent by the 1790s.

The Napoleonic war years saw major checks to European population growth. France lost perhaps 1.3 million men [22] as a result of the military campaigns. The wars with Russia brought epidemic and hunger to Sweden, Norway and Finland, with years of absolute decline between 1806–10 and almost no growth for a decade. Only the British Isles escaped, with Ireland, Scotland, and England and Wales experiencing medium-term growth at over 1 per cent per year.

The end of the war saw rapid growth almost everywhere. By 1820 every country in our area had growth approaching, or above, 1 per cent per year; Germany, England and Wales, Ireland, and Norway all approached or exceeded, for at least a decade, the extremely high level of 1.5 per cent per annum; at this rate of growth populations double in fifty years.

Thereafter, growth fell back in most countries. In the 1830s only Germany, England, Norway and Scotland reached 1 per cent per annum growth, while Ireland, Finland and France were probably below 0.5 per cent. The 1840s saw slight recovery in some of the smaller countries, but growth rates in England and Germany continued to fall slowly, and French growth remained very low, at well under 0.5 per cent. Ireland, where the population expansion was already decelerating, experienced a demographic disaster, as the failure of the staple food supply, the potato, led to massive death and emigration. The official census figures, which had been 8.125 million in 1841, fell to 6.552 million in 1851, and then fell further at each census until the 1930s. Elsewhere, excepting Denmark (where population had been sluggish in the early part of the century), and briefly Finland, rates of medium-term growth never again attained the peaks of the years after the Napoleonic wars. Europe was entering a new demographic regime.

These patterns of rise and fall were not spread evenly across the individual territories. Few even among the rural areas significantly lost population before 1800 and only the more isolated regions saw major declines much before 1850. But almost everywhere some areas grew much faster than others. In England the south-east and the industrialising areas of the north rapidly outstripped the remainder of the country, while in Scotland the central belt expanded its population share, mainly at the expense of the highland north. In Sweden, the north and west grew much faster than the east. In Switzerland the Alpine areas grew most slowly. In Germany in the first half of the nineteenth century, growth was high in the agricultural east, moderate in the industrialising west and low in the south. Similar variations occurred elsewhere.

In some countries considerable growth took place in rural areas (particularly areas of rural industrialisation), but increasingly the urban areas were the most dynamic sectors, in spite of their high levels of mortality. One estimate [5] suggests that in 1750 north-western Europe had 160 cities of at least 10,000 people, and a total city population of 4.4 million, some 7 per cent of the total. Using 10,000 population as our minimum size definition, in 1750 only the Netherlands had more than 30 per cent of its population urbanised; Belgium had around 20 per cent, England and Wales about 17 per cent. Nowhere else except Denmark exceeded 10 per cent, and Ireland, Switzerland and the rest of Scandinavia had less than 5 per cent.

By 1800 urban growth was widespread; there were 240 places of over 10,000 people in 1800, and the urban population exceeded 7.5 million. By 1850 the number of cities had risen to 552, with a population of over 20 million, 17 per cent of the total. Over two-fifths of the population of England and Wales lived in cities of over 10,000 people, as did one in three of the people of Scotland and the Netherlands, and one-fifth of all Belgians. By contrast, the figures for France were 15 per cent, for Germany 11 per cent, Ireland 10 per cent, and for the Nordic countries an average of only 6 per cent.

4

Migration

There are two ways in which a population can grow; from an excess of births over deaths; and from an excess of immigrants over emigrants. In Europe in our period the first was much more important than the second.

Internal migration, however, played a vital part in the rapid growth of cities, where deaths usually exceeded births until well into our period, and areas of rural industrial expansion were also highly dependent on immigrants. There were also some regions, particularly in the north and east, where pioneers were still moving in and establishing new areas of settlement. Nationally, however, the net direct effect on populations of most of these internal shufflings of people was zero though some inter-state migration, especially within the British Isles, and in the north and east of the continent, must have produced some now largely unmeasurable effects on national population totals.

Overseas movements, by contrast, have at certain periods in the past produced important net effects on national populations; in the fifty years before the First World War Europe permanently lost well over 20 million people to other regions of the world. In our period, however, few movements were, even relatively, on anything like this scale.

In France, small-scale immigration (especially of industrial workers) offset low emigration, leaving little net change except for deaths overseas of soldiers of the French armies during the Napoleonic wars (this was also a problem for the Swiss who, until the 1830s, provided major mercenary contingents to the armies of continental Europe). In England total net loss in any decade probably never rose above 1.5 per thousand of the population, and much of this 'emigration' was due to deaths of soldiers and sailors overseas. In Scotland, besides a flow to England of unknown proportions (until the 1840s when it was about 75,000 net for the decade as a whole), there were recurrent waves of overseas migration; none, however, is likely to have exceeded proportionally that of the 1770s which involved less than 2 per cent of the population at a time when population growth may have been approaching 1 per cent per annum. In the Nordic countries legal restrictions on emigration in the eighteenth century meant that most of those who left did so clandestinely and precise figures are lacking. Except for some small movements to Finland in the eighteenth century, however, Swedish emigration was probably insignificant until the lifting of last major restrictions in the 1840s when a considerable outflow began. In Norway emigration was low with even the peak loss, for the period 1845–50, being a mere 0.3 per cent of the 1845 population. Emigration from Denmark was equally trivial.

Elsewhere, emigration was more significant, especially in Switzerland and Germany, and particularly following the potato harvest failures of 1816–17 and 1847; in the late 1840s over 300,000 Germans emigrated, from a population of just over 30 million. But Ireland had the most dramatic population outflows. About 1.75 million people emigrated between 1780 and 1844, perhaps two-fifths to Great Britain, the rest mainly to North America; this held back population growth to around three-quarters of natural increase between 1780 and 1844. Yet this was insignificant compared with what followed. During and immediately after the famine of 1845–8, at least one million people left, around one-eighth of the 1841 population. Nowhere else in our period did emigration have this impact. Everywhere else it was the balance between births and deaths which was the main mechanism of population growth or decline.

5

Natural increase

'Natural increase' (normally computed per thousand of the population so as to allow easy comparison between populations of different sizes) is calculated by taking the difference between the 'crude birth rate' of a population and its 'crude death rate'. The 'crude birth rate' is the number of births in any year in an area, divided by the population and multiplied by 1000. The 'crude death rate' is computed in a similar way. At times, both these indicators can be misleading or inadequate, particularly during periods of rapid demographic growth when population age structures become skewed towards younger age groups. Crude rates nevertheless provide useful and widely available clues about the relative importance of fertility and mortality in overall population change.

Figure 2 sets the crude rates of our period in a longer term context for countries with precise enough information to reveal trends over a reasonable period of time. However, even these figures are often only approximate, certainly before the 1820s. For example, the Norwegian statistics used here are taken from Drake's work [21] and make rather different assumptions from those of earlier scholars [e.g. 15] about stillbirths and about the accuracy of the 1769 census. Wrigley and Schofield's figures for England [7] are subject to limitations arising from their method of estimation, and their conclusions are still disputed by some scholars who believe that the early-nineteenth-century birth rates and the later-eighteenth-century death rates are both too high [e.g. 55; 58].

Looking first at the birth rate trends as plotted in Figure 2, the most striking feature is the differences in the levels and trends

218   *Michael Anderson*

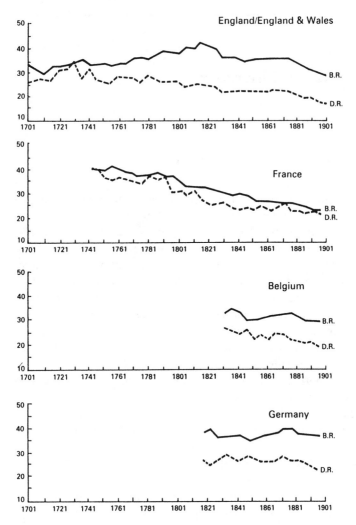

Figure 2 *Crude birth and crude death rates (per 1000 population), selected countries, 1701–1901*

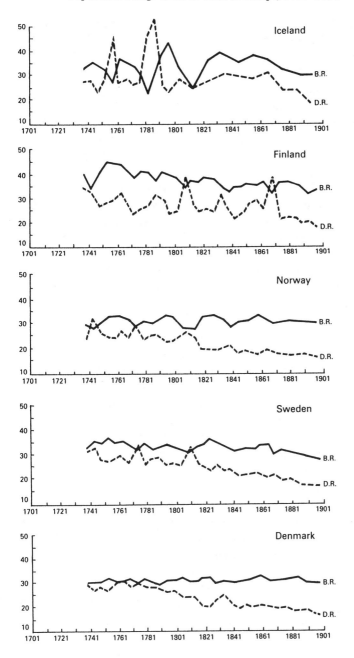

between countries. Comparing the figures, one pattern occurs in England where the birth rate was around 34 per 1000 in the 1750s, then rose, particularly from the 1780s, to over 40 by 1820, followed by a fairly rapid fall to roughly mid-eighteenth-century levels. In complete contrast was the situation of France (which differed, indeed, from any other country). The mid-eighteenth-century birth rate, at around 40 per 1000, was exceeded only by that of Finland. A slight downward tendency by the early 1790s brought the French rate below the rising English figure. There then followed a sharper fall by 1800 and a further gradual decline after 1820. The end result was that France in the late 1840s had the lowest birth rate of any country for which we have reasonable figures, the rate having fallen by over a quarter within a century.

Equally dramatic contrasts can be found in the Nordic countries, though all five countries show marked fluctuations, with Iceland and Finland the most extreme. The oscillation of the Norwegian birth rate is commented on below; parallel but less extreme fluctuations occurred in Sweden (though around a higher trend) and in Denmark, though there the quinquennial average rate lies in a narrow band between 29.0 and 32.5 per 1000 and the trend shows no marked tendency either to rise or fall.

Elsewhere, for most of the period only impressionistic results are available. The Swiss, Belgian and Dutch birth rates seem to have been between 30 and 35 for the first part of the nineteenth century, though with a tendency to fall over time. By the mid-nineteenth century, the German rate was around the relatively high English level, though there was considerable internal variation which was already present in the eighteenth century [4c].

For Scotland (where the figures are too poor to plot in Figure 2), Hollingsworth [in 11] has used the age structure from Webster's 1755 'census' to suggest a mid-eighteenth-century crude birth rate in excess of 41 per 1000, well above the estimate for England at that date; although most scholars now see this as implausibly high it is well below the contemporary rate for Finland, another northern country still recovering from the effects of devastating crises of half a century earlier. Moreover, Hollingsworth's 1755 estimate is consistent with estimates for the 1790s based on the *Old Statistical Account* which give figures for the Highland areas approaching the 1750s figure, though for the rest of the country the estimate is only around 35. The first Civil Registration figures, by contrast, give a figure for 1855–60 of 34 per thousand (around the English level for that date); by this time the most northerly Scottish countries had figures well below 30, mainly because the age structure had become distorted by heavy out-migration of the most fertile groups (though low marriage rates were also important).

In Ireland, contemporaries had an impression of a high birth rate in the eighteenth century, a view shared by most recent scholars [reviewed in 13]. The 1841 census, however, estimated a rate of only 33 per 1000, implying a fall since 1800; this figure, though widely cited, is based on the published census information on ages of infants, and this must be faulty. Had the birth rate been this low, the Irish death rate in the twenty years before the famine (at 17 per 1000) would have been the lowest in Europe, which seems very unlikely. Mokyr [47], using plausible though sweeping assumptions, has proposed a birth rate of around 40 per thousand for the years 1821–40. This, however, unreasonably implies a death rate worse than any Nordic country except Finland and is thus surely too high; nevertheless, throughout our period and certainly right up to the eve of the Famine, Ireland's fertility was at the high end of the European spectrum.

Turning now to death rates, three features are particularly striking: the wide differences in rates in the mid-eighteenth century, the tendency for most rates to fall significantly by the mid-nineteenth century (though often on rather different timings and trajectories), and the continuing fluctuations apparent in some countries even when five or ten year averages are taken. While all these aspects are clearly visible at the national levels shown in Figure 2, they are even more apparent at local and regional levels, a point which is further discussed below.

The first half of the eighteenth century saw mortality in most countries as higher than in the second half. Wrigley and Schofield's estimate [7] puts the average English crude death rate at over 31 per 1000 population for the years 1720–45, but only at around 27 per 1000 for the next 40 years; note also the relatively small amplitude of the English death rate fluctuations. Scandinavia experienced severe problems in the 1740s, with the Finnish, Icelandic and Swedish death rates over 40 in at least one year and the Norwegian exceeding 70 per 1000 in 1742. Thereafter, for the rest of the century, the Swedish and Norwegian rates fluctuated around an average level similar to the English; the Danish average was a little higher but more stable, while the Finnish and Icelandic rates fluctuated considerably but still on a medium-term trend well below 30 per 1000 [15–17].

Elsewhere, the situation in France in the mid-eighteenth century was bad; recent estimates suggest a death rate of around 40 per 1000 population in the 1740s and around 35 for the next forty years [22; 23]. In many parts of Germany, by contrast, the eighteenth-century death rate hovered around or above 30 [4c] and one interpretation of the fragmentary Scottish materials suggests a death rate for the years before 1755 of well over 35 per 1000, but a fall to below 30 by the 1790s, with rates for rural areas of below 25 [11]. Finally, for Ireland, no hard information is available and, though most demographers assume a death rate fairly well in check, there is ongoing debate over the severity of the several regional crises which clearly did occur (summary in [13]).

As is clear from Figure 2, when compared with the mid-eighteenth century, the death rates of the 1820s were almost everywhere more favourable. English mortality had fallen significantly over the previous forty years, to a medium-term trend around 22 per thousand; there it remained until well after the end of our period, though possibly rising a little in the 1840s as a result of the massive urbanisation of the previous thirty years. Scottish death rates in the 1850s were somewhat below the English levels, but Scottish mortality, particularly in the towns, may also have shifted upwards in the 1830s and 1840s. Mokyr's [47] recent estimate for Ireland for 1821–41 gives a national figure of around 24 per 1000, though he suggests that Ulster may have recorded a rate of less than 22; the argument that implies that this was below the eighteenth-century level is, however, based largely on impression (and see [6]). In the Famine years of the late 1840s the Irish situation was transformed. The number of excess deaths during these years was between one and one and a half million, producing a national death rate for the period of over 50 per 1000 [47].

On the Continent, the most dramatic changes were taking place in France. Around the turn of the century the death rate stepped down quite sharply to around 30 per 1000; it fell further before the end of the Napoleonic Wars and by the 1840s was not far above the English level. Scandinavian rates also moved downwards by the early nineteenth century, though the Nordic area was severely hit in 1808–9, and in Finland and Iceland occasional surges of mortality continued for much of the rest of the century. Nevertheless, by the end of our period Denmark, Norway and Sweden were on trend averages between 18 and 21 per 1000 population. This was in clear contrast with the lands to the south, where Germany and the Low Countries persisted with death rates only marginally below those of the late eighteenth century.

The net results of these changes in medium-term death and birth rates can be seen in the rates of natural increase, revealed by the gaps between the birth and death rate lines in Figure 2. As we have seen earlier, population grew markedly between 1750 and 1850 almost right across the continent and it increased particularly fast in the years after the Napoleonic wars. Everywhere, most of this growth came from natural increase. However, as the graphs make clear, the ways in which this natural increase was achieved varied considerably between different parts of our area.

One pattern is clearly visible in Norway, Sweden, and with slight modifications, in Denmark. In these countries, natural increase was at moderate levels in the eighteenth century and the acceleration in population growth came largely from a gradual fall in the death rate against a stable or more slowly falling birth rate; the temporary very rapid growth around 1820 was the result of a trough in the death rate coinciding with a brief surge in births.

The English pattern seems very different. A falling death rate helped to accelerate population growth in the second half of the eighteenth century, but the rising birth rate was clearly the more volatile component; in particular, the timing of the peak growth in the 1810s, and its subsequent decline to around the average European level, were mainly determined by birth rate changes. The relative importance of the birth and death rate components depends on the dates chosen for comparison. Wrigley and Schofield [7] suggest that around three-quarters of the rise in growth between the mid-seventeenth and early nineteenth centuries resulted from the birth rate side of the equation. Thus, in most modern interpretations, fertility is seen as the dominant partner; the older, and once dominant, view [e.g. 10; 42] that fertility could not possibly have been dynamic enough to play more than a minor role, is now clearly on the defensive.

France offers a third and apparently unique growth profile, where a falling death rate fails to produce more than short-term bursts of growth because of compensating and only sightly lagged falls in fertility.

Fourthly, there is Finland, where an extremely high birth rate, particularly in the eighteenth century, moved against a slowly falling underlying death rate. This produced rapid medium-term growth in spite of occasional dramatic mortality crises, a pattern which continued to the end of the nineteenth century. Possible parallels with Ireland are suggestive. One may also wonder whether parts of eighteenth-century Scotland might not have been on a similar trajectory, only being saved from the fate of Ireland and Finland by the arrival in the later eighteenth century of radically improved poor relief administration, agrarian reform and industrialisation. Iceland may also fit this pattern, though the recurrent mortality crises, and their reverberations on the birth rate, were even more severe and frequent, so that long-run growth was more controlled.

Finally, we should note that nineteenth-century Germany, with its continuing high birth and death rates, looks very different from the rest of our area.

Ten years ago, historical demographers still felt reasonably happy in extrapolating from the experience of one Western European country to another (a view exemplified by Flinn [3]). We can no longer safely think in these terms. While overall growth patterns clearly show some similarities, the factors underlying them were very different. The next sections seek to identify the causes of these different profiles of growth.

6

Fertility and nuptiality

The previous section has shown that variations in birth rates were an important mechanism of demographic change. We can distinguish four factors which may help in understanding these variations: compositional effects, illegitimacy and pre-nuptial pregnancy, changes in marital fertility, and changes in marriage patterns.

(i) Compositional effects

Compositional effects operate on crude birth rates when there are sharp variations in the proportions of populations who are females in the fertile age groups. The oscillations in the Norwegian birth rate (see Figure 2) provide a classic example, first noted by Sundt in the 1850s [79; and see 21]. Sundt argued that the crisis of the 1740s reduced fertility and also killed many children. As a result, a small age cohort entered marriage around 1770 and births fell by an eighth in ten years. When the larger cohort born in the 1760s married in the 1780s, the number of births rose again; the small 1770s cohort, by contrast, produced a 10 per cent reduction in births by 1806–10. Further fluctuations continued to the 1830s. As Sundt acknowledged, other factors were also involved; heavy taxation in the 1760s and the dearths of the 1770s played a part, while 1806–10 saw disruptive warfare. Nevertheless, the compositional factor is a major component of the cyclical changes in Norway's crude birth rates, and it influenced even the surge and slump of births which contributed to the rapid population expansion of the 1820s and the slower growth which followed it.

Oscillations in Iceland had partly similar origins, as, on a smaller scale, they did also in Sweden, Denmark and Finland. Elsewhere, however, while small variations in birth rates may have resulted from changes in population age composition, the effects were much less important.

(ii) Illegitimacy

Between 1740 and 1790, the proportion of births which occurred outside marriage rose almost everywhere [91; 92; Tomasson, *Comparative Studies in Society and History*, 1976]. In England the percentage of all births which were illegitimate (the 'illegitimacy ratio') was about 3 per cent around 1750, about 5 per cent by 1800 and 6.5 per cent by 1850. In France, the figures were initially lower (probably around 1.5 per cent in the 1750s), but they rose slowly until the 1780s, then sharply to 5.5 per cent by the 1820s and to over 7 per cent by 1850. In Sweden, illegitimate births rose very fast, from around 2 per cent of births about 1750 to 6 per cent around 1800 and 9 per cent by the mid-nineteenth century. In other Nordic countries there were broadly parallel rises; the illegitimacy ratio for the 1850s reached 14.3 per cent in Iceland, 11.1 per cent in Denmark, 8.7 per cent in Norway and 7.0 per cent in Finland. There were also rises in Scotland (probably mainly in the nineteenth century), and in most parts of Germany, where the figure for many parishes exceeded 10 per cent by the end of our period. Only in Ireland does illegitimacy seem always to have been low, perhaps one birth in forty even just before the Famine, but the fragmentary nature of the evidence cautions against too dogmatic assertion of this point.

These changes are interesting for students of social structure, but their demographic importance is minor. In England between 1750 and 1816, for example, only about 10 per cent of the rise in all births is attributable to the increase in illegitimacy. In France, the near quadrupling of illegitimacy between the 1750s and the 1820s offset only about one-eighth of the fall in legitimate births; in Sweden the increased illegitimacy offset at most one-third of the fall in legitimate births over the period.

These are the direct effects. Is it possible that rising illegitimacy (and the increasing pre-nuptial conceptions that generally accompanied it) encouraged women into earlier marriages than would otherwise have occurred, thus exposing them to lengthier marriages and consequential higher fertility? Since around half of all first births in England in the early nineteenth century were probably conceived outside wedlock, this effect could in theory have been important. In practice, however, most women who conceived outside marriage were of roughly similar ages to those conceiving their first babies inside marriage; most pre-marital conceptions probably therefore involved couples anticipating the data of ecclesiastical union, often perhaps, following local lay custom as to when a betrothed couple could legitimately commence sexual relations [7; 91]. Overall, variations in rates of pre-nuptial and extra-marital pregnancy explain little of the overall changes in population growth rates in our period.

(iii) Variations in marital fertility

When the birth rate fell in Western Europe in the last quarter of the nineteenth century, a decline in married women's fertility was the major cause. How important was change in the birth rate in our period?

Table II shows 'age-specific marital fertility rates' and 'total marital fertility ratios' for various parts of our area. Age-specific marital fertility rates are calculated for any five-year age group by the following formula:

$$\frac{\text{number of births experienced by married women in an age group} \times 1000}{\text{number of years lived by married women in that age group}}$$

Thus, if a group of women aged 25–29 lived in total for 400 years in the married state, and experienced in that period 120 births, the age-specific marital fertility rate for this age group would be:

$$\frac{120}{400} \times 1000 = 300$$

The 'total marital fertility ratio' (TMFR), is a derivation from the age-specific marital fertility rate. As used here, it shows, for any area, the number of children who would have been born to a

Table II   *Age-specific marital fertility rates and total marital fertility ratios (TMFR) (ages 20–44) for selected countries and regions*

Area		20–24	25–29	30–34	35–39	40–44	TMFR
			Marital fertility rates				
England 13 parishes	1700–49	415	364	306	238	126	7.25
	1750–99	423	356	289	237	133	7.19
Scotland national	1855	427	366	302	242	113	7.25
Sweden national	1751–80	455	381	330	232	126	7.62
	1781–1820	461	355	322	225	145	7.54
	1821–50	463	372	318	242	136	7.67
Germany 14 villages	1750–74	439	425	374	303	173	8.57
	1800–24	463	412	362	285	151	8.37
	1850–74	533	450	362	258	128	8.80
Denmark national	1760–1801	495	415	358	326	181	8.88
Belgium 6 parishes	later 18C	494	476	385	313	204	9.36
	end 18C/early 19C	543	464	433	329	178	9.75
France							
(NW) 10 parishes	1740–69	455	415	379	285	130	8.32
	1770–89	465	406	362	273	117	8.12
	1790–1819	444	366	288	189	74	6.81
(NE) 12 parishes	1740–69	486	444	396	326	149	9.00
	1770–89	488	481	425	296	131	9.11
	1790–1819	426	367	317	243	95	7.24
(SW) 9 parishes	1740–69	407	374	349	267	142	7.70
	1770–89	413	350	323	253	132	7.36
	1790–1819	381	353	312	238	99	6.92
(SE) 10 parishes	1740–69	389	393	370	286	140	7.89
	1770–89	398	382	352	274	138	7.72
	1780–1819	398	369	312	247	111	7.19

Note: The French figures are calculated as the means of the figures for the separate age-at-marriage groups and are therefore approximate and are probably slight underestimates, especially for the early years. Because the data were not published in a totally standard form there are also some minor inconsistencies between the different regions of the country.
The German figures are from Knodel's paper in [69]. Part of the increase among young women is attributable to rising pre-nuptial pregnancy. This is probably also a factor elsewhere.
The remaining figures are from [3; 9; 11; 17; 72–75].

woman who married in that area at age 20, and who experienced the area's average age-specific marital fertility rates between the ages of 20 and 44. This is not the same as average family size (that would be influenced by the proportion of women married in the different age groups); instead, TMFR provides a standard way of comparing, in a single figure, the fertility component of the marital fertility experience of different communities or countries over time.

Apart from Scandinavia, most of the figures in Table II are from family reconstitutions of a relatively small number of parishes. In France they are based on systematic sampling of rural areas [22], but the English figures are from a rather arbitrary collection of places [9].

Note first in Table II the major differences between countries in the eighteenth century. In most areas, total marital fertility ratios lay between around 8 and 9.5, but in England and, to some extent, Sweden, the figures were lower. The age-specific marital fertility figures show that this lower overall fertility is reflected in lower fertility at all ages, a point to which we shall return.

Secondly, there were significant differences in the patterns of internal variation within countries. In particular, England differed from most of the continent in the similarity of its figures across parishes. In one study of 14 parishes [70], no parish produced a total marital fertility ratio above 8.0 and, though two lie around 6.0, most cluster close to the average value. By contrast, there were substantial variations between different Swedish and Finnish parishes, larger than would result from random variation. And in France during the eighteenth century there were marked regional variations ([72–75; 23] and see Table II); completed family size of women marrying between the ages of 25 and 29 in the period 1720–39 ranged between 6.4 in the north-east quarter of the country and 5.2 in the south-west. In our period, as Table II shows, variations in age-specific and in total marital fertility continued, with the north-east by 1770–89 having a total marital fertility ratio nearly two children higher than the south-west. Women marrying at 25–29 had estimated average completed family sizes of 5.5 in the north-east, and 4.8 in the south-west.

A third feature of the changes in marital fertility patterns in our period is their different paths over time. In England, marital fertility appears remarkably constant between 1600 and 1800; the total marital fertility ratios for the four half-centuries between these two dates all lie between 7.19 and 7.27. The picture after 1800 is obscure in the absence of adequate numbers of reliable reconstitutions; this is particularly unfortunate given the birth rate surge of this period. By 1851 marital fertility was still around the late-eighteenth-century level, but the possibility remains that a temporary rise had played some role in the rapid population growth of the previous fifty years. On present evidence, however, changes in marital fertility were not important in English population changes in our period.

By contrast, in France, falls in marital fertility began at an early date. In most areas, completed family size of women who married between 25 and 29 was nearly one child lower in the years 1770–89 than it had been in the 1720s and 1730s. By 1790–1819, a further fall (plus the near disappearance of regional differences) left the north-east at one extreme with completed family size at 4.5 and the south-east at the other with families of 4.2. The total marital fertility ratios shown in Table II reveal the same pattern, with the figures down everywhere, and with the largest falls in the previously highest fertility areas. The falls occurred at almost all ages, but were proportionately largest at the older ages [for details see 72–75; 23].

It should be noted from Table II, however, that even after the falls, the total marital fertility of French women marrying in 1790–1819 was still in most areas only around the level found in England over the previous two hundred years. Controlling for age at marriage, for women marrying in the 25–29 age group, the TMFR for English women for 1600–1799 was 5.54, the same as for north-west France for 1789–1819, and below that for the north-east (5.70). Only among women marrying in the last thirty years of our period, as fertility fell still further, did France as a whole have uniquely small family sizes.

How can we explain these considerable variations in fertility levels and the changes which occurred, particularly in France, before the end of our period? Three aspects merit attention: 'fecundability' and 'fecundity', infant mortality, and conscious fertility limitation.

'Fecundability' comprises the set of factors which affect the likelihood that a woman will bear children if she is regularly exposed to intercourse and takes no steps to prevent conception. They include some which could have been relevant but which are impossible to research rigorously with the data available for our period (for example, effects of changes in health and nutrition on frequency of intercourse, declines in periods of separation of spouses, and reduction in stillbirths) [85; for a recent technical review see 69]. Fortunately, none of these seem likely to have varied enough to be very important in our period.

More significant might be changes in 'fecundity' (the physiological ability of women to bear children). Knodel points to a rise in fecundity to explain the increased marital fertility of younger women in his German villages between the mid-eighteenth and later nineteenth century (see Table II and [85]); this suggestion is strengthened by another finding: a shortening gap between marriage and first birth for women who were not pregnant at the time of their marriage. Netting [68] attributes much of the 30 per cent rise in fertility between 1750–99 and 1900–49 in a Swiss mountain village to improved fecundity, and he argues that rises in underlying fecundity were also occurring elsewhere in Switzerland. However, changes in marital fertility at younger ages in Sweden suggest a fall in underlying fecundity over the course of the nineteenth century.

The extent and causes of such changes, however, require further research. Improvements in health might have played some role in some areas. Venereal diseases were probably spreading in towns in the nineteenth century and must have held down fertility, though the size of differentials between countries and periods is unclear. Malaria, which was prevalent in parts of Scandinavia until reduced by drainage in the nineteenth century, and smallpox, which declined at the same period, can also limit fecundity; their control might have increased early-nineteenth-century birth rates. There is also an ingenious suggestion [58] that increasing potato consumption in the eighteenth century reduced exposure to the contraceptive efforts of toxins present in some grain moulds; the argument is, however, highly inferential and seems incompatible with at least some parts of the modern geographical incidence of the fungi.

Other aspects of nutrition have also been invoked to explain variations in fertility. Short-term falls in births, which occurred widely in harvest crisis years, have been linked to this factor, while improved diet has been seen as an explanation of longer term rises in birth rates (as in Switzerland) [68] and of generally high fertility (as in Ireland); in these latter cases a major role has been attributed to the potato, though recent scholarship views the evidence as inconclusive [12; 13]. However, suggestions that have been made that nutrition – or indeed fungi – was important in England seem implausible; as we have seen, English *marital* fertility seems to have been roughly constant over time, a finding inconsistent with improved fecundity unless there were compensating reductions from other causes. There are, anyway, two problems that the nutrition-fertility explanation has to confront. Firstly, as we shall see below, it is not clear that nutrition levels for the mass of the population did rise markedly over our period; in some areas they fell in the eighteenth century, though *fluctuations* in food supply diminished over time [43; 95]. Secondly, work which identified a mechanism linking critical body weight with temporary sterility has now been challenged on both data and methodological grounds, and recent work on the fecundity of women in modern less developed countries casts doubts on the importance of the nutrition hypothesis [see 69; 39a]. For example, a survey comparing the fertility of married women in Bangladesh showed average birth intervals only 10 per cent longer in the worst-fed group than in the sample as a whole. From what little we know of levels of nutrition in Western Europe in our period, it thus seems unlikely that changes and differences in access to food had any major effect on the fertility changes which we have observed earlier in this book.

Attention has instead recently focused on possible effects of variations in breastfeeding practices. Research on fertility in less developed countries suggests that women who do not breastfeed wait on average only two months before their next conception, compared with nearly 18 months for women breastfeeding for two years [69]. For most historical populations, breastfeeding changes remain poorly researched but recent work on England (where breastfeeding was probably the most important factor keeping fertility low) [87], and on Germany [82] and Sweden/Finland [88] is of interest.

Table III shows that the total marital fertility ratio in Nar on the island of Gotland was only about two-thirds of that of Petalax in Finland at roughly the same dates. In Nar breastfeeding was normal and extended for two to three years; in Petalax it was almost unknown [88]. Work on German villages in the mid-nineteenth century shows fertility implications of breastfeeding to the extent that, where lactation was short, total marital fertility ratios reached 10.6 [82].

The most extreme example of this breastfeeding-fertility link,

Table III   *Age-specific marital fertility rates and total marital fertility ratios (ages 20–44) for selected places*

Area		Marital fertility rates					TMFR	m
		20–24	25–29	30–34	35–39	40–44		
Sweden, Nar	1830–65	341	391	260	235	97	6.62	0.208
Finland,								
Petalax	1826–65	596	433	426	387	169	10.06	0.084
France,								
Vic-s-Seille	1690–1719	451	568	509	361	160	10.70	0.168
	1740–69	576	504	459	310	140	9.95	0.282
	1790–1819	483	412	333	205	96	7.65	0.453
England,								
Shepshed	1700–49	395	368	397	255	112	7.64	0.164
	1750–1824	447	344	315	256	135	7.49	0.101
Sweden,								
Alskog	1745–1820	345	337	265	174	90	6.06	0.294
Åsunda	1820–50	337	295	234	182	79	5.64	0.301

Note: The French figures are the means of age-at-marriage-specific data for age groups 15–19, 20–24, 25–29 and 30–34.
The statistic *m* indicates the divergence of an age-specific marital fertility pattern from a 'natural fertility' regime (see page 234) [47].
The data are taken from [63; 67; 74; 80; 88].

however, was in France, the widespread use of wet nurses (especially among urban populations), and short periods of breastfeeding (revealed by contemporary comment and by the seasonal patterns of infant mortality), were major factors in the high fertility of some areas in the eighteenth century [e.g. van de Walle in 91]. Detailed research on the Swedish/German model is limited for France but Flandrin [24], in particular, has argued that a rise in breastfeeding contributed significantly to the falls in infant mortality and fertility in the late eighteenth century. Similar arguments may be relevant elsewhere, though for most countries it has not been convincingly demonstrated that the well-documented medical concern over the problem of artificial feeding produced changes in actual behaviour; changes in the age pattern of infant mortality in parts of Sweden would be compatible with this interpretation [43], but apparent continued indifference elsewhere even after the mid-nineteenth century would not [43d; 43g; 86; 52].

Infant mortality declines were widespread in our period and, assuming reasonable periods of lactation, this should also have produced a more direct effect on fertility, though the precise impact of such changes requires further research. It is clear, however, that in France the areas of highest fertility had infant mortality rates at least 50 per cent above those of low fertility areas; as infant mortality fell over the later eighteenth and early nineteenth century so too did fertility; the one exceptional area, Brittany (where fertility rose), also showed an increase in infant deaths [24].

The third possible influence on marital fertility we must consider is deliberate attempts at contraception. Swedish/Finnish and German evidence shows that some women understood the contraceptive effects of prolonged breastfeeding [86; 43d] and, while mechanical techniques were unimportant, in many areas *coitus interruptus* (withdrawal before ejaculation) and abortion were clearly options open to couples who wished to restrict family size [90; 88].

There are, however, few areas where evidence on conscious use of fertility limitation is unambiguous. One such is Vic-sur-Seille, a small town in north-east France where, as can be seen from Table III, marital fertility fell significantly between marriages of the turn of the eighteenth century and marriages one hundred years later [74]. The total marital fertility ratio fell from 10.70 to 7.65, a decline of some 28 per cent; the decline was steady, and is notable because it began even before 1750 and was statistically large enough for random fluctuations to be ruled out as a possible alternative explanation.

How do we know that conscious fertility limitation was involved? Firstly, as Table III shows, it was especially among older women that marital fertility fell; this suggests attempts to 'stop' having further children once a target level had been reached (as happens with most married couples in Western societies today). In a 'natural fertility' regime (where couples make no attempt to control fertility on the basis of the number of previous births) the curve of age-specific fertility falls steadily over a woman's life as her biological fecundity declines (see the curve for the 1670–1719 cohort in Figure 3). By contrast, when older women limit their fertility, the curve tends towards an inverted S-shape, with a steep fall in the middle years of marriage (as in the 1790–1819 curve). A statistic (m) has been developed to indicate the divergence of an

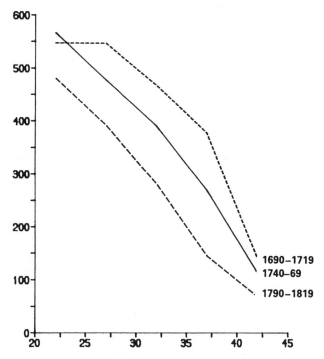

Figure 3 *Age-specific marital fertility rates of women marrying before age 25, Vic-sur-Seille, 1670–1719 to 1790–1819*

age-specific marital fertility pattern from a 'natural fertility' regime. With no fertility limitation the statistic approximates to 0.0, but m values of over 0.2 or 0.3 are taken to indicate limitation. As Table III shows, the m values for Vic-sur-Seille move away from 'natural fertility' at an early date.

Could disease, poor nutrition, a spread of prolonged breast-feeding or even disruption of married life during wartime, have produced the changes in fertility in Vic-sur-Seille? This is unlikely since it is particularly the older women who were affected and the later birth intervals which were prolonged. Of women marrying at ages 20–24 in 1720–69, 27 per cent had had their last child by age 35, but a quarter of women marrying at these ages in 1770–1818 had already stopped by 30. Median ages at the birth of last child fell from 40.5 to 36.7. Moreover, in the last period, younger marrying women had much lower fertility in their thirties than older marrying women. This is compatible with younger marriers having achieved their target family sizes and seeking to limit further births; it also reduces the possibility that the whole cohort was struck by disease or nutritional problems. Finally, the fertility of the literate (and presumably healthier and better off) fell more rapidly than that of their illiterate peers, not the predicted pattern if nutrition or disease were important.

This kind of evidence for fertility limitation appears in certain places in our area for even earlier dates. The Genevan bourgeoisie had total marital fertility ratios around 6.5 soon after 1700; women marrying in their early twenties had their last child on average at age 34; their mean last birth interval was 51 months [71]. Members of the French elite showed equally early fertility limitation (Levy and Henry, *Population*, 1960). In parts of rural France, limitation appears in marriages of the mid-eighteenth century. Average completed family size in rural areas was around 6.2 for marriages of 1720–39, 6.0 for marriages of 1740–69 and 5.6 for marriages of 1770–89. The years following 1789 showed a marked acceleration of this fall [72–75].

Could England's generally low fertility have been due to widespread fertility limitation within marriage? Almost certainly not. English marital fertility changed very little over the period 1600–1799 and a study of fourteen reconstituted parishes shows no contraceptive pattern in any of them when the period 1600–1799 is taken as a whole [70] (though this is, perhaps, hardly surprising). Where some signs of limitation occurred, as in Colyton between 1647 and 1719 (Wrigley, *Economic History Review*, 1966), the effects are not marked, and may even stem from random fluctuations due to the small numbers of events observed. Even for the framework knitting village of Shepshed [63], a careful inspection of the figures in Table III suggests a picture less clear than has been claimed.

Elsewhere in Europe the pattern is variable. A study of fifteen German villages in the century before 1850 shows evidence of limited fertility control before 1800 in only one, with two more showing some restriction among women marrying between 1825 and 1849 [82; 84]. Only in these two latter cases, moreover, is the restriction marked, with m values of 0.34 and 0.37. However, the lowest age at birth of last child for 1825–49 was only 37.9 and the longest average last birth interval 48 months. We may thus conclude that in Germany active birth control was only beginning by 1850; it did not play much role in our period.

By contrast, in Sweden, fertility restriction may have been more important from an earlier date. In Alskog, on Gotland, average completed family size for marriages of 1795–1820 was only 4.3 and the patterns of age-specific marital fertility rate (see Table III) are compatible with deliberate family limitation. Though the low fertility rates of women in their twenties might reflect the extended breastfeeding common in that part of Sweden, the differences between the fertility in their thirties of younger and older marrying women is clearly indicative of a desire to restrict family size (see [80]).

Similar evidence exists for other areas. In Åsunda in east central Sweden in the early nineteenth century age-specific marital fertility was very low at all ages; the total marital fertility ratio was 5.21 for women born in 1804–6 and average completed family size was 4.2. Breastfeeding cannot be the explanation here since the mean age at birth of last child was 36.5 [66]. However, Eriksson and Rogers are tentative about explanations for this low fertility, suggesting that almost total abstinence from intercourse (once desired family size was achieved) may have been common in an area where most marriages were arranged and couples may have had little physical or emotional attraction to each other.

This idea merits further consideration, though it is difficult to research definitively. It is clear that there were other areas (parts of Germany, for example) where deaths of older children in a family increased the subsequent fertility of the parents [83]. This suggests that couples were not reproducing at their biological maximum and that some element of choice was involved. Possibly, interpersonal attitudes changed during our period so that by 1850 (if not before) couples were really choosing on a personal basis either how much sex to have (fully realising the consequences) or even how many children to have. Flandrin's beliefs that much of the French fertility decline stemmed from changed ideas about the status of women and children [24], and various impressionistic hints that certain groups adopted a more pleasure-seeking attitude to sex [61; 65], are both compatible with this position. Fertility, however, would remain high even under these circumstances unless the costs and benefits of small families improved. Only for a few groups in our period does this seem to have become the case.

(iv) Changes in marriage patterns

The final factor to be discussed is marriage, both the ages at which women married and the proportions who did so. Recent work has strongly emphasised the significance of these variables as the most important general mechanism of constraint in largely pre-contraceptive societies, and also as key variables in changes over time. The importance of a peculiarly Western European marriage pattern as a constraint on population growth was first noted by Hajnal [2a]. Hajnal pointed out that in the later nineteenth century Western Europe was characterised by a pattern which, when compared with Eastern Europe and with most of the non-European world, showed markedly delayed marriage (average ages at first marriage for women being in their mid-twenties) and relatively high levels of celibacy (with typically 10–20 per cent of women not marrying within their fertile period). Subsequent work has suggested that in the mid-nineteenth century well over half of women's total potential fertility was being 'lost' in most countries through celibacy and delayed marriage.

Similar patterns go back in most places to medieval times or even earlier and certainly dominate the whole of our region in our period. For example, in France, women born around 1700 had a mean age of first marriage of 25 or 26 and about 8 per cent of women did not marry before the end of their fertile period; a roughly similar pattern was present in England and Sweden. Within all these countries, however, there was considerable variability between different social groups. This pattern is clearest in the Nordic countries where, partly because of superior records, the greatest effort has been made to differentiate between the experiences of different sections of the population. A number of Scandinavian studies have shown a clear tendency for lower class men to marry somewhat older wives than did the higher social groups; in a number of places a high proportion of the poorest groups actually married women older than themselves, and there is some evidence that this practice consciously reflected a desire to hold down completed family sizes [e.g. 79; 67].

The crucial importance of marriage patterns in changing national birth rates has been most dramatically demonstrated for England. In their original work on this topic Wrigley and Schofield [7; 9] suggested that the proportions never marrying fell from about 27 per cent for cohorts born around 1650 to about 10 per cent of the group born in the 1700s and below 5 per cent of those born around 1740. A subsequent rise still left the figure below 10 per cent for all groups born before 1800, and only a little higher for the rest of our period. In parallel, reconstitutions showed the mean age of marriage for women falling from about 26.8 years for the cohort born around 1640 to a low of 23.8 for those born around 1790, then rising rapidly among those who married in the second quarter of the nineteenth century. The combined effect of these changes, Wrigley and Schofield argued, explained over 80 per cent of the rise in fertility between the late seventeenth and the early nineteenth centuries (and nearly three-fifths of all the rise in population growth).

Unfortunately, there are uncertainties in the parish register data for this period, the age at marriage data come from just thirteen reconstitutions, and the proportions never married are estimated by a method which makes some substantial assumptions. More recently, Weir (*Journal of Family History*, 1984) has shown by simulation techniques that Wrigley and Schofield's estimates of birth rates, ages at marriage, and proportions never marrying are not consistent with each other, particularly for groups born around 1740 and around 1790.

Schofield [56] has taken up this point, conceding that the calculated ages at marriage for the later cohorts are the most fragile. He has produced revised estimates that involve only small changes in proportions ever married. But the revised figures stress even more strongly the crucial role of variations in the age of female first marriage as a cause of eighteenth-century population growth. In the revised figures mean age at marriage falls from 25.3 for women born around 1716 to 22.6 for women born around 1791 (the falls are particularly due to rising proportions of women marrying at young ages – see [57]); there is then a sharp rise to 25.3 for the 1816 birth cohort.

An even greater liberalisation of marriage patterns, with even more dramatic consequences, has frequently been suggested for Ireland. In particular, Connell [12] suggested that the principal cause of the rapid Irish population growth of the eighteenth and early nineteenth century was a low age of marriage which in turn produced very high levels of fertility. Connell's evidence for the eighteenth century was almost entirely of an anecdotal kind and his views have been strongly criticised (see Drake, *Economic History Review*, 1963) on the grounds that they are contradicted by the marriage age evidence which can be deduced from the 1841 census. Connell himself, however, was not unaware of this objection, and more recent scholarship has tended to support his belief that the decades immediately preceding the 1845 famine had seen a slowing of population growth associated with a rising age of marriage (for a discussion see [13]). If this was indeed so, then a mean age of marriage in the very early twenties in the later eighteenth century, but rising during the following decades, would still remain the most plausible cause of the extremely rapid population expansion in Ireland in the first half of our period.

In the case of England and Ireland, then, changing marriage patterns have been seen as a major element accelerating population growth in the eighteenth century and slowing it in the nineteenth. Elsewhere, however, changes in marriage behaviour over the first two-thirds of our period seem on balance to have acted as a brake on population growth. Extensive data for France show a mean age at first marriage for women rising by around one year over the second half of the eighteenth century, then falling back in the early decades of the nineteenth. In parallel, the proportion of women dying unmarried after the age of 50 rose from about 8 per cent of those born around 1700 to about 13 per cent of women born a century later; there then followed a small fall as fertility limitation within marriage became increasingly the prime French method of population control [76; 77]. By contrast, in Sweden, a slow rise in celibacy in the eighteenth century accelerated over the early decades of the nineteenth so that some 19 per cent of women born around 1850 remained unmarried, this being a significant factor reducing Swedish population growth over the later years of the century. The age of marriage seems also on average to have risen, though not by enough to be of much demographic significance. A

similar pattern of rising celibacy seems to have occurred in Norway
and (at least outside Flanders) in Belgium.

(v) Conclusions

Fertility was a key variable in the differing patterns of population
growth in Europe in our period. In different places, and among
different groups of the population, however, the mechanisms
underlying fertility change were rather different. The extent to
which these differences reflect different economic and social
structures and transformations will be taken up in the last two
chapters of this book.

7
Mortality

Recent research has played down the significance of mortality as the key determinant of European growth rates in our period. Nevertheless, its widespread fall remains important, though explaining it still poses considerable problems. However, one frequent cause of difficulties can largely be discounted. The crude death rate is often a poor indicator of mortality experience because it fails to allow for changes in the proportions of populations which are in the highest risk age groups. Fortunately, in our period, the limited evidence on age-specific mortality rates suggests that the major trends and turning points in mortality are well reflected by crude death rate changes, though some fluctuations in the crude rate may be due to these 'compositional effects'.

(i) Crisis mortality

Much early work focused on changes in 'crisis mortality'. Flinn [3; 41] argued that crises dominated the demographic system of Early Modern Europe, with about 3 per cent of the population dying in a 'normal' year but, perhaps as often as once a decade, this level doubling or trebling; more rarely, over restricted areas, a third or more of the population might die. For Flinn, a reduction of the incidence and severity of these mortality surges was crucial to the death rate fall of our period.

As we saw earlier, before 1700 epidemic disease was a major crisis killer and even after 1720, when plague finally disappeared from our area, local epidemics of smallpox, dysentery, typhus, measles and influenza continued. Occasionally, as in England in

1741–2, these local surges in infection spread widely enough to produce a significant crisis on a national scale. However, the greatest national mortality disasters of the Early Modern period were associated not with disease but with warfare and famine, both of which often brought epidemics in their train. The Great Northern War of 1700–21, with the disease and disruption to food supplies that followed, probably killed 20 per cent of the population of Sweden [18]. In the famines of the 1690s at least a fifth of the population of Finland, and perhaps 10 per cent of Scots, died [18; 11]. France lost around two million people in the crisis of 1693–4, and another million in 1709–10 [23].

This, however, was the last nation-wide subsistence crisis in France, though there were at least six regional crises before 1815, and food shortages occurred quite frequently right up to 1853. Some reduction in the severity of national mortality crises also occurred elsewhere, especially after the 1770s. Indeed, by the early nineteenth century, even major military operations or harvest failures often passed without serious consequences. Thus, the European-wide harvest shortages of 1816 doubled or trebled grain prices but there were major surges in mortality only in Switzerland and southern Germany, and then only of around 60 per cent above normal [45]. Prompt administrative action prevented catastrophe after the serious harvest shortages in Scotland and Sweden in 1782–3 [11; 43]; it also saved Scotland and Belgium from disaster after the potato failure of the 1840s. Except in parts of Scandinavia (where there were also problems in the 1770s and 1780s), improved army administration and tactics meant that even the vast military operations of 1792–1815 did not hit the civilian populations in the manner of the wars of a century earlier [41].

We can get some idea of the scale of crisis mortality if we compare the peak annual crude death rate in any decade with the median figure for that decade. In England between 1700 and 1750, the peaks exceeded the medians by between 17 per cent and 42 per cent; the average of the five decades was 27 per cent. For 1750–99, by contrast, no decade had a peak more than 18 per cent above its median, and the average excess was only 10 per cent; for 1800–49 the maximum excess was just 12 per cent and the average only 7 per cent (computed from [71]). Even brief crises were declining in England in this period. In only fourteen separate *months* between 1750 and 1799 did mortality move more than 25 per cent above a 25-year moving average trend. In the next half century it did so on just four occasions. Nevertheless, local mortality surges continued even in England. Precise over-time comparisons are difficult because increasing parish sizes reduced the chances of mortality surges arising from purely random fluctuations. However, on Wrigley and Schofield's figures, crises at parish level fell by nearly one-third between 1675–1725 and 1800–24, from around ten 'crisis months' per 1000 months observed to around six [7].

Elsewhere, while the situation improved, it did not in general do so as markedly as in England. France experienced a clear fall in fluctuations, but between 1800 and 1849 the peak death rates for the five decades still averaged 13 per cent above the decadal medians [from 43a]. Experience elsewhere was even less favourable. Scotland, in the trade depression years of 1837 and 1847, suffered serious epidemics of typhus and other hunger- and crowd-related diseases; these probably raised national mortality by over 50 per cent and doubled urban death rates [11]. Denmark, where decadal peaks averaged 20 per cent above decade medians for 1750–99, had peaks averaging 23 per cent above medians for 1800–49; only the 1840s had a peak of less than 10 per cent (computed from [15; 91]). The Swedish death rate doubled in the epidemics and hunger following the harvest failures of 1771 and 1772, and Sweden's experience after 1800 was boosted by the 85 per cent peak mortality of 1809; in no decade was the excess below 10 per cent [from 17]. In Iceland, volcanic eruptions spread ash on the pasturelands, and around a fifth of the population died in 1783–4 alone [16]. The Finnish death rate reached 60 per 1000 for 1809–10 and the failure of the potato in the late 1840s caused a further surge [43b]. In Ireland, in the same period, the potato crisis probably killed, directly or indirectly, over a million people [47].

When viewed across the continent as a whole, therefore, the significance of a decline in crisis mortality has perhaps been exaggerated. Certainly, by the end of our period, national or regional crises of subsistence were confined to years of major economic dislocation and, in the main, to poorer and geographically or politically peripheral areas. This, however, was largely already the case by the 1780s and had been so to a great extent even earlier. Moreover, with a few exceptions to be discussed below, local epidemics seem to have fallen only gradually. In England, 13 per cent of Wrigley and Schofield's 404 parishes had significant mortality surges between July 1783 and June 1784, and over 10 per cent in each year between July 1831 and June 1833. But even these contemporaneous local crises, in the aggregate, pushed *national* mortality rates only a few percentage points above the trend. There was, however, nothing new about this. In fact, both in England, and to a great extent elsewhere, long-run death rates had often moved against the trend in major mortality crises [7]. In our period, as in earlier times, it was thus mainly changes in non-crisis, 'background mortality' which brought the death rate down.

(ii) Background mortality

The evidence on background mortality is much more fragmentary, and we have to use comparative analysis between countries, and between areas within countries, to provide the only real clues for our interpretations.

One set of clues is provided by *changes in the age structure of mortality*. The most reliable long-run data come from Sweden where infant mortality (measured as the number of deaths in any year per thousand children born in that year) hovered around 200 for the 1750s, fell slowly until the early nineteenth century, then declined more rapidly after about 1810, reaching around 150 by the 1850s. Mortality in the 1–4 age group fluctuated in the eighteenth century, peaked in the 1770s, then fell sharply, checked around 1800, and descended rapidly after 1810; by the 1840s its level was only around 60 per cent of the 1750–99 average. Similar falls occurred in Sweden among older children and adolescents. Among adults, and particularly adult men, however, any clear decline was delayed until the 1840s, and the early-nineteenth-century mortality of older age groups was actually above the mid-eighteenth-century level [17c; 43c]. In Finland, infant mortality fell steadily over our period, from about 225 per 1000 births in

1750–75 to around 190 by 1826–50. Deaths at other ages, by contrast, showed in anything a tendency to rise [20].

French age-specific mortality data exist on a decadal basis throughout our period, but interpretation is clouded by ignorance over the age distribution of unregistered deaths. Clearly, though, French infant mortality was very high until the 1780s or 1790s, with rates of around 280 per thousand births. Thereafter a rapid decline began, to around 180 by the 1820s and 155 by the 1840s [22; 43a]. In contrast to Sweden, however, all age groups up to about 50 shared in a substantial decline; young adults were already experiencing improved survival chances by the 1780s; for children, however, as for infants, there was little amelioration before the last years of the century.

Elsewhere, information is less complete but similar trends are apparent. Infant and child mortality fell in Geneva between 1770–90 and 1800–25, the greatest improvements occurring among 1–4 year olds and in the 10–19 age group [e.g. 43a]. In thirteen English parishes, the infant mortality rate for children born between 1700 and 1749 lay in the range 169–195 (depending on assumptions about the effects of delayed baptism). For 1750–99 it was 133–165. By 1846–50, in spite of massive urbanisation in the intervening period, the *national* rate (including cities) was around 150 (after allowance for under-registration of births). Clearly, much of the English mortality decline over our period came from reduced infant mortality [9].

What happened to English *child* mortality is more uncertain. Some fall is apparent between the first and second half of the eighteenth century in the thirteen parishes studied by Wrigley and Schofield [9] (though this was mainly confined to the 5–9 age group). However, the national mid-nineteenth-century figures were significantly higher than Wrigley and Schofield's late-eighteenth-century estimates, presumably due to the rural bias in their parish collection.

It seems likely that infant mortality fell in Scotland, though the basis for this is slender [11]. Danish and Finnish infant mortality probably fell markedly between the 1780s and the 1830s [4b; 52], and the same seems true of South Flanders [4d].

In sum, reductions in infant and perhaps child deaths were an important component in national mortality declines. Even in

France, where adult mortality clearly improved, more than 80 per cent of the improvement in life expectancy between 1760–9 and 1820–9 resulted from falling mortality among children under 10; the figure for Sweden is similar [43a]. Whether infant and child mortality improvement was so important elsewhere is uncertain. In most parts of Germany, and in some local studies of other urban and industrialising areas, an opposite trend has been observed [63; 43d; 43e; Knodel and de Vos, *Journal of Family History*, 1980]; in Germany this has been attributed to increased and more continuous employment of women in field labour [43e] and elsewhere especially to increasing population densities [e.g. 63]. Mokyr's suggested figure for Ireland of 223 per thousand births for 1836–40 might also suggest a rise in the years before the Famine, but the figure seems implausibly high when compared with other areas of Europe at this date and may well be an overestimate [47].

A second set of clues comes from some unexpected patterns in *social differentials in mortality*. Peasant mortality in some parts of Sweden was not very different from that of the poor, and several local studies suggest that nineteenth-century infant mortality among farmers' children actually exceeded that of the rest of the population, while proletarian infant mortality fell faster than that of the peasantry [43c; 50; 52; 66]. At a very different social level, the European aristocracy, like much of the rest of the population, experienced improved survival prospects over the eighteenth century; for example, between 1700–49 and 1775–99 infant mortality among the children of the English peerage fell by half with a further fall of a fifth by 1825–49 [44]. Smaller falls also occurred in child mortality, though among adults improvement was slower, particularly for males.

A third set of clues, from *causes of death*, involves very uncertain ground since we frequently lack reliable information, partly because cause was seldom systematically recorded, and partly because medical diagnosis focused on symptoms since underlying causes were not understood. Even famine deaths pose problems, for few people were ever reported as dying of starvation, presumably at least in part because hunger increased case mortality from many diseases such as measles, tuberculosis and some intestinal infections [39a; 43b; 43f].

In the case of some diseases, however, the picture is now fairly clear. In particular, it now seems incontrovertible that smallpox mortality fell marked over our period, though whether from a reduced incidence of the disease or from decreased case fatality remains debatable. Before its decline, smallpox was a major killer. In Sweden, measles and smallpox together contributed at least 13 per cent of all deaths in the late 1750s, and smallpox alone at least 11 per cent in the late 1770s [43c]; by 1795–9, however, only around 6 per cent of all deaths were from smallpox, and after 1815 only 1 per cent. In Scotland, smallpox deaths probably fell somewhat in the eighteenth century, but in Glasgow it still caused 19 per cent of deaths of children under 10 in the 1790s [11]. By 1801–6, however, the Glasgow figure was only 9 per cent of all child deaths and for 1807–12 a mere 4 per cent (though, as in some other areas, there was some resurgence in the 1830s and 1840s). Smallpox deaths also fell sharply in parts of Norway and Denmark after 1800, though the disease was by no means eradicated, and the fact that Finland could produce a major epidemic in 1803 suggests strongly that the disease itself was not lessening in virulence (Turpeinen, *Annales de Démographie Historique*, 1980; [43]).

Smallpox is particularly relevant to our analysis since it killed mainly children. One review of the Swedish figures for 1779–82 [50] suggests that 28 per cent of all smallpox deaths occurred to children under one year of age, 51 per cent to children aged 1–4 and another 15 per cent to children of 5–9; in Glasgow half of all smallpox deaths involved children between six months and two years [11]. However, some scholars have argued that declining smallpox mortality was demographically unimportant, since very young children, saved from smallpox, would have died instead from other diseases (particularly measles and, later, scarlatina) [43e; 3]. In Germany, where infant mortality remained high, this could have been true, and Glasgow certainly had bad measles epidemics after smallpox declined. In Sweden, by contrast, measles and whooping cough deaths also fell in the second half of our period, further reducing child mortality [50].

On most other major killers, evidence is contradictory or almost totally lacking. Typhus may have declined somewhat but epidemics could still recur in bad years. There is no sign of any fall in water- and food-borne intestinal diseases such as dysentery and typhoid; indeed they may have increased. Finally, mortality from lung tuberculosis probably rose for much of this period, though deaths were falling in England by the 1840s; the fact that tuberculosis, which caused 11 per cent of all deaths in Sweden in 1779–82, remained so high is especially interesting because its main victims were adults, and especially older men and young women, groups whose overall mortality fell only very slowly if at all over our period [42; 50; 3; 11].

The analysis so far thus provides the following clues: there was a widespread geographical distribution to the decline in mortality; it occurred in almost all social groups; the fall was particularly vigorous among the very young while among adults the mortality reduction tended to be delayed; smallpox, an infant killer, declined, while lung tuberculosis, a killer of adults, probably increased in many areas; extreme mortality crises lessened (particularly in England and France) but smaller and more localised mortality surges remained. These, then, are the essential background facts to any valid assessment of explanations of the mortality changes of our period.

(iii) Explanation of mortality decline

For most older writers, it was simple. Our period saw substantial advances in medical education, in hospital and dispensary provision, in numbers of medical personnel, and the first major exercise in preventive medicine: inoculation and then vaccination against smallpox] [Town improvement and better personal hygiene were also important] [summary in 10].

In the 1950s and 1960s, however, McKeown demolished most of this medical interpretation [42]. With a few minor exceptions, he argued that, until well after 1850, doctors could do little to reduce mortality; this was particularly so if (as was true in the nineteenth century) the key element in the mortality decline was a fall in death from air-borne infections. Even in 1850 doctors had no real understanding of infection; before the twentieth century effective treatments were available only for a few numerically unimportant conditions; nineteenth-century hospitals were hotbeds of infection and probably increased mortality. Modern medical experience even cast doubts on the effectiveness of vaccination in the control of smallpox, unless accompanied by rigorous surveillance and isolation of contacts; until the last years of our period there was, says McKeown, insufficient coverage of the population against smallpox to be effective, and a false belief that vaccination gave lifetime immunity. Inoculation (involving the use of attenuated strains of the smallpox virus) could well have spread infection as much as it prevented it.

In assessing McKeown's writings we should note that they are based on three assumptions which have been proved questionable by recent research. Firstly, he believed that he had to find death rate explanations for most of the eighteenth-century population rise in Europe; he thus dismissed some arguments simply because they could not account for enough of the changes which occurred. Secondly, he was unable to take account of the age and cause-of-death information now available, particularly for Sweden. Thirdly, much of McKeown's interpretation relied on backwards extrapolation from often rather poor later nineteenth-century statistics, and he assumed that the eighteenth century saw the start of a single two-century process of European-wide demographic change; many would challenge that idea today [7; 4e; 43c; 59].

The role of medicine in the mortality decline must certainly have been limited and folk practices continued to have wide support among the mass of most populations. Nevertheless, eighteenth-century hospitals provided nursing care which might well have kept some of the cold and hungry alive, while the more efficient setting of fractures would have helped to get many wage-earners back to work and thus improved the nutritional levels of their families [53].

There was also increased concern by doctors and public authorities with private and public cleanliness, particularly from the late eighteenth century; however, there was little effective, legislatively supported, action, and there was also widespread evasion, at least before 1850 [43g; 49]. Increased overcrowding in older areas probably offset most of the planning benefits of new urban areas and, though agrarian reforms dispersed some Nordic populations from dense insanitary villages, relatively few people were involved. Cheaper cotton clothing and more soap may have improved personal cleanliness, but though this may have reduced typhus mortality, 'as a defence against diseases such as typhoid and cholera ... the washing of hands is about as effective as the wringing of hands' [42b, *540*]. Smallpox raises more controversy. McKeown's views have been vigorously challenged by Razzell, who originally attributed most of the English population growth to *inoculation* using the attenuated smallpox virus [49]. Subsequently, and controversially, Razzell has played down *vaccination*, using cowpox virus, arguing that inoculation continued in use; interestingly, this might have provided lifelong protection and have thus made 'vaccination' more effective than in the modern world.

There is certainly persuasive evidence of the local effectiveness of inoculation, and the introduction of widespread vaccination in Europe after 1800 closely paralleled a major fall in smallpox mortality (see Mercer, *Population Studies*, 1985). However, deaths were probably falling in Sweden before inoculation began in the 1780s, having risen in the previous half century [43c]. Deaths also dropped in eighteenth-century Norway and Denmark, even though preventive measures were not widely attempted before 1800. Anyway, the spread of vaccination in Norway was too slow to explain the mortality reduction (less than half of all children were covered before 1830) [21]; in Scania in southern Sweden effective coverage probably followed rather than preceded the mortality decline [43c].

Was better childcare or better nutrition reducing mortality? Nutritional status is not normally considered important in smallpox resistance, but, for diseases like measles, tuberculosis and cholera, modern medicine stresses its significance [39c]. McKeown [49] argued for the paramount importance of improved nutrition in the later nineteenth-century mortality decline and, by extension, for our period also. Flinn supports this view [3], pointing to extended areas of cultivation, new crops, better transportation and marketing and more sophisticated administration of food supplies. For Flinn the main improvements come from reduced starvation, but for McKeown the crucial causes were improved initial resistance to infection, a greater ability to fight the disease, and lowered susceptibility to subsequent infections.

McKeown's views have recently been questioned even for the nineteenth century, and he is vague about the levels of malnutrition involved. For our period, though there are places where nutritional improvement did occur, there are others where it almost certainly did not; moreover, generally, throughout the period, the correlation between price and mortality fluctuations is weak. It is also implausible that improvements in nutrition occurred widely enough to explain the parallelisms of timing in the fall in mortality, since the mortality decline occurred roughly simultaneously across countries and regions with very different paths of economic development [4a, 43a]. In Denmark agrarian reform and technical changes produced considerable per capita increases in food supply between 1770 and 1800 and this may have helped people to fight disease [4b]. In most areas of Sweden, however, in spite of agricultural innovations, real wages probably fell in the later eighteenth century, and in Scania the fall in mortality was slower in those places were real wages were higher [43c]. In parts of Germany where food availability increased fastest, the death rates remained high [4c]. English real wages show no clear sign of improvement between 1755 and 1810 and only modest advance before the 1820s, while agricultural output fell behind population growth for most of the period [95].

In some areas, larger average family sizes might also have offset much of the earlier standard of living improvements. Increased heights of adolescent children of London labourers, however, have been interpreted as indicating improved nutrition before 1790 and after 1810 [39b], but Scottish diet shows little improvement between the 1790s and the 1840s [6]. Possibly nutrition might have improved because the available food was more evenly spread across the population, possibly changing social attitudes meant that children benefited from a more equal distribution of food within families; but all this takes us into the realms of high speculation.

There are also other objections to a nutrition-based explanation. Tuberculosis mortality probably increased over most of our period yet tuberculosis is generally believed (especially by McKeown) to be highly nutrition-sensitive; a nutrition argument would not lead us to expect a mortality decline widely spread across all social groups; reduced exposure to infections, suggested by McKeown for the aristocracy, seems far fetched [42; 49; 43a; 43c]. However, even aristocratic children may have been underfed for customary reasons in the eighteenth century, a point meriting further research.

One version of the nutrition thesis requires special consideration: the possible life-saving effects of the potato, cultivation of
which spread across most of our area in our period. Potatoes
provided a cheap source of food readily grown even on inferior
land; they had a high calorific content and, cooked in their skins,
were a significant source of protein, of certain minerals and of
vitamin C (discussion in [4f]). By 1835 at least one-third of all the
energy intake of the Norwegian population came from potatoes,
and in Ireland and parts of Scotland and Finland they were even
more important.

Did they also provide an important insurance against grain
harvest failure, being more reliable because they could tolerate a
wider range of growing conditions than grains, and perhaps even
(as was apparently the case with maize in southern France) doing
better in years when the more traditional staple crops were poor,
and *vice versa* [3; 11]? This hypothesis is not well researched since
it needs high-quality agricultural output data. Norwegian research,
though using poor data, supports the hypothesis (discussed in
[4f]), but Mokyr's investigations of French harvest data suggest
that the potato was a *less* reliable crop overall and that it tended to
do badly in bad grain harvest years [in 48]. Anyway, grain and
potatoes were normally grown by different groups for different
purposes, and logistical and financial difficulties limited simple
substitution in bad years [47].

Moreover, there are doubts as to whether potato cultivation for
domestic use (much was grown for animal food and for spirits)
spread rapidly enough to affect the mortality decline. In Sweden,
for example, the breakthrough in potato cultivation probably came
three decades after the fall in mortality commenced [4e]; it also
seems unlikely that the potato came early enough as a field crop to
England to explain the beginnings of the death rate fall.

Under these circumstances, a number of other arguments have
been proposed, really as 'last resort' explanations. Secular climatic
changes have their proponents, but in Sweden, for example, the
later eighteenth and early nineteenth centuries were colder than
average, though after 1810 some improvement may have occurred
[43c]. Improved grain storage and more consumption of potatoes
might have reduced mortality from mould fungi, but there is at
present too little information on the distribution or the effects of

fungal infestations (particularly in the British Isles) to make this more than an intriguing idea [58].

Finally, though derided by McKeown, increasing interest has recently been shown in the possibility of genetic changes in the relationship between diseases and their human hosts as being the most plausible explanation for the widespread nature of the mortality decline across countries and social groups [43a; 43c]. A possible mechanism suggested by Schofield [42a] is that increased population mobility and greater market integration in the sixteenth and seventeenth centuries raised the killing power of certain diseases by allowing them to spread to populations not genetically equipped to resist them. Over time, however, natural selection would gradually increase the resistance of human populations while, since it is disadvantageous for diseases to produce excessive fatality, milder disease mutations also occurred. The result, by the mid-eighteenth century, was reduced case fatality for a range of diseases. Elegant though this argument is, it is a residual argument and thus impossible to verify. Also, while disease mutations can occur rapidly since generation lengths are short, too few human generations are involved for host genetic change to have played a major role.

8

Population and resources

The previous four sections have examined the various elements that contributed to population changes over our period. To understand these changes fully, however, requires an exploration of the interaction between the components, and an investigation of their relationship to long-term economic change. The model generally employed by students of animal species other than man sees short-run population movements and long-term population sizes as 'density-dependent'. As population rises, the incidence of disease and predation increases more than proportionally, while *per capita* access to resources like food and breeding sites falls. Some zoologists have argued that preventive mechanisms exist by which animal populations limit their numbers to the resources available, but this view is now discredited. Instead it is argued that animals have an inherent tendency to multiply until they meet an ecologically bounded ceiling at which high levels of disease and predation, and exhaustion of food, reduce population to a level well below the peak. The cycle then begins again.

Malthus, though not the first, is certainly the most cited scholar to have applied such principles to human populations. In his *Essay on the Principle of Population* he wrote as follows: '1. Population is necessarily limited by the means of subsistence. 2. Population invariably increases where the means of subsistence increase, unless prevented by some very powerful and obvious checks.' [35; 18] Malthus recognised that human populations could modify their ecological environment by cultivating their own food but he believed that man's ability to increase food production would always be lower than his own capacity to increase. Man's special characteristic, rationality, might allow population growth to be limited by encouraging celibacy or delayed marriage among those who could not provide for their offspring, but Malthus was pessimistic that this 'preventive check' would ultimately be powerful enough to restrain population growth. However, famine was not the only alternative check on population growth. There were other 'preventive checks' through what he calls 'vice' (he hints at prostitution, birth control and abortion or infanticide), and there were other 'positive checks' including 'excesses of all kinds, the whole train of common diseases and epidemics, wars, plague, and famine'. Indeed, Malthus seems to have seen large populations as operating under greater pressure, and consequently as more likely to succumb to a range of vices and misery.

The ambiguities yet richness of Malthus's analysis have led authors to use 'Malthusian' principles to inform many different and sometimes inconsistent styles of analysis. One approach is to seek to identify situations where populations outrun the means of subsistence and to look for correlations between high mortality and high-price/low-income years. There is, however, a general difficulty in employing Malthusian notions of positive check in this way since, for the most vulnerable sections of the population, the crucial determinants of starvation are often not the means of subsistence available to the society as a whole, but the pattern of income distribution and the effectiveness of the social welfare and crisis support system [39a; 40].

We should not, therefore, necessarily expect to find close connections between economic conditions and high mortality since many other factors can intervene. For our period, indeed, Malthusian interpretations of mortality fluctuations have in general been unfashionable; for example, Wrigley and Schofield [7] argue persuasively that the positive check was almost totally absent in England after 1700. In Sweden, however, recent research has suggested a link between real wage fluctuations and mortality fluctuations even after 1800, though these correlations seem at a local level to be strongest in the *same* year. This suggests that the crucial element may have been the weather, independently reducing the harvest and increasing mortality through disease [43h; 43i]. Moreover, since Swedish population was rising in this period, oscillations were taking place against a rising trend; any simple notion of population limited by 'the carrying capacity of the land' is thus inappropriate since, although population rose, crises did not get worse. The same phenomenon is apparent in France, and Richards (*Demography*, 1983) has argued that temporarily high wheat prices merely hastened deaths of already weak children rather than raising the trend level of mortality. How about major crises such as the Swiss mortality of 1816–18 and the Irish famine of the 1840s? Superficially these were clear retributions for overpopulation, but several authors cast doubts on this (though they adopt rather different approaches to the Malthusian analysis). Many have stressed the need in the analysis of famines to avoid judgements which employ knowledge available only with hindsight [e.g. 37]. For example, in retrospect, Iceland might have suffered less in 1783–4 had her population been smaller, but a volcanic eruption on the scale which occurred could not reasonably have been foreseen; overpopulation cannot therefore be blamed for the disaster. A similar analysis for Ireland argues that blight was an unforeseeable phenomenon and that the famine was thus exogenously induced [37]. In the Irish case, however, others have replied that only an overpopulated society would have been so dependent on a single crop and have noted that there had been sixteen partial potato failures between 1800 and 1844; there is, however, debate over whether these can legitimately be treated as warnings [see 13].

Doubt on the overpopulation of Ireland has also been cast by direct international comparisons of the availability of resources per head, and of their links to population growth. Ireland was not, in European terms, particularly densely populated and, after the Famine, lower population did not markedly increase living standards. In addition, on Mokyr's figures at least, there is no clear direct connection between density and/or poverty in any region and higher than average levels of infant mortality [47].

A Malthusian retort might be that a less populated Ireland would have been wealthier, have had better food reserves, and have been able to move more food to the starving. Clearly, the development of improved transportation and marketing did reduce famine in Europe in the eighteenth century, with the result that higher population densities could be supported [3]. Lack of surplus for storage (plus the fact that potatoes could not be stored) was obviously important in Finland, while transport distance was crucial for Iceland, and post-war disorganised markets played a part in the central European crisis of 1816–17 [43b; 16; 45]. However, as Boserup has pointed out, transport improvements and market development may in part be 'stimulated' by high population density [38]; also, high-density populations, being more difficult to control if they rioted, were more likely to engender organised assistance by elites. The connection between population density and famine relief is thus ambiguous.

Ireland, however, had food. In the early 1840s a quarter of her total agricultural output was exported, enough to feed more than a million people [48]. Exports continued even in the famine years, but they were mainly grain from the capitalist farms of the east. To a great extent, then, the problem in Ireland, Finland and the Scottish Highlands, was not so much of inadequate food in normal times as of more general economic underdevelopment, poor administrative and marketing infrastructure, and unequal distribution of resources. Ireland, argues Mokyr, starved because she was poor, but the poverty stemmed from lack of investment and low labour productivity rather than overpopulation [47].

Malthus's arguments may also apply to non-crisis situations. The model is a dynamic, self-equilibrating one, in which rising population reduces living standards and subsequent readjustment may come either through preventive checks or, more drastically, through increased mortality. Since, in either case, the link is through reduced access to resource-generating niches in society (or, more directly, through reduced income within them), much attention has focused on possible changes over time in the direct connections between population levels and resources.

The establishment of reliable measures of overpopulation and its consequences is difficult. A valuable synthesis is provided by Grigg [37]; he investigated a number of 'symptoms of over-population' including increased landlessness, subdivided farms, rising rents and falling wages, and ploughing of marginal land. Grigg's conclusion for our period is that population increase imposed considerable stress on the means of subsistence in most of Western Europe; by the 1820s and 1830s there was widespread evidence of overpopulation. Grain prices rose and real

wages were widely depressed, often only recovering to their
1750s levels around the end of our period; in many areas (and
particularly in parts of France, Ireland and much of Germany)
subdivision of farming units was rampant; landlessness became a
major concern in much of Scandinavia; in Belgium and parts of
Germany, and probably widely elsewhere on the continent,
urban workers experienced a deterioration in the quality and
range, and arguably also the quantity, of their diets. Yet major
crisis was largely avoided. Even the Irish Famine should, in
Grigg's view, be attributed to a great extent to the incompetence
and indifference of the British government's attempts to organise
relief. So, if overpopulation was widespread, how did Europe
escape?

One safety valve for overpopulation is temporary or permanent
emigration, but, as we have seen, it was not widely used until after
the end of our period (except, perhaps significantly, in Ireland).
The situation of the peasantry in some areas, and particularly in
France, was helped by a reduction in the incidence of taxation as a
result of the reduction of feudal privileges during the period of
Revolutionary rule; the extent and effects of these changes are,
however, poorly researched and it is difficult to assess their full
significance. A third ameliorating factor was the movement of
underemployed masses to the towns, where mortality was much
higher, but this, certainly by the end of our period, played only a
small role in reducing population pressure.

Instead, four other routes saved most of the continent from
calamity. Firstly, as Malthus himself recognised, in 1750 most of
the people of our area were living at significantly above a 'subsistence' level. In England, the population stagnation of the
previous hundred years had been accompanied by slow but
significant economic growth and by rising agricultural productivity; as a result, living standards had risen somewhat and could
be squeezed in the later eighteenth century without disaster striking
most of the population. A similar cushion was widely available
elsewhere as a result of the demographic crises of the first half of
the century, and through the still widely available possibilities of
taking new lands into intensive cultivation by land reclamation and
improved drainage or by carving out new plots from the forests. As
a result, the full rigour of demographic pressures generally struck

only after the Napoleonic wars, and even then were mitigated by further expansions of the cultivated area.

Secondly, in many areas a significant expansion of previously very low levels of non-agricultural employment provided incomes for those for whom there was no room on the land; because much of the new employment focused on exportable commodities, it allowed substantial imports of basic foodstuffs and thus provided a growing section of the population with the means of subsistence by routes which Malthus largely ignored. By 1850, as a result, economic growth was faster almost everywhere than population growth itself, and average living standards were rising. The areas which experienced the greatest population pressures during our period mostly lacked major industrial expansion. Ireland, indeed, suffered some de-industrialisation as cotton and linen came under competition from mainland Britain [47].

This would not have mattered if Irish agricultural output had expanded rapidly enough to feed the growing population. Boserup has argued [38] that population pressure is the greatest stimulus to agricultural change and particularly to the development of higher productivity, more intensive agriculture. This was clearly a third factor at work in our period, as rising demand across the continent encouraged both peasants and landowners to alter methods of land holding and utilisation and, particularly, to reduce the extent of fallow through the introduction of new crops and the break-up of communal systems of farming; the widespread adoption of the potato was a popular response of a similar kind.

Agricultural innovation, however, normally requires profitable markets and thus a strong cash demand for food and this was by no means everywhere apparent; certainly progress was often desperately slow, particularly in areas dominated by large numbers of small peasant landholders. In many places, had the potato not become available, it is not clear that alternative, more investment-intensive forms of enhanced food production would have developed. More likely, population growth would have slowed, either through catastrophic mortality of the kind that occurred in the late seventeenth century, or through increased operation of the preventive check. It is indeed an interesting observation on Boserup's analysis that some scholars have suggested that population pressures in France in this period, associated as they were with high density and very small landholdings, may actually have discouraged the consolidation and enclosure of open fields because of fears about the lack of viability of the ensuing plots.

The preventive check was the fourth escape route in our period, and a vital one since it kept population growth in most areas well below that of the currently developing world and thus allowed economic growth to take most of the strain of growing numbers. A cultural (and at times a legal [4c, *21*]) requirement that one should have a niche in society before entering into 'licensed' procreation meant, as we have seen in an earlier section, that late marriage and widespread celibacy were a traditional Western European device by which population and resources were maintained in some rough kind of balance [7]. Was this preventive check also variable in response to population pressure?

Certainly, in Sweden, there are suggestions that the rising celibacy of the eighteenth century was a response to population pressure, and it also seems possible that fertility limitation through nuptiality and contraception was being employed in some densely populated parts of the Netherlands by the 1840s. Some scholars have argued that the emergence of fertility limitation in France in the eighteenth century represented a different kind of phenomenon from the widespread fertility reductions of a century later, and that it had Malthusian origins. Dupaquier [23] has pointed to the rising age at marriage in France in the eighteenth century, and its parallels with falling real wages and extending subdivision; nuptiality changes were, he suggests, a traditional reaction to population pressure. However, as Wrigley has recently argued [59], even in the later eighteenth century they were inadequate to keep population growth within reasonable bounds and they were dramatically overthrown by the encouragement to marriage produced by the exemption of married men from military service during the Napoleonic wars. Under these circumstances, deliberate fertility limitation became the only alternative, though a further (debatable) factor may have been a desire among the peasantry to reduce family size to avoid the worst consequences of Napoleonic partible inheritance laws [78].

However, the chronological connection between resources and the preventive check has been explored most explicitly for England, where fertility limitation within marriage was not well developed in our period. Wrigley and Schofield [7], plotting long-term population growth against a real wage index, observe a lagged pattern in which population growth responded only slowly to changes in real wages. The key determinant of changes in population growth was the marriage rate, which lagged, they suggest, thirty to fifty years behind real wage cycles. Wrigley and Schofield explain their observation by suggesting that, because short-run fluctuations in economic conditions were considerable, long-term changes in conditions only became apparent after a considerable lapse of time; conventions about acceptable marriage circumstances thus changed relatively slowly. Thus, for example, improvements in living standards in the 150 years after 1620 were still raising marriage rates in the late eighteenth century and still producing a birth rate surge up to 1816, even though the real wage had by then been falling for at least half a century. Reactions to this fall were similarly delayed, so that only in the late eighteenth century did a stronger preventive check begin to operate on marriage, and only later still did population growth rates begin to fall.

This interpretation has been widely criticised [see e.g. 54; 55; 57]. The lags seem to some critics implausibly long and not as apparent in the evidence as the authors imply. The real wage index is an imperfect one and does not correspond well with more recent calculations. An 'average' real wage index can anyway only poorly reflect the changes in circumstances favourable to marriage which may be experienced among substantial sectors of the population. This is particularly the case in a period such as ours when substantial shifts of population were occurring into the waged sector, when dependence on new forms of wage income was increasing, and when marked changes were taking place in income distributions and standard of living expectations [57].

In a recent article, indeed, Schofield has emphasised rather different factors from those stressed in *The Population History of England* [56]. He suggests that in our period it was through changes in the *age at marriage* (rather than in the proportions marrying) that the preventive check mainly operated, and he suggests that changing expectations of long-term living standards may have been a crucial variable. Expanding opportunities in the eighteenth century encouraged a marriage age fall, but in the nineteenth century the age of marriage rose as expected standards of living increased with a shift in the occupational structure away from agricultural labour and into craft and service occupations. Even more important were the increased constraints on family support introduced by the New Poor Law of 1834 with their depressing effect on the perceptions of those contemplating marriage after that date.

Wrigley and Schofield's work also reminds us of the inverse side of Malthus's analysis: rising populations would increase misery, but exogenous increases in living standards would encourage earlier and more universal marriage and thus accelerate population growth. In many interpretations, this was the European-wide impact of the potato, since it opened up opportunities by reducing the minimum size of viable holdings; this subdivision encouraged earlier marriage which allowed population growth [3; 12; 21; 64; 65]. For Ireland, this position remains subject to debate, since long-term trends in marriage ages and the timing of the spread of the potato are obscure [46; 13]. Economic change could also expand marriage opportunities through other mechanisms. Schofield's recent paper brings him nearer some earlier writers who suggested (both for England and elsewhere) that marriage changes in our period have frequently reflected changed employment opportunities and especially the increasing availability of rural domestic handicraft (or 'proto-industrial') employment [e.g. 56; 61; 63; 64; 65].

The general argument was characterised neatly by Medick when he wrote [61] that domestic industry, organised on a putting-out basis with the putter-out providing all the materials and equipment, allowed 'the possibility of forming a family primarily as a unit of labour'. In contrast to a peasant or artisan economy where skill and capital had to be obtained before a niche could be acquired, proto-industrial families, engaged in relatively unskilled tasks, had few external constraints over the timing of their marriages; they also had incentives to marry (and to marry young) so as to establish a balanced productive unit and exploit peak earning capacities. Contemporary comment was widespread in Europe about the prevalence of 'beggar weddings' between 'people who have two spinning wheels but no bed', as one Swiss commentator wrote [cited 65].

Quantitative support for these impressions is weak but in

Flanders the ages of men and women at first marriage fell faster in the areas where domestic linen production was introduced in the eighteenth century than in areas where it did not appear [64; 2c]; marital fertility was also higher in the linen-producing areas. Similarly, in the framework knitting village of Shepshed in Leicestershire, proto-industrialisation was followed by a fall of over three years in the median age of marriage for women [63]. In both Flanders and Shepshed, however, the good times did not last. In Shepshed a glutted market for labour and increasing trade cycle insecurity produced major adjustment problems, and Levine claims (though, as we have seen, the evidence is not wholly convincing) that active fertility limitation was employed well before 1850 [63]. In Flanders where, according to Mendels, it was population pressure which encouraged the development of linen manufacture in the first place, the resultant demographic regime rapidly expanded population and symptoms of overpopulation reappeared [64]. And, more widely, and especially after 1800, disruptions of trade through war or the sudden imposition of tariffs, shifts of fashion, and competition from factory production frequently led to a collapse of incomes among densely populated and now largely landless proto-industrial workers; the result was widespread distress.

It was not only proto-industry, however, which offered opportunities of freer entry into marriage. Availability of new land through forest clearance allowed low marriage ages in Finland, agrarian reforms opened up new marriage opportunities in Denmark, and land reclamation did the same in the Netherlands. Any form of wage labour which does not require celibate cohabitation with the employer may free individuals to marry if adequate resources to house and support a family can be obtained. As Goldstone [57] has recently pointed out, a plausible explanation of the rapid rise in the proportion of women in England who married at very young ages is that development in both the industrial and the agricultural sectors of the eighteenth-century economy provided many new employment opportunities for proletarian workers. Similarly, several authors [esp. 60] have suggested that the eighteenth-century shift in England towards agricultural day labour directly produced younger marriage and lower rates of celibacy, but this assumes that constraints like housing shortages and decreasing opportunities for married women's agricultural employment did not have opposite effects. Schofield [56] suggests instead that new Poor Relief policies, focused on supporting families with children, may have been of key importance in eighteenth-century England; direct attempts to link such policies with population growth rates have not, however, proved very successful (e.g. Huzel, *Economic History Review*, 1980).

Certainly, we should not assume that proto-industrialisation and proletarianisation will automatically lower marriage ages, particularly for women (and see [62] and Jeannin, *Annales, Économies, Sociétés, Civilisations*, 1980). Changes in labour demand do seem to have lowered marriage ages in some English villages [63], but Swedish research shows that the landless tended to have older wives than did peasants; indeed, as we saw in an earlier chapter, their wives were frequently older than themselves [66; 67]. This was also noted in Norway by Sundt who was told that this was deliberate, with the object of reducing fertility to a level compatible with the appallingly low earnings of landless men [21; 79]. Freedom from property constraints, therefore, did not *necessarily* lead to younger marriage. Resources, and especially expectations about future living standards were crucial. The preventative check was thus a powerful and variable controller of Europe's population growth in our period.

9
Economic and social implications

The previous section concluded that the mechanisms of economic change and demographic control worked well enough in most places to prevent population growth from reducing the living standards of the mass of the population to a subsistence level. Some countries, however, and England in particular, did substantially better than this: there was real economic growth. England, in a period of rapid demographic change, also experienced the onset of the world's first 'industrial revolution', a shift to sustained, industry-led economic growth, associated with major changes in the scale and organisation of production. By 1850 similar transformations were also getting under way over much of the rest of Western Europe. Could the demographic growth have been a *causal* factor in these economic changes?

A number of scholars have answered in the positive, the extreme expression being Hicks's remark that 'perhaps the whole Industrial Revolution of the last two hundred years has been nothing else but a vast secular boom, largely induced by the unparalleled rise of population' [cited in 94a]. Others, more cautiously, have seen population growth as a significant contributor to economic change in England [6; 10; 60; 94c]. By contrast, few continental scholars lay much emphasis on positive economic consequences of population growth in our period (see also the judicious comments in [96, *chap.* 2]); some French writers, however (especially Chaunu writing about Normandy, *Annales, Économies, Sociétés, Civilisations,* 1972) have stressed the deleterious effects on economic development of an absence of demographic pressures. Our discussion thus follows the literature in relating particularly to the British Isles; even here, however, a more sceptical view has recently emerged [e.g. 94b].

England, of course, was, in the traditional view, exceptional. Taking the early 1750s as our starting point, a variety of recent writings may be summarised as suggesting that total measurable output (GDP) rose by about 60 per cent to 1810, by well over 150 per cent by 1830 and by well over 350 per cent by 1850. Output per head was at least a tenth higher by 1800, a quarter higher by 1830 and over 50 per cent higher by 1850.

Modern estimates such as these, it should be noted, suggest much faster growth in the nineteenth than the eighteenth century, and only a limited impact of new forms of production as late as 1850. This alone cautions against attributing too much to mid-eighteenth-century changes in population growth. Moreover, while new modes of production developed more slowly elsewhere, recent work on France, in particular, has suggested rates of economic growth not very different from those of Great Britain. The fact that the French economy could expand so rapidly in spite of France's slow population growth suggests that connections between demo-graphic and economic changes in this period are far from simple [and see 96].

Doubts have also been expressed on theoretical grounds. Older explanations particularly stressed the impact of population on demand. However, while population growth increases the total volume of *desired* goods and services within an economy, if these desires are to be translated into economic growth the 'supply side' of the economy must develop to provide resources which the extra population can employ to generate *effective* demand [e.g. 94b]. This requires supply side adjustments which are not necessarily forthcoming (the extra people may just join the starving unem-ployed). More significantly, for the extra demand to generate economic growth *per capita*, the adjustments must overcome the tendency for the marginal productivity of labour to fall; otherwise, the extra labour lowers the average productivity (and thus the average remuneration) of the economy. It is therefore essential that investment increases at a rate faster than population growth, and that substantial technical advance occurs; there is no theoretical reason why population pressure should induce these. Indeed, in the alternative view, it was only because they were taking place anyway that population growth could continue.

An alternative demand side view has seen the initial demand

stimulus of population change as operating more indirectly via entrepreneurial expectations. An economy where mortality fluctuations were reduced and where population was growing was likely to be seen as offering profitable opportunities for investment; resources which would otherwise have gone unemployed would thus be invested in capital goods of a productive kind, and this investment would stimulate further economic expansion [93].

However, while, in retrospect, it is clear that investment in Britain in the later eighteenth century was less risky than it had been earlier, this may well not have been apparent much before 1840. Such an analysis thus seems more applicable in Britain after 1840 when living standards per worker were more clearly rising. Interestingly, many modern interpretations also stress this as the crucial period of economic change [e.g. 95].

A series of supply side explanations has also been proposed. Rapid population growth leads, all other things being equal, to a fall in wages; labour inputs thus become cheaper. This encourages entrepreneurs to develop new ventures (though economic theory predicts that these would involve relatively labour-intensive forms of production); the widespread expansion of domestic industry might indeed by explained in these terms, but ready supplies of cheap labour should have acted as a deterrent to the adoption of capital-intensive but labour-saving developments associated with mechanised production; yet these developments, perhaps quite erroneously, play a major role in most interpretations of eighteenth-century economic change in England; regional labour shortages in areas like Lancashire may nevertheless have been enough to stimulate developments of this kind. However, for similar reasons to those developed above, extra labour will only generate growth *per capita* if it is either accompanied by an increase in the investment ratio or, in the short run, if it allows otherwise underexploited resources to be fully employed; the role of population is at best secondary.

There are, of course, subtler ways in which population growth may operate. Rising population reduces rigidities in labour markets by encouraging mobility of underemployed resources and by ensuring that there is a supply of new labour available for training for new jobs as they arise; as a result labour for expanding opportunities does not have to be dragged away from less productive employments. In England, rising fertility and improving child survival meant that almost one extra child per family grew to adulthood in the period 1800–25 compared to the years 1725–50 [98]. In England and many parts of Germany, and quite widely elsewhere (except, significantly, in France), new labour or productive units were bound to be arising and this clearly opened up possibilities for the introduction of new forms of production; again, however, such possibilities did not *have* to be taken up and, indeed, in many parts of our area such as Scandinavia they were largely ignored until after the end of our period.

A growing population also has a larger proportion of its members in the younger age groups and this is often seen as encouraging dynamism as well as providing a fitter and stronger labour force [93]. This is, however, offset by higher numbers of children, but they are less demanding consumers and, for most of our period, could play some productive role from a relatively young age. Interestingly, in England, the proportions of adults aged 15–59 in the population probably declined until the 1820s so that economic growth up to that point took place against a worsening dependency ratio [7]; thereafter, however, the period of more rapid growth coincided with improved dependency ratios but also with the onset of cyclical bouts of unemployment. The precise role of changing age structure is thus unclear.

Finally, two other effects of expanding populations have been suggested. Higher aggregate demand from larger populations may encourage improved productivity through economies of scale; concentrations of population may reduce 'transaction costs' per head [93]. As far as production is concerned, however, it seems that the technical, financial and organisational constraints of our period operated at such small levels that national population changes were not relevant [94b]. On the other hand, greater population densities (and particularly more concentrated markets) might have made feasible transport extensions and information developments (such as local newspapers) which would not otherwise have occurred. These developments would significantly reduce transaction costs across a range of goods and services and would well have been important, though the main source of improvement was urbanisation rather than population growth. Similarly, while the costs of most forms of public administration and of the provision of social capital such as water and sewerage and public buildings did not rise linearly with population, the great administrative and public works revolutions came to most of Western Europe, including Britain, only after the end of our period.

Even more complex arguments have been put forward, suggesting possible effects on demand for industrial products of relative shifts in agricultural and industrial incomes and costs, and of relative incomes of employees and employers [see e.g. 94c]. These arguments, however, are dependent on unknown factors such as a possible socially differential impact on consumption patterns of rises and falls in income. Falling incomes may, however, be offset by greater effort or greater involvement of women and children in the market economy. Evidence is almost totally lacking on most of these points.

At present, then, there is little reason to believe that population growth in our period played a substantial independent role in accelerating economic change. Once such changes were occurring, population change may have made a useful supporting contribution, especially once living standards began to rise significantly. Most important, however, was the fact that in most areas population growth kept below the rate of investment and of technical change; it thus did not positively inhibit growth. Ireland may be an exception, but some scholars at least have argued that Ireland's problems came more from lack of investment than from population growth. Elsewhere, in Scandinavia for example, continued high natural increase after 1850 did not prevent economic growth from occurring at rates much faster than in our period. We should not, therefore, use high population growth as a major factor holding back countries such as Sweden from economic development earlier in the century (useful summary in [4a]).

How about possible wider *social* implications of demographic change? Clearly, the expansion of national populations and the rapid growth which occurred at some local levels posed a range of administrative, economic and social problems; it also helped to dissolve older forms of production and social life (the arguments are reviewed for Britain in [98]) and arguably even played an indirect role in the onset of the French Revolution (good discussion in [96]). Many rural areas could not have stood the strain of higher population densities without compensating changes (for example, the supplementation of family incomes by rural industry, the expansion of forms of employment particularly absorptive of young persons – notably domestic service – the introduction of new foodstuffs which allowed the subdivision of plots, or the arrival of agrarian reforms which brought higher productivity from new forms of land tenure or labour exploitation). Frequently, these changes were associated with others such as a change in family labour strategies (which might involve either more or less female field labour depending on the area), and the breakdown of older village-based control over many aspects of social life [e.g. 43c; 43e; 64; 65; 96].

Population pressure (or at least the fear of it) also induced significant reforms in social welfare; these sometimes, as in eighteenth-century England, may have encouraged marriage by favouring married male employment and supporting family incomes; sometimes (as in England after 1834) they might seek actively to discourage family formation. In a number of areas more direct attempts were made to limit marriage (though this often increased cohabitation and illegitimate births) [4c, 19].

Occasionally, and particularly in Ireland in the 1840s and Germany in the 1820s, demographic events had a more dramatic effect, splitting families and communities permanently through widespread overseas emigration on a scale much larger than in previous periods; whether this permanently changed the social structure of these societies is, however, open to dispute. Even in less troubled times, one response to rising population which seems to have expanded significantly in our period was seasonal migration.

Changing birth and death rates also have more independent effects. Urban death rates generally remained substantially above those of country areas (and this acted as a major stimulus to attempts at sanitary reform), but they fell enough to allow considerable urban growth to take place through natural increase; this was vital in the rapid urban expansion after 1800 when in many areas the share of the countryside in total population was contracting and rural population surplus alone could not have produced the growth that did occur [5]. Another important side-effect, equally important in many countries in rural areas as well, was that most of the rapid expansion of the wage-earning proletariat could take place through its own natural increase. Europe's growing proletariat thus grew up in proletarian households and culture, rather than being torn away from peasant or craft production, with unpredictable results [97].

The most spectacular changes, however, occurred at the level of personal survival, though the consequences are more difficult to infer. 'Expectation of life at birth' (the average number of years lived) probably increased in England over our period from around 36 to 41 years. In Sweden the increases were from 38 to 46 years, and in Denmark, between the 1780s and the 1840s, from about 35 to 44 years. The most dramatic changes occurred in France where the rise was from 29 to 41 years. At the level of personal and family experience, however, it is more relevant to note the effect of this on *survival*, particularly among infants and children. In England about 23 per cent of boys born in the early 1740s died before their first birthday and half were dead by about age 28. By contrast, only about 16 per cent of boys born in the early 1830s died in infancy and half only by age 44 [98]. In France, where infant mortality fell from 29 per cent to 17 per cent of those born, survival of the 1830s cohort was roughly the same as in England; but this was a dramatic contrast compared with the half of those born in the 1750s who died by the age of nine [22]. These changes have led some scholars to ask whether improvements in child survival may have changed parents' perceptions of their children.

More generally, however, because adult survival changed little in our period compared with the dramatic improvement of the next hundred years, the impact through changes in social experiences, in orphanhood, in abilities to make realistic plans ahead, was probably less than it later became [98]. Nevertheless, the general reduction in major demographic crises clearly did change expectations somewhat. This is nowhere better revealed than in public reaction to those mortality surges which did occur, such as cholera in 1831–2 and 1848–9, or the threats of mass starvation in Scotland in the late 1840s [51; 11; 3]. People were no longer *expected* to die in massive numbers from sudden and unpredictable causes. This fact alone, perhaps demonstrates the significance of the population changes of north-western Europe in the century before 1850.

Select bibliography

This list of works is intended to provide a basic introduction to the literature (particularly the literature in English) on topics covered by this book; it is not an exhaustive list of the works used in preparing the text. The place of publication is London unless otherwise stated.

(a) General collections and surveys

[1] E. A. Wrigley (1969) *Population and History*. Still the best general introduction to the historical demographer's task.
[2] D. V. Glass and D. E. C. Eversley (1965) *Population in History*. A major collection of essays of continuing significance. Note especially chapters by Hajnal [2a], Utterström [2b], and Deprez [2c].
[3] M. W. Flinn (1981) *The European Demographic System 1500–1800* (Brighton). A masterly synthesis which, however, underplays the variations demonstrated by more recent work.
[4] W. R. Lee (ed.) (1979) *European Demography and Economic Growth*. A useful collection. Note especially the introduction [4a], and the chapters by Andersen [4b], Lee [4c], Deprez [4d], Fridlizius [4e], and Drake [4f].
[5] J. de Vries (1984) *European Urbanization, 1500–1800*.

(b) National surveys

[6] N. L. Tranter (1985) *Population and Society, 1750–1940*. A useful if uneven survey, best on sources, on migration and on economic and social implications.
[7] E. A. Wrigley and R. S. Schofield (1981) *The Population History of England, 1541–1871: a Reconstruction*. Though this pioneering masterpiece is written with great clarity, the density and range of material covered can be daunting on first reading. The overall argument can be fairly well grasped by focusing initially on the introduction,

followed by chapters 6, 7 (up to page 269), 10 and 11. Useful reviews are in *Social History* (1983), *Population Studies* (1983), *Journal of Economic History* (1983) and *Population* (1983). See also [54] and [55].

[8] E. A. Wrigley (1983) 'The growth of population in eighteenth-century England: a conundrum resolved', *Past and Present*, XCVIII. A summary, for our period, of the core of the argument of [7].

[9] E. A. Wrigley and R. S. Schofield (1983) 'English population history from family reconstitution: summary results 1600–1799', *Population Studies*, XXXVII. An essential companion to [7]

[10] M. W. Flinn (1970) *British Population Growth 1700–1850*. Mostly now superseded by [7], but still excellent on source problems and useful on economic implications.

[11] M. W. Flinn *et al.* (1977) *Scottish Population History from the Seventeenth Century to the 1930s*. Shows, comprehensively, how much is yet to be learnt.

[12] K. H. Connell, (1950) *The Population of Ireland, 1750–1845* (Oxford). Still the fundamental work on Ireland from which all others start.

[13] J. Mokyr and C. Ó Gráda (1984) 'New developments in Irish population history, 1700–1850', *Economic History Review*, XXXVII. A useful survey of research since [12].

[14] J. M. Goldstrom and L. A. Clarkson (eds) (1981) *Irish Population, Economy and Society* (Oxford). The chapters by Clarkson [14a] and Lee [14b] are especially useful on source problems.

[15] H. Gille (1949) 'Demographic history of the North European countries in the eighteenth century', *Population Studies*, III.

[16] R. F. Tomasson (1977) 'A millennium of misery: the demography of the Icelanders', *Population Studies*, XXXI.

[17] *Historical Statistics of Sweden* (1955) Part 1: *Population 1720–1950* (Stockholm).

[18] G. Utterström (1954) 'Some population problems in pre-industrial Sweden', *Scandinavian Economic History Review*, II.

[19] A. Lassen (1966) 'The population of Denmark, 1660–1960', *Scandinavian Economic History Review*, XIV.

[20] O. Turpeinen (1979) 'Fertility and mortality in Finland since 1750', *Population Studies*, XXXIII.

[21] M. Drake (1969) *Population and Society in Norway 1735–1865*.

[22] 'Démographie Historique' '(1975) *Population* special number to XXX. Contains a series of important summaries of the French aggregative project.

[23] J. Dupaquier (1979) *La Population française aux XVII et XVIII siècles* (Paris). An excellent short survey.

[24] J-L. Flandrin (1979) *Families in Former Times*. Mainly on French

family life, but with interesting if controversial ideas on fertility and mortality reduction.

[25] W. R. Lee (1977) *Population Growth, Economic Development and Social Change in Bavaria, 1750–1850* (New York).

[26] K. B. Mayer (1952) *The Population of Switzerland* (New York).

(c) Sources and techniques

See also [7, 11, 14, 21, 23]

[27] T. H. Hollingsworth (1969) *Historical Demography.* Rather fragmented, but invaluable on sources.

[28] P. G. Spagnoli (1977) 'Population history from parish monographs: the problem of local demographic variations', *Journal of Interdisciplinary History*, VII.

[29] E. A. Wrigley (ed.) (1966) *An Introduction to English Historical Demography.* On methods for aggregative analysis and family reconstitution with English records. See especially chapters 3 and 4.

[30] A-S. Kälvemark (1977) 'The country that kept track of its population: methodological aspects of Swedish population records', *Scandinavian Journal of History*, II.

[31] K. Pitkanen (1977) 'The reliability of the registration of births and deaths in Finland in the eighteenth and nineteenth centuries', *Scandinavian Economic History Review*, XXV.

[32] P. Thestrip (1972) 'Methodological problems of a family reconstitution study in a Danish rural parish', *Scandinavian Economic History Review*, XX.

[33] M. P. Guttman and P. Wyrick (1981) 'Adapting methods to needs; studying fertility and nuptiality in 17th and 18th century Belgium', *Historical Methods*, XIV. Short cuts for partial family reconstitution.

[34] J. Knodel and E. Shorter (1976) 'The reliability of family reconstitution data in German villages', *Annales de Démographie Historique.* On *Ortssippenbücher.*

(d) The general determinants of population size

[35] T. R. Malthus (1803) *An Essay on the Principle of Population*, 2nd edn [references are to the Dent 1958 edition]. Remains essential reading for all serious students of historical demography.

[36] W. Petersen (1979) *Malthus.* Useful background to [35].

[37] D. Grigg (1980) *Population Growth and Agrarian Change.* Very useful on the conceptual issues; some flaws in the historical accounts.

[38] E. Boserup (1981) *Population and Technology* (Oxford). Inspiring if controversial. In part an alternative view to [35].

(e) Mortality

See also [7, 11, 12, 13, 15, 16, 23]

[39] R. R. Rotberg and T. K. Rabb (eds) (1983) *Hunger and History*. A very useful collection of papers. Note especially chapters by Watkins and van de Walle [39a], by Fogel *et al.* [39b], and by 'the Conferees' [39c].

[40] A. K. Sen (1981) *Poverty and Famines* (Oxford). Important conceptual and theoretical insights.

[41] M. W. Flinn (1974) 'The stabilisation of mortality in pre-industrial Western Europe', *Journal of European Economic History*, III. An excellent early survey of the issues.

[42] T. McKeown (1976) *The Modern Rise of Population*. See also review by Schofield in *Population Studies*, 1977 [42a], and McKeown's replies to critics in *Population Studies*, 1978 [42b]. This controversial book summarises work published by McKeown and his colleagues in *Population Studies* in 1955 and 1962.

[43] T. Bengtsson *et al.* (1984) *Pre-industrial Population Change* (Stockholm). An extremely useful recent collection, particularly on Sweden. Note especially chapters by Perrenoud [43a], Kaukiainen [43b], Fridlizius [43c], Imhof [43d], Lee [43e], Fridlizius and Ohlsson [43f], Goubert [43g], Bengtsson and Ohlson [43h], and Bengtsson [43i].

[44] T. H. Hollingsworth (1956) 'The demography of the British peerage', *Population Studies*, Supplement to vol. XVIII.

[45] J. D. Post (1977) *The Last Great Subsistence Crisis in the Western World*.

[46] L. M. Cullen (1968) 'Irish History Without the Potato', *Past and Present*, XL.

[47] J. Mokyr (1983) *Why Ireland Starved*. Important, imaginative, but controversial in parts.

[48] P. Solar (1983) 'Agricultural productivity and economic development in Ireland and Scotland in the early nineteenth century', in T. M. Devine and D. Dickson, *Ireland and Scotland 1600–1850*.

[49] P. E. Razzell (1965) 'Population change in eighteenth-century England: a reinterpretation', *Economic History Review*, XVIII. Stresses smallpox inoculation and vaccination.

[50] L. Widén (1975) 'Mortality and causes of death in Sweden during the eighteenth century', *Statistik Tidskrift*, XII.

[51] R. J. Morris (1976) *Cholera 1832*.

[52] O. Turpeinen (1979) 'Infant mortality in Finland, 1479–1865', *Scandinavian Economic History Review*, XVII.

[53] S. Cherry (1980) 'The hospitals and population growth', *Population Studies*, XXIV, i & ii. A counter to [42].

(f) National and local population dynamics

See also [3, 4, 7, 8, 11, 12, 21, 23, 47]

[54] *Journal of Inter-disciplinary History* xv (1985) contains a symposium on English population history organised around [7]. Among many useful papers note especially those by Schofield, Lee and Lindert.

[55] P. H. Lindert (1983) 'English living standards, population growth and Wrigley–Schofield', *Explorations in Economic History*, xx.

[56] R. S. Schofield (1985) 'English marriage patterns revisited', *Journal of Family History*, x. Some revised data and a rather different interpretation from [7].

[57] J. A. Goldstone (1986) 'The demographic revolution in England: a re-examination', *Population Studies*, xl.

[58] M. K. Matossian (1984) 'Mold poisoning and population growth in England and France, 1750–1850', *Journal of Economic History*, xliv. Provocative though probably wrong.

[59] E. A. Wrigley (1985) 'The fall of marital fertility in nineteenth-century France: exemplar or exception?' *European Journal of Demography*, i (i & ii).

[60] H. J. Habakkuk (1971) *Population Growth and Economic Development since 1750* (Leicester). Still worth reading for insights.

[61] H. Medick (1976) 'The proto-industrial family economy', *Social History*, iii. Conceptually important.

[62] R. Houston and K. D. M. Snell (1984) 'Proto-industrialization? Cottage industry, social change, and industrial revolution', *Historical Journal*, xxvii. A useful corrective to some of the wilder ideas on this topic.

[63] D. Levine (1977) *Family Formation in an Age of Nascent Capitalism*. A pioneering study of English villages.

[64] F. F. Mendels (1981) *Industrialisation and Population Pressure in Eighteenth Century Flanders* (New York).

[65] R. Braun (1978) 'Early industrialization and demographic change in the Canton of Zurich' in C. Tilly (ed.), *Historical Studies of Changing Fertility* (Princeton). Fascinating but impressionistic data.

[66] I. Eriksson and J. Rogers (1978) *Rural labour and population change* (Uppsala). An imaginative Swedish study.

[67] C. Winberg (1978) 'Population growth and proletarianization' in S. Åkerman *et al.*, *Chance and Change: Social and Economic Studies in Historical Demography in the Baltic Area* (Odense).

[68] R. M. Netting (1981) *Balancing on an Alp: Ecological Change and Continuity in a Swiss Mountain Community*.

278 *Michael Anderson*

(g) Fertility and nuptiality

See also [7, 9, 12, 23, 59, and 61–68]

[69] R. A. Bulatao and R. D. Lee (eds) (1983) *Determinants of Fertility in Developing Countries*. A collection of papers with the latest data and ideas on the general determinants of fertility. See especially vol. 1, chapters 1–7.

[70] C. Wilson (1984) 'Natural fertility in pre-industrial England 1600–1799', *Population Studies*, XXXVIII.

[71] L. Henry (1956) *Anciennes Familles Genevoises* (Paris). The pioneering family reconstitution study, and the first to show significant fertility limitation in pre-industrial populations.

[72] L. Henry (1972) 'Fécondité des mariages dans le quart sud-ouest de la France de 1720 à 1829', *Annales Economie, Société, Civilisation*, XXVII. The first regional report from the important French family reconstitution project. For the rest of the country see [73–75].

[73] L. Henry and J. Houdaille (1973) 'Fécondité des mariages dans le quart nord-ouest de la France de 1670 à 1829'. *Population*, XXVII.

[74] J. Houdaille (1976) 'La fécondité des mariages de 1670 à 1829 dans le quart nord-est de la France', *Annales de Démographie Historique*.

[75] L. Henry (1978) 'Fécondité des mariages dans le quart sud-est de la France de 1670 à 1829', *Population*, XXXIII.

[76] L. Henry and J. Houdaille (1978) 'Célibat et age au mariage aux XVIIIe et XIXe siècles en France, I: célibat définitif', *Population*, XXXIII.

[77] L. Henry and J. Houdaille (1979) 'Célibat et age au mariage aux XVIIe et XIXe siècles en France, II: age au premier mariage', *Population*, XXXIV.

[78] A. I. Hermalin and E. van de Walle (1977) 'The civil code and nuptiality: empirical investigation of a hypothesis', in R. D. Lee (ed.), *Population Patterns in the Past*. On France.

[79] E. Sundt (1855) *On Marriage in Norway* [translation by M. Drake, Cambridge, 1980]. A pioneering piece of sociological investigation.

[80] D. Gaunt (1973) 'Family planning and the pre-industrial society: some Swedish evidence', in K. Ågren *et al.*, *Aristocrats, Farmers, Proletarians: Essays in Swedish Demographic History* (Uppsala).

[81] D. Gaunt (1977) 'Pre-industrial economy and population structure', *Scandinavian Journal of History*, II.

[82] J. Knodel (1978) 'Natural fertility in pre-industrial Germany', *Population Studies*, XXXII.

[83] J. Knodel (1982) 'Child mortality and reproductive behaviour in German village populations in the past', *Population Studies*, XXXVI.

[84] J. Knodel (1979) 'From natural fertility to family limitation: the onset of fertility transition in a sample of German villages', *Demography*, XVI.

[85] J. Knodel and C. Wilson (1981) 'The secular increase in fertility in German village populations', *Population Studies*, xxxv.

[86] J. Knodel and E. van de Walle (1967) 'Breast feeding, fertility and infant mortality: an analysis of some early German data', *Population Studies*, xxi.

[87] C. Wilson (1986) 'The proximate determinants of marital fertility in England, 1600–1799', in L. Bonfield *et al.* (eds), *The World We Have Gained* (Oxford). Fascinating and important.

[88] U-B. Lithell (1981) *Breastfeeding and Reproduction: Studies in Marital Fertility and Infant Mortality in 19th Century Finland and Sweden* (Uppsala).

[89] A. McLaren (1978) 'Abortion in France: women and the regulation of family size, 1800–1914', *French Historical Studies*, x.

[90] A. McLaren (1981) ' "Barrenness against nature": recourse to abortion in pre-industrial England', *Journal of Sex Research*, xvii.

[91] T. P. R. Laslett *et al.* (1980) *Bastardy and its Comparative History*. A collection of essays with a full bibliography.

[92] E. Shorter (1973) 'Illegitimacy, sexual revolution and social change in modern Europe', in T. K. Rabb and R. I. Rotberg (eds), *The Family in History* (New York). Controversial. Useful graphs.

(h) Economic and social implications

See also [4, 6, 10, 24, 46, 47, 51]

[93] S. Kuznets (1966) *Economic Growth and Structure: Selected Essays*. Interesting theoretical ideas, especially in chapter 3.

[94] R. Floud and D. N. McCloskey (eds) (1981) *The Economic History of Britain since 1700*, vol. 1. See especially chapters by Schofield and Lee [94a], McCloskey [94b] and Cole [94c].

[95] N. F. R. Crafts (1985) *British Economic Growth during the Industrial Revolution* (Oxford).

[96] A. Milward and S. B. Saul (1973) *The Economic Development of Continental Europe, 1780–1870*. A wide-ranging survey with useful, often comparative discussions of social and demographic relationships with economic change.

[97] C. Tilly (1984) 'Demographic origins of the European proletariat', in D. Levine (ed.), *Proletarianization and Family History* (New York).

[98] M. Anderson (1990) 'The social implications of demographic change', in F. M. L. Thompson (ed.), *Cambridge Social History of Britain*, vol. 2.

5 The population of Britain in the nineteenth century

Prepared for the Economic History Society by

Robert Woods
University of Liverpool

Contents

Figures

Tables

Author's preface

This is a study in historical demography written by a geographer. It focuses on the form and nature of long-term population change in Great Britain (not Ireland, for which see Ó Gráda, 1994), but it does so, where necessary, by stressing the geographical variability of demographic forms and the role of population re-distribution. Demography is a technical subject which is inherently quantitative and rather empirical in outlook. It often rests uneasily with social theory and social history, but without the detailed evaluation, description and analysis of population statistics which demography provides, one cannot hope even to begin to understand the causes and consequences of the rise of Victorian cities, the wider significance of marriage, family planning and the sanitary revolution. This pamphlet has been written for economic and social historians in a way that should prove accessible, but it does introduce demographic indices as descriptive devices, hence the brief *Glossary of Demographic Terms*, and it does dwell on the changing nature of that shifting sand created by official statistics. It is, therefore, not only a brief introduction to a body of literature, but also an opinionated guide to certain fundamental research questions to which that literature relates either explicitly or implicitly. Most of these questions remain only partially answered, the victims of inadequate data or unsophisticated theories, but herein lies the interest and the challenge.

I should like to express my thanks to those historical demographers who have provided help, support and advice on matters associated with the population of Britain in the nineteenth century, but especially Gerry Kearns, Paul Laxton, Graham Mooney, Naomi Williams, Sally Sheard, Chris Galley, Chris Smith, Andy

Hinde, Eilidh Garrett, Patti Watterson, Nicola Shelton, Clare Holdsworth, John Woodward, Dick Lawton, Chris Wilson and Michael Anderson. Finally, I owe a special debt to Alison, Rachel and Gavin.

March 1995

1
Malthus's Britain

When, in 1803, Malthus completed his chapters on England, Scotland and Ireland for the much enlarged second edition of *An Essay on the Principle of Population* (Malthus, 1803) he was able to create a picture of great variety in terms of form and shade. In England the checks to population were much affected by social class, the opportunities for employment and the physical environment. The restraint on marriage which led to high levels of celibacy and a substantial gap between age at sexual maturity and age at marriage was most obvious among sons of tradesmen and farmers, clerks in counting houses and servants who lived with the families of the rich. Even 'those among the higher classes, who live principally in towns, often want the inclination to marry, from the facility with which they can indulge themselves in an illicit intercourse with the sex'. This self-imposed restraint on marriage operated with 'considerable force throughout all the classes of the community'.

Malthus was also clear in the way he depicted the level of mortality in England and especially the manner in which it varied with the extent of urbanisation. Using what we would now call a mortality ratio or the crude death rate (CDR) he showed that while the great towns had CDRs per thousand population from 44 to 53, 'moderate' towns had 36 to 42 and 'country villages' only 22 to 25.

There certainly seems to be something in great towns, and even moderate towns, peculiarly unfavourable to the very early stages of life; and the part of the community on which the mortality principally falls seems to indicate that it arises more from the closeness and foulness of the air, which may be supposed to be unfavourable to the tender lungs of children, and the greater confinement which they almost necessarily experience, than from the superior degree of luxury and debauchery usually and justly attributed to towns. A married pair with the best constitutions, who lead the most regular and quiet life, seldom find that their children enjoy the same health in towns as in the country (Malthus, 1803, pp. 256–7).

Since great cities and manufacturing centres were growing rapidly in the late eighteenth century it was clear to Malthus that the void created by excessive urban mortality had to be filled by 'a constant supply of recruits flowing in from the redundant births of the country'.

Aspects similar to the English scene were also to be found in Scotland, although the contrast was probably even sharper. For example, in rural Scotland:

those parishes where manufactures have been introduced, which afforded employment to children as soon as they have reached their 6th or 7th year, a habit of marrying early naturally follows; and while the manufacture continues to flourish and increase, the evil arising from it is not very perceptible; though humanity must confess with a sigh that one of the reasons why it is not so perceptible is that room is made for fresh families by the unnatural mortality which takes place among the children so employed (Malthus, 1803, p. 283).

Malthus found examples of the excessive subdivision of land holdings and landlord exploitation in the Highlands and Islands. Observations were also made on how prolific Scottish women were; the advantages of the Scottish system of voluntary poor relief which obliged the common people to be self-reliant, to care for relatives in sickness and old age and only to turn to the parish 'as a last resource in cases of extreme distress'; and that 'half the surplus of births was drawn off in emigration'. 'Scotland is certainly still over-peopled, but not so much as it was a century or half a century ago, when it contained fewer inhabitants.'

On Ireland, Malthus was also quite clear.

The details of the population of Ireland are but little known. I shall only observe, therefore, that the extended use of potatoes has allowed of a very rapid increase of it during the last century. But the cheapness of this nourishing root, and the small piece of ground which, under this kind of cultivation, will in average years produce the food for a family, joined to the ignorance and barbarism of the people, which have prompted them to follow their inclinations with no other prospect than an immediate bare subsistence, have encouraged marriage to such a degree that the population is pushed much beyond the industry and present resources of the country; and the consequence naturally is, that the lower classes of people are in the most depressed and miserable state. The checks to the population are of course chiefly of the positive kind, and arise from the disease occasioned by squalid poverty, by damp and wretched cabins, by bad and insufficient clothing, by the filth of their persons, and occasional want. To these positive checks have, of late years, been added the vice and misery of intestine commotion, of civil war, and of martial law (Malthus, 1803, pp. 291–2).

There are several good reasons for allowing Thomas Robert Malthus (1766–1834) to introduce us to the population of Britain in the early nineteenth century, some of which will already be apparent. Malthus was an extremely shrewd and, by 1803, well-informed observer of his times. He was also able to combine a facility for statistical analysis with a reading of the considerable literature available to him drawn from the work of fellow political economists. But Malthus was much more than a commentator. His primary intention in the first edition of *An Essay on the Principle of Population*, published anonymously in 1798, had been to demonstrate the imperfectability of human kind consequent upon society's inability to rid itself of misery and vice. These two sentinels at the cemetery gate were themselves, in his view, the direct consequences of population's ability to grow at a rate that followed a geometrical progression while food supplies could only be expanded at an arithmetical rate.

For illustrative purposes Malthus applied Benjamin Franklin's calculations on the rate of population growth of the United States – doubling every twenty-five years – to his own estimate of the current population of 'this Island', seven millions (Malthus, 1798, p. 74). Malthus chose the United States because it provided an example of relatively unchecked population growth. After fifty years of such geometrical increase Britain's population would be 28 millions and after a century, 112 millions. But even assuming that agricultural production could support those initial seven millions, in fifty and one hundred years it would only be able to cope with 21 and 35 millions, leaving at least seven and seventy-seven millions, respectively, 'totally unprovided for', the victims of misery and vice, starvation and disease, or future emigrants.

This natural inequality of the two powers of population and production in the earth, and that great law of our nature which must constantly keep their effects equal, from the great difficulty that to me appears insurmountable in the way to perfectibility of society. All other arguments are of slight and subordinate consideration in comparison of this. I see no way by which man can escape from the weight of this law which pervades all animated nature (Malthus, 1798, p. 72).

Let us set aside the question of Malthus's logic and the manner in which he derived the geometrical and arithmetical series, and turn to that aspect of the *Principle of Population* which became most significant in the second and subsequent editions, namely the checks to population growth. Although the ultimate check to population appeared to be want of food arising from the different ratios according to which population and food supplies increase, the immediate checks 'are all resolvable into moral restraint, vice and misery' (Malthus, 1803, p. 18). Of these, the 'positive checks', as Malthus called them, included 'all unwholesome occupations, severe labour and exposure to the seasons, extreme poverty, bad nursing of children, great towns, excesses of all kinds, the whole train of common diseases and epidemics, wars, plague, and famine'. The preventive checks could largely be equated with 'restraint from marriage which is not followed by irregular gratifications', while 'promiscuous intercourse, unnatural passions, violations of the marriage bed, and improper arts to conceal the consequences of irregular connections, are preventive checks that clearly come under the head of vice'. Having outlined the reasons for their existence and described their principal characteristics Malthus proceeded to document their workings in a wide range of societies, including England, Scotland and Ireland. But before doing so he also made what proved to be another telling observation in the 1806 edition of his essay: the positive and preventive checks will tend to be inversely related. In countries with high mortality, the preventive check will not be prominent while in those that are naturally healthy, where mortality is low, the preventive check will be found to prevail with considerable force.

When, finally, Malthus did turn to discuss the population of Great Britain and Ireland he found, as we have already seen, many illustrations of his principle. The preventive check was strong among all classes, but especially among farmers' sons and clerks;

mortality was rather low, but not in the great cities, the manufacturing centres or among the lowest classes, and in Ireland, where the preventive check was weak, the situation was dire, or about to become so.

Without doubt, Malthus is Britain's most celebrated, but also most controversial, demographer. In the nineteenth century his works were at one and the same time an inspiration to Charles Darwin and anathema to Karl Marx. In the twentieth century, but especially since the 1960s, historians and demographers alike have come to regard *An Essay on the Principle of Population* as providing a model for the study of pre-industrial societies in western Europe and to see Malthus not only as one of the first economists, but also one of the great Georgian historians.

The model that characterises Malthus's principle, at least the one embodied in the second *Essay*, is best represented in diagrammatic form. Figure 1 shows a systems model in which the rate of population growth is influenced by mortality, fertility and net migration (Wrigley, 1983a). The diagram should be read in the following way: if the rate of population growth begins to accelerate the price of food will be increased thus reducing the level of real wages; lower real wages may lead to increased mortality or adversely affect the prospects of marrying which will automatically increase the level of both temporary and permanent celibacy; fertility will accordingly be reduced and population growth decelerate as it would if mortality were to be increased. The narrow-lined arrows in figure 1 are used to represent the positive check while the broader-lined arrows show the preventive check. The arrows made up of dashed lines are not strictly part of a Malthusian system while the arrows to mortality, real wages, food prices and marital fertility represent influences from outside the closed system marked by the rectangular outer box. Malthus's *Principle of Population* reduces very easily to a closed systems model dominated by negative feedback loops in which either mortality or fertility, influenced by nuptiality, provide routes by which population growth may be brought into balance with resources and prevailing economic conditions. The system is said to be 'homeostatic' or self-regulating and, if the mortality-positive check circuit dominates, to be a 'high-pressure system', but if the nuptiality/fertility-preventive check is more influential then to be a 'low-pressure

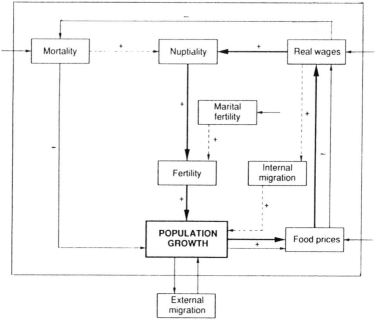

Figure 1   *A model of a demographic system*

system' (Wrigley and Schofield, 1981, pp. 454–84). The purpose of this distinction is to separate those societies in which misery and vice are endemic and those where moral restraint removes the need for a positive check. It is also logical to argue from figure 1 that if fertility is effectively controlled via nuptiality, the rate of population growth is not only kept in harmony with prevailing resource supply, but the ratio of resources to population is actually improved, food prices should then fall and real wages increase. Thus there may be not only short-term economic advantages to be had from a well-adjusted preventive check, but for those societies having persistently high levels of celibacy, there may be long-term structural advantages for income per head and capital accumulation (Wrigley, 1988, pp. 20–22). As can be readily imagined, it has proved tempting to take the spirit of this argument further and to speculate that a contributory cause of early industrialisation in Britain and north-west Europe was related to the comparative advantage conferred by the presence of a culturally embedded and thus rigidly adhered to form of the preventive check which condoned marriage only when financial means were sufficient for the establishment of a new and independent household by the newlyweds (Macfarlane, 1986, pp. 35–48; Anderson, 1988a).

Figure 1 shows three other relationships which were not part of Malthus's original principle, but are nonetheless worthy of special comment. First, in agrarian societies one would expect the opportunity to marry to be associated with the supply of farms to be allocated via the rules for inheritance. If adult mortality were to increase for any reason it should serve to release more farms. In these particular circumstances it is possible to envisage real wages falling, mortality increasing and the opportunity to marry also increasing. Secondly, migration internal to the system will be stimulated by geographical inequalities in real wages. Thirdly, marital fertility, that is the birth of legitimate children to married women, will also contribute to the general level of fertility. In Malthus's scheme marital fertility is not linked with real wages and controls on it are not part of the preventive check. Fertility in marriage is not limited by deliberate human intervention; this would be an immoral act to be classed as vice.

The final reason for beginning with the *Principle of Population* and the systems model that so neatly summarises its salient features is that during the nineteenth century ways were found to escape from the weight of Malthus's law. What we have in figure 1 provides a benchmark against which we may judge some of the most significant demographic changes to occur before the First World War. First, and of fundamental importance for the *Principle*, the association between population growth and food prices appears to have been broken during Malthus's lifetime (Wrigley and Schofield, 1981, p. 405; Wrigley, 1983b; 1987, pp. 215–41; 1988, p. 63).

Secondly, while the inverse association between mortality and real wages persisted, the latter began a long-run improvement. Mortality was probably reduced as a consequence, but differences between classes persisted and may even have been at their most accentuated towards the end of the nineteenth century. Improving standard of living was only one of many potential contributors to falling mortality.

Thirdly, marital fertility took the place of nuptiality as the principal influence on changes and variations in the general level of fertility. Family limitation came to be widely practised (Wilson and Woods, 1991).

Fourthly, the closed demographic system described by Malthus was thrown open to new forms of destabilising influences. Cities grew at the expense of villages; America and the Empire at the expense of Britain. The volume of internal migration rose rapidly; many thousands left for new worlds while others came to Britain seeking one.

Malthus could not have envisaged these changes. No one could in 1803, but his description of the race between the hare of population and the tortoise of subsistence is still of profound importance. His classification of the checks to population, but especially the stress he placed on the distinctive demographic role of marriage in western Europe, have only recently begun to be fully appreciated. He was probably unwise to lay so much emphasis on the inverse association between the preventive and the positive checks, since the two may work together, and to imply that economic as well as moral superiority could be conferred on those societies effectively using that form of the preventive check which stressed the age at which sexual activity commenced rather than when it stopped or how it was rationed.

2
What do we know and how do we know it?

Among the many epithets applied to the nineteenth century, the 'age of statistics' would seem one of the most appropriate. The first British population census was conducted in 1801 and repeated every ten years thereafter. The civil registration of births, deaths and marriages was begun in England and Wales in 1837 and 1855 in Scotland. While civil registration did not replace the recording of ecclesiastical events, particularly baptisms and burials, it did mean that parish registers lost their position as the principal source for demographic enquiry. In the second half of the nineteenth century information on the population's age structure, for example, drawn from the censuses, could be matched with data on age or cause of death from vital registration to create a relatively clear account at least of the pattern of mortality.

The availability of several guide books to sources of demographic and social statistics for the nineteenth century makes it unnecessary to dwell on the details of content, availability and accuracy (Wrigley, 1966, 1972; Lawton, 1978; Nissel, 1987; Higgs, 1989), but it may prove useful to provide some illustrations of how certain changes in content and reliability have affected the ability of contemporary and twentieth-century demographers to construct an accurate and comprehensive picture. As all historical demographers know only too well: sources condition interpretations.

First, the availability of a series of population censuses makes it a far more simple task to chart the changing size, composition – in terms of age and sex – and distribution of population. The problem Malthus had in his first *Essay* of knowing the true size of 'this Island's' population was thus removed by 1803 (Malthus, 1803, p. 14). Table 1 gives totals for the population of England

Table 1 *The population of England and Wales, Scotland and Ireland (in thousands)*

	England and Wales	Scotland	Ireland
Estimates			
1601	4,460		
1651	5,608		
1701	5,448	1,040	2,000
1751	6,222	1,265	2,250
1791			4,500
Censuses			
1801	8,893	1,608	
1811	10,164	1,806	
1821	12,000	2,092	6,802
1831	13,897	2,364	7,767
1841	15,914	2,620	8,178
1851	17,928	2,889	6,554
1861	20,066	3,062	5,799
1871	22,712	3,360	5,412
1881	25,974	3,736	5,175
1891	29,003	4,026	4,705
1901	32,528	4,472	4,459
1911	36,070	4,761	4,390
1931	39,952	4,843	
1951	43,758	5,096	4,332
1981	49,155	5,131	4,953
1991			

Percentage share of British Isles population	*1800*	*1900*
England	55	73
Wales	4	5
Scotland	10	11
Ireland	31	11

Source: based on Mitchell (1988)

and Wales, Scotland and Ireland based on the 1801 to 1911 censuses, as well as those for 1931, 1951 and 1981. It also shows estimates for dates prior to 1801. Great Britain's population was about 6.5 millions in 1701, 7.5 millions in 1751, 11 in 1801, 21 in

1851 and 37 in 1901, of which England's share increased from 77 per cent in the mid-eighteenth century to 82 per cent in 1901. Within this London's share increased from 9 per cent to 12 per cent over the same period. By 1901 London's population was more than twice that of Wales and slightly more than that of Scotland. Although it is not a simple matter to define urban places, the 1850s is by convention taken as the decade in which half Britain's population can be classified as urban. The growth of London certainly made a substantial contribution to urbanisation, but it was the expansion of provincial industrial and commercial centres, which created the great Victorian cities, that made a crucial difference to the national scene (Law, 1967; Lawton, 1972, 1983; Armstrong, 1981).

Secondly, the operation of a hundred years rule restricting the disclosure of information about individuals recorded in the nineteenth-century censuses has effectively limited public access to the more recent census enumerators' books. In the 1841 and subsequent censuses the enumerators were obliged to make copies of the household census schedules in specially printed ledgers. These books now provide invaluable information on named individuals, arranged by address and also relationship to head of household. Data on age, sex, marital status, occupation and place of birth are also provided (Lawton, 1978). The ability to consider household structure, occupation, life-time migration, and to trace the characteristics of individuals and households from census to census has remarkably enhanced our knowledge of mid-Victorian society, but especially urban society.

Thirdly, the establishment of General Register Offices in London in 1837 and Edinburgh in 1855, the need for full-time specialist staffs well versed in statistical methods, and efficient nation-wide administrations created a statistical bureaucracy with wide-ranging implications for both the collection and analysis of demographic data (Newsholme, 1889; Nissel, 1987; Szreter, 1991). For example, the compilers of statistics at the London GRO – William Farr, William Ogle, John Tatham and T. H. C. Stevenson – were men of great distinction, all medically qualified, who brought a sense of rigour and purpose to what otherwise might have been merely a matter of data collection. The contribution of William Farr (1807–1883) must be singled out for special mention (Eyler, 1979). He was Compiler of Abstracts at the London GRO from 1839 to 1880, where for thirty-seven of those years he worked closely with George Graham, the Registrar General. Farr was responsible for calculating the first official English life tables, preparing special reports on cholera, devising classifications of cause of death and innumerable other small yet, in combination, significant improvements in the system of recording, its detail and accuracy (Farr, 1864, 1885).

In England and Wales the registration system was organised in the following way. The country was divided into registration divisions, counties and districts, many of the most populous of which were further divided into sub-districts. Each registration district had a Superintendent Registrar whose responsibility it was to gather the required information on births, deaths and marriages and forward it to London where it would be compiled, tabulated and to some extent interpreted in the *Annual Reports and Decennial Supplements*. The sub-districts, districts (over 600 by 1851) and counties (45) provided the units for reporting, but convention varied with GRO interest and administrative convenience.

Farr himself was probably responsible for the emphasis on mortality statistics which were derived from death certificates. Since the age, sex, occupation and cause of death of the deceased were all recorded on these certificates, fairly detailed tables giving numbers dying classified by age, sex, occupation, cause and place of death could be created. Compared with the tables that could be derived from the birth certificates, these are truly rich veins to be mined. Fertility was not a subject of great public concern in Victorian Britain, although it became so in the early 1900s. The number of births, their sex and legitimacy was reported, but not the age of the mother or further details about her previous pregnancies, the duration of her marriage, her and her husband's occupations etc. In Scotland in 1855 the practice of recording maternal age was begun, but it was discontinued in 1856. The effects of these major lacunae on our ability to reconstruct nineteenth-century fertility patterns will be obvious. Crude and indirectly standardised rates may be calculated, but little more. Marriage was of rather more concern to Victorians, largely because of its standing in law, but here too there are limitations. From the marriage certificates, the GRO regularly tabulated the number of marriages, the form of solemnisation (civil or ecclesiastical and thence denomination) and whether the bride and groom were able to put their own signatures to the certificate. Estimates of literacy levels have been based on the last-mentioned piece of information (see figure 6 for example). Despite these various problems, the development of civil registration from 1837 or 1855, coupled with considerable improvements in the population censuses from 1841, means that it is the demography of the first third or half of the nineteenth century that remains obscure in comparison with later decades.

Having outlined the origins and development of population data gathering in the nineteenth century, we are now able to return to the question: what do we know about the changing demography of Britain?

Population, its composition and distribution

We have already seen in table 1 that the population of Britain increased substantially in the nineteenth century, but it also changed in composition and distribution. While it is no simple matter to trace the changing employment, occupation and social class structure of Britain between 1801 and 1911 via the census, a start may be made for certain distinctive groups of occupations and considerable detail is possible for the last fifty years. Of the major categories of employment, agriculture was in steep relative decline at mid-century representing only about 20 per cent of those employed; manufacturing was holding steady at about 33 per cent; domestic service contributed 14 to 15 per cent and the remaining 32 per cent was made up from mining, building, transport, dealing, and the professions and public service in roughly equal measure. By the end of the century agriculture's contribution to employment was no more than 10 per cent. These figures do, of course, conceal major differences in the sexual division of labour. Domestic servants were overwhelmingly young women while agricultural labourers were generally male; agricultural servants and the female gangs of the eastern counties of England and Scotland used especially in harvesting vegetables and root crops were the major exceptions. Those engaged in manufacturing were

Table 2 *The social class composition of England and Wales*

Social class	1881	(%)	1911	(%)	Change index
1951 classification					
I	159,756	(2)	302,753	(3)	126
II	1,089,498	(15)	1,729,865	(15)	105
III	2,972,127	(40)	4,863,747	(43)	108
IV	2,276,383	(30)	3,303,648	(29)	96
V	974,034	(13)	1,101,402	(10)	75
1911 classification					
VI	361,928		428,658		78
VII	407,532		881,716		142
VIII	740,554		595,600		53
Example occupations					
Doctors	15,091		24,553		107
Civil servants	19,556		61,152		206
Commercial clerks	173,161		353,622		134
Farmers	203,308		208,750		68
Grocers	99,434		161,528		107
Railway employees	194,541		425,588		144
Carpenters, joiners	226,214		207,253		60
Tailors	98,919		120,494		80
Tramway service	2,591		41,219		1,047
Electricity supply	2,447		98,089		2,637

The 1951 classification
I – professional and managerial occupations
II – intermediate non-manual
III – skilled manual
IV – intermediate manual
V – unskilled manual
The 1911 classification used three special groups
VI – textile workers
VII – miners
VIII – agricultural workers
Change index: $[(1911/1881)/k] \times 100$, where k is the ratio of total classified in 1911 to 1881 (i.e. 1.52).
Source: based on Banks (1978)

also predominantly male, female textile workers represent the principal exception. Most women employees, at least those recorded in the census, were not married (Hewitt, 1958; Roberts, 1984).

Table 3 *Population redistribution and urbanization in England and Wales (figures are given in parts per thousand)*

	Rural	In towns of:				Urban
		2,500–10,000	10,000–50,000	50,000–100,000	Over 100,000	
1801	662	99	94	35	110	338
1811	634	108	94	37	137	366
1821	600	109	92	43	156	400
1831	557	106	111	40	186	443
1841	527	100	121	55	207	483
1851	460	99	135	58	248	540
1861	413	98	140	61	288	587
1871	348	108	162	56	326	652
1881	300	105	160	73	362	700
1891	255	102	163	86	394	745
1901	220	89	181	74	436	780
1911	211	88	183	80	438	789

Urban plus Rural equals 1,000 and the sum of the four town size categories equals Urban.
Source: based on Law (1967)

The information on occupations in the 1851 and 1911 censuses is sufficiently detailed to encourage those interested in defining broad social classes; yet all those tempted to engage in social grading have faced considerable problems in making their classifications (Szreter, 1984). Table 2 provides evidence for the continued rise of the middle class, the growth of bureaucracy and transport services; the further decline of agricultural employment; the decline of certain skilled trades dominated by the self-employed; and the dramatic expansion of the new energy industries. However, table 2 does not provide evidence for radical change in the class structure, merely a shift of the unskilled into other occupations, many of which required more skill and certainly more specialisation. At least 75 per cent of late Victorian Britain's population was made up of the urban industrial working class and their children (Booth, 1886; Banks, 1978; Routh, 1987).

Table 3 shows the changing distribution of population between urban and rural places, large and small towns. It complements the points illustrated in table 2. By 1911 Britain was overwhelmingly an urban country in which large commercial and industrial cities predominated. None could compete with London, yet each held sway in its own region (Weber, 1889; Lawton, 1958, 1983).

Demographic change

Apart from the rise of great cities the nineteenth century was also a period of significant if not dramatic demographic change. Mortality began its secular decline, to be reinforced at the turn of the century by the rapid decline of infant mortality. General fertility rates were in decline throughout the century, but from the 1870s marital fertility also began its secular decline. The causes of these revolutionary changes are still not understood with any degree of certainty, as we shall see in later chapters; nor can their trends and characteristics be charged with the precision and confidence one would wish (Glass, 1951; Teitelbaum, 1974). Table 4 makes a start. It gives estimated series for the crude birth and death rates (CBR, CDR), life expectation at birth (e_0), infant mortality (IMR), the gross reproduction rate (GRR) and the index of overall fertility (I_f). All of the measures reported in table 4, but especially those for periods 1 to 12, need to be treated with extreme caution; they are merely guides to approximate orders of magnitude.

Despite these reservations table 4, accompanied by figure 2 which shows long-run fertility and mortality trends (measured by GRR and e_0), helps us to place the nineteenth century in context. It was a period of transition from an old demographic regime characterised by the form of system illustrated in figure 1 and associated with Malthus, to a new regime in which mortality is now very low, almost all deaths occur in old age and average life expectation at birth is approaching its maximum at about 90 to 92 years. Contraceptives are available, effective and used to achieve small completed family sizes and to time conceptions in order to maximise women's employment opportunities. Marriage is of less economic necessity for women and divorce is common. Several of these radical changes began and became obvious before the First World War; others have only emerged in the last three decades (Anderson, 1985, 1990).

Table 4 *Demographic indices for England, 1551–1850, and England and Wales, 1851–1975*

Twenty-five year periods		CBR	CDR	e_0	IMR	GRR	I_f
1	1551–75	34.94	28.42	35	190	2.41	0.345
2	1576–1600	33.22	24.22	39	162	2.29	0.336
3	1601–25	32.72	24.82	39	162	2.25	0.324
4	1626–50	31.46	26.22	36	178	2.11	0.310
5	1651–75	28.58	28.36	35	189	1.91	0.271
6	1676–1700	31.22	30.28	33	199	2.07	0.311
7	1701–25	31.74	27.86	36	180	2.23	0.327
8	1726–50	33.74	30.50	33	203	2.25	0.335
9	1751–75	34.24	27.26	36	180	2.38	0.348
10	1776–1800	35.56	26.46	37	175	2.64	0.389
11	1801–25	40.18	25.38	39	167	2.91	0.423
12	1826–50	36.04	22.54	40	151	2.57	0.365
13	1851–75	35.82	22.22	41	154	2.49	0.360
14	1876–1900	32.28	19.26	46	149	2.07	0.313
15	1901–25	24.02	14.26	53	105	1.42	0.233
16	1926–50	16.16	12.24	64	55	0.95	0.174
17	1951–75	16.76	11.72	72	22	1.15	0.188

CBR – crude birth rate
CDR – crude death rate
e_0 – life expectation at birth in years
IMR – infant mortality rate
GRR – gross reproduction rate
I_f – index of overall fertility
See the *Glossary of demographic terms* for definitions
Sources: based on Wrigley and Schofield (1981) and Wilson and Woods (1992)

It is also worth emphasising at this point that some of the most important changes in demographic structure were not particular to Britain alone. Figure 3 shows the influence of changes in fertility and mortality on the intrinsic rate of natural population increase (*r*) for England, France and Sweden between 1751 and 1981. The diagonal lines join points with equal rates of natural population increase allowing the relative contributions of fertility and mortality to be judged more easily (Wrigley and Schofield, 1981, p. 246). In each case fertility and mortality have declined since the late eighteenth century almost to the point of convergence in the late

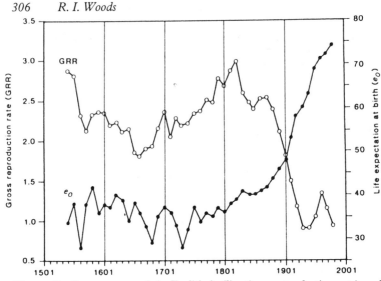

Figure 2 *Long-term trends in English fertility (gross reproduction rate) and mortality (life expectation at birth).*

twentieth century, but the time paths for the three countries so traced vary quite markedly. In France fertility and mortality declined together from an early date and natural growth remained at a low level throughout the nineteenth century. In Sweden mortality declined before fertility in a way that has come to be regarded as normal and coincidental with the predictions of the classic demographic transition model. But in England the modern rise of population was initiated by the increase of fertility in the late eighteenth century, as figure 2 also makes clear, and was only supported by the secular decline of mortality. These differences of form, pattern and the timing of change suggest the diversity of demographic structures in Europe in the nineteenth century, but they also illustrate aspects of a broader picture of conformity. Fertility and mortality were higher and are now much lower everywhere in Europe. Most people lived in the countryside and depended for their livelihood on agriculture, now most Europeans share a common urban life style.

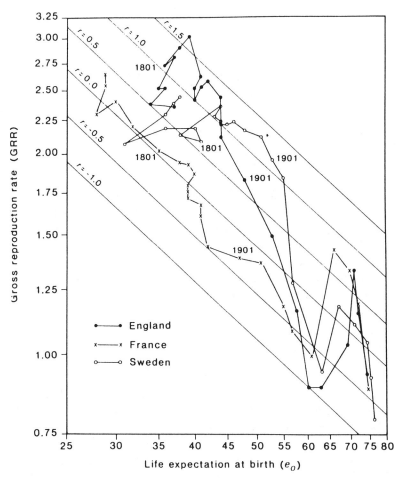

Figure 3 *The influence of changes in fertility (gross reproduction rate) and mortality (life expectation at birth) on the intrinsic rate of natural population increase (r) for England, France and Sweden, 1751 to 1981.*

3
Whether to move and where to go

In any consideration of nineteenth-century population history pride of place should go to mobility and migration, both internal and international. Not only did Britain's population experience radical redistribution, but the age-, sex- and skill-selective nature of migration also changed society, economy and environment in several very important respects, some of which will be considered separately in chapters four and six.

Four aspects are of particular significance. First, the outer rural periphery – especially the west of Ireland and the Scottish Highlands – experienced massive emigration which caused general depopulation (Flinn, 1977; Anderson and Morse, 1990; Withers and Watson 1991). Although the Irish case is often linked to famine migration in the 1840s, the history of Irish emigration to North America and Great Britain is a long one which famine probably only exacerbated (see table 1). Secondly, the countryside in general suffered net loss to the towns (Saville, 1957; Lawton, 1967). From Cornwall to Norfolk, Dorset to Anglesey and Aberdeen agricultural labourers, servants and small tenants left and were not replaced, except by machines. In a few rural counties, such as Kent, this did not lead to absolute population decline because natural growth exceeded net out-migration, but in most counties the downward spiral of decline was not arrested until after the Second World War (Lawton, 1968). Thirdly, the great industrial and commercial centres of central Scotland, the English North and Midlands, and South Wales, not only increased their citizenry, but also expanded physically until they coalesced into the amorphous conurbations so well known in the twentieth century. These Victorian cities grew particularly rapidly both by net migration and natural growth, despite high mortality. Intra-urban migration also fuelled suburban expansion which eventually affected whole cities primarily through the depopulation of their inner areas. In the cases of certain Scottish and Northern industrial towns this process was obvious even in the late nineteenth century (Lawton, 1983; Morris, 1990). Fourthly, London should probably be treated as a special case since it not only maintained its British primacy, but also its share of the total population. The new problems associated with managing and servicing such a massive concentration of people – nearly five millions by 1901 – imposed many strains not least in terms of transport, social inequalities which were made more obvious by their juxtaposition, and sanitation. The engineering problems were solved in time; the others still remain (Porter, 1994).

Of course this is a very simple view of migration which, while acceptable in outline, is thwarted by paucity of sources and complexity of process when more detail is required. In the 1991 census migration was recorded by asking respondents where they were living one year ago, but for Victorian Britain place of birth must suffice. International migration must be counted by using embarkation lists. Although the general flow of migrants has turned from rural–urban to urban–urban to urban–rural over the past two hundred years, the pattern of any one individual's moves through his or her lifetime might include many addresses and several towns or villages. Step, chain and return migration are all appropriate terms, as is circulatory movement. However, migration need not be regarded as a series of random walks; there is order in the chaos once one deals with aggregates.

Emigration

The broad picture of European emigration shows that from 1821 to 1915 44 millions left, of which Great Britain accounted for 10 and Ireland for 6 millions. More detailed estimates suggest that between 1853 and 1900 4,675,100 persons left England and Wales for a non-European destination while 896,000 left Scotland. In both cases more than half went to the USA with a further fifty to

Australasia (Carrier and Jeffrey, 1953; Easterlin, 1961; Baines, 1985, 1991; Hatton and Williamson, 1994).

Although these figures are impressive in their own right, the impact of emigration needs to be assessed with some caution. For example, if the annual rate of emigration per thousand population for England and Wales in the second half of the nineteenth century was to be set at 1, then the corresponding figures for Scotland and Ireland would be 1.4 and 3.1, with 2 and 4 in several decades. Emigration was far more important for Irish and Scottish populations than it was for England. Between 1853 and 1900 net emigration represented 9 per cent of natural increase in England and Wales, but more than 25 per cent for Scotland. It is also important to note that of the 4,675,100 who left England and Wales between 1853 and 1900 only about 2,250,000 were permanent migrants, giving England and Wales what was probably an unusually high rate of return migration compared with Scotland, Ireland and the rest of Europe (Baines, 1985).

To continue our catalogue of complications, let us briefly consider the Irish in Great Britain. In 1851, 7.2 per cent of the population of Scotland and 2.9 per cent of the population of England and Wales had been born in Ireland. The other nineteenth-century censuses give averages of 5.5 and 2.0 per cent, respectively, for Scotland, and England and Wales (Lawton, 1959). Within Britain the towns of the west of Scotland, the northwest and Midlands of England, and London were particularly popular temporary or permanent destinations. But cities like Liverpool and Glasgow were also important ports for re-embarkation to America, thus allowing Irish-born migrants to become emigrants from England or Scotland (Lawton, 1956; Lees, 1979; Swift and Gilley, 1985).

Urbanisation

Although it is now useful to consider inter-regional migration in its own right, in nineteenth-century Britain movement was more specifically to the cities, coastal resorts and the coalfields. Any region possessing one or a number of these was likely to receive migrants from its neighbours. It is therefore appropriate to consider internal migration in terms of selective urban growth and rural decline (Redford, 1926; Cairncross, 1953; Friedlander and Roshier, 1966).

Even in 1801 England was highly urbanised with about 30 per cent of its population living in urban places and perhaps another 36 per cent living in rural areas, but not directly engaged in agriculture. (The rural agricultural population of France was still nearly 60 per cent of the total at this time.) The 'half urban' mark had been crossed by 1851 in England and Wales, slightly later in Scotland, and by the early years of the twentieth century at least three-quarters of the population were urban residents. Most migrants came from the same or neighbouring counties. The rural surplus population of the countryside was often replaced if not actually displaced by new labour-saving technology or else attracted by expanding industries offering higher wages to work in the factories or mines. Many migrants, the more skilled in particular, changed place of employment and residence without changing the nature of their jobs. Coal to coal, iron to iron, port to port, kitchen to kitchen, loom to loom: this was an important element in the process of internal redistribution and economic development. Labour was as mobile and as adept as capital at seeking out and responding to relative advantage.

However, it must be emphasised that although migration was an important contributor to urbanisation, most nineteenth-century towns and cities also grew by natural increase. This was itself a reflection of biases in the age- and sex-selective nature of rural to urban migration which tended to pick out the young and active, and to leave behind the elderly or less ambitious. In England and Wales the total population living in urban registration districts increased by some 182 per cent between 1841 and 1911, of which 151 per cent was due to natural increase and 31 per cent to net migration. In rural registration districts there was a 13 per cent overall gain in population made up of 86 per cent natural increase and 73 per cent net migration loss (Lawton, 1967, 1968, 1980, 1983). Of the non-rural districts the very large cities, the resorts and residential centres, and the coalfield settlements grew most rapidly because natural growth was supplemented by migration gain; this was at the expense not only of rural areas, but of the smaller and middle-sized towns, many of which failed to expand by net migration and some were net exporters of people. By the end of the nineteenth century the rural share of Britain's population had begun to stabilise; migration had changed to become largely inter-urban or intra-urban and directed towards the upper end of the urban settlement hierarchy, or to be distinctly residential and short distance in character reflecting changes of residence, but not necessarily places of employment (Lawton, 1979; Pooley, 1979; Dennis, 1984). While the purely demographic impact of migration declined, the social and environmental legacy remained. Places created and filled in the nineteenth century have been rejected and depleted in the twentieth.

'Laws' and causes

Although we shall never know the particular form of motivations that led individuals to migrate, it is reasonable to infer some of the principal causes from the most obvious patterns of mass movement. When E. G. Ravenstein (1834–1913) defined his 'laws of migration' in the 1870s and 1880s he saw the major causes of migration as economic in nature, leading young adults to the great centres of industry and commerce (Ravenstein, 1885, 1889). In general there seems little reason to doubt this conclusion, but points for debate remain over whether the migrants were pushed or pulled, the extent to which entire families were involved, the balance between men and women, the stepped nature of the movement, and the extent to which localised changes of address outweighed, in volume if not in significance, the longer-distance rural–urban migration with which Ravenstein was so concerned (Grigg, 1977).

It is clear from both historical studies and recent surveys that the volume of migration will increase when both push and pull factors are working, but also when origins and potential destinations are well connected by both easy access and a ready flow of information. If there is no transport, only the brave or the very desperate will pioneer the route; no information and the move depends on serendipity; no push and inertia will hold sway; no pull and alternative destinations may prove more attractive. The late nineteenth century Atlantic economy seems to have provided all the necessary conditions (Thomas, 1954; Baines, 1985, 1991). The British and American economic cycles were out of phase, British slump coincided with American boom; steamships made the passage cheaper and somewhat more comfortable; friends and relatives established in the USA and Canada provided information and assistance. The same observation could also be made regarding internal migration in the British Isles. The longer-distance pioneer migrants were largely motivated by employment prospects, whether that meant rural–urban movement in the early decades of the nineteenth century or urban–urban in later years. The spread of the railway network was a great boon, but the bicycle also played its part by enhancing local mobility (Perry, 1969). Relatives and friends followed the pioneers and those simply looking for a better place to live, without necessarily changing jobs, made up the numbers.

4

Marriage

We know from earlier chapters that the preventive check and moral restraint played an important part in Britain's demography. The marriage pattern of north-western Europe was rather distinctive, not to say eccentric, in comparison with other southern or eastern European, or non-European societies. Marriage was not universal and it did not take place very quickly after menarche. Generally, it was not arranged by parents, but was a matter of free choice between eligible partners heavily constrained by social and geographical barriers. Marriage usually, at least for women, coincided with the start of sexual activity, and led to the establishment of a new household distinct from both sets of parents. While marriage may have required their approval, it also signalled independence from parental control and responsibility. However, this may prove to be a rather idealised picture. A substantial minority of brides were pregnant. Many young people had already left their parental home and its influence long before getting married. Others retained close social contacts in the same community even after forming a separate household (Anderson, 1980; Wall, Robin and Laslett, 1983).

This chapter is primarily concerned with the timing of marriage and the extent of nuptiality, their temporal and geographical variations and their influence on fertility. The next chapter deals with the limitation of fertility within marriage and the more intimate relations between husbands and wives.

What should our expectations be with respect to Georgian and Victorian marriage patterns? Many of our perceptions have been encouraged by Jane Austen and her characterisation of the Bennet family of Longbourn, Hertfordshire, and others in similar social positions. During 24 years of marriage Mr and Mrs Bennet had been blessed with five daughters. The youngest, a well-grown girl of 16, eloped with a soldier who was only obliged to marry her after the negotiation of a financial settlement. The eldest, a sweet girl of 23 who smiled too much, made a good match with a young man from the North of England, the recent inheritor of industrial wealth. The second at 21 made a brilliant match with a man of great substance, much of it located in Derbyshire. The marital fortunes of the other daughters remain obscure, but it is to be supposed that the third, a plain girl, remained a spinster at home reading, adjusting her ideas and caring for her parents. Now, of course, one must not be tempted to think the Bennets typical of their age, but their fears and prejudices probably reflect closely a preoccupation with the need for a woman to marry carefully, if not well.

Without thinking highly either of men or of matrimony, marriage had always been her object; it was the only honourable provision for well-educated young women of small fortune, and however uncertain of giving happiness, must be their pleasantest preservative from want. This pre-servative she had now obtained; and at the age of twenty-seven, without having ever been handsome, she felt all the good luck of it.

Thus the thoughts of a friend of the Misses Bennet on accepting the proposal of a cleric whom she regarded as neither sensible nor agreeable, and whose society was irksome to her.

In wider society the prospects for marriage were affected by the size of the pool of eligibles, its composition and the circumstances in which those eligibles found themselves. To complicate matters, we must also remember that many young women left home in their late teens to become domestic or farm servants (Higgs, 1983; Anderson, 1984; Hinde, 1985; Litchfield, 1988); that in certain areas of the country most women spent some time employed in the textile industry (Hewitt, 1958; Garrett, 1990); that a significant group of young women was obliged to marry because they had become pregnant; that widows and widowers often remarried; and that just because divorce was restricted we should not think separation uncommon (Stone, 1990).

In broad terms, the level of nuptiality declined throughout the nineteenth and early twentieth centuries in England and Wales, but it did so from the high peak of the late Georgian years (Wilson and Woods, 1991). After the 1850s in both England and Wales, and Scotland, the rate of change was relatively slow until the increase of the late 1930s and 1940s. Increasingly, marriage was postponed until the mid- to late twenties and many did not marry at all. In itself this is an interesting, if imprecise, observation yet it is the geography of Victorian marriage patterns that holds the key to our understanding of nuptiality's variable demographic contribution, at least in the late nineteenth century, rather than its slow change over time. Regional, but especially local, variations would appear to reflect some of the influences outlined above. If this does prove to be the case, then a consideration of the geography of nuptiality will not only assist our appreciation of how fertility declined in late Victorian Britain, but it will also provide a simple summary of the effects of age- and sex-selective migration; occupational specialisation; employment opportunities; the distribution of eligible partners; and local customs.

The geography of nuptiality

Using the index I_m, the proportion of females married, table 5 shows the extent of nuptiality in the late nineteenth century. It quotes I_m for England and Wales, Scotland and selected registration counties. Its purpose is to illustrate slow change during the fifty years as well as the extent of regional diversity. As is often the case, extremes are of most interest. The highest levels of nuptiality were to be found among those populations living in coalmining communities where there was usually a surplus of eligible men whose wages peaked early in their working lives and where alternative employment for women was scarce (Friedlander, 1973). West Lothian and Durham provide good examples. At the other extreme we have rural populations which had been exposed to very substantial emigration and in which there were few economic opportunities either in or outside agriculture. Sutherland, in the north of Scotland, was the most striking example. The other examples drawn from rural Scotland, Wigtownshire and Aberdeenshire, show higher levels of nuptiality, but in the former the level was increasing while in the latter it was in decline

Table 5 *Index of proportion married, I_m*

	1861	1891	1911
England and Wales	0.502	0.477	0.479
London	0.483	0.459	0.444
Lancashire	0.504	0.482	0.478
County Durham	0.593	0.564	0.552
Norfolk	0.498	0.492	0.469
Wiltshire	0.499	0.487	0.488
Scotland	0.422	0.420	0.418
Sutherland	0.295	0.322	0.319
Aberdeenshire	0.393	0.383	0.325
Wigtownshire	0.370	0.373	0.380
Midlothian	0.394	0.397	0.391
West Lothian	0.569	0.563	0.573
Ireland		0.336	0.339

See the *Glossary of demographic terms* for definitions
Source: based on Coale and Watkins (1986).

(Anderson and Morse, 1990). In the English rural counties of Norfolk and Wiltshire there was very slow decline.

While the index I_m does capture the general volume of marriage, it also obscures the individual effects of age at marriage and proportion ultimately marrying. For, while one would expect late marriage and low proportions marrying to be related, the association need not be a perfect one. While we cannot be absolutely certain, it seems most likely that the geographical variation in nuptiality, conveniently captured by I_m, was due mainly to differences in the proportion of women who remained unmarried during their thirties and forties rather than to differences in the proportion of women who had married by the age of twenty-five. While the mean age at marriage might vary very little, those left unmarried at thirty could account for from five to 30 per cent or more of women (Anderson, 1984).

The importance of these distinctions may be clarified by imagining particular forms of economy and society. Consider the differences between Sutherland or western Ireland, a textile town like Keighley in the West Riding of Yorkshire, and a city such as

Bath with many wealthy residents and visitors employing substantial numbers of domestic servants. In Sutherland the opportunity to marry would be limited for financial reasons even if the sex ratio of eligibles was balanced. Many holdings were not sufficiently large to support a wife and children. In Keighley young women would usually spend some time, perhaps ten years, working in the mills before they married (Garrett, 1990). The mean age at first marriage might be increased, but not necessarily the ultimate proportion getting married. And in Bath, where female domestic servants were numerous, being 'in service' would have represented a 'stage in the life cycle' prior to marriage and starting a family as well as a source of refuge for the widowed or abandoned. Here Sutherland, Keighley and Bath stand proxy for other equivalent areas in the rest of Britain.

Among London's registration districts there was a very close inverse relationship between I_m and the percentage of women employed in domestic service. In Hampstead I_m was 0.274 while in Poplar, in the East End, it was 0.638 in 1861 and little changed in 1891 (Woods, 1984). Indeed, the range of I_m values between London registration districts was greater than among registration counties in the British Isles.

So far in this chapter we have taken note of certain social conventions in marriage, at least as portrayed in literature, considered variations in the extent of nuptiality, particularly its geographical manifestation, and noted the contribution certain forms of labour organisation can have for both age- and sex-selective migration and for the prospects of marrying. But since this pamphlet is largely concerned with demographic issues, we must now turn to consider the influence of nuptiality on fertility. In Britain in the early 1990s up to a third of babies were born outside marriage and about a third of marriages ended in divorce. In the last century marriage set the bounds for sexual activity; of course that does not mean that illegitimacy, bridal pregnancy, prostitution and adultery were not common especially in certain localities, but it does give nuptiality a direct demographic significance which it has all but lost by now.

Table 6 illustrates the point using another fertility index I_h, illegitimate or non-marital fertility. If we begin by taking these figures at their face value and do not consider their level simply a

Table 6 *Index of illegitimate fertility, I_h*

	1861	1891	1911
England and Wales	0.046	0.026	0.019
London	0.025	0.018	0.016
Lancashire	0.048	0.025	0.017
County Durham	0.062	0.035	0.027
Norfolk	0.074	0.043	0.030
Wiltshire	0.051	0.027	0.020
Scotland	0.056	0.042	0.031
Sutherland	0.022	0.024	0.020
Aberdeenshire	0.089	0.069	0.056
Wigtownshire	0.074	0.076	0.057
Midlothian	0.047	0.034	0.024
West Lothian	0.084	0.072	0.041
Ireland		0.010	0.010

See Table 5

reflection of attitudes to bastardy (where it is frowned upon, registration may be avoided) then they should suggest some interesting observations regarding the potential contribution of nuptiality to fertility rates. In post-famine Ireland virtually all births were to married women, but in north-east and south-west Scotland, East Anglia and eastern England in general, the extent of illegitimacy in 1861 was sufficiently large for one to begin to doubt the importance of marriage as a social and legal event with strong demographic significance (16 per cent of births were illegitimate in Aberdeenshire) (Leneman and Mitchison, 1987; Mitchison and Leneman, 1989). But elsewhere in Britain, and especially off the coalfields, non-marital fertility was low enough at mid-century (only 5 or 6 per cent of births were illegitimate) for the institution of marriage still to be accepted as having particular significance as a regulator of fertility rates. But table 6 also shows that by the early twentieth century I_h had fallen everywhere (only 4 per cent of births were illegitimate in England and Wales in 1911). Were those forces which initiated the decline of marital fertility also leading to the reduction of non-marital fertility?

5
How many children should we have?

The origins of the secular decline of marital fertility in Britain, as in much of western Europe with the exception of France, are to be found in the second half, but especially the last quarter, of the nineteenth century. This much at least is clear from the available vital statistics, but there are many aspects of this fundamental change in demographic structure that remain obscure. By what means was the size of families limited? Why did marital fertility decline from this period and not earlier or later? Were the reasons economic or social in origin, of necessity or through the choice of fashion? Who controlled their fertility first and did others learn from their behaviour? Hypotheses abound, but the evidence remains tantalising in its vagueness or insecurity.

We do know that until the 1870s English, and by implication British, marital fertility was consistent with 'natural fertility', that is it was largely biologically determined with little sign of parity-specific control. Children came by God's will. In general, their births were neither deliberately spaced nor were there attempts to prevent conception or live birth once a particular number of children had already been born. A woman's fertility was influenced by her physiological ability to conceive, her proneness to spontaneous abortion, and the frequency of coitus. The first mentioned declined with age, the second increased, while the last mentioned declined with the duration of marriage (Bongaarts and Potter, 1983; Wilson, 1984, 1986; Reay, 1994).

Figure 4 shows age-specific marital fertility schedules for rural England (marriage cohorts 1550 to 1849) (Wilson and Woods, 1991); Scotland in 1855 (Hinde and Woods, 1984); the Hutterite marriage cohorts of 1921–30 (Coale and Watkins 1986); and for

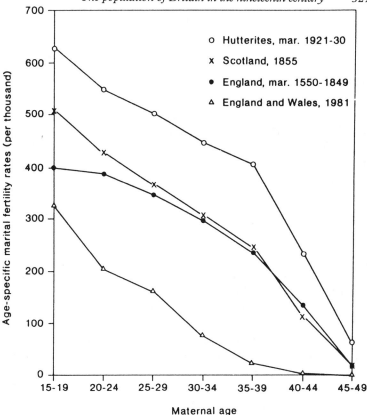

Figure 4   *Age-specific marital fertility curves*

comparison England and Wales in 1981. The height of each curve gives the level of total marital fertility, while the shape indicates whether any form of parity-specific control, or stopping behaviour, is present. The concave form of the modern England and Wales curve shows that effective family limitation is widespread, especially among married women in their thirties and forties. The convexity of the other three indicates that such stopping behaviour was either absent or unusual. Between the 1850s and the 1930s such behaviour became widespread in Britain; the level of age-specific marital fertility was much reduced and the shape of the resulting curve radically altered. Unfortunately, it is not possible to chart the exact course of the changing age pattern of marital fertility because the recording of mother's age at the birth of her

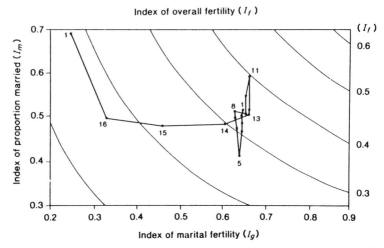

Figure 5   *The changing contribution of nuptiality (I_m) and marital fertility (I_g) to overall fertility (I_f) in England. (Each point represents a twenty-five year period as in Table 4. Point 1 is for 1551–75, 11 for 1801–25, 14 for 1876–1900 and 17 for 1951–75.) Source: Wilson and Woods (1992)*

children did not become part of the regular registration system until the late 1930s. The first year of civil registration in Scotland, 1855, was the one and only exception. Thus, it is impossible to say with complete certainty whether married couples began by fixing on some ideal family size and then attempted to limit conceptions in order to meet that ideal (i.e. stopping behaviour – 'four and no more') or whether, at least initially, they sought to lengthen the intervals between births and thereby to affect the completed family size, for example, consciously practising sexual abstinence in marriage (i.e. spacing behaviour). In the absence of contrary evidence, stopping behaviour is assumed more likely (Seccombe, 1990; Woods, 1992; Garrett and Reid, 1994).

Despite the paucity of data in a form that would be ideal for our purposes, it is nonetheless possible to be clear on the following points. First, unlike the increase in fertility in the late eighteenth and early nineteenth centuries, the experience of the late Victorian period was dominated by the secular decline of marital fertility and not a cyclical, perhaps isolated, movement in nuptiality (Woods, 1987; Wilson and Woods, 1991; see also figures 2 and 3). Figure 5 plots *(I_m)* against *(I_g)* to reveal the highly distinctive nature of new trends originating in the third quarter of the nineteenth century (point 13 for 1851–75) when (I_m) (nuptiality) gave way to (I_g) (marital fertility) as the driving force of temporal changes in the level of fertility. Secondly, we may now assume in a way that was not open to contemporaries that marital fertility was reduced as the direct consequence of changed behaviour rather than some general decline in fecundity. Patterns of thought and action changed rather than physiology (Teitelbaum, 1984). Thirdly, and here we are on less sure ground, it is unlikely that the phenomenon was merely a result of the invention, marketing, adoption and effective use of new appliance methods of birth control. The rubber condom, Dutch cap and douche all became available during the last decades of the nineteenth century, but they were rather expensive for general use until the 1920s and 1930s when even the results of retrospective surveys reveal their far more widespread adoption (Peel, 1963). Since it is known that marital fertility was significantly reduced, it must be assumed that some combination of sexual abstinence, *coitus interruptus*, accurate use of the safe period (not properly understood until the twentieth century) and induced abortion were the most likely means by which family limitation was brought about. None of these methods was new to Victorians, but the desire and confidence to use them were innovatory (Shorter, 1973; McLaren, 1978; Sauer, 1978; Soloway, 1982; Mason, 1994).

If the foregoing represents sound, if unsubstantiated, reasoning, then how should we proceed to explain the obvious demographic trends? Let us, for the sake of clarity, oversimplify and consider only three possible approaches: the demographic, the economic and the sociological.

There is a persistent line of argument in demographic theory which holds that high levels of fertility are necessary to match high levels of mortality, and thus that when infant or childhood mortality begins to decline, marital fertility will also be reduced without adversely affecting the effective level of fertility, that is the supply of new adults capable of reproducing (Brass and Kabir, 1980; Teitelbaum, 1984; Woods, 1987). Thus mortality decline not only facilitates the reduction of fertility, it also acts as a strong inducement. Setting aside for the time being any consideration of what causes mortality patterns to vary, it is still obvious that for this particular demographic mechanism to work there must be a distinct time lag between the decline of mortality and fertility during which average family size will increase. Married couples would be impelled to limit their fertility thereby avoiding the accompanying financial burdens which the survival of larger numbers of children would bring. This interpretation assumes that there is a distinct chronology to demographic change and that a sophisticated adjustment mechanism is created requiring considerable foresight on the part of married couples and a degree of reproductive planning. In Britain, early childhood mortality (ages 1 to 4) certainly did decline at the same time as marital fertility, but infant mortality did not begin its secular decline until 1899–1900 (Woods, Watterson and Woodward, 1988). it seems likely that the reduction of infant and childhood mortality did eventually help to sustain lower marital fertility, but that mortality decline was not an initiating factor (Reves, 1985; Coale and Watkins, 1986, pp. 201–33).

Economists have provided one of the most important theoretical contributions to the study of fertility. Their focus has tended to emphasise the costs and returns of having children, the costs and availability of contraceptive methods, inter-generational wealth flows, and the conflict between investing in children or consumer durables. Children, especially in traditional peasant societies, represent a source of labour, income and security for their parents. But in nineteenth-century urban Britain the economic value of children to their parents was far less obvious and presumably far less likely to enter any accounting framework for reproductive planning. In general, if parents were not attempting to maximise their fertility in order to reap financial gains for the family wage economy, they were also not attempting, until after the 1870s, to restrict their fertility in order to avoid the liability of childrearing (Haines, 1979; Crafts, 1984a, 1984b). Remember also that it was rather unusual at this time and in most areas for married women to be employed outside the home, for reasons of tradition and lack of opportunity, and thus that childbearing and rearing did not represent alternatives to wage earning as they do today. The sexual division of labour was clear; while he earned, she looked after him, home and children.

Set against this rather confusing picture we have the concepts of 'relative income compression' and 'social diffusion'. During the late nineteenth century, it is claimed, middle class parents were obliged to devote increasing proportions of their incomes to the education of their children in order to provide them with competitive advantage in the labour market (Banks, 1954).

They were also tempted to alter their spending patterns towards status-conferring consumer goods, the maintenance of appearances via servants and a respectable address (Banks, 1981), all of which exerted pressure on family finances and encouraged the rearing of small numbers of what economists have called higher-quality children. Even if the middle classes, but especially the lower middle classes of shopkeepers and clerks, were experiencing relative economic pressure in their efforts to attain or retain social respectability and were thus more inclined to plan their families, at least three quarters of Britain's population would conventionally be classified as 'working'. Were there similar pressures on working class couples? It would seem not. Perhaps instead, members of the working class learned from the innovatory class via that group's domestic servants who imparted the ideals and values of the small family rather than the means by which it might be brought about (Banks, 1954).

There is little reason to doubt that economic pressures, whether relative or absolute, played an important part in influencing the decision of many couples to limit their fertility in the late nineteenth century, but what still remains in doubt is why that pressure only took tangible effect in the last quarter of the century and why the secular decline of marital fertility occurred so rapidly that different occupations, status groups and social classes all appeared to be reducing their family size at about the same rate and time, although from rather different levels (Stevenson, 1920; Innes, 1938; Woods, 1987; Haines, 1989). The notion of social and indeed spatial diffusion is difficult to sustain with the available evidence.

Of those occupational groups that are relatively easy to identify, coalminers provide interesting illustrations of the difficulties encountered in developing purely economic explanations of fertility decline (Friedlander, 1973; Haines, 1979). Coalmining districts and families are known to have had higher fertility longer and to have been among the last areas and social groups to attempt family limitation. A commonly held account holds that the income curve for coalminers peaked in the early to mid-twenties; there were few employment opportunities for women; such areas contained a surplus of men; and marriage for women was early and general. The demand for male labour was usually buoyant, but the work was dangerous, accidents and injuries common and often fatal. There was, therefore, little economic incentive, as there was in the lower middle classes, to restrict fertility. But it is also likely that these rather closely knit communities perpetuated an ethos which was strongly oriented towards men's values and women's obligations and thus less compatible with that degree of foresight and co-operation between the sexes necessary for successful family limitation before the development of effective intra-uterine devices and oral contraceptives. (Compare West Lothian and County Durham with the other counties in tables 5 and 6.)

This leads us on to consider the sociological approach. Here the emphasis is on attitudes and values; the ability of women to negotiate and of men to insist. The process might be thought analogous to a massive and irreversible electoral swing in which there are many polling days, but the results are not immediately obvious. Soon all eligible adults decide to act in the same manner, some copy others, but most make independent decisions based on their own self-interest. If this analogy is close, then it is also necessary to establish what self-interest dictated for most married couples and whether that changed, and also the nature of the constraints on implementation and whether they disappeared in the late nineteenth century. It would seem likely that the balance of costs and returns tipped against large families at an early stage in the process of urban and industrial growth. One might even argue that in such an individualistic society as Britain's, but also one in which the state, as well as the family, had traditionally taken some responsibility for supporting the poor and the old, the investment in children could only be recovered when those children were employed but unmarried (a period of perhaps ten to fifteen years), and not necessarily when the parents were unwell, infirm or aged. In British society, certainly in the eighteenth and nineteenth centuries, children were born and raised 'for their own sakes' rather than for any rationally calculated long-term financial return or insurance. Self-interest should have dictated the practice of moral restraint and direct family limitation by whatever means available among rich and poor alike. Relative economic pressure felt by the middle classes and the decline of child mortality in the late nineteenth century would have confirmed views on what self-interest should imply. What were the constraints on behaviour that deflected the attainment of this self-interest? The belief that sexual intercourse was only intended for procreation, and the prevailing moral code of which that was a part, made the question of how many children a married couple should have not only unanswerable, but unthinkable. Children were the gifts of God, and God could only be thwarted by postponing marriage (*à la* Malthus) or practising a degree of celibacy in marriage. Condoms, widely applied as a prophylactic, were not for use with respectable married women. By the last quarter of the nineteenth century these aspects of the dominant moral code had probably lost their force partly because the Christian theology on which they were founded had become increasingly more divorced from urban working-class culture and because women had become more assertive in their attitude to marital relations. The secularisation of nineteenth-century British society accompanied urbanisation and can be indexed by the decline in church attendance and the increasing popularity of civil marriage in England and Wales after 1837 (Anderson, O., 1975). For women, their increased involvement in formal education, even before the 1870 Education Act, and their improved literacy are likely to have both caused and symbolised changes in confidence and thus their bargaining power. In the early twentieth century this process also included emancipation and far greater involvement in the non-domestic labour force (Banks and Banks, 1964; Roberts, 1984; Woods, 1992).

Figure 6 shows one index of marital fertility (I_g) and three other indices for female literacy, living standards and civil marriages. It would be unwise to conclude that merely because the trends in these four indices combine to tell the same story that cause may be inferred, but the story is certainly plausible. In parts of Scotland and much of Ireland high marital fertility persisted into the twentieth century. On the coalfields and in north-east Scotland, I_g was still in excess of 0.7 in 1901, but it declined thereafter. In the far north and the Scottish islands marital fertility was also high, but there, like Ireland, nuptiality was at a particularly low level and rates of natural population growth were kept in check. In England

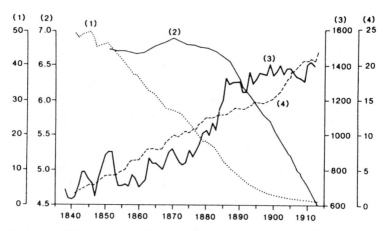

Figure 6   *The percentage of brides signing the marriage register with a mark (1); the index of marital fertility, I_g (2); an index of real wages (3); and the percentage of civil marriages (4) in England and Wales. Source: Woods (1987, 308)*

and Wales, to which figure 6 applies, the coalfields were also the most conspicuous areas of persistently high marital fertility, but there too, as with equivalent districts in Scotland, France, Belgium and Germany, attitudes and behaviour eventually came to favour family limitation (Anderson and Morse, 1990, 1993; Teitelbaum, 1984; Woods, 1987).

However, it should also be stressed that the British experience of the secular decline of marital fertility was merely part of a Europe-wide movement in which Britain was later than most of France, but in step with much of Germany and Italy (Coale and Watkins, 1986; Watkins, 1991; Gillis, Tilly and Levine, 1992; see also figure 3). The most important structural barriers to change appear to have been the major linguistic and cultural divisions as well as the strength of pro-natalist religious feeling. Just as in Britain, it is not possible to say in detail how or why family limitation began to be practised, but the most plausible interpretations also stress the importance of changes in attitude and the removal of constraints on behaviour emphasised in the sociological approach rather than the after-effects of industrialisation and urbanisation or the prior decline of infant and child mortality. The electoral swing was Europe wide, relatively rapid, and has not been reversed.

6

Mortality

The works of two men have come to dominate our understanding of mortality patterns in the nineteenth century: William Farr and Thomas McKeown. The former, as we have already seen, was largely responsible for shaping the Victorian system of civil registration, while the latter's account of the course of mortality changes in Britain since the eighteenth century relies heavily on Farr's legacy of cause of death reporting. Both were medically trained and perhaps, as a consequence, they tended to see demographic change virtually exclusively in terms of mortality, morbidity and health, to the neglect of other factors. For McKeown, in particular, the modern rise of population was almost entirely a matter of mortality decline. Despite the fact that such a view is demonstrably no longer tenable, the set of arguments with which McKeown is most closely associated are still worth careful scrutiny. But before we consider these problems of interpretation and method, let us first follow Farr and search for empirical 'laws of vitality'.

Farr himself was occupied with the problem of calculating accurate English life tables which would not only provide much-needed material for the life assurance companies to assess premiums, but would also chart one of the fundamental 'laws of mortality', namely its regular variation with age (Farr, 1864). Figure 7 shows results from two examples of Farr's work, the 1841 table for Liverpool and the Third English Life Table for 1838–54, as well as one for Glasgow, 1870–72, and the Eighth English Life Table for 1910–12 (Woods and Hinde, 1987). The curves show the number of survivors to any age left from 1,000 live births. They are matched by life expectations at birth (e_0) and infant mortality rates (IMR) of 26 and 253 for Liverpool, 32 and 170 for Glasgow,

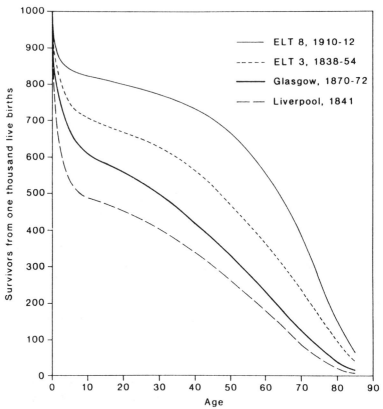

Figure 7   *The numbers surviving to each age out of 1,000 live births*

41 and 149 for English Life Table 3, 53 and 109 for ELT 8. Mortality was obviously higher in Liverpool and Glasgow than England and Wales as a whole; infant and childhood mortality in combination could have been responsible for from 15 to 30 per cent of all deaths, and mortality certainly did decline by at least 20 per cent between mid-century and 1911: these are the three principal findings illustrated in figure 7.

During the nineteenth century life expectation at birth in Britain improved from the mid-thirties to the upper forties and the low fifties by 1911. It is now at least 75 years (table 4 and figure 2). Of the change, most occurred in the latter part of the nineteenth century and was particularly obvious among those aged from 2 to 25. There was little or no secular decline either in national infant mortality levels or in mortality rates for those aged 35 plus before 1900 (Luckin, 1980; Woods and Woodward, 1984, p. 39). But there were important local and social variations in mortality. The local differences were closely tied to environmental conditions, but especially urban/rural differences. The lowest levels of life expectation were invariably in urban places, and especially in what would now be called the inner cities inhabited by the poorest families in the worst housing with the most inadequate sanitation. Even in 1841 when life expectation at birth was 26 in Liverpool and 37 in London, it was 45 in Surrey and probably 50 years in the most salubrious rural areas (Woods and Hinde, 1987). By 1911 the national average had increased and the urban–rural differential had narrowed substantially. It is far more difficult to assess the pattern of occupation and social-class related mortality, although Farr was also responsible for the first tabulations of occupation-specific mortality rates (McDowall, 1983; Woods and Williams, 1995). It remains a matter of speculation whether the wealthy urban middle classes or the poor agricultural labourers experienced the lower level of mortality. Table 7 provides an example of the problems to be resolved. It gives estimates of the class-specific infant mortality rates for 1895–7 and 1910 using the 1911 classification first introduced in table 2. It shows not only that levels declined for every class, but also that compared with the national trend for England and Wales, they did so at different rates. Class VIII (agricultural labourers) was overtaken by class I (professionals and managers) (Watterson, 1986, 1988; Williams, 1992). The children of the largely urban middle classes came to fare better than those of the rural working classes. Equally, the extent of morbidity and its relation to mortality are still a matter for debate despite the fact that work-preventing illhealth was regularly recorded for members of the Friendly Societies (Riley, 1987a, 1987b; Alter and Riley, 1989).

These are the basic regularities of Victorian mortality which Farr did so much to reveal to his contemporaries: mortality varied with age in a regular fashion (figure 7); for most ages male mortality was in excess of that for women, although the Third English Life Table (1838–54) shows excess female mortality between the ages of 10 and 40; strong urban–rural and inner city–suburban contrasts were broadly associated with environmental quality; certain occupations – including the medical profession – were especially

Table 7 *Estimated class-specific infant mortality rates by father's social class for England and Wales*

		1895–7	1910	Change index
I	Professionals	121	59	159
II	Intermediate	138	92	103
III	Skilled workers and clerical	147	97	106
IV	Intermediate	149	105	91
V	Unskilled workers	166	127	72
VI	Textile workers	164	123	78
VII	Miners	169	132	68
VIII	Agricultural labourers	110	87	65

The 1911 classification for I to V is similar to that for 1951, but VI to VIII are dealt with separately (see Table 2).
Change index: $\{[(1895\text{--}7\text{--}1910)/1895\text{--}7]/k\} \times 100$, where k is the equivalent rate of change of national infant mortality between 1895–7 and 1910 (i.e. 0.32).
Source: based on Woods, Watterson and Woodward (1988, *364*)

unhealthy, dangerous or accident prone; and mortality rates tended to mirror differences of wealth and social class. Although these often observed regularities assist the search for order, additional perspectives are necessary if the origins and causes of the secular decline in mortality are to be interpreted successfully. It is here that we turn to McKeown, but especially the paper he published with R. G. Record in 1962, 'Reasons for the decline of mortality in England and Wales during the nineteenth century', and his 1976 book, *The Modern Rise of Population* (McKeown and Record, 1962; McKeown, 1976). In reading these and other works by McKeown on the same theme it is worth bearing in mind the following points. First, McKeown overemphasised the importance of mortality decline for the modern rise of population in Britain compared with fertility; it is also likely that he overdramatised the fall in mortality that was particular to the nineteenth century. Secondly, his method of accounting, working backwards from cause of death data to infer the most likely ultimate causes, whether environmental, economic, epidemiological or medical for example, assumes that the data are sound, that there is little need for corroborating evidence and that the contribution of these ultimate causes may thus be quantified. All of these assumptions must be treated with caution. Thirdly, despite these problems,

McKeown's central conclusion that, 'with the notable exception of vaccination against smallpox, specific preventive or curative measures could have had no significant influence on mortality before the twentieth century', is still valid (McKeown and Record, 1962, p. 94). Fourthly, relatively little notice is taken of the 'laws of vitality' which were apparent to Farr as well as other Victorian medical statisticians, and which have been outlined above (Newsholme, 1889). In particular, McKeown did not disaggregate the pattern of mortality change by region or locality in such a way that the slow decline in rural areas could be contrasted with the more rapid fall from higher levels in the larger cities at the same time that those very cities were housing an increasing share of Britain's population (Woods, 1985; Williamson, 1990).

The critical focus for McKeown's analysis is summarised in table 8. Over 90 per cent of the late nineteenth-century mortality decline in England and Wales was due to conditions attributable to micro-organisms with 33 per cent associated with respiratory tuberculosis; 17 per cent with typhoid and typhus (quite different diseases, but not separated in official statistics until 1869); 12 per cent from cholera, diarrhoea and dysentery; 12 per cent from scarlet fever and diphtheria; 5 per cent from smallpox and 4 per cent from non-respiratory tuberculosis. Working backwards from these immediate causes McKeown argued that 'the specific changes introduced by the sanitary reformers were responsible for about a quarter of the total decline of mortality in the second half of the nineteenth century'. The remainder of the improvement, mainly associated with tuberculosis, must be attributed to the rise of living standards brought about by the industrial revolution, that is, 'perhaps half of the total reduction of mortality' (McKeown and Record, 1962, p. 120). The last quarter could be attributed to changes in the character of diseases, but especially scarlet fever (Eyler, 1987). The argument for the attribution of the first quarter is relatively easy to follow, how else could the water-borne diseases have declined, but what of tuberculosis? The direct effects of specific therapeutic measures can be ruled out; conditions of exposure to the disease, diet, physical and mental stress remain. McKeown excluded the last-mentioned and claimed that exposure via crowding at home and at work was not reduced before 1900.

Table 8 *Cause-specific standardized death rates for England and Wales (figures in parts per million)*

Cause of death	1848–54	1901	1971	Percentage reduction*
A Conditions attributable to micro-organisms				
1 Airborne diseases	7,259	5,122	619	44
2 Water- and food-borne diseases	3,562	1,931	35	33
3 Other conditions	2,144	1,415	60	15
	12,965	8,468	714	92
B Conditions not attributable to micro-organisms	8,891	8,490	4,670	8
Total all diseases	21,865	16,958	5,384	100

* In the period 1848–54 to 1901 and attributable to each category.
Source: McKeown (1976, 54)

Thus diet remained the most likely influence on the downward trend of tuberculosis mortality.

Now that we have seen McKeown's full hand, and suspect it to be of variable quality, how might it be strengthened? First, one might seek direct evidence for improvements in living standards, but especially diet, and thereby assess their influence. The available indices of real wages show an upward movement in the second half of the nineteenth century denoting rising living standards which should be associated with improvements in the quantity and quality of food consumed, just as they should with the amelioration of poor housing conditions (figure 6). However, it is extremely difficult to trace the direct links to their influence, especially on respiratory tuberculosis. Recent efforts in this area have dwelt on problems rather than solutions by stressing the indissolubility of the various influences involved.

The changing nutritional status of Britain's population is particularly difficult to assess not only because of problems relating to sources, but also the need to select statistical measures that capture both trends in the average position and the relative distribution of experience. The analysis of data on average heights drawn from a wide variety of population samples may help to resolve the matter. Floud, Wachter and Gregory (1990) provide evidence of the steady increase in average heights between 1860 and 1914 which they take to reflect improving nutritional status. The close correlations with rising real wages and falling mortality in this period are also noted. But for the period from 1750 to 1850, when available evidence for real wage and mortality trends are less reliable, data for average heights 'suggests that there was significant improvement in nutritional status over the whole of the century', and that 'significant inequalities within the working class, as shown by height differentials, narrowed during the late eighteenth and early nineteenth century and then remained roughly constant' (Floud, Wachter and Gregory, 1990, p. 305). But the second quarter of the nineteenth century is shown to be a period in which average heights declined so breaking the long-run trend. Between the 1820s and the 1850s gains in real wages may have been offset by the effects of 'urbanisation, diet and possibly work intensity'. The decline of mortality also stabilised or went into reverse during these years (table 4 and figure 2). Even if the nutritional status of the British population did improve in the long-term, what implications would this have had for the decline of tuberculosis and the McKeown interpretation in general? How responsive was tuberculosis to improvements in diet? The conclusion to F. B. Smith's study of tuberculosis in the nineteenth century captures the essence of the problem.

Better nutrition, housing, nurture, lessening of fatigue, smaller family size acting synergistically in varying permutations through time and place hold the answer, although that answer remains vague because its chronology and linkages are little traced or understood (Smith, 1988, p. 244).

Further efforts in this area should probably begin by re-examining the contribution of tuberculosis decline to the fall of mortality.

Secondly, one might look more closely at local variations in mortality decline and consider the way in which the mortality gradient between urban and rural places began to narrow by the early years of the twentieth century (Pelling, 1978; Szreter, 1988, 1994; Guha, 1994). Certainly this aspect was neglected by McKeown, but it too is not free from the problems that are always to be encountered in the analysis of multivariate associations. The urbanisation of Britain's population had important consequences for public health, but it also meant that once the technology for sanitary engineering became available, and the need for a constant supply of pure water and effective sewerage recognised, then investment could bring direct and immediate benefits to large numbers very quickly. Once the investment had been made, the carriage systems put in place; the streets cleaned, paved and lighted, and the worst slums swept away; then one's expectations of material advances in health and mortality should certainly be raised. But these investments were the results of political decisions and attitudes which came in a slow and halting fashion to recognise public health as a priority for direct intervention by national and local government (Wohl, 1983; Woods, 1991). The story of how public health became a priority and its rise on the political agenda is intriguing in its own right for it reflects the combination of initiatives made by individuals (Sir Edwin Chadwick, Dr John Snow and Sir John Simon, for example) as well as changes in attitude among the political elite and their supporters. The latter were influenced by, on the one hand, the successive extension of the electoral franchise and, on the other, by self interest. Public opinion also came to see the value of direct state intervention, collective action and regulation. Even members of the medical profession played an increasingly confident and interventionist role, especially through the army of Medical Officers of Health which constituted a local health bureaucracy (Frazer, 1947; Hardy, 1988, 1993).

The implications for that one quarter of the mortality decline in the last half of the nineteenth century attributed by McKeown to the sanitary reformers are several in number. Above all the course of the sanitary revolution was politically motivated; it did not always take notice of need and was often confounded by vested interest. Certainly reformers did make important contributions, especially in the moulding of public opinion, but the process of change was far wider and probably owed less to inspired individuals than to political expedience in the face of overwhelming evidence for the hazards to health of poor hygiene coupled with growing technical competence (Hassan, 1985; Kearns, 1985).

Thirdly, it may also prove instructive to consider those aspects of the 'laws of vitality' which do not appear to have altered substantially in the nineteenth century. The most obvious example must surely be the persistently high rate of infant mortality (Woods, Watterson and Woodward, 1988–89; Williams and Mooney, 1994). In the late nineteenth century between 15 and 20 per cent of deaths in Britain occurred to those under the age of one year with about 25 per cent for those under five years. National trends showed little sign of continued decline until the late 1890s or 1900. Variations between urban and rural places were clear and persistent, with the former two to two and a half times the latter at the extremes, as were the rates related to father's occupation and thereby social class (table 7). The mortality of infants born to unmarried mothers was substantially higher than that to legitimate children and roughly one third of all infant deaths occurred during the first months of life.

These regularities were all well known to contemporaries and became the subject of particular concern during the 1890s and 1900s when the health of the population, but especially mothers and young children, was the subject of much debate. Sir George Newman's *Infant Mortality: A Social Problem* (1906) set the scene and the tone of where the causes of persistently high infant mortality should be sought. But it was probably the work of Sir Arthur Newsholme, while Medical Officer of Health for Brighton (1888–1908) and Medical Officer of the Local Government Board (1909–19), that most helped to lay a sound foundation for the analysis of infant mortality variations and changes (Newsholme, 1889).

Table 9 arranges the factors suggested by Newsholme in a convenient form. Newsholme, himself, was particularly concerned with the sanitary environment and epidemic diarrhoea which in summer months had been an important, yet avoidable, cause of infant deaths especially in poor urban environments. In the 1890s diarrhoea appeared to emphasise the need for further sanitary improvements at a time when general infant mortality rates were rising, even though non-diarrhoeal infant mortality rates were already in decline. Much was also made at the time of the movement away from breastfeeding to the use of artificial feeds and the involvement of mothers in the non-domestic labour force (Dyhouse, 1978; Smith, 1979; Dwork, 1987).

However, it is unlikely that sewerage alone could have made the

Table 9 *Influences on infant mortality*

Care			
(A) Mother	(B) Of mother	(C) Of child	(D) Poverty
Age Work Family size Legitimacy	Ante-natal Post-natal Maternal mortality	Delivery (midwifery) Visiting (care, advice) Feeding (i) breast (ii) artificial -form -preparation	Housing Unemployment Wife's work Other children's work
(E) Housing	(F) Sanitary environment	(G) Personal factors	
Type Crowding	Pure water Excreta removal Scavenging Paving		

Source: Woods, Watterson and Woodward (1989, *114*)

difference. Mortality among two, three and four year olds was already in decline from the 1870s at least, perhaps partly as a result of changes in disease patterns normally associated with scarlet fever. It is very difficult to chart in any generalised form changes in the practice of infant and child care during this period. What evidence there is suggests that infants were usually breastfed, unless their mothers were physiologically unable, for six or seven months, but that artificial foods did become more popular during the first half of the twentieth century and that many babies experienced a mixed diet of breastmilk and other solids. The evidence on advances in obstetric, ante- and post-natal care is similarly ambiguous. The training and registration of midwives certainly improved in the 1900s and many local authorities established clinics for maternal and child care, but neonatal mortality changed very little at 40 to 50 per thousand live births throughout the 1890s, 1900s and 1910s, and maternal mortality also stayed remarkably constant until the 1930s (Loudon, 1988, 1992). It would seem that if child-care practices did improve then the beneficiaries were infants aged one month and older.

The role of fertility decline must also be considered at this point (Reves, 1985). Certainly the reduction in illegitimate births would have depleted the most at-risk category of infants, but it is also reasonable to expect that efforts at family limitation not only reduced the sizes of completed families, but also served to lengthen the intervals between births rather more. Mothers would have been able to provide better care for fewer children and, if birth intervals were also increased to three, four or more years, the problem of competition for care between very young siblings would also have been avoided. If this outline is valid then we are left to ask once again, what caused the decline of fertility in late nineteenth-century Britain? Of the various factors already reviewed, the improvement in standards of education, but especially those of women, would seem of special significance not only for family limitation, but also the possibility of child care training via special literature, by nurses and health visitors (Woods, Watterson and Woodward, 1988–89).

All of this is highly speculative yet the story it suggests is credible and complements a similar one emerging in Third World countries. Fertility control programmes work most effectively when they operate alongside schemes to improve maternal and child health. In Britain the control of fertility, by whatever means, probably helped to initiate the decline of infant mortality, a connection obscured by high rates of diarrhoeal infant mortality in the 1890s, but the secular decline was reinforced by improving urban sanitation and eventually better obstetric facilities and targeted child health care programmes.

The course of infant mortality decline suggests certain implications for the fall of mortality in general and the manner in which McKeown's interpretation may be extended. First, it reinforces the need to search for connections between a wide range of factors which may not only support, or even amplify each other's contribution, but may also operate in a sequential fashion so that their relative importance will change during a period of several decades. Secondly, it emphasises the benefits of tracing temporal changes in a disaggregated fashion which allows for regional, local and social trends to emerge. But it also highlights the danger of generalising from the experience of just one age group, for infant mortality was not only of special significance for the rise of life expectation at birth, its secular decline also followed a separate and rather distinctive course.

Farr's tireless work on the vital statistics of England and Wales have made it possible to describe in some detail the pattern of mortality variation in the nineteenth century, but we are still some way off providing a full explanation of the origins of the secular decline of mortality during the nineteenth century. We know that direct medical science could have had only a minor influence on the decline of mortality before the 1930s and that the cleansing of great cities was a special problem in a country like Great Britain which had a particularly high level of urbanisation, but once the sanitation and public health problem in general had been solved then the positive effects would have been immediate and lasting. We also know that poverty, poor diet and thus low nutritional status, and inadequate housing persisted and were then, as now, closely related to variations in mortality rates. The significance of and reasons for the decline of mortality from tuberculosis continues to be an area for enquiry, but few now follow McKeown's lead and argue from mortality via tuberculosis to improved living standards, especially diet. Few would be bold enough to attach precise weights to the various factors apparently in operation. Many would now regard the nineteenth century as a period in which the foundations of modern medical science were laid, but that most of the fruits have only been available in this century (Pickstone, 1985; Bynum, 1994).

7
1911

If Malthus had returned to survey Britain's population in 1911 he would have been struck by its size, the extent of its concentration in large towns and the apparently effortless way in which real wages had been rising in recent decades. Misery and vice were still in evidence, moral restraint was practised, but new forms of restraint were used by married couples to limit their fertility. Differences in health and mortality between urban and rural environments and social classes persisted, but the former at least had recently shown marked signs of narrowing as the urban penalty weakened under the influence of public health reforms. Malthus would also have been shocked by Ireland's experience and at the state of the workhouses. He would have enjoyed the wealth of new statistics and been frustrated by their lacunae. Finally, he would probably have been startled by the pace not only of demographic change, but also of politics, the economy and society, and would doubtless have been apprehensive about what the future held in store now that some of the old certainties had lost their meaning.

The year 1911 is a convenient one with which to close. It was a census year and one with a hot, dry summer which tested public health to the limit. It was also the year in which the English and Welsh local authorities became the new units for civil registration. By 1911 the secular decline of both mortality and fertility, even infant mortality, were well underway and largely irreversible. The age of great cities had not yet yielded to the motor car and the long-distance commuter train, to counter-urbanisation and *urbs in rure*, nor had slum clearance depopulated the inner city so completely. There were horses in fields, bicycles in lanes; but women feared pregnancy as the old did the workhouse, and more than one in ten babies died before reaching their first birthday.

Certainly our understanding of these phenomena has improved considerably in recent years, largely because we now have estimates of demographic indices for periods before the first population census was taken and civil registration was introduced, at least in England, and can determine how the modern rise of population occurred. There is also some indication that old sources are being put to better effect using large databases and computer-assisted nominal record linkage. Single-discipline perspectives are also becoming less popular as historians and social scientists attempt to develop a common language. For the historical demography of the nineteenth century this will mean the integration of space with time and greater emphasis on the interaction between migration, fertility and mortality, environment and social class.

If the conundrum of English population growth in the eighteenth century has been resolved (Wrigley, 1983b), what remains of its nineteenth-century equivalent for Great Britain? The so-called McKeown problem has not yet been solved in the absence of a satisfactory method of ascribing numerical influence to those factors affecting mortality decline. Without reliable information on the means by which family limitation was brought about and a strategy for inferring motivation, the fertility transition will ultimately remain the subject for speculation in the absence of adequate evidence. The conflict between the free will of individuals and their obligation to conform to group social norms is still an intriguing issue in the study of migration, marriage and fertility control. The need to maintain a consciously comparative perspective also remains pressing and thereby to place Britain's demographic experience in a wider international context.

When the late M. W. Flinn completed his pamphlet on the population of eighteenth-century Britain in 1970 much still remained obscure. Now the course of English population history is reasonably clear. Equivalent substantial advances in our understanding of the processes and causes of demographic change in the nineteenth century are possible in the years to come, but they are most likely to stem from more imaginative use of familiar sources, the release of new material and above all the ability of scholars to think beyond the bounds set by disciplines back into the minds of their Georgian and Victorian ancestors.

Glossary of demographic terms

Although readers should refer to Roland Pressat's *Dictionary of Demography* (edited by Christopher Wilson, Oxford, 1986) for more detailed information on demographic terms, a brief introduction may prove useful.

Crude rates – live births (crude birth rate, CBR) or deaths (crude death rate, CDR) per 1,000 population (e.g. table 4)

Infant mortality rate – infant deaths (under one year of age) per 1,000 live births in a year (e.g. tables 4 and 7; Woods, 1993)

Princeton or A. J. Coale's fertility indices (Coale and Watkins, 1986) – the four indices are overall fertility (I_f), marital fertility (I_g), illegitimate fertility (I_h) and proportion married (I_m). They are indirectly standardised measures which use the marital fertility of Hutterite women married 1921–30 (figure 4) as their standard against which to estimate the expected number of births against which the actual is then compared. They enable the influence of variations in age structures and marriage patterns to be taken into account even where age-specific marital fertility cannot be calculated directly (e.g. tables 4, 5 and 6, figure 6). The indices are related in the following way:

$$I_f = I_m \times I_g + I_h(1 - I_m)$$

and if I_h is zero then $I_f = I_m \times I_g$ (figure 5 uses this property to construct the curved isolines for I_f).

Gross reproduction rate (GRR) – the average number of daughters that would be born to a woman during her lifetime if she passed through the childbearing ages experiencing the average age-specific fertility pattern of a given period, often a year (figures 2 and 3).

Age-specific marital fertility – The number of legitimate births per 1,000 married women by five-year age groups (e.g. figure 4)

Natural fertility – that fertility which is not influenced by deliberate attempts at that form of family limitation which takes account of the number of previous live births, that is fertility which is not the subject of parity-specific control (Hinde and Woods, 1984)

Life tables – a system for expressing the probability of dying by age, survivorship (figure 7) and life expectation at age x (e_x) (Woods and Hinde, 1987; Woods, 1993)

Life expectation at birth (e_0) – the average number of years a newly-born baby may be expected to live (table 4 and figures 2 and 3).

Intrinsic rate of natural population growth (r) – the annual rate at which a closed stable population grows when it is not affected by migration. Figure 3 has been so constructed to reveal the changing contribution of fertility (via GRR) and mortality (via e_0) to r.

Bibliography

The bibliography is arranged in sections that relate to the seven chapters. Material referred to in each chapter will be listed in that chapter's section along with other useful items. The bibliography begins with some of the most valuable general references.

General references

Anderson, M. (1988a) *Population Change in North-Western Europe, 1750–1850* (London).

Deane, P. and Cole, W. A. (1967) *British Economic Growth* (Cambridge).

Flinn, M. W. (1970) *British Population Growth, 1700–1850* (London).

Flinn, M. W. (ed.) (1977) *Scottish Population History: From the Seventeenth Century to the 1930s* (Cambridge).

Flinn, M. W. (1981) *The European Demographic System, 1500–1820* (Brighton).

Fraser, W. H. and Morris, R. J. (eds) (1990) *People and Society in Scotland, Volume II, 1830–1914* (Edinburgh).

Ó Gráda, C. (1994) *Ireland: A New Economic History, 1730–1939* (Oxford).

Smout, T. C. (1986) *A Century of the Scottish People, 1830–1950* (London).

Thompson, F. M. L. (ed.) (1990) *The Cambridge Social History of Britain, 1750–1950 Volume 2: People and their Environment* (Cambridge).

Wrigley, E. A. (1987) *People, Cities and Wealth* (Oxford).

Wrigley, E. A. (1988) *Continuity, Chance and Change* (Cambridge).

Wrigley, E. A. and Schofield, R. S. (1981) *The Population History of England, 1541–1871: A Reconstruction* (London; Cambridge, 1989).

Chapter 1: Malthus's Britain

Anderson, M. (1988a) *Population Change in North-Western Europe, 1750–1850* (London).

Coleman, D. and Schofield, R. S. (eds) (1986) *The State of Population Theory: Forward from Malthus* (Oxford).

Macfarlane, A. (1986) *Marriage and Love in England, 1300–1840* (Oxford).

Malthus, T. R. (1798 and 1803) *An Essay on the Principle of Population* (First edition (1798) edited by A. Flew, Harmondsworth, 1970; second (1803) and subsequent editions edited by P. James, Cambridge, 1989).

Wilson, C. and Woods, R. I. (1991) 'Fertility in England: a long-term perspective', *Population Studies*, 45, pp. 399–415.

Wrigley, E. A. (1983a) 'Malthus's model of a pre-industrial economy' in J. Dupâquier and A. Fauve-Chamoux (eds) *Malthus Past and Present* (London), pp. 111–24.

Wrigley, E. A. (1983b) 'The growth of population in eighteenth-century England: a conundrum resolved', *Past and Present*, 98, pp. 121–50.

Wrigley, E. A. (1988) *Continuity, Chance and Change* (Cambridge).

Wrigley, E. A. and Schofield, R. S. (1981) *The Population History of England, 1541–1871: A Reconstruction* (London; Cambridge, 1989).

Chapter 2: What do we know and how do we know it?

Anderson, M. (1985) 'The emergence of the modern life cycle in Britain', *Social History*, 10, pp. 69–87.

Anderson, M. (1990) 'The social implications of demographic change' in F. M. L. Thompson (ed.) *The Cambridge Social History of Britain, 1750–1950. Volume 2: People and their Environment* (Cambridge), pp. 1–70.

Armstrong, W. A. (1974) *Stability and Change in an English County Town: A Social Study of York, 1801–50* (Cambridge).

Armstrong, W. A. (1981) 'The flight from the land' in G. E. Mingay (ed.) *The Victorian Countryside* (London), pp. 118–35.

Banks, J. A. (1978) 'The social structure of nineteenth century England as seen through the census' in R. Lawton (ed.) *The Census and Social Structure* (London), pp. 179–223.

Craig, J. (1987) 'Changes in the population composition of England and Wales since 1841', *Population Trends*, 48, pp. 27–36.

Eyler, J. M. (1979) *Victorian Social Medicine: The Ideas and Methods of William Farr* (Baltimore).

Farr, W. (1864) *English Life Tables. Tables of Lifetimes, Annuities, and Premiums* (London).

Farr, W. (1885) *Vital Statistics* (London).

Glass, D. V. (1951) 'A note on the under-registration of births in Britain in the nineteenth century', *Population Studies*, 5, pp. 70–88.

Hardy, A. (1994) ' "Death is a cure for all diseases": using the General

Register Office cause of death statistics for 1837–1920', *Social History of Medicine*, 7, pp. 472–92.

Hewitt, M. (1958) *Wives and Mothers in Victorian Industry* (London).

Higgs, E. (1989) *Making Sense of the Census: The Manuscript Returns for England and Wales, 1801–1901*, Public Record Office Handbooks No. 23 (London).

Hinde, P. R. A. (1987) 'The population of a Wiltshire village in the nineteenth century: a reconstitution study of Berwick St James, 1841–71', *Annals of Human Biology*, 14, pp. 475–85.

Law, C. M. (1967) 'The growth of urban population in England and Wales, 1801–1911', *Transactions of the Institute of British Geographers*, 41, pp. 125–43.

Lawton, R. (1958) 'Population movements in the West Midlands, 1841–1861', *Geography*, 43, pp. 164–77.

Lawton, R. (1972) 'An age of great cities', *Town Planning Review*, 43, pp. 199–224.

Lawton, R. (ed.) (1978) *The Census and Social Structure: An Interpretative Guide to Nineteenth Century Censuses for England and Wales* (London).

Lawton, R. (1983) 'Urbanization and population change in nineteenth-century England' in J. Patten (ed.) *The Expanding City* (London), pp. 179–224.

Laxton, P. (1981) 'Liverpool in 1801: a manuscript return for the first national census', *Transactions of the Historic Society of Lancashire and Cheshire*, 130, pp. 73–113.

Lee, R. D. and Lam, D. (1983) 'Age distribution adjustments for English censuses, 1821 to 1931', *Population Studies*, 37, pp. 445–64.

Malthus, T. R. (1803) *An Essay on the Principle of Population* (Second edition edited by P. James, Cambridge, 1989).

Mitchell, B. R. (1988) *British Historical Statistics* (Cambridge).

Newsholme, A. (1889) *The Elements of Vital Statistics* (London).

Nissel, M. (1987) *People Count: A History of the General Register Office* (London).

Roberts, E. (1984) *A Woman's Place: An Oral History of Working-Class Women, 1890–1940* (Oxford).

Routh, G. (1987) *Occupations of the People of Great Britain, 1801–1891* (London).

Szreter, S. R. S. (1984) 'The genesis of the Registrar-General's social classification of occupations', *British Journal of Sociology*, 35, pp. 522–46.

Szreter, S. R. S. (ed.) (1991) 'The General Register Office of England and Wales and the Public Health Movement 1837–1914, a comparative perspective', *Social History of Medicine*, Special Issue 4(3).

Teitelbaum, M. S. (1974) 'Birth under-registration in the constituent counties of England and Wales, 1841–1910', *Population Studies*, 28, pp. 329–43.

Weber, A. F. (1899) *The Growth of Cities in the Nineteenth Century: A Study in Statistics* (New York; Ithaca, 1963).

Welton, T. A. (1911) *England's Recent Progress: An Investigation of the Statistics of Migrations, Mortality, etc in the Twenty Years from 1881 to 1901* (London).

Wrigley, E. A. (ed.) (1966) *An Introduction to English Historical Demography* (London).

Wrigley, E. A. (ed.) (1972) *Nineteenth Century Society: Essays in the Use of Quantitative Methods for the Study of Social Data* (Cambridge).

Chapter 3: Whether to move and where to go

Anderson, M. and Morse, D. (1990) 'The people' in W. H. Fraser and R. J. Morris (eds) *People and Society in Scotland Volume II, 1830–1914* (Edinburgh), pp. 8–45.

Baines, D. (1985) *Migration in a Mature Economy: Emigration and Internal Migration in England and Wales, 1861–1900* (Cambridge).

Baines, D. (1991) *Emigration from Europe, 1815–1930* (London).

Carrier, N. H. and Jeffrey, J. R. (1953) *External Migration: A Study of the Available Statistics, 1815–1950*, Studies on Medical and Population Subjects No. 6 (London).

Cairncross, A. K. (1953) 'Internal migration in Victorian England', in *Home and Foreign Investment, 1870–1913* (Cambridge), pp. 65–83.

Dennis, R. J. (1984) *English Industrial Cities of the Nineteenth Century* (Cambridge).

Easterlin, R. A. (1961) 'Influences on European overseas emigration before World War I', *Economic Development and Cultural Change*, 9, pp. 331–51.

Flinn, M. W. (ed.) (1977) *Scottish Population History: From the Seventeenth Century to the 1930s* (Cambridge).

Friedlander, D. and Roshier, D. J. (1966) 'A study of internal migration in England and Wales', *Population Studies*, 19, pp. 239–79 and 20, pp. 45–59.

Grigg, D. B. (1977) 'E. G. Ravenstein and the "laws of migration"', *Journal of Historical Geography*, 3, pp. 41–54.

Hatton, T. J. and Williamson, J. G. (1994) 'What drove the mass migrations from Europe in the late nineteenth century', *Population and Development Review*, 20, pp. 533–59.

Kearns, G. and Withers, C. W. J. (eds) (1991) *Urbanizing Britain* (Cambridge).

Law, C. M. (1967) 'The growth of urban population in England and

Wales, 1801–1911', *Transactions of the Institute of British Geographers*, 41, pp. 125–43.

Lawton, R. (1956) 'The population of Liverpool in the mid-nineteenth century', *Transactions of the Historic Society of Lancashire and Cheshire*, 107, pp. 89–120.

Lawton, R. (1959) 'Irish migration to England and Wales in the mid-nineteenth century', *Irish Geography*, 4, pp. 35–54.

Lawton, R. (1967) 'Rural depopulation in nineteenth-century England' in R. W. Steel and R. Lawton (eds) *Liverpool Essays in Geography* (London), pp. 227–55.

Lawton, R. (1968) 'Population changes in England and Wales in the later nineteenth century: an analysis of trends by registration districts', *Transactions of the Institute of British Geographers*, 44, pp. 55–74.

Lawton, R. (1979) 'Mobility in nineteenth-century British cities', *Geographical Journal*, 145, pp. 206–24.

Lawton, R. (1983) 'Urbanization and population change in nineteenth-century England' in J. Patten (ed.) *The Expanding City* (London), pp. 179–224.

Lees, L. H. (1979) *Exiles of Erin: Irish Emigrants in Victorian London* (Ithaca).

Morris, R. J. (1990) 'Urbanization in Scotland' in W. H. Fraser and R. J. Morris (eds) *People and Society in Scotland Volume II, 1830–1914* (Edinburgh), pp. 73–102.

Perry, P. J. (1969) 'Working class isolation and mobility in rural Dorset, 1837–1936: a study of marriage distances', *Transactions of the Institute of British Geographers*, 46, pp. 115–35.

Pooley, C. G. (1979) 'Residential mobility in the Victorian city', *Transactions of the Institute of British Geographers, New Series*, 4, pp. 258–77.

Pooley, C. G. (1983) 'Welsh migrants to England in the mid-nineteenth century', *Journal of Historical Geography*, 9, pp. 287–306.

Porter, R. (1994) *London: A Social History* (London).

Ravenstein, E. G. (1885 and 1889) 'The laws of migration', *Journal of the Royal Statistical Society*, 48, pp. 167–227 and 52, pp. 241–301.

Redford, A. (1926) *Labour Migration in England, 1800–1850* (Manchester).

Saville, J. (1957) *Rural Development in England and Wales, 1851–1951* (London).

Swift, R. and Gilley, S. (eds) (1985) *The Irish in the Victorian City* (London).

Thomas, B. (1954) *Migration and Economic Growth: A Study of Great Britain and the Atlantic Economy* (Cambridge).

Weber, A. F. (1899) *The Growth of Cities in the Nineteenth Century: A Study in Statistics* (New York; Ithaca, 1963).

Withers, C. W. J. and Watson, A. J. (1991) 'Stepwise migration and

Highland migration to Glasgow, 1852–1898', *Journal of Historical Geography*, 17, pp. 35-55.

Chapter 4: Marriage

Anderson, M. (1971) *Family Structure in 19th Century Lancashire* (Cambridge).

Anderson, M. (1976) 'Marriage patterns in Victorian Britain: an analysis based on registration district data for England and Wales, 1861', *Journal of Family History*, 1, pp. 55–78.

Anderson, M. (1978) 'Sociological history and the working-class family', *Social History*, 3, pp. 317–34.

Anderson, M. (1980) *Approaches to the History of the Western Family, 1500–1914* (London).

Anderson, M. (1984) 'The social position of spinsters in mid-Victorian Britain', *Journal of Family History*, 9, pp. 377–93.

Anderson, M. (1988b) 'Households, families and individuals: some preliminary results from the national sample from the 1851 census', *Continuity and Change*, 3, pp. 421–38.

Anderson, M. and Morse, D. (1990) 'The people' in W. H. Fraser and R. J. Morris (eds) *People and Society in Scotland Volume II, 1830–1914* (Edinburgh), pp. 8–45.

Anderson, O. (1975) 'The incidence of civil marriage in Victorian England and Wales', *Past and Present*, 69, pp. 50–87 and 84, pp. 155-62.

Coale, A. J. and Watkins, S. C. (eds) (1986) *The Decline of Fertility in Europe* (Princeton).

Crafts, N. F. R. (1978) 'Average age at first marriage for women in mid-nineteenth century England and Wales: a cross-sectional study', *Population Studies*, 32, pp. 21–5.

Friedlander, D. (1973) 'Demographic patterns and socioeconomic characteristics of the coal-mining population in England and Wales in the nineteenth century', *Economic Development and Cultural Change*, 22, pp. 39–51.

Garrett, E. M. (1990) 'The trials of labour: motherhood versus employment in a nineteenth-century textile centre', *Continuity and Change*, 5, pp. 121–54.

Hewitt, M. (1958) *Wives and Mothers in Victorian Industry* (London).

Higgs, E. (1983) 'Domestic servants and households in Victorian England', *Social History*, 8, pp. 201–10.

Hinde, P. R. A. (1985) 'Household structure, marriage and the institution of service in nineteenth-century rural England', *Local Population Studies*, 35, pp. 43–51.

Hinde, P. R. A. (1989) 'The marriage market in the nineteenth-century

English countryside', *European Journal of Economic History*, 18, pp. 383–92.

Kabir, M. (1980) 'Regional variations in nuptiality in England and Wales during the demographic transition', *Genus*, 36, pp. 171–87.

Leneman, L. and Mitchison, R. (1987) 'Scottish illegitimacy rates in the early modern period', *Economic History Review, 2nd Series*, 40, pp. 41–63.

Litchfield, R. B. (1988) 'Single people in the nineteenth-century city: a comparative perspective on occupations and living situations', *Continuity and Change*, 3, pp. 83–100.

Mitchison, R. and Leneman, L. (1989) *Sexuality and Social Control: Scotland, 1660–1780* (Oxford).

Ogle, W. (1890) 'On marriage rates and marriage ages, with special reference to the growth of population', *Journal of the Royal Statistical Society*, 53, pp. 253–80.

Stone, L. (1990) *Road to Divorce: England, 1530–1987* (Oxford).

Tranter, N. L. (1985) 'Illegitimacy in nineteenth century rural Scotland. A puzzle resolved', *International Journal of Sociology and Social Policy*, 5, pp. 33–46.

Wall, R., Robin, J. and Laslett, P. (eds) (1983) *Family Forms in Historic Europe* (Cambridge).

Wilson, C. and Woods, R. I. (1991) 'Fertility in England: a long-term perspective', *Population Studies*, 45, pp. 399–415.

Woods, R. I. (1984) 'Social class variations in the decline of marital fertility in late nineteenth-century London', *Geografiska Annaler*, 66B, pp. 29–38.

Woods, R. I. and Hinde, P. R. A. (1985) 'Nuptiality and age at marriage in nineteenth-century England', *Journal of Family History*, 10, pp. 119–44.

Chapter 5: How many children should we have?

Anderson, M. and Morse, D. (1990) 'The people' in W. H. Fraser and R. J. Morris (eds) *People and Society in Scotland Volume II, 1830–1914* (Edinburgh), pp. 8–45.

Anderson, M. and Morse, D. (1993) 'High fertility, high emigration, low nuptiality: adjustment processes in Scotland's demographic experience. Parts I and II', *Population Studies*, 47, pp. 5–25 and 319–43.

Anderson, O. (1975) 'The incidence of civil marriage in Victorian England and Wales', *Past and Present*, 69, pp. 50–87 and 84, pp. 155-62.

Banks, J. A. (1954) *Prosperity and Parenthood: A Study of Family Planning Among the Victorian Middle Classes* (London).

Banks, J. A. (1981) *Victorian Values: Secularism and the Size of Families* (London).

Banks, J. A. and Banks, O. (1964) *Feminism and Family Planning in Victorian England* (Liverpool).

Bongaarts, J. and Potter, R. J. (1983) *Fertility, Biology and Behavior: An Analysis of the Proximate Determinants* (New York).

Brass, W. and Kabir, M. (1980) 'Regional variations in fertility and child mortality during the demographic transition in England and Wales' in J. Hobcraft and P. H. Rees (eds) *Regional Demographic Development* (London), pp. 71–88.

Coale, A. J. and Watkins, S. C. (eds) (1986) *The Decline of Fertility in Europe* (Princeton).

Crafts, N. F. R. (1984a) 'A time series study of fertility in England and Wales, 1877–1938', *European Journal of Economic History*, 13, pp. 571–90.

Crafts, N. F. R. (1984b) 'A cross-sectional study of legitimate fertility in England and Wales, 1911', *Research in Economic History*, 9, pp. 89–107.

Davies, M. (1982) 'Corsets and conception: fashion and demographic trends in the nineteenth century', *Comparative Studies in Society and History*, 24, pp. 611–41.

Friedlander, D. (1973) 'Demographic patterns and socioeconomic characteristics of the coal-mining population in England and Wales in the nineteenth century', *Economic Development and Cultural Change*, 22, pp. 39–51.

Friedlander, D. (1983) 'Demographic responses and socioeconomic structure: population processes in England and Wales in the nineteenth century', *Demography*, 20, pp. 249–72.

Friedlander, D., Schellekens, J. and Ben-Moshe, E. (1991) 'The transition from high to low marital fertility: cultural or socioeconomic determinants', *Economic Development and Cultural Change*, 39, pp. 331–51.

Garrett, E. M. (1990) 'The trials of labour: motherhood versus employment in a nineteenth-century textile centre', *Continuity and Change*, 5, pp. 121–54.

Garrett, E. M. and Reid, A. (1994) 'Satanic mills, pleasant lands: spatial variation in women's work, fertility and infant mortality as viewed from the 1911 census', *Historical Research*, 67, pp. 156–77.

Gillis, J. R., Tilly, L. A. and Levine, D. (eds) (1992) *The European Experience of Declining Fertility: A Quiet Evolution, 1850–1970* (Oxford).

Glass, D. V. (1938) 'Changes in fertility in England and Wales, 1851–1931' in L. Hogben (ed.) *Political Arithmetic* (London), pp. 161–212.

Haines, M. R. (1979) *Fertility and Occupation: Population Patterns in Industrialization* (New York).

Haines, M. R. (1989) 'Social class differentials during fertility decline: England and Wales revisited', *Population Studies*, 43, pp. 305–22.

Hinde, P. R. A. and Woods, R. I. (1984) 'Variations in historical natural fertility patterns and the measurement of fertility control', *Journal of Biosocial Science*, 16, pp. 309–21.

Innes, J. W. (1938) *Class Fertility Trends in England and Wales, 1876–1934* (Princeton).

Litchfield, R. B. (1978) 'The family and the mill: cottonmill work, family work patterns and fertility in mid-Victorian Stockport' in A. S. Wohl (ed.) *The Victorian Family* (London), pp. 180–96.

McLaren, A. (1977) 'Women's work and the regulation of family size', *History Workshop Journal*, 4, pp. 70–81.

McLaren, A. (1978) *Birth Control in Nineteenth-Century England* (London).

Mason, M. (1994) *The Making of Victorian Sexuality* and *The Making of Victorian Sexual Attitudes* (Oxford).

Newsholme, A. and Stevenson, T. H. C. (1906) 'The decline of human fertility in the United Kingdom and other countries as shown by corrected birth rates', *Journal of the Royal Statistical Society*, 69, pp. 34–87.

Peel, J. (1963) 'The manufacture and retailing of contraceptives in England', *Population Studies*, 17, pp. 113–25.

Reay, B. (1994) 'Before the transition: fertility in English villages, 1800–1880', *Continuity and Change*, 9, pp. 91–120.

Reves, R. (1985) 'Declining fertility in England and Wales as a major cause of the twentieth century decline in mortality: the role of changing family size and age structure in infectious disease mortality in infancy', *American Journal of Epidemiology*, 122, pp. 112–26.

Roberts, E. (1984) *A Woman's Place: An Oral History of Working-Class Women, 1890–1940* (Oxford).

Sauer, R. (1978) 'Infanticide and abortion in nineteenth century Britain', *Population Studies*, 32, pp. 81–93.

Seccombe, W. (1990) 'Starting to stop: working-class fertility decline in Britain', *Past and Present*, 126, pp. 151–88.

Shorter, E. (1973) 'Female emancipation, birth control and fertility in European history', *American Historical Review*, 78, pp. 605–40.

Soloway, R. A. (1982) *Birth Control and the Population Question in England, 1877–1930* (Chapel Hill).

Soloway, R. A. (1990) *Demography and Degeneration: Eugenics and the Declining Birth Rate in Twentieth Century Britain* (Chapel Hill).

Stevenson, T. H. C. (1920) 'The fertility of various social classes in England and Wales from the middle of the nineteenth century to 1911', *Journal of the Royal Statistical Society*, 83, pp. 401–32.

Teitelbaum, M. S. (1984) *The British Fertility Decline: Demographic Transition in the Crucible of the Industrial Revolution* (Princeton).

Watkins, S. C. (1991) *From Provinces to Nations: Demographic Integration in Western Europe, 1870–1960* (Princeton).

Wilson, C. (1984) 'Natural fertility in pre-industrial England', *Population Studies*, 38, pp. 225–40.

Wilson, C. (1986) 'The proximate determinants of marital fertility in England, 1600–1899' in L. Bonfield, R. M. Smith and K. Wrightson (eds) *The World We Have Gained* (Oxford), pp. 203–30.

Wilson, C. and Woods, R. I. (1991) 'Fertility in England: a long-term perspective', *Population Studies*, 45, pp. 399–415.

Woods, R. I. (1987) 'Approaches to the fertility transition in Victorian England', *Population Studies*, 41, pp. 283–311.

Woods, R. I. (1992) 'Working-class fertility decline in Britain', *Past and Present*, 134, pp. 200-7.

Woods, R. I. and Smith, C. W. (1983) 'The decline of marital fertility in the late nineteenth century: the case of England and Wales', *Population Studies*, 37, pp. 207–25.

Woods, R. I., Watterson, P. A. and Woodward, J. H. (1988–89) 'The causes of rapid infant mortality decline in England and Wales, 1861–1921. Parts I and II', *Population Studies*, 42, pp. 343–66 and 43, pp. 113–32.

Chapter 6: Mortality

Alter, G. and Riley, J. C. (1989) 'Frailty, sickness, and death: models of morbidity and mortality in historical populations', *Population Studies*, 43, pp. 25–45.

Anderson, O. (1987) *Suicide in Victorian England* (Oxford).

Bynum, W. F. (1994) *Science and the Practice of Medicine in the Nineteenth Century* (Cambridge).

Dwork, D. (1987) 'The milk option: an aspect of the history of infant welfare movement in England, 1898–1908', *Medical History*, 31, pp. 51–69.

Dyhouse, C. (1978) 'Working-class mothers and infant mortality in England, 1895–1914', *Journal of Social History*, 12(2), pp. 248–67.

Eyler, J. M. (1976) 'Mortality statistics and Victorian health policy: program and criticism', *Bulletin of the History of Medicine*, 50, pp. 335–55.

Eyler, J. M. (1979) *Victorian Social Medicine: The Ideas and Methods of William Farr* (Baltimore).

Eyler, J. M. (1987) 'Scarlet fever and confinement: the Edwardian debate over isolation hospitals', *Bulletin of the History of Medicine*, 61, pp. 1–24.

Farr, W. (1864) *English Life Tables. Tables of Lifetimes, Annuities, and Premiums* (London).

Floud, R., Wachter, K. and Gregory, A. (1990) *Height, Health and History: Nutritional Status in the United Kingdom, 1750–1980* (Cambridge).

Frazer, W. M. (1947) *Duncan of Liverpool: An Account of the Work of Dr W. H. Duncan Medical Officer of Health of Liverpool, 1847–63* (London).

Guha, S. (1994) 'The importance of social intervention in England's mortality decline: the evidence reviewed', *Social History of Medicine*, 7, pp. 89–113.

Hardy, A. (1983) 'Smallpox in London: factors in the decline of the disease in the nineteenth century', *Medical History*, 27, pp. 111–38.

Hardy, A. (1988) 'Public health and the expert: the London Medical Officers of Health, 1856–1900' in R. MacLeod (ed.) *Government and Expertise: Specialists, Administrators and Professionals, 1860–1919* (Cambridge), pp. 128–42.

Hardy, A. (1993) *Epidemic Streets: Infectious Disease and the Rise of Preventive Medicine* (Oxford).

Hassan, J. A. (1985) 'The growth and impact of the British water industry in the nineteenth century', *Economic History Review, 2nd Series*, 38, pp. 531–47.

Kearns, G. (1985) *Urban Epidemics and Historical Geography: Cholera in London, 1848–9*, Historical Geography Research Series No. 15 (Norwich).

Kearns, G. (1988) 'Private property and public health reform in England, 1830–1870', *Social Science and Medicine*, 26, pp. 187–99.

Kearns, G. (1991) 'Class, biology and the urban penalty' in G. Kearns and C. W. J. Withers (eds) *Urbanizing Britain* (Cambridge).

Lee, C. H. (1991) 'Regional inequalities in infant mortality in Britain, 1861–1971: patterns and hypotheses', *Population Studies*, 45, pp. 55–65.

Logan, W. P. D. (1950) 'Mortality in England and Wales from 1848–1947', *Population Studies*, 4, pp. 132–78.

Loudon, I. (1986) 'Deaths in childbed from the eighteenth century to 1935', *Medical History*, 30, pp. 1–41.

Loudon, I. (1988) 'Maternal mortality: 1880–1950. Some regional and international comparisons', *Social History of Medicine*, 1, pp. 183–228.

Loudon, I. (1991) 'On maternal and infant mortality', *Social History of Medicine*, 4, pp. 29–73.

Loudon, I. (1992) *Death in Childbirth: An International Study of Maternal Care and Maternal Mortality, 1800–1950* (Oxford).

Luckin, B. (1980) 'Death and survival in the city: approaches to the history of disease', *Urban History Yearbook*, pp. 53–62.

McDowall, M. (1983) 'William Farr and the study of occupational mortality', *Population Trends*, 31, pp. 12–14.

McKeown, T. (1976) *The Modern Rise of Population* (London).

McKeown, T. (1979) *Role of Medicine: Dream, Mirage or Nemesis?* (Oxford).

McKeown, T. and Brown, R. G. (1955) 'Medical evidence related to English population changes in the eighteenth century', *Population Studies*, 9, pp. 119–41.

McKeown, T. and Record, R. G. (1962) 'Reasons for the decline of mortality in England and Wales during the nineteenth century', *Population Studies*, 16, pp. 94–122.

McKeown, T., Record, R. G. and Turner, R. D. (1975) 'An interpretation of the decline of mortality in England and Wales during the twentieth century', *Population Studies*, 29, pp. 391–422.

Mercer, A. (1990) *Disease, Mortality and Population in Transition: Epidemiological-Demographic Change in England since the Eighteenth Century as part of a Global Phenomenon* (Leicester).

Newsholme, A. (1889) *The Elements of Vital Statistics* (London).

Pelling, M. (1978) *Cholera, Fever and English Medicine, 1825–1865* (Oxford).

Pickstone, J. V. (1985) *Medicine and Industrial Society: A History of Development in Manchester and its Regions, 1752–1946* (Manchester).

Reves, R. (1985) 'Declining fertility in England and Wales as a major cause of the twentieth century decline in mortality: the role of changing family size and age structure in infectious disease mortality in infancy', *American Journal of Epidemiology*, 122, pp. 112–26.

Riley, J. C. (1987a) 'Disease without death: new sources for a history of sickness', *Journal of Interdisciplinary History*, 17, pp. 537–63.

Riley, J. C. (1987b) 'Ill health during the English mortality decline: the Friendly Societies' experience', *Bulletin of the History of Medicine*, 61, pp. 563–88.

Riley, J. C. (1989) *Sickness. Recovery and Death: A History and Forecast of Ill Health* (London).

Smith, F. B. (1979) *The People's Health, 1830–1910* (London).

Smith, F. B. (1988) *The Retreat of Tuberculosis, 1850–1950* (London).

Szreter, S. R. S. (1988) 'The importance of social intervention in Britain's mortality decline c. 1850–1914: a re-interpretation of the role of public health', *Social History of Medicine*, 1, pp. 1–37.

Szreter, S. R. S. (1994) 'Mortality in England in the eighteenth and nineteenth centuries: a reply to Sumit Guha', *Social History of Medicine*, 7, pp. 269–82.

Watterson, P. A. (1986) 'Role of the environment in the decline of infant mortality: an analysis of the 1911 Census of England and Wales', *Journal of Biosocial Science*, 18, pp. 457–70.

Watterson, P. A. (1988) 'Infant mortality by father's occupation from the 1911 Census of England and Wales', *Demography*, 25, pp. 289–306.

Williams, N. (1992) 'Death in its season: class, environment and the mortality of infants in nineteenth-century Sheffield', *Social History of Medicine*, 5, pp. 71–94.

Williams, N. and Mooney, G. (1994) 'Infant mortality in an "Age of Great Cities": London and the English provincial cities compared, c. 1840–1910', *Continuity and Change*, 9, pp. 185–212.

Williamson, J. G. (1982) 'Was the industrial revolution worth it? Disamenities and death in 19th century British towns', *Explorations in Economic History*, 19, pp. 221–45.

Williamson, J. G. (1984) 'British mortality and the value of life, 1781–1931', *Population Studies*, 38, pp. 157–72.

Williamson, J. G. (1990) *Coping with City Growth During the British Industrial Revolution* (Cambridge).

Wohl, A. S. (1983) *Endangered Lives: Public Health in Victorian Britain* (London).

Woods, R. I. (1985) 'The effects of population redistribution on the level of mortality in nineteenth-century England and Wales', *Journal of Economic History*, 45, pp. 645–51.

Woods, R. I. (1991) 'Public health via hygiene and sanitation: the urban environment in the late nineteenth and early twentieth centuries' in R. S. Schofield, D. Reher and A. Bideau (eds) *The Great Mortality Decline: A Reassessment of the European Experience* (Oxford), pp. 232–47.

Woods, R. I. (1993) 'On the historical relationship between infant and adult mortality', *Population Studies*, 47, pp. 195–219.

Woods, R. I. and Hinde, P. R. A. (1987) 'Mortality in Victorian England: models and patterns', *Journal of Interdisciplinary History*, 18, pp. 27–54.

Woods, R. I., Watterson, P. A. and Woodward, J. H. (1988–89) 'The causes of rapid infant mortality decline in England and Wales, 1861–1921. Parts I and II', *Population Studies*, 42, pp. 343–66 and 43, pp. 113–32.

Woods, R. I. and Williams, N. (1995) 'Must the gap widen before it can be narrowed? Long-term trends in social class mortality differentials', *Continuity and Change*, 10, pp. 103–37.

Woods, R. I. and Woodward, J. H. (eds) (1984) *Urban Disease and Mortality in Nineteenth Century England* (London).

Chapter 7: 1911

Flinn, M. W. (1970) *British Population Growth, 1700–1850* (London).

Wrigley, E. A. (1983b) 'The growth of population in eighteenth-century England: a conundrum resolved', *Past and Present*, 98, pp. 121–50.

6 British population history, 1911–1991

Michael Anderson

Professor of Economic History
University of Edinburgh

1
Introduction

The aim of this essay is to take the history of British population up to 1991. The period from 1911 to 1991 was one of major change, and only the broad outlines can be covered here. Those needing more detail should consult the supplementary reading listed in the bibliography and indicated in the text by numbers in square brackets.

There are, in general, fewer problems in describing population change in the twentieth century than in the earlier periods. In particular, there is no shortage of available source material, directly focused on the issues of concern. Regular and increasingly sophisticated censuses [1] and other questionnaire surveys [especially 13] are available. The dynamics of population change can be explored in the detailed published summaries from the registration of births, deaths and marriages [2–12], and by study of offshoots from administrative processes (for example, information on population movement obtained from changes in registration with general practitioners [28]). Particularly after key reforms to vital registration in 1938, the available sources provide most of the tools needed to estimate basic demographic rates, but gaps remain in some areas (for example, mortality by occupation among married women, and cohabitation). Restrictions imposed by confidentiality restrict our ability to construct the detailed birth histories needed to understand differences in couples' family-building strategies. However, starting in the 1930s, and expanding significantly from the 1960s, an increasing number of sociological inquiries provides evidence on people's perceptions and motivations, of a kind that is almost totally lacking for earlier periods.

2

Population change: trends and patterns and movement

Between 1851 and 1911, the population of Great Britain nearly doubled, from 20.8 million to 40.8 million. Between 1911 and 1971 it grew by a further third, to 54.4 million, but over the next twenty years only another 3% was added (mostly in the 1980s). The 1991 population was 56.2 million.

Figure 1 shows these trends, broken down by country and, within England, into standard regions. The graph is plotted on a logarithmic vertical scale, which has the useful property that, regardless of initial population size, similar rates of change have identical angles of slope. Particularly marked is the stagnant twentieth-century demographic growth of Scotland, with the 1991 figures being 1.5% lower than in 1971 (only 7.3% up on 1911). Wales saw a growth of 16.2% for 1911–1971 and a further 5.5% for 1971–1991, and England 37.8% and 3.9% respectively. Elsewhere within the European Community, no national state saw a fall in population between 1971 and 1991; only Belgium and Denmark had growth rates (marginally) lower than those of England and Wales, and the EC average growth for the period was 7.7% [3 (1994)].

Within England there are contrasting trends, though the recent figures are subject to some inconsistencies because of boundary changes. Three regions show continuing strong growth throughout the century right up to 1991: the East Midlands, East Anglia and the South-west (which grew especially rapidly after 1950) [16 chap. 3]. By contrast, the North, the North-west and Yorkshire/Humberside shared Scotland's experience of modest growth between 1911 and 1951, followed by slow increase for the next twenty years, and subsequent stagnation or decline, reflecting their increasingly

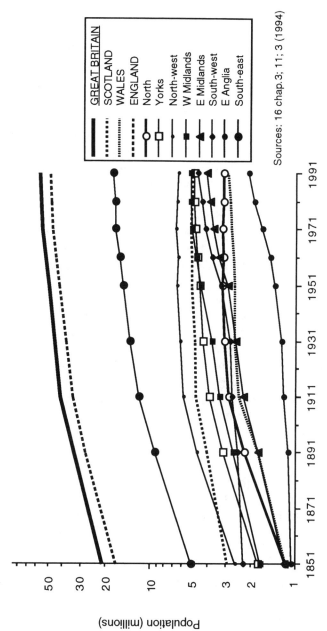

Figure 1 *Population of Great Britain and its constituent countries, and of the regions of England, 1851–1991*

Sources: 16 chap.3; 11; 3 (1994)

depressed industrial base [16 chap 3; 23; 24]. The West Midlands, markedly more dynamic up to 1971, also saw its economy and population depressed thereafter. Even the South-east replaced rapid population growth – up by nearly a half between 1911 and 1971 – by stagnation in the 1970s; between 1971 and 1991, the South-east's population grew by 3.7%, but this conceals a fall of 8.4% in the population of Greater London and a 12.0% rise elsewhere in the region.

A similar pattern, of a declining metropolitan core accompanied by rising population in surrounding areas, characterised most of Britain throughout the second half of the twentieth century [16 chap. 3; 24; 25]. Britain's 19 largest urban centres all saw their populations undergo inter-censal decline at least once before 1981, though absorption of suburbs through boundary changes sometimes caused recorded populations to continue to rise. Liverpool and Manchester were among several cities which reached their census peak as early as 1931, and Greater London, Birmingham and Glasgow all declined by the 1950s (Inner London's population had peaked in 1901) [16 chap. 10]. Between 1971 and 1981, Glasgow's population fell by 22%, Manchester's by 17% and Liverpool's by 16%; Greater London lost almost a tenth of its population in the 1970s, though in the 1980s the rate of loss slowed significantly. In parallel with this process of 'decentralisation', populations of remoter rural areas continued until the 1970s a decline which had typically begun well before 1900. As a result, population became increasingly concentrated in rings surrounding the major urban centres, and, within the more rural areas, focused on their principal towns. However, in the early 1970s, as metropolitan decline continued, many remote areas saw population growth, and this process of 'counter-urbanisation' continued, particularly in the Western and Northern Isles of Scotland, through most of the 1980s [26; 27; 28; 29].

Populations grow or decline through the net result of changes in numbers of births, deaths, and in- and out-migrants. Taking England and Wales first, at the start of the twentieth century, birth rates were 65% higher than death rates, and the differential increased to 73% in the years immediately before the First World War. As a result, even at a time of high emigration, population grew rapidly, rising by nearly 11% between 1901 and 1911. After the War, birth rates fell much faster than death rates, and the gap between births and deaths narrowed to just 17% in 1933. The post-1945 period saw a resurgence of births, while the overall death rate remained almost constant, as improved survival of the young was offset by the impact of an ageing population. The result was an acceleration in population growth after 1945, with births exceeding deaths by about 50% throughout the 1960s. From the early 1970s, however, the number of births fell back dramatically, from an annual average of around 863,000 between 1961 and 1971 to an average of only around 650,000 between 1971 and 1991. With the net balance of international migration playing only a small role after World War One, the prime determinant of English and Welsh demographic history at national level between 1921 and 1991 was thus the erratic path of fertility change.

In Scotland, the situation was rather different. Fertility and mortality broadly followed the English/Welsh trends, with both birth and death rates rather higher until 1983. However, as Figure 2 shows, Scotland's population grew much more slowly than England's, almost entirely due to the much higher rates of Scottish emigration. In the 1920s, the decade with the highest levels of loss, around 390,000 more people left than entered Scotland, and, in spite of a 54% excess of births over deaths, the country experienced a small net decline of population. The high birth rates of the 1950s and 1960s were almost totally offset by the loss over the two decades of more than half a million emigrants (roughly balanced between those who moved overseas and those who moved elsewhere within the United Kingdom). Thereafter, with net emigration running at almost 15,000 per year, Scotland suffered a loss of population in every year but two between 1971 and 1989.

Historical geographers have debated at length the factors that underlie the different balance of in- and out-migration between regions [26]; they have not always been helped by problems (some of their own making) of defining consistent and socially meaningful geographical boundaries across which movements are measured. In most accounts, distinctions are made between processes of decentralisation (movement from core metropolitan areas) and more general regional flows, notably a continuing tendency for the balance of migration in England to be from north to south, and for the west of Scotland to have the highest rates of population loss [30].

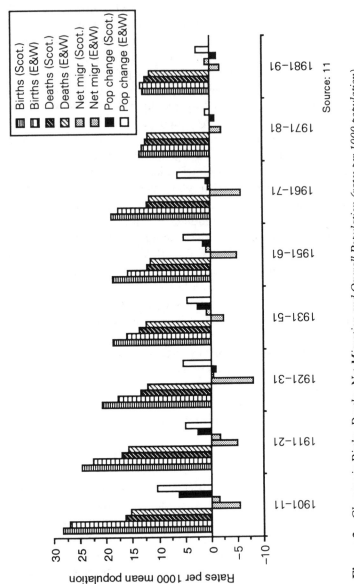

Figure 2 *Changes in Births, Deaths, Net Migration and Overall Population (rates per 1000 population), Scotland, and England and Wales, 1901–1991*

In considering major regional flows, most emphasis is laid on the shifting balance of the national economy, with continued out-migration since the 1920s from the areas (mainly in northern Britain) which had dominated the industrial expansion of the nineteenth century, and inmigration to areas (mostly in the southern half of the country) where new industries established themselves from the 1930s and where the major expansion of government and financial services took place after the Second World War [16 chap. 10; 24]. It would be wrong, however, to see this movement simply as one in which northerly unemployed or poorly paid workers pursued new opportunities in the south. The unemployed themselves had relatively low migration propensities, and the net moves had little impact on regional inequalities in unemployment. Throughout the period, a major constraint on this kind of movement was rigidity in the housing market, initially as a result of legal controls on rented property and local government policy on council housing, and, since the 1960s, because of large house-price differentials.

A second factor which produced apparent shifts in population at regional level is a by-product of the processes of decentralisation noted above. Rising incomes, markedly improved transportation (especially by road since the Second World War), and restrictions on building in the immediate surroundings of major cities at a time when the number of households rose rapidly, all encouraged outward movements in residence, accompanied by long-distance commuting, a growing share of which was across regional boundaries [31]. Decentralisation was accentuated by an increasing tendency among elderly people to move to cheaper housing in rural areas on retirement [32; 33]. In addition, especially in the 1970s, many companies relocated parts of their manufacturing and servicing activities to non-metropolitan areas with lower cost and less cramped industrial sites and with local supplies of available labour [26; 28; 30]. A further impetus to dispersed settlement was the development of North Sea oil and gas installations in the 1970s.

These were all factors which encouraged a shift of population out of cities and their immediate peripheries. However, they are not the whole explanation, nor do they explain that element of counter-urbanisation which led to a reversal of more than a century of population decline in the most remote rural areas of the country [26; 30]. This migration runs counter to the dominant neo-classical economists' explanation, because it involved movement away from areas with higher wages and lower unemployment, and towards areas with lower wages and higher unemployment or under-employment. In part it reflected a shift in values among a sector of the population who expressed in this way their preferences against the values of capitalist city life. At the same time, high levels of unemployment in all parts of the national economy made attractive a more self-dependent life with an element of security derived from multiple occupations, in areas of the country where housing was relatively cheap. In addition, particularly in areas like the Highlands and Islands (where net in-movement from England continued through the 1980s), inmigration was probably encouraged by improved transport, services, and mass communications, which allowed residents even in more remote communities to remain in contact with most amenities of late twentieth-century life.

A final element in overall population change both nationally and regionally has been the balance between immigration and emigration [16 chap. 11; 34; 35]. We have already noted the significant net outflow of population from Scotland throughout the period. Scottish emigration was among the highest in Europe in the years before World War One and overseas emigration from Scotland (but not from England) continued to be heavy for much of the inter-war period, focused particularly on the Old Commonwealth. After World War Two, emigration from Great Britain actually exceeded immigration in most years before the 1980s, with a significant flow of skilled talent to non-Commonwealth countries in Europe and the USA.

One particularly characteristic feature of Scottish migration history in the twentieth century has been that, with the exception of the Irish, no major immigrant group located itself in Scotland on any appreciable scale. In England and Wales, however, large-scale immigration has been much more important (though Irish citizens always made up the largest single group of 'foreign' nationals in Great Britain, their numbers rising by about half a million between 1939 and 1971). Taking Great Britain as a whole, adding the Irish to over 850,000 white British/UK nationals born overseas, and including nearly half a million foreign nationals from the USA, Australasia and other parts of Europe, the total white immigrant population in the mid-1980s was about 1.8 million [16 chap. 12]. By the mid-1980s, there were also 1.5 million immigrants from ethnic minority groups, and about one million members of these groups born in the UK.

In 1950 there were probably fewer than 20,000 non-white residents in Britain, but by 1961, in part encouraged by active recruitment of labour particularly in Jamaica, there were about 200,000 born in the West Indies and well over 50,000 born on the Indian sub-continent. The 1962 Commonwealth Immigrants Act, significantly strengthened in 1968, 1971, 1986 and 1988, imposed strict limits on immigration, making entry for most adult male Commonwealth citizens dependent on prior acquisition of a work voucher, and increasingly restricting access by dependents. The threat of the 1962 Act encouraged a further 98,000 immigrants from the Caribbean and 92,000 from the Indian sub-continent between January 1961 and June 1962. Thereafter the immigration rate fell, though nearly a million further New Commonwealth and Pakistan-born immigrants entered the UK between 1965 and 1984. Overall, ethnic minority immigrants made up about 2.4% of the British population in the mid-1980s, and the share of the ethnic minority population as a whole was about 4.4% of the total.

3
Mortality

Trends

As Figure 3 shows, the female crude death rate in England and Wales initially continued its nineteenth-century decline, but it levelled out in the 1920s, as falls in 'age-specific mortality'[1] were offset by a steadily ageing population. The rates for males followed roughly the same path as for females, typically about 20 per 10,000 higher [9; 16 chap. 7]. For most periods, Scottish death rates modestly exceeded those for England and Wales, though, in the 1980s, female death rates in Scotland turned upwards at a time

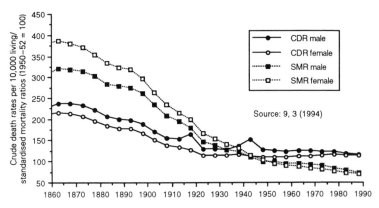

Figure 3 *Crude death rates, and standardised mortality rates (1950–52 = 100), (quinquennial averages), England and Wales, 1860–1990*

---

[1] Age-specific mortality rates are normally generated by calculating the number of people dying in any year in each five-year period of life for every thousand people alive in that age group on one date in that year.

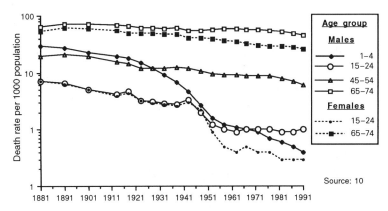

Figure 4   *Death rates (per 1000 population, decennial averages), selected ages, Scotland, 1881–1991*

when in England and Wales they were modestly declining. Civilian death rates rose during both the World Wars, and there were about 723,000 military deaths between 1914 and 1918, and 265,000 between 1939 and 1945 [16 chap. 7].

However, crude death rates are strongly influenced by population age structure, and Figure 3 takes this into account by also showing 'standardised mortality ratios'.[2] These SMRs show rapid decline until the late 1940s, limited reduction until the late 1970s, then a rapid further fall in the 1980s; by 1990, the SMR was 25% below the 1966–70 level for males and 19% lower for females [9].

Figure 4 explores the age pattern of mortality further, examining selected Scottish age/sex groups (the patterns for England and Wales were broadly similar though Scottish mortality was generally higher) [9; 16 chap. 7]. Death rates for children beyond their first year of life fell from the mid-nineteenth century, with younger children benefiting particularly from the widespread use of anti-biotics in the post-Second World War period. Death rates for

---

[2]   Standardised mortality ratios control for variations in age and sex structures between different geographical areas (or social groups) by: first calculating age/sex-specific mortality for any area (or social group) for each age group separately; next estimating the total number of deaths that these rates would together produce if the area (or group) studied had the same age and sex structure as the national population; and finally comparing the age/sex-standardised death rate for the area (or group) with that of the national population. Changed age structures can also be controlled in this way.

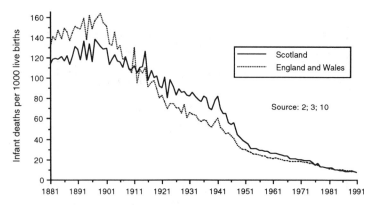

Figure 5 *Infant mortality, Scotland, and England and Wales, 1881–1991*

Scottish males aged 1–4 fell by 70% between 1900–2 and 1936–40; by 1990–92 they were less than 2% of their 1900–2 rate. From the late nineteenth century there was also a steady and continuing reduction in deaths among young adults. There were very fast falls in the 1940s and 1950s, but, especially in Scotland, little if any subsequent reduction. Among older middle-aged adults and, above all, among the elderly, improvements in survival were modest everywhere and relatively slow to emerge. Among men aged 45–54, the death rate fell in Scotland from about 20 per 1000 around 1900 to 12.0 in 1921–25. It was still 8.7 in 1975–79, then fell more rapidly to 6.1 by 1989–91. In England and Wales the trend was similar though at a lower level throughout. At the highest ages, among men aged 75–84, there was improvement north and south of the border only in two short periods, the 1940s and the 1980s, but older women experienced modest reductions in mortality throughout the century, with the 1990–92 death rates for ages 65–74 and 75–84 roughly half those of 1900–2.

Figure 5 shows changes in infant mortality from 1881 to 1991. Starting around the turn of the century, infant mortality fell erratically and with considerable regional variation. The fall was much steeper in England and Wales than in Scotland, for reasons which are still not understood [36]. Scotland also experienced sharper leaps at the start of both World Wars. The 1940s saw rapid improvement, especially in Scotland, and the trends continued downwards more gradually from the mid-1950s. The Scottish rate eventually equalled the English in the 1980s.

These transformations in mortality reflect fundamental shifts in the principal causes of death which occurred throughout the developed world in the twentieth century (though, in considering all data on changes in causes of death, it is important to be aware of changing fashions and competence in diagnosis and recording) [16 chap. 7; 37; 38; 36]. In 1911–13, 'communicable diseases' (mostly infectious diseases directly attributable to viruses and bacteria) still dominated reported mortality, and they struck particularly at the young. In Scotland, six percent of all deaths (and more than a third of deaths at ages 1–4) were attributed to measles, scarlatina, whooping cough, diphtheria or croup. Infant diarrhoea caused at least another 3% of all deaths (at least one in eight of infant deaths). Lung tuberculosis was directly involved in at least 7% of all deaths, but in a third of deaths in the 25–34 age group. Other tubercular conditions generated another 4% of deaths, and bronchitis and pneumonia 15%. By contrast with the second half of the century, the so-called 'noncommunicable' or 'degenerative' diseases were of less importance. In 1911–13, cancers were recorded as causing a mere 7% of all deaths, and heart disease just 9%, but cancers and all circulatory conditions, like most other degenerative diseases, are certainly under-recorded in the statistics of the period [16 chap. 7; 38; 39].

Figure 6 shows trends for Scotland for selected diseases from 1890 to 1980. Within the 'childhood disease' category, measles,

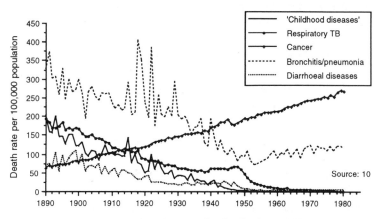

Figure 6 *Death rates by selected causes, Scotland, 1890–1980*

scarlatina and croup almost disappeared as major killers by 1939, and the inter-war reduction in whooping cough and diphtheria mortality accelerated during World War Two; by 1950 they had ceased to be of major concern. Diarrhoeal diseases were brought under a greater degree of control. Deaths from all kinds of TB fell by half between 1900 and 1939 and almost disappeared after the 1950s.

Other trends were less encouraging. Recorded bronchitis and pneumonia deaths fell until the 1950s, and the years of sudden mortality surges disappeared as smoke and industrial pollution were brought under control. Thereafter, however, there was little further fall even in age-specific mortality, and the death rate rose overall because of the rising share of the population who survived to the older and more susceptible age groups. Recorded cancer mortality for men, driven upwards by the spread of cigarette smoking and accentuated by an ageing population, almost trebled from 110 per 100,000 people in the early 1920s, to 206/100,000 in the early 1950s and 307/100,000 in 1991, though improvement in the smoking-related conditions was visible from the 1970s; lung cancer death rates for men aged 55–64 were 18 per 100,000 in the early 1930s, 326/100,000 in the early 1960s and 220/100,000 in 1991 [10].

Recorded cancer mortality rates for women also rose, with breast cancer rates doubling between the 1930s and 1990. Lung cancer deaths for women aged 55–64 continued to rise throughout the period. Much of the rise in female cancer mortality was due to the ageing population, though age-standardised rates in England and Wales were about 15% higher in 1990 than in the early 1950s. This was in spite of some major improvements, notably the reduction of stomach and intestine cancer death rates, which fell by more than two thirds for Scots women aged 65–74 between the 1930s and the 1980s. Reported heart and cerebrovascular disease mortality, controlling for age, having changed little throughout the first half of the century, fell by two fifths between the 1940s and the late 1980s. By this time, in spite of the appearance of a range of 'new' infectious diseases (of which AIDS is only the most pub-licised), mortality rates throughout the industrialised world were dominated by so-called 'non-communicable' rather than 'commu-nicable' conditions, with nine out of ten deaths in England due to circulatory disease, bronchitis and cancer [16 chap. 7; 39].

Differential mortality

In part, these changes in mortality reflected changing social conditions. Though there is some debate over the extent and direction of change in mortality by area [40], significant regional differences persisted. Mortality at most ages declined fairly uniformly across the country, so that areas with high death rates at the start of the period also had them at the end [16 chap. 8]. Compared with East Anglia, the North-west had infant mortality 37% higher in 1961 and 33% higher (on slightly different regional boundaries) in 1991. In Scotland, because of the faster decline in urban death rates, urban–rural differences did fall considerably. Large burghs had SMRs 38% above the 'landward' areas in 1911, but only 10% above in 1971. Nevertheless, in 1991, the death rate in Eastern Glasgow, even after controlling for differences in the age and sex composition of the population, was still 36% higher than the Western Isles and 77% above the middle-class suburbs of Bearsden and Milngavie; Eastern Glasgow's death rate from lung cancer was 143% above Bearsden and Milngavie, and its rate for cerebrovascular disease was 89% higher. However, significantly, the Eastern Glasgow rate for breast cancer – normally considered a disease of affluence – was marginally lower [10].

Not surprisingly, these regional and local differences were paralleled by differences in mortality by occupation and social class. In the nineteenth century, working conditions were an important direct source of excess mortality for many groups, but, by the early twentieth century, they were of less importance than the adverse economic, housing and general environmental conditions which many urban families endured. As a result, in Scotland in the 1920s, while workers in coal mines in the age group 25–44 had death rates only 8% above the national average for males of that age, general labourers, many of whom lived in considerable poverty, had death rates 24% above the mean (and solicitors' death chances were 59% below)[10 (supplement to 78th Report)]. Overall, in England and Wales the standardised mortality ratio for men in Social Class 1 was 18% below the mean in 1921–23, while the ratio for Social Class 5 was 25% above it, a differential of 52% [15b].

Subsequent trends in class differentials are difficult to trace, as occupational classifications changed over time, and there are inconsistencies in reporting and measurement [13; 16 chap. 8; 41; 42]. However, differential mortality probably declined in the inter-war period, then increased sharply as general mortality fell in the second half of the century. By 1959–63 in England and Wales, Social Class 1 mortality for men aged 15–64 was 25% below the population mean, while Social Class 5 mortality was 27% above it, a differential of 69% [42]. In the early 1970s the chances that an unskilled man would die before retirement were more than double that of a professional [43] and there is some evidence that the gap increased further in the 1970s and 1980s [42]. In England, at least, significant differential mortality also existed among immigrants depending on country of birth [41; 44].

Explanations

There is much debate over these marked patterns in recorded differential mortality, some scholars even arguing that they largely arise because illness leads to downward social mobility or unemployment, so that occupations recorded at censuses do not match with those reported at time of death [45; for further discussion see 42; 43; 46]. There are, however, now three dominant interpretations of mortality differentials: material disadvantage; differences in culture, beliefs and knowledge and their impact on behaviour; and differential exposure to infective conditions. A parallel debate exists over the causes of mortality decline (improved living standards and wider access to more advanced medicine; the impact of the spread of new beliefs about healthy living; and changes in levels of exposure to infection). A fourth factor, changes in the biology of disease-causing microorganisms, often considered important for some periods in the past, is of less importance in the twentieth century (the apparent decline in the severity of scarlatina is an exception). However, recent literature has pointed to possible long-term effects of interactions between different disease conditions, suggesting that exposure earlier in life to infective conditions (particularly perhaps to influenza) may predispose victims to later degenerative diseases [38; 39]. This makes interpreting the causes of long-term mortality change particularly complex.

There is now general agreement that the direct impact of new medical treatments was limited before the introduction of sulphonamides in 1935 and, much more dramatically, of modern antibiotics from the later 1940s [16 chap. 7; 47]. New vaccines also became available after World War Two and these, much more accessible to the mass of the population through the new National Health Service, almost eliminated the modest residual mortality from various childhood diseases and tuberculosis.

Surgical and medical advances offered significantly improved survival for under-weight babies from all social classes (especially over the second half of the century), and also for children and young adults suffering from such conditions as appendicitis (almost always fatal until the early twentieth century), diabetes (after the introduction of insulin treatment in the 1920s), serious accidents, and childhood leukaemia (especially since the 1970s) [16 chap. 7]. However, none of these conditions was a major cause of mortality in the past. Among older people, the impact of science-based medicine was much less dramatic, though from the 1960s early diagnosis and subsequent drug, radiation or surgical intervention did have modest effects, mainly by extending life among middle-aged sufferers from cardiovascular conditions and cancer. However, the effect of these direct medical interventions on life expectancy remained modest until the 1980s. Their impact on the lower social classes was also reduced by less effective access (in spite of their generally higher sickness levels) to some of the available services [42; 43].

Overall, therefore, the impact of medical and surgical intervention on mortality was relatively limited, though it had some effect on survival of infants, children and younger adults. However, the indirect effects of medical advance were more notable, particularly in reducing exposure to situations in which disease was caused or spread. The growing credibility of medical science provided the State with a justification for health and safety interventions at work and environmental improvements in the community [16 chap. 7; 39 chap. 7]. While, individually, identification and prevention of any one occupationally-specific disease had only limited and often delayed impact on overall mortality, collectively they were significant by the 1980s. More important, and much earlier, was the elimination from food and water supplies of the most generally

378   *Michael Anderson*

lethal microorganisms. The introduction (mostly before 1914) of modern sewage transport and treatment systems was significant in reducing the spread by flies of infant diarrhoeas, particularly in the large cities where mortality fell fastest. However, while smoke pollution control (mostly introduced well after World War Two) made cities nicer places in which to live and removed sudden surges in mortality associated with periods of 'smog', its main effect was to spread deaths from chest conditions throughout the year, rather than markedly reducing total deaths from bronchitis and related diseases [39 chap. 7]. Administrative measures based on medical knowledge about the spread of disease also played a crucial role, notably through meat and milk inspection and its impact on tuberculosis in the inter-war period, and in tracing contacts of smallpox and tuberculosis, and isolating infected persons so that they could not infect others.

Some scholars also emphasise changes and differentials in living standards (and especially in access to more and better food and clothing, better housing, and new methods of keeping people and their environment clean) [41; 42; 43]. This argument was used extensively by McKeown [47] in interpreting the downward trend in mortality, and Winter develops a similar case, but stressing the need to take account of long-term rather than immediate consequences of changing nutrition and welfare provisions [48]. The continued or even growing mortality differentials since World War Two have similarly been explained in terms of unequal access to sanitary improvement and hygiene-related technologies such as hot running water, refrigerators and easy-to-clean surfaces. Until the 1960s, large areas of overcrowded and poorly serviced housing certainly showed higher mortality at almost all ages. The apparent rise in mortality from circulatory conditions during and after the inter-war depression has also been related to material deprivation and the long-term effect of the First World War [36; 39; 49]. Wilkinson sees the stress and social isolation of life among the poorest sections of the population as a main cause of what he believes is a strong connection between rising mortality differentials and growing relative poverty since 1951 [50].

However, the availability of larger quantities of non-contaminated food does not mean that all sections of the population will understand the need, and be willing to spend the money and effort required, to prepare and preserve it properly; even in the 1980s there was widespread ignorance of the basic principles of food hygiene. Also, while medical scientists discovered the basic principles of nutritional deficiencies in the 1920s, it proved difficult to persuade people to change their eating and drinking habits, a task made even harder by the fact that advice over diet frequently conflicted with popular beliefs about what constituted 'a real man' or a 'healthy baby'. Thus, much of the resistance even among those aware of medical advice is culturally linked to class-based suspicions and misunderstandings, and to the impracticality of the recommendations for working class mothers on low incomes [41; 43; 51].

However, programmes of public education have sometimes had significant effects on mortality among sections of the population. The class differences which emerged in tobacco smoking from the 1970s (probably the most important residual source of mortality differentials) were a direct result of middle class reaction to a medically-inspired campaign, which also produced a reversal over the same period of the rising tide of male lung cancer, and the widening of mortality differentials from a range of circulatory and other respiratory diseases [16 chap. 8; 39 chap. 6; 43]. Infant welfare propaganda and the spread of clinics and mother-and-baby welfare programmes were a major factor reducing infant mortality over the first thirty years of the century [48; 52; 53].

Thus, some social-class differentials in mortality are not directly attributable to poverty and deprivation. Nor was all the reduction in mortality due to the ability of individuals and the State to pay more for a healthy life style and for medical treatment. Changes in attitudes, education and advice were important. There is also a view that differential mortality, especially from the now-dominant cancers and circulatory diseases, results in part from long-term differences in behaviour which are a direct reaction to the economic and psychological stresses of life in the poorer parts of industrialised societies [41; 42; 43; 51; 54]. To this may be added the probability that a significant element of differential adult mortality from degenerative diseases is a consequence of infectious diseases caught in childhood [39]. Reduced perinatal mortality appears to be linked in part to the quality of the mother's environment around the time of *her own* birth [48], and poor living standards during childhood seem to increase risks of heart and other diseases in adulthood [55]. Equally indirectly, one factor in the fall in infant and child mortality in the first thirty years of the century was the marked but socially differentiated reduction in family size, which reduced exposure to diseases of childhood as well as allowing parents to focus more care and resources on a smaller number of children [39 chap. 5; 53; 56].

4
Fertility and nuptiality

Fertility trends

Of the three variables of fertility, mortality and migration, fertility has been most responsible for medium-term demographic change in twentieth century Western Europe. Figure 7 shows, for England and Wales for the period 1891 to 1991, the 'total period fertility rate' (TPFR). TPFR may be viewed as the average number of children who would have been born to a group of women who experienced throughout their child-bearing years the age-specific fertility rates[3] of the year in question. TPFR, though widely used by demographers since the 1980s to obtain up-to-date information on fertility change, accentuates short-term fluctuations, so Figure 7 also shows estimates of the average number of children actually born to women who reached age 45. Scottish figures show broadly similar trends, though with lower TPFRs in the 1980s.

In the 1980s, TPFRs of around 2.1 were required for population replacement (after allowing for the sex imbalance at birth and for mortality between birth and the average age of child-bearing). For earlier years, population replacement TPFRs were roughly 2.2 for the 1950s and 2.6 for the 1920s. In fact, TPFR was 3.5 in 1900–2, then fell steadily to below replacement level in the mid-1930s (TPFR was 1.8 in 1931–35). It rose sharply during and after

---

[3] Age-specific fertility is usually calculated as the number of births in any year to each five-year age group of women, per thousand women alive in that age group on one specific date in that year. To calculate the total period fertility ratio, the single-year figures for each separate five-year age group are first multiplied by five to provide an estimate of total births over a five-year period; the five-year figures for each of the age groups are then summed to estimate fertility over the whole of a woman's fertile period.

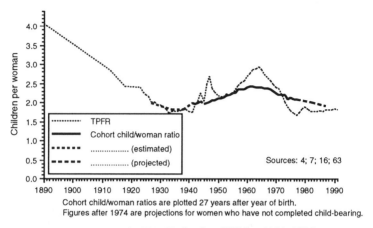

Figures after 1974 are projections for women who have not completed child-bearing.

Figure 7   *Estimates of fertility, England and Wales, 1891–1991*

World War Two, fell back in the early 1950s, then rose strongly to peak at 2.9 in 1964. Thereafter it declined to only 1.7 in 1977, then rose to around 1.8 in the late 1980s and early 1990s [4; 7]. Meanwhile, average live births per married woman after 25 years of marriage fell from 4.3 in marriages of the 1890s to 2.0 in marriages of 1936–40, rising to 2.4 for marriages of 1956–60, and with a steep fall predicted thereafter. Similar trends occurred elsewhere in Western Europe [15a].

These overall figures arise from significant underlying changes in four factors: marriage patterns; the balance between fertility inside and outside marriage; numbers of families of different sizes; and the ages at which women bore children.

Marriage patterns, marital breakdown, and cohabitation

For 1901–10, the mean age at first marriage in Scotland was 27.5 for males and 25.6 for females; as in most of the period, the figures for England and Wales were marginally lower. In Scotland in 1901, 13% of men aged 20–24 were or had been married (17% in England and Wales) and 85% had been married by age group 45–49 (88% in England and Wales). The comparable figures for women were 24% (and 27%), and 80% (and 86%). In the early

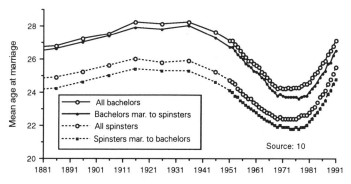

Figure 8 *Mean ages at first marriage, Scotland, 1881–1991*

1930s, proportions married were slightly lower, but by 1951 there were signs of a marriage boom. In 1971, 38% of men aged 20–24 in Scotland were married (36% in England and Wales); the proportions of women ever married at ages 20–24 were the highest ever recorded, at 58% and 60% respectively [2; 10].

After the early 1970s, proportions married at younger ages declined rapidly, and the average age at first marriage rose. The median marriage age in England and Wales reached a low of 23.2 for men and 21.3 for women in 1970; one spinster bride in three was a teenager. By 1991, the medians were 26.5 for men and 24.6 for women; in 1990, only 13% of men were married in the age group 20–24 (27% of women) [3; 5; 8]. Trends in Scotland ran in parallel (mean ages at marriage are shown in Figure 8). However, in spite of these recent declines, in the depressed early 1990s the mean marriage ages and the proportions never married at all ages were still around the 1900 levels, and significantly above those of the depressed 1930s.

The later 1960s and early 1970s saw major changes not only in marital fertility and nuptiality but also in marital dissolution [16 chap. 5]. As Figure 9 shows, the number of divorces, which had been low until the 1930s, rose in the War and post-War years, then fell back until the mid-1960s when they began twenty years of rapid increase. Latest estimates suggest that, at 1987 rates, about 33% of marriages of the late 1970s will end in divorce within twenty years, compared with about 7% of marriages of the early 1950s [57]. Remarriage rates, which had moved broadly in line

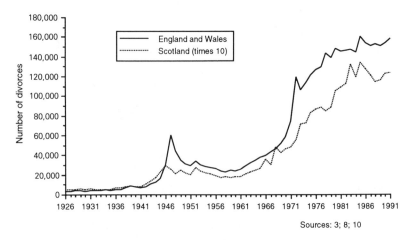

Sources: 3; 8; 10

Figure 9 *Divorces, Scotland, and England and Wales, 1926–1991*

with divorces until the early 1970s, also fell away somewhat after 1972, and the average time gap between divorce and remarriage grew [16 chap. 5; 17].

By the 1980s, as elsewhere in Europe, declining marriage rates and high divorce rates were accompanied by rapid growth of a largely new phenomenon: widespread cohabitation, which did not just precede marriage but, for many couples (for some years at least), substituted for it [16 chap. 5; 58]. Survey evidence of 1991 (which from its retrospective nature probably underestimates earlier trends) suggested that only 3% of women marrying under the age of 30 in the late 1960s had cohabited before marriage. Ten years later, the figure had risen to 19%, for 1980–84 it was 33% and, for 1985–89, 51% [12 (1991)]. Less than a fifth of currently non-married women aged 25–29 were cohabiting in 1979, but nearly one third in 1989 [59]. Increased cohabitation also accounted for half of the fall between 1973 and 1980 in the proportion of those aged 20–24 who were married [60].

Legitimate and illegitimate fertility

Figure 10 shows total births for Great Britain from 1901 to 1991, subdivided into births within and outside marriage. The sharp

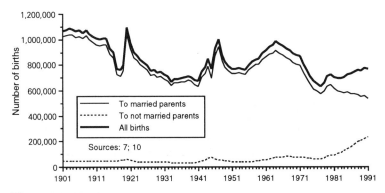

Figure 10 *Number of births, and number of births within and not within marriage, Great Britain, 1901–1991*

fluctuations in births during and after the two World Wars, and the inter-war trough, are clear. So, too, is the fertility surge of the early 1960s, the marked fall in child-bearing after the peak year of 1964, and stabilisation and modest recovery after 1977. Also shown is the rapid rise, particularly after 1976, in the share of births to not-married parents, from 9.2% in 1976 to 21.3% in 1986 and 30.1% in 1991 [and see 61]; by contrast, the peacetime pre-1939 non-marital birth ratios in England and Wales were consistently around 4%.

Until the 1980s, overall fertility change was almost entirely driven by variations in marital fertility, largely resulting from changes in one or more of four factors: age profiles of married women; proportions of the female population who were married; average number of children born; average ages at child-bearing. Of these four factors, the changing age profile of the female population was particularly significant in the rising birth rate of the 1950s and 1960s, reflecting the larger numbers born in the early 1940s compared with the 1930s. Some part of the fertility reduction after 1964 came from a shifting age-profile – but by then other factors were also at work.

Across the period as a whole, the most important shifts resulted from changes in the second and third of the four factors listed above. After 1900, almost all sections of British society completed a transition, begun in the 1860s, from largely unrestricted fertility within closely regulated marriage to strong fertility control within

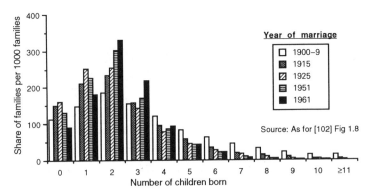

Figure 11   *Family size by year of marriage, England and Wales, 1900–1961*

much less regulated marriage. Had family sizes remained unchanged between 1901 and 1961, the upward shifts in nuptiality
and the fall in marriage ages, discussed in the previous section,
would have produced a 47% increase in fertility in England and
Wales, and a 54% rise in Scotland. In fact, because marital fertility
fell between 1901 and 1961 (by 48% in England and Wales and
46% in Scotland), overall English/Welsh fertility in 1961 was 22%
(and Scottish 19%) below the 1901 level. Non-marital fertility only
marginally changed between the two dates [62].

Figure 11 shows how families of more than six children (42% of
all marriages of 1870–79) had almost disappeared by marriages of
1915 and had become extremely rare by the 1950s. More than
four-fifths of marriages of the mid-1920s produced three children
or fewer. Of uninterrupted first marriages of 1921–25, 43% were
childless or had only one child. Marriages of the early 1960s, with
their low proportion childless, produced on average 2.4 children,
compared with 2.2 for those of the mid-1920s. Many subsequent
marriages have not yet completed their fertility, but latest estimates
suggest an average of about 1.9 children for women in their late
twenties in the late 1980s [63].

At the start of the twentieth century, there was an inverse
relationship between average family size and social class. At the
extreme, marriages of professionals in 1900–9 had a mean of 2.3
children and those of labourers 4.5. Marriages of the 1920s
showed falls in all classes (though particularly in the lower middle

classes), and after 1945 social class differentials narrowed further [16 chap 4].

Information on fertility by birthplace is only available from the 1970s. It shows that the share of all births which were to New Commonwealth immigrants rose from 6.1% in 1973 to a peak of 8.5% in 1980, then fell back to 7.1% by 1991. This partly reflected shifts in age composition, but total period fertility rate figures for all immigrant groups showed a marked fall in the 1980s. In 1971, the TPFR for those born in the United Kingdom was 2.3, while for New Commonwealth and Pakistan immigrants it was 4.0 (those born in India 4.3, Pakistan/Bangladesh 9.3, Caribbean 3.4) [16 chap. 12]. In 1991, the figures were 1.8 for the UK-born, and 2.5 for New Commonwealth-born (2.1, 4.6, and 1.5 for those born in India, Pakistan/Bangladesh, and the Caribbean, respectively) [64].

Interpreting medium-term change in British fertility is complicated by significant changes in the fourth factor noted above: the ages at which women had children. Information on this has been available only since 1938. In 1938–40 the mean age of women at first birth was 26.6 and at all births was 29.0. Both these statistics fell steadily after World War Two, with lows for first births of 23.9 in the late 1960s and for all births of 26.2 in the early 1970s. By the late 1970s both were rising again, reaching 25.6 for first births in 1991 and 27.7 for all births. Overall, the gap between marriage and the birth of a first child grew from 20 months in 1971 to 28 months in 1991, and these delays in starting child-bearing pushed down fertility rates, artificially accentuating the apparent flight from child-bearing [4 (1992); 7]. However, as in the 1930s, their long-term effect was not just delayed child-bearing, but also an increase in permanent childlessness.

A further complicating factor was the rapid spread in the 1980s of child-bearing within cohabitations. As late as 1971, only 22% of conceptions in England and Wales were outside marriage. Of every 100 such conceptions, 30 ended in abortion, 36 were followed by marriage, thus legitimating the child, and 34 produced an illegitimate birth, only 16 of which were jointly registered by both parents. By 1991, the share of conceptions outside marriage had risen markedly, to 43%. Of every 100 extra-marital conceptions, 36 ended in abortion, 9 were followed by marriage before the birth, leaving 55 to be registered as to non-married parents, 41 of which were jointly registered, three quarters by parents living at the same address. On this basis, by 1991, one in every six babies was being registered by two unmarried partners living at the same address. [4 (1992); 7]

Explaining the fertility and nuptiality trends

Over the past sixty years, many mutually contradictory interpretations have been offered for the changes outlined above, but none have wholly stood the test of time. Most analysis has used national average data and, as a result, has not been adequately sensitive to changes in patterns of family building between different age groups of the population [65]. Three classes of interpretations are particularly influential, linked to welfare (in the broad sense of 'well-being'), to new technologies, and to value changes.

(a) Welfare

Economists have mostly explained demographic change by reference to changes in real disposable incomes and wealth, to new opportunities for consumption, and to patterns and levels of unemployment and of married women's employment. People's sense of material security was also affected in our period by the prospect of war in the 1930s and the high levels of marital breakdown since the 1960s.

The proposition that marriage and fertility are influenced by economic conditions and prospects has a long pedigree. Many interpretations of fertility and nuptiality changes in the first sixty years of the fertility decline saw low fertility as a reaction to pressures on living standards [66; 67; 68], and, at least up to the 1950s, birth and death rates fluctuated with the trade cycle [e.g. 69; 70]. Figure 12 plots marriage rates and unemployment in Scotland between 1880 and 1965; a broadly similar pattern occurred in England and Wales. Until 1914, short-term fluctuations in employment and the marriage rate moved closely together, and after World War Two the upward trend in marriages was checked in less prosperous years. The high unemployment years of

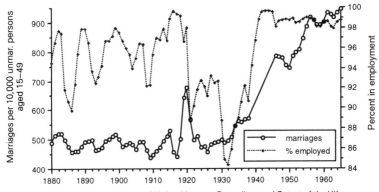

Sources: Feinstein, *Statistical Tables of National Income, Expenditure and Output of the UK,*
1855–1965; P Flora *et al. State Economy and Society in Western Europe 1815–1975,* Part II

Figure 12 *Marriages (Scotland) and employment rate (100 minus percent*
unemployed) (UK), 1880–1965

the 1920s saw a depressed marriage market, while the improving
economy in the 1930s coincided with a rise in marriages which was
sustained at a high though fluctuating level throughout the decades
of stable prosperity after 1940, only finally falling back with the
recession of the mid-1970s – and doing so dramatically in the
more depressed 1980s. For births, the inter-war period saw
depressed economy and fertility, the latter accentuated by the
imminent threat of war. In the 1950s and 1960s, both economy
and fertility were relatively buoyant, and family-building occurred
in a context of relative economic security, backed by expanded
state insurance systems [cf. also 72]; by contrast, the economic
insecurity of the 1980s coincided with reduced fertility.

However, at a more detailed level, fertility fell back in the late
1960s and early 1970s while economic opportunities remained
strong, then turned up and stabilised in and after the recession of
the later 1970s. On closer inspection, therefore, simple economic
interpretations offer less clear results and, in particular, provide no
explanation of the differences between fertility and nuptiality in the
scale and timing of their variations since 1945.

Recent years have seen a sharpening of conceptualisation and
analysis, beginning with Easterlin's proposition [73] that a couple's
willingness to marry and have children is dependent on their
economic status relative to their economic aspirations, with the

latter influenced by the relationship between their current lifestyles and those they experienced in adolescence, and with both heavily influenced by the relative sizes of their birth cohorts. This interpretation offers a good fit with the high fertility and high nuptiality of the prosperous 1960s, but it fails to explain the rapid fall in fertility in the early 1970s (when wage trends continued to favour younger workers) and its subsequent rise after 1977 (when wage trends went against them).

More recent work on fertility has incorporated gender variables using insights from 'the New Home Economics' [67]. One hypothesis is that fertility is pushed up by rising male earnings, but is constrained when a household's income depends on married women's earnings – in a context where married women's employment and, for much of the period, their earnings relative to men's, have been increasing, but where child-bearing and child-rearing involves substantial time and financial costs for women [16 chap. 4; 74; 75]. A related hypothesis suggests that rising employment of married women, and improved women's earning power relative to men's, discouraged some women from marriage [75; 76]. For the 1930s and since World War Two, these hypotheses provide superficially plausible accounts of short-run change in nuptiality and fertility, of fertility differentials between working and non-working wives, and of timing of births within marriage [75; 77]. Until the 1960s, rising real wages stimulated and sustained higher fertility by encouraging earlier childbirth and fewer small families, but thereafter the wage effect was increasingly offset by the depressive effect on timing of first birth and on large families of expanding female employment, accelerated by rising relative wages for women following the 1971 Equal Pay Act. Greater labour-force commitment of large numbers of married women also encouraged delayed onset of childbearing [75; 78].

However, more recently, even the proponents of this approach have been more cautious in their claims about its ability to explain overall changes in fertility (as opposed to shifts in timing of births), and the whole approach has been questioned, notably by Murphy [65] and by Lesthaeghe and Surkyn [79], who adopt a sociologically informed scepticism of the assumptions and methodology employed.

Any statistically based interpretation faces major problems in measuring fertility in ways sensitive enough to capture underlying trends. Changes in the context of family building (such as the introduction of the contraceptive pill) are difficult to incorporate in these analyses if their impact is gradual over a period of years. There is also a major difficulty of finding reliable and valid aggregate measures of concepts like 'relative income', 'ability to achieve material aspirations', 'costs of children', and 'women's commitment to lifetime earning'. Many of the variables that are needed relate not to current income and employment but to people's perceptions of likely future trends, and not to absolute experience but to the way people's own lives compare with others' lives at the same time, and to their own and others' experiences in the past [65]. There is also a problem of direction of causality: for example, in distinguishing the impact of married women's employment on fertility, from the impact of small family sizes on women's ability to enter the labour force on a long-term basis [65; note also 77].

A final problem in most economists' analysis is that changes in people's perceptions of the relative priority of different aspects of their lives (changes in 'cultural factors' or in 'tastes') are largely discounted; yet it is clear that part of the shift in the relationship between married women's employment and marital fertility arose from new attitudes to labour-market opportunities. For mothers of the 1950s the primacy of child-rearing produced low employment expectations; but their daughters who were of child-bearing age after 1970 grasped the growing employment opportunities available to them [80] and coped with the stresses by lengthening their birth intervals as they returned to work between babies [81].

Finally, economists' models have been primarily focused on the income rather than the expenditure side of family budgets, and have thus played down the role of changing patterns of consumption. Work on the first stages of the fertility decline emphasised rising costs of children [66], accentuated by improving child survival as mortality fell [82], and by consumer goods that had to be foregone by those with large families [18]. The balance between expenditure on children and expenditure on consumer durables influenced discussion of the post-Second World War 'baby boom' [67], and recently attention has been paid to the rising costs of what is considered 'appropriate' child-rearing ('quality' rather than 'quantity'). It has also been suggested that new and competing consumption opportunities, notably in the form of leisure activities not easily shared with young children, may have inhibited child-bearing in the 1980s [70; 80].

In sum, the fact that economists' models have proved poor predictors of medium-term fertility variation tells us more about the validity of available data and the unresolved complexity of the underlying social processes, than it does about the real importance of economic factors affecting couples' family-building in this period. The broad correlations in medium-term trends suggest that it is too soon to discount welfare interpretations entirely.

(b) Technology

New technology transformed many aspects of the household economy in British society. New cooking and cleaning methods, new fibres and plastic surfaces, and faster and more flexible transport, allowed husbands and wives to enter the labour force while still being able to care for infants and small children; it has also been suggested that the availability of labour-saving consumer durables was one factor encouraging larger families in the 1950s and early 1960s [83]; while, financially, the opportunity costs of child-bearing were high for married women, rising incomes allowed many other personal difficulties to be offset.

There is increasing consensus over the impact on medium-term trends in fertility of improved and better-known contraceptive technology. The early fertility decline, until after World War One, was achieved with little recourse to artificial contraception, and only about half even of those marrying in the 1930s claimed to have used mechanical birth control techniques [84]. Indeed, many women lacked knowledge of or access to any effective means other than abortion, and husbands were often resistant to contraceptive use [68]. Though there was a considerable extension among those marrying after World War Two [16 chap. 4; 84], contraceptive innovation probably had little impact on fertility until the 1960s. Thereafter, it played a greater role, as old methods became more freely available, and as new, highly reliable, methods emerged. The greater security provided by the contraceptive pill (first available for married women in the early 1960s and much more freely after

1974) and by contraceptive sterilisation (almost non-existent in 1959-60 but used by 15% of couples by 1976 [84]) reduced the number of accidental pregnancies and, aided by extremely low child mortality, allowed women to integrate planned family-building into a coherent life plan. This ability to plan securely, quite unavailable to earlier generations [68; 85], changed both levels and life-time profiles of child-bearing [70; 77; 86; 87]. Murphy [87] has even argued that the history of pill use provides a plausible explanation for all the major shifts in fertility between 1964 and 1980, including close links between scares about pill safety and upturns of fertility in 1970 and after 1977.

It has also been argued that modern contraception influenced marriage trends by offering opportunities for apparently risk-free sexual activity, thus reducing the attractions of early marriage [70]. Certainly, the period saw a dramatic rise in pre-marital sex. From at least the 1930s until the late 1950s (with the possible exception of World War Two), well under a third of women were sexually experienced before marriage. By 1970 the figures approached half and, by the early 1980s, they probably significantly exceeded 80% [58; 88].

(c) Value change

The existence of technology does not mean that people will use it, and people do not jump at every economic opportunity available to them, especially if it means challenging longstanding values such as those stressing the primacy of women's domestic roles [79; 89]. In interpreting population change in the twentieth century, we cannot ignore value changes in addition to the changes in tastes and in aspirations for child quality already noted above [16 chaps. 2 and 4].

While considerable emphasis is now placed on cultural factors in explaining the first sixty years of the fertility decline [18 chap. 5; 62], for the post-1945 period there is, unfortunately, little direct evidence for Britain. Much discussion is therefore based on inference, on analogy from broader cultural change, and on survey work from the United States [summarised in 70]. One suggestion is that British youth and young adult culture between the 1950s and the 1980s was characterised by a growing emphasis on personal choice and an active rejection of external controls whether by community, church, family or even law. Rising divorce, cohabitation, and premarital sex are seen as part of a wider cluster of activities including experimenting with drugs, driving cars at excessive speed, post-1950s popular music, and football hooliganism. Significant changes in family behaviour since 1945 are then attributed to this 'de-regulation of personal relationships' and growing emphasis on 'self-generated morality' [90; 79]. With particular reference to fertility, Simons [e.g. in 91; 92] suggested that changes since 1945 show strong correlations with levels of adherence to 'fundamentalist' values, manifested in levels of church attendance and conversion, and survey indicators of national pride. The fertility boom of the 1950s and 1960s coincided with strong public support for such values and behaviour, which was increasingly replaced in the 1970s by more 'pragmatist' approaches to all aspects of personal life, involving declining interest in institutionalised religion and disenchantment with all kinds of traditional social institutions [cf. also 79].

In these perspectives, legislation assisted the trend by providing 'an expanded set of choices' over areas like abortion and divorce, but typically followed rather than preceded the fundamental shifts in attitudes, in a world where individual consent replaced public morality, and where the search for personal fulfillment through relationships inside and outside marriage replaced marriage as an institution based on the achievement of limited extrinsic ends [90; 93; 94].

From a rather different perspective, Aries [72] rejects personal hedonism as a motive for restricted fertility but sees a growing wish among adults to fit children within their own life-plans and to organise children around their lives rather than their lives around children; for some this will inevitably mean remaining childless. And Preston [70] sees fundamental cultural changes, notably increasing concerns with global over-population and environmental responsibility, as inhibiting child-bearing from the late 1960s. Nevertheless, only 5% of women interviewed at ages 16–21 in 1986 expected to remain childless and their expected mean completed family size of 2.2 was little different from that anticipated by older women interviewed at the same time [95].

Conclusion

It would be wrong to conclude that the 1970s and 1980s saw a complete overturning of older family values. Of a sample of single women born in 1958 and interviewed in 1981, 90% expected eventually to marry, and as Murphy [62] argues, while it is helpful conceptually to present the three classes of explanation as discrete, in practice they are closely interrelated. For example, even if cultural factors play a major role in encouraging people to think in new ways about family life, the magnitude of the shifts may well be influenced by labour market changes, and the possibility of achieving new ambitions be heavily dependent on shifts in contraceptive technology. Future work will surely seek increasingly to integrate these different interpretations.

5

Economic and social implications of demographic change

The previous sections considered changes in each of the separate demographic variables. This section reviews the combined impact of these changes on demographic structures and on some other aspects of the economic and social history of the period.

Changing age structures

We have already noted the varying patterns of fertility over the twentieth century, against a background of falling mortality especially at younger ages and, for Great Britain as a whole, relatively modest net migration. Figure 13 shows the resulting population age structures, plotting the number of males and females alive at each individual year of age in 1911, 1951 and 1991 [cf. 19]. The 1911 plots show a pattern typical of a society in transition from a regime of high fertility and high mortality to one of low fertility and low mortality. The fall in the numbers alive at each successive age is relatively smooth, reflecting high mortality at all ages and little annual variation in numbers born; the fluctuations are mainly due to inaccuracies in age reporting on census returns and, significantly for young men, the consequences of the then recent surge of emigration.

By 1951, a very different pattern appeared. Widespread family limitation, combined with low child and young adult mortality, produced a pattern where, on average, the population contained only marginally more children than middle-aged adults. However, even after the temporary absence overseas of men on National Service is taken into account, there were marked fluctuations in

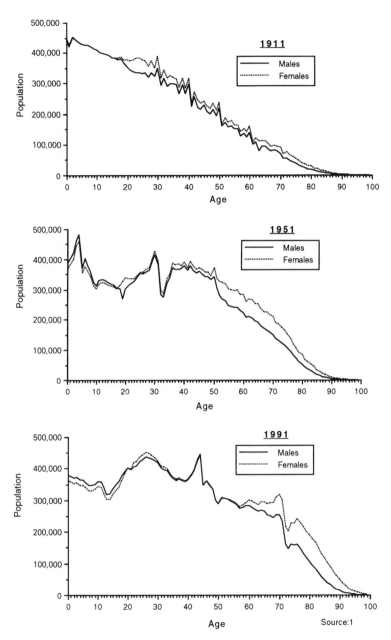

Figure 13   *Age structures of the population, Great Britain, 1911, 1951, 1991*

numbers alive at different ages. Note the consequences of the restrained fertility of World War One and the 1930s; also the results of the sudden surges of fertility at the end of the two Wars, reflected in peaks at around ages 4 and 30.

The volatility in fertility had even more impact by 1991. The post-War birth surges are still visible, as also are the consequences of the baby-boom of the mid-1960s and its subsequent fall, which bottomed out in the later 1970s, as the small birth cohort of the early 1950s reduced the numbers reaching child-bearing age.

The wider consequences of these trends are considerable. For example, in the late 1980s there were fewer children alive than at any period since the 1840s, and this, combined with the short-period volatility in births which had been apparent for a quarter of a century, posed significant problems for the long-term planning and rationalisation of maternity and educational services [96]. By contrast, the number of 16–24 year olds, which had been around 7 million in 1931, rose from 4.9 million in 1956 to 6.4 million in 1967 and after 1977 rose again to 7.4 million by 1985, before falling back, eventually, to about the 1960s level by the late 1990s; these trends have considerable impact on employment prospects, demand for higher education and housing, and the ages at which people can achieve financial autonomy [73; 96; 97; 98].

Improved survival, especially for older women, combined with low fertility since World War Two, also produced a society in which a growing proportion of the population was of pensionable age, with rising numbers of very old people. From the 1980s there were concerns over rising social and economic burdens from this growth of 'dependency'. In 1911, shortly after the introduction of an old-age pension (payable at age 70), just 5.2% of the population of Great Britain was aged 65 and over. By 1951 that figure had risen to 10.9% and was 16.0% by 1991. However, as a result of the falling numbers of children, people aged 15–64 made up 63.9% of the population in 1911, 66.7% in 1951, and 65.1% in 1991, so there had been, up to 1991, little change in overall dependency as conventionally defined [and see 99]. Moreover, much of the increased dependency arose from changes in employment practices, as earning opportunities for the elderly were restricted by age-linked retirement schemes and, from the 1970s, by early retirement which was often a surrogate for redundancy [99; 100]. However, the costs of supporting the elderly tend to rise exponentially with age, and the share of the aged who were 85 and older (increasingly cared for by relatives who were themselves nearing or beyond retiral age) rose fast, reaching 1.5% of the population by 1991 compared with just 0.2% in 1911 [1; 16 chap. 13]. The age profile of those already alive also suggests that, without major changes in working patterns, there may be significant problems of providing pensions for the elderly between 2010 and 2030 [101].

Changing survival and its implications

Changes in mortality improved survival, so more children reached adulthood, fewer marriages were broken by death in the child-bearing years, orphanage and step-parenthood through parental death became relatively rare, and couples could expect more years of life together after all their children had grown up [85; 102].

For example, of babies born in 1891, one in six did not reach their first birthday and nearly one in four died before they were five. Around a third of women aged 25 in 1900 died before their sixty-fifth birthday. By 1946, however, only about 3% of babies died before their first birthday, and by the 1970s the loss in the first year of life was around 1% and fewer than 3% of all those born did not reach twenty-five. The proportion of women who died between ages 25 and 65 fell by about half between 1900 and 1975, and was little more than one in seven by 1980 [102]. If we look at 'typical' children (defined as those born at their mothers' generation's median age at child-bearing) about 26% of those born in 1891 lost their father before age 25, 22% their mother, and 6% both. The median age at which they lost their father was about 37 and their mother 41. Those born in 1946 fared very differently. Only around 10% lost father by age 25, 7% mother and 1% both. The median age at which this cohort could expect to lose their fathers was about 45 and for their mother it was 53. As a result, the first generation with a majority of parents as home-owners (and therefore having something significant to leave) only inherited well past the most expensive phases of child-rearing [102].

A changing life course

Declining fertility until the 1930s, and the increased tendency until the 1980s to cluster children early in marriage, plus a marked tendency until the 1970s for marriage itself to take place at younger ages, meant that women finished child-bearing at significantly younger ages than in the past (about age 28 for a typical woman born in 1946 compared with 36 for a typical woman born in 1891). Delayed marriage and child-bearing among some women in the 1980s only partly reversed this pattern. Together with increased survival and the greater predictability of new contraceptive technologies, these changes transformed women's life-course experiences, in particular by freeing them to devote much more effort to employment in the years when child-care pressures were largely behind them [85; 102].

The same changes also opened up new possibilities and problems for relationships between parents, children and grandchildren. A typical woman born in 1861 might expect, on average, to die within five years of the birth of her last grandchild; her husband, on average, died at about the time that that grandchild was born. Under these circumstances, at the start of our period, only a minority of children knew all four of their grandparents – indeed, of couples born in the early 1860s when their mothers were in their early thirties, only about a quarter would have had all four parents alive on their wedding day. By contrast, women born in 1921 could expect to live for about 16 years after their youngest grandchild's fifth birthday and four parents could have been at the first wedding of about three quarters of those adults born of parents who were in their late twenties in the late 1940s. By the 1980s, increasing numbers of children knew at least briefly not merely their grandparents but at least one great-grandmother. Meanwhile, as old people lived longer, the number of children in a position to look after them in old age was reduced. Modelling this for typical women born in 1831 suggests approximately 3.5 children surviving to age 25, with their mothers expecting on average to live for only three years after the age of 65; on average, therefore, the burden of care in old age for a majority of children was relatively trivial. By contrast, a similar model suggests that, for typical women born in 1921, 2.1 of their children survived to age

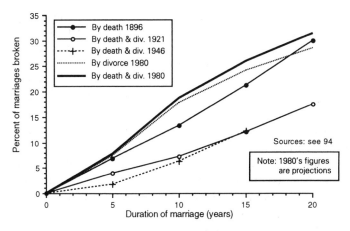

Figure 14   *Dissolution of marriage by death and divorce, by duration and year of marriage, England and Wales, 1896–1980*

25, while they themselves on average would live for about 14 years after the age of 65. The burden of caring was thus much increased, even without the markedly increased employment among middle-aged women, made possible by the changes in marriage and child-bearing practices outlined above [102].

Marital break-up and lone parenthood

Over the course of the twentieth century, lone parenthood as a result of marital dissolution and extra-marital births markedly increased, but lone parenthood as a result of premature parental death fell. As a result, as Figure 14 shows, the proportion of 'typical' marriages (those taking place at around the average marriage age) which terminated within twenty years was not markedly different for marriages of the later 1890s and of 1980. Nor, indeed, was the proportion of children not living in two-parent families much higher in 1991 than in 1851 (the last date before the mid-twentieth century when reliable figures are at present available). However, if the late 1980s are compared even with 1971, the situation is very different, and the associated consequences for family poverty and the Welfare State were considerable [103; 104]. In 1971, about 8% of families with dependent children had a lone parent, but this rose to 19% by 1991 [12], with most of the increase coming from partnership break-up rather than non-marital births. In 1971, 0.7% of dependent children lived with a single mother, 2.5% with a separated mother, 1.9% with a divorced mother, 1.6% with a widowed mother and 0.9% with a lone father. In 1991, the respective percentages were 5.1%, 4.0%, 6.5%, 1.0%, and 1.2% [105]. This marked growth in lone-parent households, together with rising numbers of lone elderly persons, regional shifts in population, and a tendency from the 1950s for children to leave home earlier [97] also produced a continued growth in the number of households (and changes in the kinds of houses in demand), in spite of the slow rise of national populations [98; 106].

Migration and immigration

The emergence of retirement communities as a consequence of differential migration by age was identified above as a source of stress on welfare services [33]. Another very prominent aspect of differential migration, and one often associated with inter-community tension, was the concentration in particular parts of some English cities (through outflow of the more affluent and inflow of immigrants) of poor people and particularly of members of certain immigrant groups. This arose from chain migration, bolstered by employment and housing availability and sometimes by direct recruitment in the country of origin [24; 30]. This pattern, with its associated social polarisation, may be observed among Irish immigrants right up to the 1950s, and among Jewish immigrants before the two World Wars. More recently, in 1987, 46% of all births in Tower Hamlets in London and 42% of births in Brent were to mothers born in the New Commonwealth or in Pakistan, as were 31% of births in Leicester. This compared with just 8% for England and Wales as a whole [16 chap. 12] and with the very low numbers of non-white immigrants in all parts of Scotland [34; 107]. But the complexity of the long-term social and economic impact of these patterns remains a major problem for future research [108].

Further Reading

(Starred items have particularly useful bibliographies; note particularly [16]. Place of publication is London unless otherwise stated.)

Statistical Reports and Series

Basic material, sometimes with limited commentary, can be found as follows:

(a) For population change, structure and movements: [1] *Censuses of Population* (most separately for England and Wales and for Scotland; decennial since 1801, except for 1966, and none in 1941).

(b) For vital statistics for England and Wales: [2] the *Annual Reports of the Registrar-General for England and Wales* until 1973 and thereafter in [3] *Population Trends* (Office of Population Censuses and Surveys (OPCS), quarterly); also contains useful articles on developments in British population.

(c) More detailed tabulations since 1974 in a group of annual publications published by OPCS, including: [4] *Birth Statistics*, series FM1; [5] *Marriage and Divorce Statistics*, series FM2; [6] *Mortality Statistics: general*, series DH1.

(d) Sets of long-run series, including [7] *Birth Statistics: historical series of statistics from the registers of births in England and Wales, 1837–1983*, OPCS, FM1, no. 13, 1987; [8] *Marriage and Divorce Statistics: historical series of statistics on marriages and divorces, 1837–1983*, OPCS, FM2, no. 16, 1990; [9] *Mortality Statistics, 1841–1990*, OPCS, DH1, no. 25, 1992.

(e) For Scottish vital statistics: [10] *Annual Reports of the Registrar-General for Scotland.*

(f) Other summary statistics: [11] *Annual Abstracts of Statistics*; [12] *Social Trends* (since 1974); [13] *General Household Survey* (since 1971).

General surveys, commentaries and collections

[14]* B. Benjamin, *Population Statistics: a review of UK sources* (Aldershot, 1989).

[15] A. H. Halsey, *British Social Trends since 1900* (1988), especially [15a] chapter 2 (by D. Coleman on 'Population') and [15b] chapter 11 (by K. McPherson and D. Coleman on 'Health').

[16]* D. A. Coleman and J. Salt, *The British Population: patterns, trends, and processes* (Oxford, 1992).

[17]* R. M. Smith, 'Elements of demographic change in Britain since 1945', in J. Obelkevich and P. Catterall (eds.), *Understanding Post-War British Society* (1994), pp. 19–30.

[18] R. I. Woods, *The Population of Britain in the Nineteenth Century* (1992) [reproduced in this volume].

[19] M. Anderson, 'Population and family life', in T. Dickson and J. H. Treble, *People and Society in Scotland* – III, *1914–1990* (Edinburgh, 1992) pp. 12–47.

[20] J. Hobcraft and P. Rees (eds.), *Regional Demographic Development* (1977).

[21] H. Joshi (ed.), *The Changing Population of Britain* (1989).

[22] M. Murphy and J. Hobcraft (eds.), *Population Research in Britain*, Supplement to *Population Studies* 45 (1991).

Migration and Population Distribution

[23] E. C. Willatts and M. G. C. Newton, 'The geographical pattern of population change in England and Wales, 1921–1951', *Geographical Journal*, 99 (1953) pp. 442–50.

[24] P. A. Compton, 'The changing population' in R. J. Johnston and J. C. Doornkamp (eds.), *The Changing Geography of the United Kingdom* (1982) pp. 37–73.

[25] A. G. Champion, 'Evolving patterns of population distribution in England and Wales, 1951–1971', *Transactions of the Institute of British Geographers*, New Series, 1 (1976) pp. 401–20.

[26] A. J. Fielding, 'Counterurbanisation' in M. Pacione (ed.), *Population Geography: Progress and Prospect* (1986), pp. 224–56.

[27] A. G. Champion (ed.), *Counterurbanisation: the changing pace and nature of population deconcentration* (1989).

[28] J. Stillwell, P. Rees and P. Boden (eds.), *Migration Processes and Patterns,* Volume 2II, *Population redistribution in the United Kingdom* (1992).

[29] H. Jones, 'Evolution of Scottish migration patterns', *Scottish Geographical Magazine*, 102 (1986) pp. 151–64.

[30] A. G. Champion, 'Internal migration and the spatial distribution of population' in [20] pp. 110–32.

[31]   R. Lawton, 'Regional population trends in England and Wales, 1750–1971', in [21] pp. 29–70.
[32]   C. M. Law and A. M. Warnes, 'The changing geography of the elderly in England and Wales', *Transactions of the Institute of British Geographers*, New Series, 1 (1976) pp. 453–71.
[33]   A. M. Warnes and C. M. Law, 'The elderly population of Great Britain: locational trends and policy implications', *Transactions of the Institute of British Geographers*, New Series, 9 (1984) pp. 37–59.
[34]   I. Diamond and S. Clarke, 'Demographic patterns among Britain's ethnic groups' in [20] pp. 177–98.
[35]   C. Holmes, 'The promised land? Migration into Britain 1870–1980', in D. A. Coleman (ed.), *Demography of Immigrants and Minority Groups* (1982) pp. 1–21.

Mortality

[36]* R. M. Mitchison, *British Population Change since 1860* (1977).
[37]   M. A. Heasman and I. Lipworth, *Accuracy of Certification of Causes of Death*, Studies on Medical and Population Subjects (General Register Office, 1966).
[38]   T. B. Gage, 'The decline of mortality in England and Wales 1861 to 1964: decomposition by cause of death and component of mortality', *Population Studies*, 47 (1993) pp. 47–60.
[39]   A. Mercer, *Disease Mortality and Population in Transition: epidemiological-demographic change in England since the eighteenth century as part of a global phenomenon* (Leicester, 1990).
[40]   J. Anson, 'Regional mortality in Britain, 1931–87', *Journal of Biosocial Science*, 25 (1993) pp. 383–95.
[41]   M. Whitehead, *The Health Divide: inequalities in health in the 1980s* (Health Education Council, 1987) reprinted in an extended edition by Penguin (1988) along with [43].
[42]* M. Blaxter, 'Fifty years on: inequalities in health', in [22] pp. 69–94.
[43]* *Report of the Working Group on Inequalities in Health (the Black Report)*, (HMSO, 1980), abbreviated edition reprinted by Penguin (1988) together with [41] and a new introduction.
[44]   M. G. Marmot et al., *Immigrant Mortality in England and Wales 1970–78: causes of death by country of birth*, OPCS Studies on Medical and Population Subjects No. 47 (HMSO 1984).
[45]   R. Illsley, 'Occupational class, selection, and the interpretation of social class mortality differentials', *Quarterly Journal of Social Affairs*, 22 (1986) pp. 151–65.
[46]   A. J. Fox et al., 'Social class mortality differentials: artefact, selec-

tion or life circumstances', *Journal of Epidemiology and Community Health* 39 (1985) pp. 1–8.
[47] T. McKeown, *The Modern Rise of Population* (1976).
[48] J. M. Winter, 'Unemployment, nutrition and infant mortality in Britain, 1920–50', in J. M. Winter (ed.), *The Working Class in Modern British History: essays in honour of Henry Pelling* (Cambridge, 1983) pp. 232–56.
[49] J. M. Winter, 'The decline of mortality in Britain, 1870–1950', in T Barker and M. Drake (eds.), *Population and Society in Britain, 1850–1980* (1982) pp. 100–20.
[50] R. Wilkinson, 'Class mortality differentials, income distribution and trends in poverty 1921–81', *Journal of Social Policy* 18 (1989) pp. 307–35.
[51] H. Graham, *Women, Health and the Family* (Brighton, 1984).
[52] J. M. Winter, *The Great War and the British People* (1985).
[53] R. I. Woods *at al.*, 'The causes of rapid infant mortality decline in England and Wales 1861–1921', *Population Studies*, 42 (1988) pp. 343–66 and 43(1989) pp. 113–32.
[54] M. G. Marmot and M. E. McDowally, 'Mortality decline and widening social inequalities', *Lancet* (1986 ii) pp. 274–6.
[55] D. J. Barker, 'Rise and fall of Western diseases', *Nature*, 338 (1989) pp. 371–2.
[56] R. Reves, 'Declining fertility in England and Wales as a major cause of the twentieth century decline in mortality', *American Journal of Epidemiology* 122 (1985) pp. 112–26.

Fertility and nuptiality

[57] J. Haskey, 'Current prospects for the proportion of marriages ending in divorce,' in [3] (1989) pp. 34–7.
[58] K. E. Kiernan, 'The family: formation and fission', in [21] pp. 27–41
[59] J. Haskey and K. E. Kiernan, 'Cohabitation in Britain – characteristics and estimated numbers of cohabiting partners' in [3] (1989) pp. 23–32.
[60] K. E. Kiernan and S. M. Eldridge, 'Inter and intra cohort variation in the timing of first marriage', *British Journal of Sociology* 38 (1987) pp. 44–65.
[61] J. Cooper, 'Births outside marriage: recent trends and associated demographic and social changes', in [3] (1991) pp. 8–18.
[62] A. J. Coale and S. C. Watkins (eds.), *The Decline of Fertility in Europe* (Princeton, 1986).
[63] J. Cooper and C. Shaw, 'Fertility assumptions for the 1991-based national population projections', in [3] (1993) pp. 43–9.

[64] P Babb, 'Birth statistics 1992', in [3] (1993) pp. 7–11.

[65] M J Murphy, 'Economic models of fertility in post-War Britain: a conceptual and statistical re-interpretation', *Population Studies* 47 (1992) pp. 235–8.

[66] J. A. Banks, *Prosperity and Parenthood* (1954).

[67] G. S. Becker, *A Treatise on the Family* (Cambridge Mass., 1981).

[68] W. Seccombe, 'Men's "marital rights" and women's "wifely duties"': changing conjugal relations in the fertility decline', in J R Gillis *et al.* (eds.), *The European Experience of Declining Fertility* (1992).

[69] M. Silver, 'Births, marriages and income fluctuations in the United Kingdom and Japan', *Economic Development and Cultural Change* 14 (1966) pp. 302–15.

[70] S. H. Preston, 'Changing values and falling birth rates', in [71] pp. 176–95.

[71] K. Davis *et al.*, *Below Replacement Fertility in Industrial Societies: causes, consequences, policies* (Cambridge, 1987).

[72] P. Aries, 'Two successive motivations for the declining birth rate in the West', *Population and Development Review* 6 (1980) pp. 645–50.

[73] R. A. Easterlin, *Birth and Fortune: the impact of numbers on personal welfare* (University of Chicago Press, 1980).

[74] H. Joshi, 'The cash opportunity costs of childbearing: an approach to estimation using British data', *Population Studies* 44 (1990) pp. 41–60.

[75] J. F. Ermisch, *The Political Economy of Demographic Change* (1983).

[76] J. F. Ermisch, 'Economic opportunities, marriage squeezes and the propensity to marry: an economic analysis of period marriage rates in England and Wales', *Population Studies* 35 (1981) pp. 347–56.

[77] J. F. Ermisch, *Fewer Babies, Longer Lives* (York, 1990).

[78] E. de Cooman *et al.*, 'The next birth and the labour market: a dynamic model of births in England and Wales', *Population Studies* 41 (1987) pp. 237–68.

[79] R. Lesthaeghe and J. Surkyn, 'Cultural dynamics and economic theories of fertility change', *Population and Development Review* 14 (1988) pp. 1–45.

[80] N. Keyfitz, 'The family that does not reproduce itself' in [71] pp. 139–54.

[81] M. Ní Brolcháin, 'The interpretation and role of work-associated accelerated childbearing in post-War Britain', *European Journal of Population* 2 (1986) pp. 135–54.

[82] R. I. Woods, 'Approaches to the fertility transition in Victorian England', *Population Studies* 41 (1987) pp. 283–311.

[83] M. Kirk, 'The problem of fertility 1936–86' in [22] pp. 31–48.

[84]   C. M. Langford, 'Birth control practice in Great Britain: a review of evidence from cross-sectional surveys', in [22] pp. 49–68.

[85]   M. Anderson, 'The emergence of the modern life-cycle in Britain', *Social History* 10 (1986) pp. 69–86.

[86]   M. Ní Brolcháin, 'The contraceptive confidence idea: an empirical investigation', *Population Studies* 42 (1988) pp. 205–25.

[87]   M. J. Murphy, 'The contraceptive pill and female employment as factors in fertility change in Britain 1963–80: a challenge to the conventional view', *Population Studies* 47 (1993) pp. 221–44.

[88]   M. Bone, 'Trends in single women's sexual behaviour in Scotland, in [3] (1986) pp. 7–14.

[89]   P. A. David, 'Comment' on G. S. Becker and R. J. Barro 'Altruism and the economic theory of fertility' in [71], pp. 77–86.

[90]   J. Lewis, *Women in Britain since 1945* (Blackwell, 1992).

[91]   J. Simons, 'Developments in the interpretations of recent fertility trends in England and Wales', in [20] pp. 117–38.

[92]   J. Simons, 'Culture, economy and reproduction in Europe', in D. A. Coleman and R. Schofield (eds.), *The State of Population Theory: forward from Malthus* (1986) pp. 256–78.

[93]   L. Roussel, 'Types of marriage and frequency of divorce' in E Grebenik *et al.* (eds.), *Later Phases of the Family Cycle* (Oxford, 1989).

[94]   M. Anderson, 'The relevance of family history' in M Anderson (ed.) *Sociology of the Family: selected readings* (1980) pp. 33–63.

[95]   C. Shaw, 'Recent trends in family size and family building', in [3] (1989) pp. 19–22.

Wider implications

[96]   I. Diamond, 'Education and changing numbers of young people', in [21] pp. 72–89.

[97]   K. E. Kiernan, 'Transitions in young adulthood in Great Britain', in [22] pp. 95–114.

[98]   M. J. Murphy, 'Housing the People: from shortage to surplus', in [21] pp. 90–109

[99]   P. Thane, 'Old age: burden or benefit', in [21] pp. 56–71.

[100]   J. Falkingham, 'Dependency and ageing in Britain: a reexamination of the evidence', *Journal of Social Policy* 18 (1989) pp. 211–33.

[101]   J. A. Kay, 'The welfare crisis in an ageing population' in M. Keynes *et al.* (eds.), *The Political Economy of Health and Welfare* (1988) pp. 136–45.

[102]* M. Anderson, 'The social implications of demographic change' in F. M. L. Thompson (ed.), *The Cambridge Social History of Britain, 1750-1950* 2 (Cambridge, 1990) pp. 1–70.

[103] J. Millar, 'Lone mothers' in C. Glendinning and J. Millar (eds.), *Women and Poverty in Britain* (Brighton, 1987) pp. 159–77.

[104] J. Popay *et al.*, *One Parent families: parents, children and public policy*, Study Commission on the Family Occasional paper 12 (1983).

[105] J. Haskey, 'Trends in numbers of one-parent families in Great Britain', in [3] (1993) pp. 26–33.

[106] D. Eversley and W. Köllmann (eds.), *Population Change and Social Planning* (1982).

[107] G. C. K. Peach, 'The growth and distribution of the black population in Britain, 1945–80' in D. A. Coleman (ed.), *Demography of Immigrant and Minority Groups in the UK* (1982) pp. 23–42.

[108]* C. Holmes, 'The impact of immigration', in T. Barker and M. Drake (eds.), *Population and Society in Britain, 1850-1980* (1982) pp. 172–94.

Index

Entries under England are restricted to instances where England is being compared with other countries.

New Studies in Economic and Social History

Edited for the Economic History Society by
Michael Sanderson
University of East Anglia, Norwich

This series, specially commissioned by the Economic History Society of Great Britain, provides a guide to the current interpretations of the key themes of economic and social history in which advances have recently been made or in which there has been significant debate.

In recent times economic and social history has been one of the most flourishing areas of historical study. This has mirrored the increasing relevance of the economic and social sciences both in a student's choice of career and in forming a society at large more aware of the importance of these issues in their everyday lives. Moreover specialist interests in business, agricultural and welfare history, for example, have themselves burgeoned and there has been an increased interest in the economic development of the wider world. Stimulating as these scholarly developments have been for the specialist, the rapid advance of the subject and the quantity of new publications make it difficult for the reader to gain an overview of particular topics, let alone the whole field.

New Studies in Economic and Social History is intended for students and their teachers. It is designed to introduce them to fresh topics and to enable them to keep abreast of recent writing and debates. All the books in the series are written by a recognised authority in the subject, and the arguments and issues are set out in a critical but unpartisan fashion. The aim of the series is to survey the current state of scholarship, rather than to provide a set of prepackaged conclusions.

The series has been edited since its inception in 1968 by Professors M. W. Flinn, T. C. Smout and L. A. Clarkson, and is currently edited by Dr Michael Sanderson. From 1968 it was published by Macmillan as *Studies in Economic History*, and after 1974 as *Studies in Economic and Social History*. From 1995 *New Studies in Economic and Social History* is being published on behalf of the Economic History Society by Cambridge University Press. This new series includes some of the titles previously published by Macmillan as well as new titles, and reflects the ongoing development throughout the world of this rich seam of history.

1. M. Anderson
   Approaches to the history of the Western family, 1500–1914

2. W. Macpherson
   The economic development of Japan, 1868–1941

3. R. Porter
   Disease, Medicine, and society in England: second edition

4. B. W. E. Alford
   British economic performance since 1945

5. A. Crowther
   Social policy in Britain, 1914–1939

6. E. Roberts
   Women's work 1840–1940

7. C. O'Grada
   The great Irish famine

8. R. Rodger
   Housing in urban Britain 1780–1914

9. P. Slack
   The English Poor Law 1531–1782

10. J. L. Anderson
    Explaining long-term economic change

11. D. Baines
    Emigration from Europe 1815–1930

12. M. Collins
    Banks and industrial finance 1800–1939

13. A. Dyer
    Decline and growth in English towns 1400–1640

14. R. B. Outhwaite
    Dearth, public policy and social disturbance in England, 1550–1800

15. M. Sanderson
    Education, economic change and society in England 1780–1870: second edition

16. R. D. Anderson
    Universities and elites in Britain since 1800

17. C. Heywood
    The development of the French economy, 1700–1914

Previously published as

Studies in Economic History

Titles in the series available from the Macmillan Press Limited

5. J. R. Harris
    The British iron industry, 1700–1850

6. J. Hatcher
    Plague, population and the English economy, 1348–1530

7. J. R. Hay
    The origins of the Liberal welfare reforms, 1906–1914

8. H. McLeod
    Religion and the working classes in nineteenth-century Britain

9. J. D. Marshall
    The Old Poor Law 1795–1834: second edition

10. R. J. Morris
    Class and class consciousness in the industrial revolution, 1750–1850

11. P. K. O'Brien
    The economic effects of the American civil war

12. P. L. Payne
    British entrepreneurship in the nineteenth century

13. G. C. Peden
    Keynes, the treasury and British economic policy

14. M. E. Rose
    The relief of poverty, 1834–1914

15. S. B. Saul
    The myth of the Great Depression, 1873–1896: second edition

16. J. Thirsk
    England's agricultural regions and agrarian history, 1500–1750

17. J. R. Ward
    Poverty and progress in the Caribbean, 1800–1960

which
numbers around 5,000 members, publishes the *Economic History Review* four times a year (free to members) and holds an annual conference.

Enquiries about membership should be addressed to

The Assistant Secretary
Economic History Society
PO Box 70
Kingswood
Bristol
BS15 5TB

Full-time students may join at special rates.